Time Out

Global Perspectives on Sport and the Covid-19 Lockdown

Time Out

Global Perspectives on Sport and the Covid-19 Lockdown

Jörg Krieger
April Henning
Lindsay Parks Pieper
Paul Dimeo

First published in 2021
as part of the *Sport & Society* Book Imprint
http://doi.org/10.18848/978-1-86335-230-7/CGP (Full Book)

Common Ground Research Networks
2001 South First Street, Suite 202
University of Illinois Research Park
Champaign, IL
61820

Copyright © 2021 Jörg Krieger, April Henning, Lindsay Parks Pieper, and Paul Dimeo

All rights reserved. Apart from fair dealing for the purposes of study, research, criticism or review as permitted under the applicable copyright legislation, no part of this book may be reproduced by any process without written permission from the publisher.

Library of Congress Cataloging-in-Publication Data

Names: Krieger, Jörg, editor. | Henning, April, editor. | Dimeo, Paul, editor. | Parks, Lindsay Pieper, editor.
Title: Time out : global perspectives on sport and the Covid-19 lockdown / Edited by Jörg Krieger, April Henning, Lindsay Parks Pieper, and Paul Dimeo
Description: Champaign, IL : Common Ground Research Networks, 2020. | Includes bibliographical references. | Summary: "In the edited collection, Time Out: Global Perspectives on Sport and the Covid-19 Lockdown, practitioners and international scholars explore the impact of the global Covid-19 health pandemic on sport from a global perspective. It is part of a two-volume Covid-19 and Sport series that tackles the effects of the global lockdown on sport during March and April 2020, when restrictions were at their most severe and the human toll at its peak in many countries. The twenty chapters provide a comprehensive overview of the immediate consequences of the Covid-19 lockdown on global sport from a variety of perspectives"-- Provided by publisher.
Identifiers: LCCN 2020050049 (print) | LCCN 2020050050 (ebook) | ISBN 9780949313423 (hardback) | ISBN 9781863352291 (paperback) | ISBN 9781863352307 (adobe pdf)
Subjects: LCSH: Sports--Social aspects. | COVID-19 (Disease)--Social aspects. | Sports administration. | Epidemics--Social aspects. | Globalization.
Classification: LCC GV706.5 .T56 2020 (print) | LCC GV706.5 (ebook) | DDC 306.4/83--dc23
LC record available at https://lccn.loc.gov/2020050049
LC ebook record available at https://lccn.loc.gov/2020050050

Cover Photo Credit: Kyle Krisko

Table of Contents

Introduction   1
    Jörg Krieger, April Henning, Lindsay Parks Pieper, and Paul Dimeo

List of Contributors   5

Global Sport Stakeholders

Chapter 1   15
    Let the Games Begin? The Decision to Postpone the Tokyo 2020 Summer Olympics
       Helen Jefferson Lenskyj

Chapter 2   29
    How Covid-19 Exposed the Limitations of a Technocratic Anti-Doping System and the Need for Diversification of Responsibility
       Daniel Read

Chapter 3   47
    Analyzing the "Position Paper on the Impact of the Covid-19 Crisis on the Sport Sector"
       Mariann Bardocz-Bencsik, Niki Koutrou, and Rachel May

Chapter 4   65
    Containing the Virus, Killing Sports Journalism: How Rugby League in Australia Muscled its Way out of Lockdown
       Tracey Lee Holmes

Chapter 5   79
    Covid-19 and the Instrumental Use of Sport: What Does the Future Hold for Sport-for-Development Organizations?
       Haydn Morgan, Jeremy Hapeta, Rochelle Stewart-Withers, and Justin Coleman

Chapter 6   93

Time Out: How is the Media Industry Using the Covid-19 Lockdown to Rethink its Coverage of Women and Sport?
    Gina S. Comeau and Barbara Ravel

Sport Participants

Chapter 7   107

Working out Covid-19: Being a Les Mills Instructor and Managing Health in Times of Quarantine
    Karin Andersson, Ulrike Vogl, and Jesper Andreasson

Chapter 8   119

Swolecial Distancing: Gym Closures and the Quarantine Workout
    Broderick D.V. Chow

Chapter 9   133

Havocking a Dream: The Impact on Athletes of the Suspension of Tokyo 2020
    Marjorie Enya and Katia Rubio

Chapter 10   147

Interruption of Training, Sedentary Behavior, Resilience, and Mood State Among Female Catchball Players During the Covid-19 Social Isolation Period
    Hilla Davidov

Chapter 11   171

Africa's International Sports Icons as Role Models and Activists During the Covid-19 Lockdown
    Cecil G.S Tafireyi

Chapter 12   183

A Unique and Special Solution for a Unique and Special Time: Training Professional Football Referees Virtually
    Yuya Kiuchi, Bill Dittmar, and Scott Matteson

Individual Sports

Chapter 13   197

Between Self-Interest and Solidarity: European Football and the Covid-19 Lockdown
    Alan McDougall

Chapter 14 211

Covid-19: How Football Closed in South America
Jorge Tovar

Chapter 15 227

The Zwift Pace: How Elite Cycling Faced the Covid-19 Lockdown
Bertrand Fincoeur, Serena Bongiovanni, and Vincent Gesbert

Chapter 16 241

Analyzing Boxing's Most Extended Break Between Rounds: The Impact of the Covid-19 Pandemic on National Boxing Federations and Innovative Responses
Ria Ramnarine and Kalyn McDonough

Chapter 17 257

The Lift Seen Around the World: Hafþór Björnsson and Legitimacy in Strongman
Conor Heffernan

Chapter 18 271

Rise of the Machine: On the Prevalence of Indoor Rowing Records Under Covid-19
Alec S. Hurley

Chapter 19 285

A Handbrake Turn in Mexico: Crisis Management of a Global Motorsport Event
Hans Erik Næss

Chapter 20 297

Crisis for Sport, Opportunity for eSports?
Hee Jung Hong

Introduction

Jörg Krieger, April Henning, Lindsay Parks Pieper, and Paul Dimeo

Like any leap year, 2020 was a much-anticipated year among sport enthusiasts. In Japan the preparations for the 2020 Tokyo Olympic Games were speeding along. In Europe, football fans looked forward to the first European Championships staged on the entire continent to celebrate the sixtieth anniversary of the competition. Across the world of sports, annual, biannual, and quadrennial elite and recreational sporting events were planned and eagerly awaited.

However, just as in many other sectors around the world, all sporting activities were brought to an abrupt halt in March 2020. This halt was due to the rapid spread of the coronavirus disease 2019, or Covid-19, caused by a virus named SARS-CoV-2. Originating in Wuhan, China, in late 2019, the World Health Organization (WHO) declared Covid-19 a global pandemic on March 11, 2020. By that time, China, Germany, France, Iran, Italy, Spain, and the United States had each already reported more than one thousand infections with rapidly rising death figures. In an attempt to prevent the further spread of the virus, national governments began to balance economic consequences against health protection. This led leaders to impose drastic measures on public life, including social distancing regulations, mask requirements, curfews, school closings, and travel restrictions. By the beginning of April 2020, large parts of the world's population found themselves in what became known as the global lockdown of Spring 2020.

The introduction of these measures also forced sport into a global "time out." One of the most decisive turning points came in an announcement on March 24, when the International Olympic Committee and Japanese organizers rescheduled the 2020 Olympic Games. Organizers and officials initially held out hope that they would be able to maneuver around the pandemic. However, athletes, National Olympic Committees, and international sport federations pressured the organizers into postponing the Games when it became increasingly clear that it would be impossible to guarantee a smooth staging of the event during such a crisis. The postponement of the Olympics to August 2021 caused a wave of cancellations and the rescheduling of international sport events. The Union of European Football Associations quickly postponed its European Championships to 2021, World Athletics moved the athletics world championships from 2021 to 2022 to avoid conflicting with the Olympics, and other annual sporting events such as cycling's crown jewel event, the Tour de France, and the tennis Grand Slam tournaments were postponed until later that year. Taken together, the decisions made during the Covid-19 lockdown will impact the international sporting calendar for years to come.

All elite sport stakeholders were heavily affected by the lockdown. Athletes could not undertake their usual training regimes and were forced to try to keep in shape from their individual homes, with some teams working out together via video calls. For some athletes, however, training was the least of their worries as they faced significant financial crises. Sport clubs also faced economic consequences with large portions of their incomes from sponsorships, broadcasting rights, and ticketing immediately dissolved in the absence of competitive events. Similarly, large sport organizations not only had to restructure their events, but also step into negotiations with their commercial partners to secure the short-term financial future of their sports. Sectors closely linked to sport also suffered from the cancellation of elite and leisure sport. For example, sports-related travel to follow elite sport teams, attend youth competitions on a local level, or to participate in leisure sport events dropped with severe costs for businesses across the entire sector.

The lockdown did not only hit those involved in sport at the elite level. The leisure sport industry had to absorb and adjust to the consequences of the Covid-19 crisis as well. Thousands of recreational sport participants transformed their homes into gyms or took on new outdoor sporting activities in attempts to remain active. Online mail orders of gym equipment saw a sudden spike as regular gym goers were forced to train at home. In contrast, commercial gyms faced considerable financial losses that led some branches to bankruptcy. Similarly, local sport clubs that did not have deep economic reserves but survived off the income from ticketing and hosting smaller events found themselves in financial straits. In many cases, those clubs had to seek governmental support in order to secure their survival.

Finally, as schools and universities closed during the lockdown, physical education (PE) suffered immensely from the restrictions. When online distance learning became the primary tool to deliver education, schools around the world quickly erased PE from the schedules to make way for "essential" school subjects and eliminate the issue of close physical contact required for sporting activities. Kinesiology and sport studies instructors similarly had to develop innovative solutions in order to sustain classes where physical activity components were required. University educators therefore instructed via online video channels, with physical examinations taking place under strict conditions.

The idea for a book series on sport and the Covid-19 crisis emerged early in the global lockdown period. With sport all over the globe being so heavily affected by the Covid-19 pandemic, we considered it necessary to provide practitioners and scholars many of whom carried on with innovative research strategies to understand the effects of the pandemic in their own areas of study with a forum for their analyses in order to understand the impact of the global pandemic on sport as a whole. As the spread of the virus continues to impact our societies, we decided to address the crisis at two distinct phases and from two different perspectives. The first two volumes of our Covid-19 and Sport series tackle the effects on sport during the global lockdown during March and April 2020, when restrictions were at their most severe and the human toll at its peak in many countries. In this volume, authors explore the impact of lockdowns and other social distancing measures on the global sport context. The simultaneously published volume addresses national and local contexts.

This book of international perspectives on sport and the Covid-19 lockdown is organized around three main themes. The first section explores the reactions of international stakeholders within the global sport system. This includes international sport organizations, as well as affected sectors such as sport media and the sport-for-development sector. In section two, the authors focus on the impact of the Covid-19 crisis on sporting participants within an international context. Both the effects on elite athletes and leisure sport participants are discussed. In the final section, the chapters explore the impacts on individual sports.

We do not claim that this book, and indeed the entire series on sport and the Covid-19 crisis, captures all facets of sport during the time of Covid-19. Indeed, the long-term consequences will likely only be seen over the next few years and the lasting impacts may take many more years to be fully felt and understood. Rather, it is our objective to present a variety of perspectives that allows us to study the immediate consequences of the Covid-19 lockdown on sport as comprehensively as is currently possible. Thus, we have tried to include a broad sample of academic disciplines and wide geographical distribution among the authors of this edited collection. We are keen to support the development of young scholars and we specifically encouraged early career researchers (ECRs) to submit contributions. Around half of the chapters in this book have been written by ECRs and we believe that their work provides insightful and innovative perspectives on the crisis. Finally, we have authors from different backgrounds including sport journalists and policy-makers who took a variety of approaches in their writing. This allows for a broader understanding of the Covid-19 lockdown's impact on sport with all contributors undertaking reflective analysis and discussion.

List of Contributors

Karin Andersson is a PhD student at the University of Vienna, Austria. She has worked as a research assistant at the Austrian Academy of Sciences, and as a Lecturer at the University of Vienna. Her interdisciplinary dissertation is situated at the intersections of sport sociology, gender studies, and cultural studies.

Jesper Andreasson is an Associate Professor of Sport Science at Linnaeus University, Sweden. He holds a PhD in Sociology and has published articles and books in the field of gender studies, sociology of sport, health, and gym and fitness culture.

Mariann Bardocz-Bencsik holds a master's degree in International Studies and a Bachelor's degree in Sport Management. She is currently enrolled in the PhD programme of the University of Physical Education in Hungary, her research topic is the role of sport in international development. She works as a communications professional with various sports organizations, including the World Curling Federation.

Serena Bongiovanni holds an MSc in Biochemistry from the University of Geneva, Switzerland, and an MSc in Sports Sciences from the University of Lausanne, Switzerland. Her graduate project focused on integrity issues in e-cycling. Bongiovanni has also been extensively involved in women's football over the last ten years.

Broderick D.V. Chow is Reader and Interim Deputy Dean of Learning and Teaching at the Royal Central School of Speech and Drama, University of London, United Kingdom. His research looks at the intersections of theater, performance, and sport. He is co-editor with Eero Laine and Claire Warden of *Performance and Professional Wrestling* (Routledge, 2016) and is co-editing a new collection with Laine entitled *Sports Plays*. His forthcoming book *Dynamic Tensions* explores the origins of men's fitness practices in the popular theater in the U.K. and U.S. Broderick is a competitive Olympic weightlifter and qualified coach.

Justin Coleman is Co-Founder and Chief Operations Officer of the Alliance of Sport in Criminal Justice. In addition, he is an Ambassador for EPALE UK, and a VAMHN Lived Experience Advisory Group member. These roles provide support for, and learning from, various communities of practice that support both social and criminal justice reform. Coleman has over two decades of experience in the Youth, Health, Social, and Criminal Justice Systems, earning multiple national and international awards for his contribution to social and criminal justice research, and for his expertise in program development, design, and "mass case management" delivery.

Gina S. Comeau is an Assistant Professor in the Department of Political Science at Laurentian University, Canada. Her research centers on the governance of civil society organizations and the role these play in public policy formulation processes in the sport and cultural policy sectors. Other research interests include the representation of women in political and popular culture. She is the author of several articles and chapters on these subjects and has presented her work at a number of national and international conferences. She is currently working on a book project examining the representation of gender in popular culture.

Hilla Davidov was part of the Israeli Olympic delegations from 2004 to 2016 and was an active member of the Judo professional Olympic entourage helping support the national team in winning three Olympic medals. Davidov has a BEd in Physical Education and an MBA (Marketing). Currently, she is a PhD candidate in the Olympic Studies program at German Sport University Cologne. Davidov was a member of the Israel Advisory Committee for re-designing the National Curriculum in Physical Education and received the World Fair Play Award in 2016. Davidov is a member of the International Pierre de Coubertin Committee.

Bill Dittmar is the co-founder of Executive Fusion, Inc. with his wife Heidi since 1991. Executive Fusion's main mission is to "Help Businesses Tell Their Story" through various marketing channels. He is also the co-owner of Synergy Global 4U, a private Virtual Campus. Dittmar was a Major League Soccer Referee (MLS) from 1996 to 2015 and is currently a MLS Referee Coach for the Professional Referees Organization. He is currently both a NCAA Soccer Official and a Virginia High School Soccer Coach since 1985.

Marjorie Enya is a member of the Olympic Studies Group at the University of São Paulo, Brazil and a master's student at the International Olympic Academy in Greece. She holds a bachelor's degree in History from the University of São Paulo, Brazil, and an MBA in Project Management from *Fundação Getúlio Vargas*. Enya has extensive experience in high performance sports team management and organization of sports mega events and was awarded the 2018 World Rugby Executive Scholarship for the Development of Women Leaders. She currently serves as an executive board member at the Brazilian Rugby Union and represents South America on the World Rugby Council.

Bertrand Fincoeur is a Senior Lecturer in Sport Sociology and Sport Management at the Institute of Sports Sciences at the University of Lausanne, Switzerland. He is also a Lecturer at the College of Humanities at the Swiss Federal Institute of Technology in Lausanne. His research areas primarily cover sports ethics and integrity.

Vincent Gesbert is a Lecturer in Sports Psychology at the Institute of Sports Sciences at the University of Lausanne, Switzerland. He holds a PhD in Sport Science from University of Rennes 2, France. His research areas primarily cover team performance, talent development, and use of technologies in elite sport.

Jeremy Hapeta is a Physical Education Lecturer and the Research Development Advisor Māori, at Massey University, New Zealand. Previously a fully registered teacher, Hapeta has taught in primary, intermediate, and secondary schools. He also played top-level rugby in New Zealand, Japan, and France, and has coached rugby in Italy and New Zealand. His research interests include Kaupapa Māori methodologies, sport for development, sport for social change and inclusion, team culture, games for understanding, and games sense. Hapeta is on Sport NZ's Physical Literacy Academic Reference Group and a member of Sport NZ's Tertiary Sport Research Collaboration group.

Conor Heffernan is an Assistant Professor of Physical Culture and Sport Studies at the University of Texas at Austin, United States. His research interest is late nineteenth and early twentieth century body cultures in Great Britain and the United States. Outside of academia, Heffernan also runs Physical Culture Study, a website dedicated to the history of health and fitness and provides content for several fitness outlets.

Tracey Lee Holmes is a senior journalist who has lived in numerous countries working for some of the world's most well-known media organizations. Currently at the Australian Broadcasting Corporation in Sydney, Australia, she is presenter of the award-winning podcast, The Ticket, focused on sport's intersection with society, politics, and global affairs. She is an experienced board director, university lecturer, and mentor. She has a master's degree in Communications and is currently studying for a Graduate Diploma in Sports Law at the Melbourne Law School, Australia.

Hee Jung Hong is a Lecturer in Sport at the University of Stirling, United Kingdom. She completed her PhD in Sport Psychology and her main research interests include career transitions in sport, life after sport, dual careers of athletes, athletes' career development and management, athletes' welfare and well-being, and sport psychology in eSports. She is the principal investigator on the eSports research project, "An International Analysis of Organisational Support for Esports Players' Mental Health and Physical Activity," funded by the International Olympic Committee. She is also a project manager for the Dual Career for Junior Athletes (DCJA) project funded by the European Commission.

Alec S. Hurley is a PhD candidate in the Physical Culture and Sport Studies program at the University of Texas at Austin. His research focuses on the intersection of sport, empire, and identity.

Yuya Kiuchi is an Assistant Professor in the Department of Human Development and Family Studies at Michigan State University, United States, and the Graduate Director for GPIDEA's graduate programs in Youth Development and Family Community Services. His interests include African American Studies and History, and Popular Culture Studies. He serves on the Editorial Advisory Board for the *Journal of Popular Culture* and the Endowment Committee for the Popular Culture Association. He is also a former professional-level football referee in Japan and is a National Referee Coach for the U.S. Soccer Federation.

Niki Koutrou is a Senior Lecturer in Sport Management in the Department of Sport and Event Management at Bournemouth University. She has established a growing international research and scholarship profile in the areas of sport volunteering and participation legacies of mega-sport events, volunteer management, sport program evaluation, sport policy and sustainability, and Olympic Studies. Koutrou is also the Principal Investigator of a project funded by the Olympic Studies Centre of the IOC that aims to explore and evaluate the volunteering legacy of the Athens 2004 Games.

Helen Jefferson Lenskyj is Professor Emerita at the University of Toronto, Canada where she taught sociology. Her work as a researcher and activist on gender and sport issues began in the 1980s, and she has published eight books critiquing the Olympic industry, as well as five books on gender and sport. Her most recent publication is *The Olympic Games: A Critical Approach* (Emerald, 2020). Lenskyj completed her PhD. at the University of Toronto in 1983 and was a Professor from 1986 until retiring in 2007. Her website is www.helenlenskyj.ca.

Scott Matteson is an Instructor in the Department of Human Development and Family Studies at Michigan State University, United States. He is currently pursuing a Doctorate in Education from the University of South Carolina in curriculum and instruction, with a concentration in educational technology. His research focus includes how the implementation of technology into classrooms influences student engagement through motivation, choice, and voice.

Rachel May studied Middle Eastern Studies and Politics at the University of Edinburgh, United Kingdom, and has since worked as a manager for various international sport for development projects and organizations. She has recently launched an enterprise called Mhor Outdoor in Scotland to promote wellbeing and reduce inequalities through outdoor and mountain sports.

Kalyn McDonough is a doctoral candidate in the Biden School of Public Policy and Administration at the University of Delaware, United States. Her research interests focus on social determinants of health and health equity, physical activity as a determinant of health, and the role of public policy in achieving health equity. The majority of her research is applied in nature, with a strong commitment to grounding studies in a robust literature base as well as the expertise of practitioner communities, to support evidence-based decision-making in practice and to inform policy.

Alan McDougall is Professor of History at the University of Guelph, Canada. He is the author of *The People's Game: Football, State and Society in East Germany* (Cambridge University Press, 2014) and *Contested Fields: A Global History of Modern Football* (University of Toronto Press, 2020).

Haydn Morgan is a Lecturer in Sport Management at the University of Bath, United Kingdom. His research explores the connection between participation in sport and the enhancement of social inclusion within marginalized populations. More specifically, her research seeks to examine how engagement with sport and physical activity may facilitate access into education, employment, and training; develop citizenship qualities; or enable young people to accumulate and enhance various forms of capital.

Hans Erik Næss holds a PhD in Sociology from the University of Oslo, Norway. He is an Associate Professor in Sport Management at the Department of Leadership and Organization, Kristiania University College, Norway. His research interests are sport governance, sporting events, and the relation between sport and politics. He has published articles on these topics in journals such as *Journal of Global Sport Management* and *European Journal for Sport and Society*. His latest book is *A History of Organizational Change. The Case of Fédération Internationale de l'Automobile, 1946-2020* (Palgrave Macmillan, 2020).

Ria Ramnarine is a former professional boxing world champion who transitioned from athlete to an AIBA 3-Star coach and an International Technical Official. She volunteers as a coach at the Fine Line Fight Factory gym and is the Founder of Boxing Beyond the Ring, a female empowerment boxing program. She is an employee at the University of Trinidad and Tobago and a sport columnist.

Barbara Ravel is an Associate Professor in the School of Human Kinetics at Laurentian University, a bilingual institution located in Sudbury, Ontario, Canada. She received her PhD and M.Sc. in Human Kinetics from Université de Montréal, after completing a master's and an undergraduate degree in Lyon, France. Her research focuses on gender and sexuality in sport with a particular interest in soccer/football and ice hockey. She has presented and published on these topics in both French and English.

Daniel Read is a Lecturer in Sports Business at the Institute for Sports Business at Loughborough University in London, United Kingdom. Having completed his PhD focusing on the legitimacy of the World Anti-Doping Agency, he has broad multidisciplinary research and enterprise interests in sports governance, competition integrity, and athlete welfare.

Katia Rubio is Associate Professor at the School of Education at the University of São Paulo (USP), Brazil, where she coordinates the Olympic Studies Group. She is also a Researcher at the Institute of Advanced Studies at USP, and holds a bachelor's degree in Journalism and Psychology, a master's degree in Physical Education, and a PhD in Education. She completed a post-doctorate in social psychology at the Autonomous University of Barcelona, Spain. She is founding president of the Brazilian Association of Sport Psychology and editor of *Olimpianos Journal of Olympic Studies*, has published thirty-two books, and dedicates her research to the memory of Brazilian Olympic athletes.

Rochelle Stewart-Withers (Te Āti Awa Tribe) is Head of Programme for the Institute of Development Studies at Massey University in Palmerston North, New Zealand. She is an Indigenous scholar and her research critically explores the potential of sport as a means for improving economic and social outcomes in developing countries, especially at the community and household level. She has been particularly interested in how sport is used as an entry point into communities when looking to address gender and Indigenous social and economic disparities, as well as how athletes and communities see sport to be a livelihood option.

Cecil G.S. Tafireyi is a PhD candidate in Sport Science at the University of KwaZulu-Natal, South Africa, and has an MA in Olympic Studies from the German Sport University. He also holds a Master of Sport Science degree from the University of KwaZulu-Natal. His research interests are in sport and politics/international diplomacy, physical education, and health promotion. Tafireyi is one of the founders of the sports management consultancy Sports Forum International, registered in Eswatini, and is a Physical Education and Sport textbook writer for the Zimbabwean new curriculum.

Jorge Tovar is an Associate Professor in the Economics Department at Los Andes University in Bogota, Colombia. He holds a PhD in economics from the University of California, Berkeley, United States. His current research covers the intersection of industrial organization, international trade, and sports economics, with an additional interest in the economic and social history of football. He teaches courses on social and economic issues in sports, including an advanced sports economics class at the University of Wisconsin, Madison, United States, while being the Spring 2020 Tinker-Nave Professor. His publications include the 2014 book, *Números Redondos*, and articles in the *Journal of Quantitative Analysis in Sports*, *Economic Inquiry*, and *Soccer and Society*.

Ulrike Vogl is an Assistant Professor of Linguistics at Ghent University, Belgium. She has published on language ideologies, historical pragmatics, and the history of language teaching. Recently her research focuses on discourse analysis, including a wide range of socially relevant topics such as multilingualism, migration, gender, fitness, and health.

Global Sport Stakeholders

CHAPTER 1

Let the Games Begin? The Decision to Postpone the Tokyo 2020 Summer Olympics

Helen Jefferson Lenskyj

INTRODUCTION

In 2013, when the International Olympic Committee (IOC) selected Tokyo as the host city of the 2020 Summer Olympics, Japanese organizers could not have predicted the global catastrophe that would hit seven years later. Boosters were promoting a Tokyo bid just two years after some of the country's worst natural disasters: the earthquake and tsunami of 2011 and the subsequent Fukushima nuclear accident. The Olympic industry's public relations machine saw an opportunity to exploit these events, by rebranding these Olympics the "Recovery Games." Displaced residents from the Fukushima region, together with their allies and advocates, were vocal in their critique of this spin, pointing to the incontrovertible evidence that neither the people nor the environment had "recovered" in any significant way (Lenskyj 2020, 55-57).

Predictably, the IOC and the Tokyo organizing committee (OC) continued to capitalize on Fukushima in 2020. A January 10 *Olympic News* item, for example, reported that "six inspirational students" from Fukushima were sampling the Olympic "spirit" and witnessing "the magic of the Opening Ceremony of the Youth Olympic Games" in Lausanne (IOC 2020a).

A few months earlier, presidents of international federations had complained about the "cheap appearance" of Tokyo 2020 Olympic sites. Heat was a more serious concern; the 2019 marathon trial events had to start at midnight to avoid extreme temperatures and humidity. On December 19, *Olympic News* announced a revised marathon course, moving the events to the cooler city of Sapporo, about 800km north of Tokyo (IOC 2019).

In November 2019, the world first heard of a public health crisis in China's province of Hubei, caused by Covid-19. Unsurprisingly, Olympic industry officials initially refused to see the pandemic as a threat. After all, the last time there had been an interruption to the inexorable Olympic cycle was caused by a world war, which had necessitated cancellations in 1940 and 1944. With some important variations, the IOC's responses loosely followed Kubler-Ross's five stages of grief, overlaid with the hubris that characterizes every Olympic industry position: denial, anger, bargaining, depression, and acceptance (Kubler-Ross and Kessler 2014).

The five stages of grief were first developed by Kubler-Ross and her colleagues in an attempt to understand and support individuals with terminal illnesses, and, like other stage theories, they were descriptive, rather than prescriptive. Applied to the IOC, the model is useful insofar as it demonstrates how Olympic industry powerbrokers' response to the pandemic followed some of the same stages, skipped over others, and even developed a stage of their own creation. And while some individuals within the Olympic industry displayed anger and depression, the IOC's official pronouncements as an organization cannot necessarily be slotted into categories intended to capture human emotions.

The following discussion will critically examine the responses of IOC members and other key stakeholders in the period December 1, 2019, to April 30, 2020. Official *Olympic News* items on the IOC's website <olympic.org> comprise the main primary source. These were the carefully worded messages that the Olympic industry presented to the outside world. These are supplemented by mainstream media reports of interviews, some conducted by *Associated Press* (AP) journalist Stephen Wade, with Olympic industry officials: members of the IOC, Tokyo 2020 OC and Japanese politicians. Additionally, the concerns and actions of athletes are documented and analyzed.

The IOC issued dozens of Covid-19-related pronouncements in March and April 2020. At first, these revealed a blending of the denial and anger stages. Unsurprisingly, overt displays of emotion were rare at their carefully staged press conferences and interviews, and the bland Olympic News items were usually accompanied by reassuring images of IOC President Thomas Bach. Bargaining, depression and acceptance stages were brief, followed by a unique self-congratulatory stage generated by the Olympic industry's well-oiled propaganda machine.

1. Denial and Anger Stages

Covid-19 is Not a Serious Problem, Plans for Tokyo 2020 Summer Olympics Are Proceeding Normally, There Is No "Plan-B."

On February 1, Japan had banned visitors from Hubei, and on February 12 added a second Chinese province. Meanwhile, Australia and the US had restricted entry to all Chinese travelers. Japan's prime minister (PM) Shinzo Abe was the target of widespread criticism for his weak leadership on the pandemic, allegedly in an attempt to minimize its significance and the potential threat to his Olympic "dream." As one commentary explained, Tokyo 2020 "offered a potent symbol of national recovery and of his "Abenomics" policies of revitalization and reform" (Lewis and Ahmed 2020).

A February 3 *Reuters* item reported that Abe and the Olympic Minister, Seiko Hashimoto, were not considering cancellation, but were in "close contact" with the

IOC and the World Health Organization (WHO) "to keep the coronavirus from affecting the Olympics." At this point, Japan had twenty cases, while China had reported 361 deaths (Lies 2020).

In mid-February, the IOC, Tokyo Organizing Committee (OC), the host city and Japanese governments, and the WHO set up a joint task force. The IOC Executive Board's statement of March 3 pointed to safety and security measures in place, praised "the great unity and solidarity" of athletes, sports organizations and governments, and urged athletes to keep on training (IOC 2020c). The next week saw the lighting of the flame in Olympia, and two IOC statements confirming its commitment to "delivering [2020] Olympic Games that can bring the world together in peace" (IOC 2020d). Tokyo 2020, it was claimed, would show that "our shared humanity is stronger than the forces that want to divide us"—as if the virus were equivalent to some kind of malicious political interference that threatened the autonomy of sport and the "supreme authority" of the IOC. The pseudo-religious "beacon of hope" metaphor made the first of many appearances at this time (IOC 2020e).

Reality soon prevailed over rhetoric, and the Greek legs of the torch relay were canceled after only two days, as a result of decisions made by the Greek Olympic Committee and the Greek Ministry of Health. The IOC assured Greek officials that "We fully understand the decision," while at the same time confirming its "full commitment" to Tokyo 2020 (IOC 2020f).

On February 14, following a two-day visit to Tokyo, John Coates, head of the IOC inspection team, announced that there were no plans to change the dates. *AP* quoted his explanation: "the advice we've received externally from the WHO is that there's no case for any contingency plans or cancelling the Games or moving the Games." However, the Chinese team of 600 athletes would be closely monitored, Coates said. Tokyo OC president Yoshiro Mori and CEO Toshiro Muto concurred. Meanwhile, WHO chief of emergencies Dr. Mike Ryan avoided media questions by stating that it was "not the role of the WHO to call off—or not call off—any event." The IOC's medical director, Richard Budgett, declined AP's request for an interview. By this date, *AP* reported that China had about 1,400 deaths (Wade and Yamaguchi 2020). However, since it was not until March 11 that the WHO declared the pandemic, Coates' position was not out of line with the general global view.

In the same spirit of denial, along with "the show must go on" message, a February 17 *Olympic News* item celebrated the release of Tokyo 2020's official motto "United by Emotion." In addition to the predictable reference to Olympic sport's unifying power, the article pointed to "the 2020 zeitgeist in the urban environment of Tokyo" (IOC 2020b). This was probably a nod to the post-disaster mood and emotion felt in the city, and 1,000 km to the north, in Fukushima. Regardless of ongoing radiation hotspots, this region was selected as the start of the torch relay and the site of several events.

Journalists seeking out IOC members for unofficial predictions targeted outspoken Canadian Dick Pound. In a February 25 interview with *AP* News, he claimed that a decision had to be made by late May, or else the event would be canceled, not postponed (Wade 2020a). Regardless of their merit, his comments had the effect of stealing Bach's thunder, which was probably the intent of the éminence grise of the "Olympic family."

On February 28, Bach took the unusual step of holding a conference call with three major Japanese media outlets, during which he confirmed the IOC's full commitment to holding the Tokyo Olympics in July 2020. On the issue of Pound's prediction, Bach repeatedly refused to "add fuel to the flame of speculation" (CBC 2020).

2. Bargaining Stage

Covid-19 is a Problem, but the IOC and Japan Can Mitigate its Impacts with Careful Planning.

By early March, dozens of international sports governing bodies were postponing or cancelling events on their 2020 calendar, both within and outside Asia. These included Six Nations rugby, F1 races, Euro 2020, Copa America, World Athletes Indoor Championships, Asian Athletics Indoor Championships, Asian Football Confederation league matches, Formula E, International Tennis Federation Cup Asia, Badminton Asia Championships, LPGA, Skiing World Cup, and X Games.

Talk of Tokyo's postponement prompted mainstream media to react, and, in a February 28 article (updated March 11), *Toronto Globe and Mail* sportswriter, Cathal Kelly, displayed the mindless boosterism that has long characterized the media's approach to all things Olympic. Foreshadowing Bach's "beacon of hope" rhetoric and endorsing the "bread and circuses" principle of diverting the masses, he asserted: "It's times like these we need sport most." Even if spectators are banned, Kelly said, "there will still be the agony, ecstasy, controversy, jingoism, outbursts of extreme goodwill that make us love the Olympics" To proceed with Tokyo 2020 works "far, far better than any number of reassuring updates from politicians or public health officials" He concluded by calling the Olympics a reminder that "we're all still together, and that we're all going to make it out okay" (Kelly 2020) —a prediction that did not age well, given the high number of fatalities over the next few months. In the same vein, on February 26, an American sportwriter claimed, "It's far too early to freak out about the coronavirus ruining the Tokyo Olympics," pointing to the WHO's recent review and the "clinical trials on a possible treatment" being held in China and the U.S. (Armour 2020).

Eventually, the media began to question the Olympic industry's promises that all would be well, and some sources published athletes' reactions to a possible postponement. "Cancelling the Olympics may seem like a no brainer for some, but for most of the athletes, it is unthinkable," according to retired U.K. Olympic field hockey player Sam Quek. In a March 1 article, she claimed that "even if there was a

100% chance, I would contract the virus, I would still want to go." However, she said she would opt for a "closed-door Olympics" so that spectators were not at risk. If she had not been able to compete at the Rio 2016 Olympics because of a cancellation, she stated that she would feel that her life "from the age of 16 to 27 had been stolen away and a complete waste" (Quek 2020). Many other Olympic athletes echoed her views, a graphic reminder of the levels of indoctrination and exploitation experienced by young athletes in the service of elite sport, as tragically illustrated in recent investigations into the sexual abuse of American gymnasts (Ropes and Gray 2018; Moran and Blumenthal 2019).

A March 2 Guardian article took a more critical approach. Sportswriter Jonathan Liew pointed out that, even at that late stage, with Japan in lockdown, Tokyo 2020's official website made no mention of Covid-19. Liew asked what message would be conveyed if the Games proceeded as planned: "That the bloated and entitled modern Olympic movement is simply too enormous to be thwarted. That corporate contracts and vested interest must take precedence over human wellbeing?" (Liew 2020). Over the following three weeks, his forecasts proved true. "You can't postpone the Olympic Games like a football match," Bach told a German radio interviewer on March 22, justifying the IOC's reluctance to postpone the games (Bagratuni 2020).

Some athletes were ambivalent, wanting the games to be held but concerned about the health and safety of athletes and spectators, while a small number were outspokenly critical of the IOC's failure to announce postponement. Outstanding among these was Canadian IOC member Hayley Wickenheiser. In a March 17 tweet, she called the IOC's insistence on proceeding "insensitive and irresponsible" in the context of a "crisis that is bigger than even the Olympics." As an athlete, she pointed to the uncertainty for those who were training for Tokyo 2020, while, as a trainee emergency room doctor, she saw the impacts of the virus firsthand. Others pointed to the dangers of training at the time and accused the IOC of being "tone deaf to the situation" (Prominent athletes, 2020).

On March 17, with news that the deputy head of Japan's Olympic Committee had tested positive, PM Abe insisted that the games would proceed, but with no spectators permitted on the torch relay route (ABC News 2020b). At this point, Canadian Olympic industry officials exemplified the "bargaining" approach. Pound claimed that the IOC could mitigate risks by screening spectators or filling stadiums to half-capacity, while Canada's chef de mission Marnie McBean encouraged athletes to be ready for July, even if they competed in front of empty stands. Both Pound and McBean issued assurances that health and safety were paramount (Prominent athletes 2020). In a March 18 statement, the Australian Olympic Committee (AOC) announced that it supported the IOC, and claimed that Australian athletes were "happy to go" (ABC News 2020a)

For the IOC, it was still "business as usual" on the question of Tokyo 2020. A March 17 communique and March 18 news item reported on planned consultations with stakeholders, while stating that all should work towards "containment of the virus." At the same time, the IOC's commitment to Tokyo 2020 was emphasized, along with the implicit message that everything was under control: "with more than four months to go there is no need for any drastic decisions at this stage; and any speculation at this moment would be counter-productive" (IOC 2020g). In the following week, Bach, in particular, repeatedly rejected "speculation" as unwelcome interference on the part of uninformed media and the public.

The communique included details of planned adaptations to test events, torch relay, transport, crowd movement planning, and qualifications systems. Of course, no IOC pronouncement during the crisis would be complete without references to athletes' health and safety, and to Olympic values and ideals. Abe provided a quotable statement, "I want to hold the Olympics and Paralympics perfectly, as proof that the human race will conquer the new coronavirus" (IOC 2020g). As the stakeholder consultations proceeded, Olympic News provided appropriately supportive quotes from selected representatives of Olympic organizations in Asia, Africa, Europe and Oceania, all speaking positively about "commitment" and "hope" (IOC 2020i).

In an unusual move on March 18, Bach and several IOC directors held a two-hour conference call with 220 members of the IOC Athletes' Commission (AC), a group comprising a mixture of appointed and elected athlete representatives. Bach subsequently reported that he and his colleagues had been "*confronted* with many questions," but that the call "was very constructive and gave us a lot of insight" (IOC 2020h, emphasis added). The official account on the AC website <athlete365> emphasized "the health and safety of athletes and everyone involved," while repeating the IOC's commitment to proceeding as planned. "It is not the right time to make drastic decisions," it stated. Bach later claimed that "there was not a single voice asking for the cancellation of the Games" (IOC 2020n). However, if he was referring to postponement, rather than cancellation, mainstream media gave voice to significant numbers of athlete calling for that outcome.

According to AC chair Christy Coventry's report of the conference call and related Facebook post, the IOC acknowledged that athletes' training had been interrupted by quarantine restrictions and that they may feel "isolated and overwhelmed." Athletes were told, "It is vital that you remain in good mental health" by contacting friends and family remotely, or by looking at the "Well-being" section of the Athlete 365 website, not particularly helpful or empathetic advice. Coventry claimed that qualification-related questions were athletes' top concerns (IOC 2020h).

In contrast, AC member and outspoken athlete advocate, Fan Xiao (U.S.), described the shortcomings of the call, telling *New York Times* journalists that the IOC's message was not "Protect yourselves and protect your community," and that officials had failed to answer key questions about safety, training, and alternative scenarios. Xiao reported that one AC representative from Europe had blamed the media for exaggerating the risks and had even dismissed the virus as "not a deadly disease." When IOC's medical director Richard Budgett reportedly failed to correct that statement, Seyi Smith, chair of Canada's AC, emphasized the seriousness of the situation, and Budgett later agreed (Keh and Panja 2020). In a subsequent article in a special issue of *Human Rights Defender*, Xiao reported that the IOC officials on the conference call did not adequately explain timelines, the conditions required for the games to proceed, impacts on Japan's health care system, and safety provisions for the athletes' village, which would be housing 11,000 international visitors (Xiao 2020). Writing in response to Xiao's critique, the IOC predictably issued a boilerplate statement, devoting a full page to athletes' involvement in decision-making and a second page to the IOC's longstanding support and respect for athletes' rights ("The Response" 2020).

One day later, Bach conceded that they were "considering different scenarios" and generating "many different prognoses," but that it was "too early to make a decision" four and a half months in advance (Futterman 2020). On March 22, two days before the official postponement, *Olympic News* reported that the IOC "will step up its scenario-planning" because of the accelerated spread of cases globally. For the first time, it was reported that the task force would address the possibility of postponement, with these discussions to be finalized within four weeks. Even at this late stage, the IOC tried to shift responsibility to the Tokyo OC, the Japanese authorities, national Olympic committees and international federations, as well as broadcasters, corporate sponsors, partners, suppliers and contractors, all of whom, the IOC emphasized, would have to demonstrate their "full commitment and cooperation" (IOC 2020j). There was, in fact, little evidence of lack of commitment; rather, most of these organizations and individuals were waiting for clear directives from the IOC instead of a stream of evasive press releases.

Also, on March 22, Bach addressed athletes in a letter published on <Athlete 365>. Exhorting them to "never give up," he pointed to "improvements" in Japan's status that strengthened IOC's confidence "in our Japanese hosts that we could, with certain safety restrictions," proceed with Tokyo 2020, again implying that this responsibility fell primarily upon the host city and country. He claimed, however, that it was still "premature" to make a decision about dates. Finally, he expressed the hope that "the Olympic flame will be a light at the end of this tunnel" (IOC 2020k).

The same day, the Canadian Olympic Committee announced that it would not send athletes to Tokyo, followed on March 23 by Australia's swift reversal, then by Norway, Brazil, and other countries. Numerous national and international sports governing bodies were calling for postponement, and, on March 22, Abe first hinted that this was a possibility if the games could not be held in a "complete form" (Nikkei Asian Review 2020).

3. Depression and Acceptance Stages

The Pandemic is a Serious Problem, and the IOC and Tokyo OC Have Decided to Postpone the Games, in the Best Interests of the Athletes.

The joint statement from the IOC and the Tokyo OC, issued on March 24, announced that Tokyo 2020 would be rescheduled for a date not later than summer of 2021. The postponement had no doubt been discussed internally in the preceding weeks, but, as demonstrated above, IOC insiders had consistently denied that this was a possible scenario, and many observers were surprised at this sudden turnaround over a period of two days. According to the joint statement, "The leaders agreed" that the Olympics could serve as "a beacon of light" and the flame could be "the light at the end of the tunnel," and so on (IOC 2020m). Significantly, public manifestations of the depression and acceptance stages only lasted for one short day, before morphing into the self-congratulatory stage.

4. Self-Congratulatory Stage

The IOC Has Made the Right Decision.

Using a convenience sample of athletes' responses to the postponement on Twitter and Instagram, *Olympic News* reported general support for "a good decision," "excellent and right decision," made "for all the right reasons." While many athletes expressed personal disappointment, they pointed to "the bigger picture" (IOC 2020l). One short day later, in yet another example of shifting responsibility, Bach exhorted all stakeholders, "It will require everybody's efforts to make these games a symbol of hope." He explained that the IOC's earlier discussions with Tokyo OC had made members "pretty confident that by adapting these protective and mitigating measures, Japan could be able to organize the Games." However, in view of the rapid growth of international outbreaks, Bach explained that he had called an emergency meeting in order to make a joint decision "because it could not be unilateral by the IOC" (IOC 2020n). He repeated this sentiment in a March 25 letter to IOC members, detailing every step of the extensive discussions and consultations that he had personally and masterfully initiated. His four-page letter pointed to the IOC's rapid responses to every aspect of "this dynamic situation" that "kept evolving by the day," while portraying every action on the part of the IOC in the best possible light. In short, the letter appears to be answering the unspoken question, "Why did you wait so long?" (IOC 2020).

In view of the mounting pressure to postpone the games, it was hardly surprising to see widespread approval of the IOC's belated decision. In what *Olympic News* termed "an extraordinary statement," G20 leaders expressed their full support, as well as commending "Japan's determination to host Tokyo 2020 in their complete form as a symbol of human resilience." Bach used this opportunity to repeat his favorite "light at the end of the tunnel" metaphor (IOC 2020p).

Apparently, the stepped-up scenario-planning committee had been hard at work between March 22 and March 30, when new 2021 dates were announced (IOC 2020q). The 2021 event would still be called Tokyo 2020, probably because of a significant stockpile of merchandise bearing that logo. Using easily accessible social media posts again, Olympic News quickly published the positive reactions of four athletes and three organizations (IOC 2020r).

After a very short pause, Bach featured in two more news items, firstly, to support the UN's #BeActive campaign, and secondly, to praise doctors, nurses, health workers and volunteers on World Health Day (IOC 2020s; IOC 2020t). Interestingly, the accompanying photos showed Bach in casual clothes instead of business attire, as was customary for the Covid-19-related news items that required a more authoritative image.

By April 10, the first cracks in the 2021 plan were appearing, with Tokyo OC's CEO Yoshiro Mori stating that no one could say whether the pandemic would be under control by 2021, while expressing the hope that "mankind will manage to overcome the coronavirus crisis [by developing] treatments, medicines and vaccines" (Wade 2020b). A few days later, a lengthy Olympic News item explained all the challenges associated with the postponement, ending with the assurance that the task was "difficult, but possible" (IOC 2020u).

Veteran U.S. sportswriter Christine Brennan's *USA Today* opinion piece of April 21 explored the issues further, citing uncertainty on the part of medical experts, administrators, coaches, administrators and athletes (Brennan 2020). By April 28, a growing number of media reports echoed these concerns, citing, amongst other sources, the Japanese Medical Association, whose president warned that a vaccine was essential for global control of the pandemic in 2021. In response, a Tokyo OC spokesman dismissed what he termed "a variety of insights, opinions" from medical experts, noting that some claimed it was too early to make "a judgment." Mori, quoted in the same article, resorted to the Bach-like rhetoric: "If the world triumphs over the virus and we can hold the Olympics, then our games will be so many times more valuable than any past Olympics" (Wade 2020c).

Finally, on April 29, *Olympic News* published Bach's lengthy letter to the "Olympic movement," titled "Olympism and corona." [Olympism, according to the Olympic Charter, is "a philosophy of life, exalting and combining in a balanced whole the qualities of body, will and mind"] Covering crisis management, the post-Covid-19 world, and social, economic and political impacts, Bach's letter ended with the assertion that "the post-coronavirus world will need sport, and we are ready to contribute to shaping it with our Olympic values" (IOC 2020v).

On the topic of ideals and values, it was disappointing, but not surprising, to see many critics invoke these (largely mythical) "values" as evidence that the Olympic industry was failing to live up to its high moral reputation in dealing with the pandemic. In practice, there is little in the IOC's long history to support the notion that "values" of any kind animate its dealings with athletes (Lenskyj 2020). One notable exception to the "values" discourse was the critique by Enya et al. (2020), who argued that the IOC's "unilateral decision" provided further evidence of its lack of transparency and ongoing governance problems. They identified key questions that the IOC has a responsibility to address, most notably, whether or not national Olympic committees and athletes' representatives had any significant opportunities to participate in the discussion. Details of the possible scenarios and the actual voting process had not been revealed, nor had the involvement and influence of sponsors, broadcasters and other stakeholders, as well as the Japanese government. Enya et al. suggested that the IOC may have "ended up putting commercial interests (theirs and those of different IFs [international federations] before athletes' welfare," and the evidence certainly supports this possibility (Enya et al. 2020, 61).

CONCLUSION

The IOC's responses to this unprecedented threat loosely followed Kubler-Ross's five stages of grief, in that they progressed from a long period of denial and anger to a short bargaining and depression stage and an even shorter acceptance stage, followed by a unique display of self-congratulations. Although there were occasional lapses in the official response, the message remained consistent: the IOC is "the supreme authority of the Olympic movement."

These events amply illustrate how the Olympic industry's generously financed public relations machine controlled global messages about the pandemic and its impact on the 2020 Olympics. Initially, it was successful in silencing critics, and its belated postponement announcement was received with a mixture of relief and cynicism. By March 24, the day that the IOC eventually announced the postponement, dozens of international sports governing bodies had already adjusted their own calendars, postponing or cancelling more than 300 major events, with the possibility of a canceled 2020 Olympics undoubtedly guiding their decisions (ESPN 2020). Voices of the women and men at the heart of the event—the athletes—were largely silenced throughout the process, and, outside of the Olympic industry's inner circles, the world may never know which factors were responsible for the final decision.

REFERENCES

ABC News. 2020a. "Australian Olympic Committee Backs IOC 2020 Tokyo Go-Ahead Despite Coronavirus Fears." *ABC News*, March 18, 2020. abc.net.au/news/2020-03-19/australian-olympic-committee-backs-tokyo-2020-coronavirus/12069870.

———. 2020b. "Deputy Head of Japan's Olympic Committee Tests Positive for Covid-19." *ABC News*, March 17, 2020. abc.net.au/news/2020-03-18/japanese-olympic-official-tests-positive-coronavirus/12065664.

Armour, Nancy. 2020. "Opinion: It's Far Too Early to Freak Out About the Coronavirus. *Greenville Online*, February 26, 2020. greenvilleonline.com/story/sports/columnist/nancy-armour/2020/02/26/tokyo-olympics-perspective-needed-coronavirus-impact/4880176002/.

Bagratuni, John. 2020. "Bach Wants Tokyo Games Because of Athletes but Criticism Mounts." *DPA International*, March 21, 2020. dpa-international.com/topic/bach-wants-tokyo-games-athletes-criticism-mounts-urn%3Anewsml%3Adpa.com%3A20090101%3A200321-99-420368.

Brennan, Christine 2020. "Uncertainty, Not Optimism, Takes Hold in Japan." *USA Today*, April 21, 2020. usatoday.com/story/sports/christinebrennan/2020/04/21/coronavirus-uncertainty-over-2021-olympics-takes-hold-japan/2997544001/.

CBC. 2020. "IOC President Tries to Boost Olympic Morale in Japan." *CBC Sports*, February 28, 2020. cbc.ca/sports/olympics/tokyo-olympic-organizers-bach-interview-1.5479312.

Enya, Marjorie, Mateus Nagime, and Dominik Gusia. 2020. "Postponing the Tokyo 2020 Olympics." *Journal of Olympic Studies* 4 (1): 49-63.

ESPN. 2020. "List of Sporting Events Canceled Because of Coronavirus." ESPN, March 23, 2020. espn.com/olympics/story/_/id/28824781/list-sporting-events-canceled-coronavirus.

Futterman, Matthew. 2020. "Olympics President: 'Of Course We Are Considering Different Scenarios'." *New York Times*, March 19, 2020. nytimes.com/2020/03/19/sports/olympics/olympics-coronavirus-bach-ioc.html.

IOC. 2019. "Revised Tokyo 2020 Marathon Course Approved." *Olympic News*, December 19, 2019. olympic.org/news/revised-tokyo-2020-marathon-course-approved.

———. 2020a. "Fukushima Students Using YOG Experience to Promote Reconstruction." *Olympic News*, January 10, 2020. olympic.org/news/fukushima-students-using-yog-experience-to-promote-reconstruction.

———. 2020b. "'United by Emotion' to Be the Tokyo 2020 Games Motto." *Olympic News*, February 17, 2020. olympic.org/news/-united-by-emotion-to-be-the-tokyo-2020-games-motto.

———. 2020c. "IOC Executive Board Statement on the Coronavirus." *Olympic News*, March 3, 2020. olympic.org/news/ioc-executive-board-statement-on-the-coronavirus-covid-19-and-the-olympic-games-tokyo-2020.

———. 2020d. "IOC Statement on the Olympic Flame Lighting and the Olympic Games Tokyo 2020." *Olympic News*, March 12, 2020. olympic.org/news/ioc-statement-on-the-olympic-flame-lighting-and-the-olympic-games-tokyo-2020.

———. 2020e. "Olympic Flame for Tokyo 2020 Provides Beacon of Hope." *Olympic News*, March 12, 2020. olympic.org/news/olympic-flame-for-tokyo-2020-provides-beacon-of-hope-following-lighting-cermony-in-ancient-olympia.

———. 2020f. "IOC Statement on the Greek Leg of the Olympic Torch Relay." *Olympic News*, March 13, 2020. olympic.org/news/ioc-statement-on-the-greek-leg-of-the-olympic-torch-relay.

———. 2020g. "Communique from the International Olympic Committee Regarding the Olympic Games Tokyo 2020." *Olympic News*, March 17, 2020. olympic.org/news/communique-from-the-international-olympic-committee-regarding-the-olympic-games-tokyo-2020.

———. 2020h. "IOC Athletes' Commission Lead Global Call with Athlete Representatives." Athlete 365, March 18, 2020. olympic.org/athlete365/voice/ioc-ac-global-call-coronavirus.

———. 2020i. "Quotes from the IOC's stakeholder Consultations Regarding the Olympic Games Tokyo 2020." *Olympic News*, March 18, 2020. olympic.org/news/quotes-from-the-ioc-s-stakeholder-consultations-regarding-the-olympic-games-tokyo-2020.

———. 2020j. "Health and Safety Paramount as IOC Executive Board Agrees to Continue Scenario Planning." *Olympic News,* March 22, 2020. olympic.org/news/health-and-safety-paramount-as-ioc-executive-board-agrees-to-continue-scenario-planning-for-the-olympic-games-tokyo-2020.

———. 2020k. "Letter from President Thomas Bach OLY to Athletes." *Olympic News,* March 22, 2020. olympic.org/athlete365/voice/22-march-letter-president-thomas-bach-athletes/.

———. 2020l. "Athletes and NOCs React to Postponement." Olympic News, March 24, 2020. olympic.org/news/athletes-react-to-postponement-of-tokyo-olympic-games.

———. 2020m. "Joint Statement from the International Olympic Committee and the Tokyo 2020 Organising Committee." *Olympic News,* March 24, 2020. olympic.org/news/joint-statement-from-the-international-olympic-committee-and-the-tokyo-2020-organising-committee.

———. 2020n. "IOC President: 'It will require everybody's efforts to make these games a symbol of hope'." *Olympic News,* March 25, 2020. olympic.org/news/ioc-president-it-will-require-everybody-s-efforts-to-make-these-games-a-symbol-of-hope.

———. 2020o. "IOC President Updates IOC Members on Steps and Considerations Regarding Tokyo 2020 Postponement." *Olympic News,* March 27, 2020. olympic.org/news/ioc-president-updates-ioc-members-on-steps-and-considerations-regarding-tokyo-2020-postponement.

———. 2020p. "IOC Thanks G20 Leaders for their Support for the Olympic Games Tokyo 2020." *Olympic News,* March 27, 2020. olympic.org/news/ioc-thanks-g20-leaders-for-their-support-for-the-olympic-games-tokyo-2020.

———. 2020q. "IOC, IPC, Tokyo 2020 Organising Committee and Tokyo Metropolitan Government Announce New Dates:" *Olympic News,* March 30, 2020. olympic.org/news/ioc-ipc-tokyo-2020-organising-committee-and-tokyo-metropolitan-government-announce-new-dates-for-the-olympic-and-paralympic-games-tokyo-2020.

———. 2020r. "Athletes React to New Dates for Tokyo 2020 Olympics." *Olympic News,* March 31, 2020. olympic.org/news/athletes-react-to-new-dates-for-tokyo-2020-olympics.

———. 2020s. "President Joins Olympic Athletes and Fans in Call to Stay Active." *Olympic News,* April 6, 2020. olympic.org/news/ioc-president-joins-olympic-athletes-and-fans-in-call-to-stay-active.

———. 2020t. "IOC President to Doctors, Nurses, Health Workers and Volunteers." *Olympic News,* April 7, 2020. olympic.org/news/ioc-president-to-doctors-nurses-health-workers-and-volunteers-you-are-our-true-champions.

———. 2020u. "What Goes into Postponing the Olympic Games." *Olympic News,* April 17, 2020. olympic.org/news/what-goes-into-postponing-the-olympic-games.

———. 2020v. "President Bach Writes to Olympic Movement." *Olympic News,* April 29, 2020. olympic.org/news/ioc-president-bach-writes-to-olympic-movement-olympism-and-corona.

Keh, Andrew, and Tariq Panja. 2020. "IOC's Reassurance About Tokyo Olympics Rankles Some Athletes." *New York Times,* March 18, 2020. nytimes.com/2020/03/18/sports/olympics/olympics-coronavirus-athletes-training.html?action=click&module=RelatedLinks&pgtype=Article.

Kelly, Cathal. 2020. "Don't Cancel the Olympics Because of the Coronavirus. *Globe and Mail,* February 28, 2020. globeandmail.com/sports/article-dont-cancel-the-olympics-because-of-the-coronavirus-its-times-like/.

Kubler-Ross, Elizabeth, and David Kessler. 2014. *On Grief and Grieving: Finding the Meaning of Grief Through the Five Stages.* New York: Scribner.

Lewis, Leo, and Murad Ahmed. 2020. "Japan: How Coronavirus Crushed Abe's Olympic Dream. *Financial Times,* March 30, 2020. fr.com/content/c343aa5e-702a-11ea-9bca-bf503995cd6f.

Lies, Elaine. 2020. "Japan Will Make Utmost Efforts to Keep Virus from Affecting Olympic Games PM Abe." *US News,* February 3, 2020. usnews.com/news/world/articles/2020-02-03/japan-will-make-utmost-efforts-to-keep-virus-from-affecting-olympic-games-pm-abe.

Liew, Jonathan. 2020. "The Spectre of a Cancelled Olympics Belongs to a Different, Scarier World." *The Guardian,* March 2, 2020. theguardian.com/sport/2020/mar/02/the-spectre-of-a-cancelled-olympics-scarier-world-coronavirus?utm_term=Autofeed&CMP=twt_gu&utm_medium=&utm_source=Twitter" \l "Echobox=1583172964.

Moran, Jerry, and Richard Blumenthal. 2019. "The Courage of Survivors." July 30, 2020. moran.senate.gov/public/index/cfm/u-s-olympics-sexual-abuse-investigation.

Nikkei Asian Review. 2020. "Abe Says Postponing Olympics Is an Option." *Nikkei Asian Review*, March 23, 2020. asia.nikkei.com/Spotlight/Tokyo-2020-Olympics/Abe-says-postponing-Olympics-is-an-option-due-to-coronavirus.

Prewitt, Alex. 2020. "How Hayley Wickenheiser Is Using Her Unique Platform in Global Fight Against Covid-19." *Sports Illustrated*, April 11, 2020. si.com/olympics/2020/04/11/hayley-wickenheiser-ice-hockey-medical-school-doctor-coronavirus.

Quek, Sam. 2020. "Sam Quek: Cancelling the Olympics Because of Coronavirus Is Unthinkable for Athletes." *Mirror Online*, March 1, 2020. mirror.co.uk/sport/other-sports/sam-quek-cancelling-olympics-because-21612577.amp.

Ropes and Gray Law Firm. 2018. "Report of the Independent Investigation." Ropes and Gray Law Firm, December 10, 2018. ropesgray.com>media>Files>USOC>ropes-gray-full-report.pdf.

"The Response from the International Olympic Committee." 2020. *Human Rights Defender* 29 (2): 22-24.

USA Today. 2020. "Tokyo Olympics CEO Hints Games Could Be in Doubt Even in 2021." *USA Today*, April 10, 2020. usatoday.com/story/sports/olympics/2020/04/10/tokyo-olympic-ceo-hints-games-could-be-in-doubt-even-in-2021/111531604/.

Wade, Stephen. 2020a. "IOC senior member." *AP News*, February 25, 2020. apnews.com/afsContent8539951776.

———. 2020b. "Tokyo Olympic CEO." *AP News*, April 10, 2020. apnews.com/e25f9d7370ceda0b4794df5bbd79f7b3.

———. 2020c. "Japan Medical Assn." *AP News*, April 28, 2020. apnews.com/cae4ce17ce524a211ccd5b1944372491.

Wade, Stephen, and Mari Yamaguchi. 2020. "No 'Plan B' for Olympics." *AP News*, February 14, 2020. apnews.com/936a921979a504cb9d4056dc44b2830a.

Xiao, Han. 2020. "Athletes First? The Right to Health and Safety in Postponing the Tokyo Olympic Games." *Human Rights Defender* 29 (2): 19-21.

CHAPTER 2

How Covid-19 Exposed the Limitations of a Technocratic Anti-Doping System and the Need for Diversification of Responsibility

Daniel Read

THE ANTI-DOPING SYSTEM DURING COVID-19

There can be no doubt that the spread of Covid-19 globally and ensuing social distancing protocols constituted a significant shock to the sports industry as leagues and competitions ground to a halt (see Introduction to this book). The anti-doping system was no exception as those responsible for testing were presented with significant operating restrictions, not least to conducting out-of-competition testing. Unannounced out-of-competition testing specifies how athletes "may be required to provide a sample at any time and at any place by any Anti-Doping Organization with testing authority over him or her" (WADA 2019c, 37). The ability to test athletes at random, 365 days of the year, is based on the argument that some performance enhancing substances are only detectable for a short time, therefore, in-competition testing alone is insufficient (Borry et al. 2018). Problematically, government mandated social distancing rules as well as increased travel and border restrictions designed to limit the transmission of Covid-19 severely impeded the ability to reach athletes and conduct out-of-competition testing. Accordingly, questions were raised by athletes, experts, and journalists about the opportunity reduced testing provided to athletes willing to use prohibited substances (Futterman 2020; Nestler 2020; Sridhar 2020).

Out-of-competition testing is a fundamental pillar of the moral technopreneurialism approach to anti-doping (Henne 2014; Park 2005). Moral technopreneurialism refers to how scientific processes and developments have been used by regulators to construct and pursue "the moral underpinnings of the anti-doping agenda" (Henne 2014, 885). Scientific processes, such as testing, are used to present subjective moral beliefs as objective truths. Testing became a dominant feature of anti-doping under the International Olympic Committee Medical Commission as it enabled the group to push their moral agenda of protecting Olympic sport's "purity" by detecting physical impurity (i.e., doping) (Henne 2014). As detection capabilities improved and athletes were found to be using prohibited substances at the Olympics, this evidence confirmed preconceptions about doping and was used to rationalize further research and testing. Current anti-doping efforts under the World Anti-Doping Agency (WADA), the chief regulator of anti-doping in Olympic sport, are still justified on the perspective that doping violates the values of Olympism, fair play, and athlete health (Mazanov and Connor 2010; World Anti-Doping Code 2019). WADA's "technocratic" system (Meier and Reinold 2018) privileges continued innovation in testing, science, technology, and surveillance to detect and punish athletes using prohibited substances (Henne 2014; Sefiha and Reichman 2016).

Anti-doping policy development has historically been punctuated by high-profile events, such as scandals, that expose shortcomings in the system and stimulate debate and change (Hunt 2011; Read, Skinner, Lock, and Houlihan 2019; Ritchie and Jackson 2014). Covid-19 has served as a "focusing event" having encouraged scholars and practitioners to reflect on the current anti-doping system (e.g., Pitsiladis, Muniz-Pardos, Miller, and Verroken 2020; WADA 2020e). However, commentary has been limited to considering new approaches that reinforce the technocratic system. Drawing from data provided by interviews in digital and print media sources as well as organizational press releases, this chapter will demonstrate how the restrictions imposed by Covid-19 on testing capabilities exposed an existing fundamental limitation with the technocratic anti-doping system, namely the dependence on testing and a lack of strategic diversity. Consequently, there is space for new anti-doping systems to emerge. Accordingly, this chapter provides a critical reflection on how the anti-doping system has responded to Covid-19 arguing that the pandemic should serve as a catalyst for evolving regulation away from a unidimensional, detection-oriented technocratic model. Instead, a model that diversifies and connects responsibility for anti-doping to multiple levels is proposed. A diversified responsibility model is argued to promote prevention, reduce the burden on athletes to self-regulate their behavior, reduce dependence on scientific innovation and increase resilience to any future environmental or geo-political events that impede out-of-competition testing.

The Response to Covid-19 from the Anti-Doping System

The anti-doping system is defined in this chapter as the stakeholders responsible for anti-doping policy implementation as specified by the World Anti-Doping Code (2019). This includes but is not limited to international federations, national anti-doping organizations, regional anti-doping organizations, Olympic and Paralympic committees, and major event organizers. These are collectively referred to as anti-doping organizations (WADA 2019c). Covid-19 prompted different levels of response from anti-doping organizations ranging from trialing novel non-contact testing approaches to temporary cessation of all testing.

The most common response from national anti-doping organizations was to reduce or stop all testing. For instance, a survey by the Monitoring Group of the Council of Europe Anti-Doping Convention found that 65% of the forty-eight

European countries surveyed stopped all out-of-competition testing and a further 33% reduced testing (Petrou and Pakhnotskaya 2020). As U.K. Anti-Doping Chief Executive, Nicole Sapstead, explained, "With the cancellation of sporting events and recent U.K. Government advice concerning the control of the virus, we have reviewed our operational activity and are announcing a significant reduction in our testing program" (U.K. Anti-Doping 2020). Other major Olympic nations also reduced levels of testing due to social distancing protocols and welfare concerns as China suspended all domestic testing and Russia suspended testing for ten days (Morgan 2020; The Independent 2020). Meanwhile the United States reduced operations to "mission-critical testing of athletes in sports still competing, and as absolutely needed for those preparing for the Tokyo Olympic and Paralympic Games" (U.S. Anti-Doping Agency 2020) and Australia only engaged with "critical" testing (Australian Anti-Doping Agency 2020). The full extent testing was reduced is not yet known, but the German Anti-Doping Organization speculatively estimated that testing had been reduced by 90% to 95% (Oelmaier 2020). Anti-doping organizations attached to sports bodies were equally restricted. For instance, the President of the International Cycling Union, David Lappartient, highlighted that there had been a 95% reduction in the number of tests in cycling (Farrand 2020). Likewise, the Athletics Integrity Unity reduced operations to "priority testing missions in those places where it is feasible and safe to do so" (Athletics Integrity Unity 2020). The International Testing Agency, which has multiple agreements in place to partially or fully manage anti-doping programs on behalf of International Federations, also stated that it would be postponing testing missions in light of restrictions imposed due to Covid-19 (International Testing Agency 2020).

Considered together, the reduction and, in some instances, complete absence of testing can be considered a prime opportunity for athletes contemplating or already using prohibited substances due to the reduced likelihood of being tested. As Travis Tygart, CEO of the U.S. Anti-Doping Agency responded when asked about Covid-19, "What we worry about is those who otherwise may not be willing to compete clean and will try everything to get away with it. It does for a period of time at least open that window of opportunity" (BBC 2020). This concern is supported by other anti-doping advisors who recognized the incompatibility of social distancing with testing and the opportunity this affords athletes to use prohibited substances (Leventhal 2020). Notwithstanding the speculated added difficulties athletes would have faced in obtaining substances under social distancing protocols and planning their substance use for peaking at a specific competition (Benson 2020; Oelmaier 2020), Covid-19 exposed a significant shortcoming in the technocratic system, the dependence on detection via testing and the lack of alternative strategies. This manifested in a window of opportunity for doping that demanded a response from anti-doping organizations.

Solutions to Covid-19 Provided by the Anti-Doping System

To circumvent the challenges posed by Covid-19 some anti-doping organizations fast-tracked novel and innovative technological practices. For example, the U.S. Anti-Doping Agency trialed whether athletes could self-administer urine and blood test kits posted to their home under the guidance of doping control officers present via video-call. The blood sample was taken using "dried blood-spot testing," a procedure that involves an athlete pricking their finger to collect blood droplets. Dried blood-spot testing has been publicized by WADA as a "game-changer" due to its potential benefits that include a simple and less-invasive method, improved sample stability and reduced transportation and storage demands (WADA 2019). Ultimately, this may allow increased testing capability of athletes training in hard to reach locations (WADA 2019), a tactic often used by those trying to avoid detection. Similarly, the German Anti-Doping Agency indicated that it piloted dried blood-spot testing whilst out-of-competition testing capabilities were reduced (Nationale Anti-Doping Agentur 2020). The development of dried blood-spot testing and the search for alternatives is commendable under the circumstances, but the fundamental issue remained that under the technocratic system solutions were dependent upon further technological innovation. Other concerns about the vulnerability of video-call platforms to hacking and the potential for packages being lost raise additional questions about liability and safety of remote testing.

The messaging about alternative strategies was consistent from anti-doping organizations and WADA to assuage concerns about the lack of testing and deter athletes considering doping in the "window of opportunity." Anti-doping organizations and WADA officials specifically emphasized that other technological mechanisms were still in place (Keating 2020; O'Flynn 2020). Athletes were still required to report their whereabouts information, ensure they had valid therapeutic use exemptions, reminded that the athlete biological passport was in operation, and that intelligence and investigation methods were still in place (WADA 2020a). Upon individual inspection, these mechanisms reveal significant limitations. Firstly, athletes were still required to provide whereabouts information for out-of-competition testing, but the likelihood of being tested was negligible due to travel restrictions and concerns for doping control officer welfare (Benson 2020; Leventhal 2020). Athletes were advised that failure to provide a sample would constitute a rule-violation, but should an athlete declare that they were 1. self-isolating due to presenting Covid-19 symptoms, 2. a high-risk individual, or 3. lived with a high-risk individual, then this could potentially lead to the test being canceled (Leventhal 2020; WADA 2020b). Secondly, the need to maintain a valid therapeutic use exemption for any prohibited substances used for medicinal purposes is important to ensuring athletes do not provide inadvertent analytical rule-violations, but it does not function as a deterrent to doping.

Thirdly, WADA (2020b) emphasized the athlete biological passport as a pivotal tool at their disposal. Through the collection of blood and urine tests, the athlete biological passport monitors change in steroidal and hematological markers over time in an athlete to identify "unnatural" changes that may be due to doping. Athletes can then be targeted for testing or sanctioned based on an abnormal profile without having provided a sample containing a specific prohibited substance (WADA 2019c). The athlete biological passport has experienced some success since its introduction (Devriendt, Chokoshvili, and Borry 2019), for example, there was a significant decrease in female 800m, 1500m, 5,000m and 10,000m performance after implementation indicating a reduction in doping (Ilujkov, Chokoshvili, and Borry 2019). Opposingly, both the hematological and steroidal athlete biological passport modules can be hard to interpret, influenced by a myriad of confounding factors and manipulated through certain techniques (Mahendru, Kumaravel, Mahalmani, and Medhi 2020; Ponzetto et al. 2019). Evidence of this is provided by an Austrian police investigation in 2019 that has since implicated "21 athletes from eight countries and five sports" (Pavitt 2020) in blood doping as evidence suggested that athletes had not produced abnormal passport profiles (Benson 2019). Further, anti-doping experts have commented that there is little utility to the athlete biological passport under limited testing frequency imposed by Covid-19 (Benson 2020). Acknowledging that the athlete biological passport has had some success, evidence suggests that the combination of a lack of testing and sophisticated doping programs during the window of opportunity still left the anti-doping system vulnerable.

Lastly, WADA (2020b) as well as national anti-doping organizations (Nationale Anti-Doping Agentur 2020; U.K. Anti-Doping 2020) emphasized ongoing intelligence work as a deterrent. There is no doubt that intelligence gathering has been beneficial to the anti-doping system and the Austrian case previously provided demonstrated how intelligence driven investigations can buttress the limitations of testing. Further, there is growing support for intelligence work profiling changes in athlete performance in conjunction with the athlete biological passport to indirectly identify potential doping behaviors (Hopker et al. 2018). Specific to the window of opportunity provided by Covid-19, greater integration of intelligence processes into the anti-doping system should function as a potential deterrent to using prohibited substances. Problematically though, intelligence and investigation processes primarily serve to support testing by, in theory, helping target the right person at the right time for testing. This is evident in the International Standard for Testing and Investigations:

> Code Article 5.8 requires Anti-Doping Organizations to obtain, assess and process anti-doping intelligence from all available sources, to be used to help deter and detect doping, by informing the development of an effective, intelligent and proportionate Test Distribution Plan and/or the planning of Target Testing, and/or by forming the basis of an investigation into a possible anti-doping rule violation(s). (WADA 2020c, 53)

In this sense, rather than offering an opportunity to approach doping from a different perspective (Marclay et al. 2013), intelligence becomes another part of the technocratic system to anti-doping reinforcing the prioritization of detection and testing.

Beyond the tools discussed, consideration of new approaches to managing the challenges posed by Covid-19 were minimal. Pitsiladis, Muniz-Pardos, Miller, and Verroken (2020) commented on the opportunity Covid-19 provided for developing approaches to sports integrity, however, this was limited to how technology could enable more targeted and frequent testing. WADA did indicate that it would be increasing the availability of educational resources and suggested to other anti-doping organizations that "On-line and virtual education should be considered where possible (and where needed)" (WADA 2020d, 4). However, the extent to which educational materials increased is unclear and the primary guidance given to anti-doping organizations trying to handle Covid-19 focused on technocratic procedures (WADA 2020d) to resume testing as quickly as possible if safe to do so (WADA 2020b). WADA's commitment to regulating prohibited substance use via a technocratic system is most clear in the words of its President, Witold Bańka,

> What this pandemic has demonstrated is the need for further innovation in anti-doping. WADA knows that to make anti-doping more effective, we continually need to innovate. Our work, in collaboration with the wider anti-doping community, researching new sample collection and analytical techniques has been ramped up, in particular in the areas of dried-blood-spot analysis and artificial intelligence. (WADA 2020e)

This statement is indicative of the approach WADA is taking to the dependence on testing exposed by Covid-19, which is to innovate new tests and technology, therefore further entrenching the anti-doping systems dependence on a technocratic system. As Bańka has reiterated on how Covid-19 has encouraged reflection, "DBS [dried blood-spot testing], artificial intelligence, and strong cooperation with law enforcement are, I think, the future of anti-doping" (Ryan 2020). It is fairly safe to conclude that although new tools are being developed under an innovation-driven technocratic system, there is less chance of a fundamental re-evaluation of the aims and philosophy underpinning policy. The arguments presented so far about the limitations of the technocratic systems are not exceptional to the pandemic context either and can be situated in broader criticisms of the technocratic system.

The Problem with the Technocratic System

It is noted that there have been significant technological developments in anti-doping testing in recent years to improve prohibited substance detection (Thevis, Walpurgis, and Thomas 2020). Likewise, artificial intelligence and law enforcement investigations can help address shortcomings in testing (Ellingworth 2020). However, the technocratic system suffers further limitations related to the dependence on testing and innovation even when considered to be working at "full" capacity.

The glaring limitation is the disparity between recent estimates of athletes who have used prohibited substances calculated from randomized response techniques (a survey method that provides individual respondents confidentiality) ranging from 3.1% to 57.1% (Duiven and De Hon 2015; Elbe and Pitsch 2018; Ulrich et al. 2018) and the 1.42% of accredited tests globally in 2018 that reported an adverse analytical finding[1] (WADA 2019b). Official figures only provide the percentage of tests that return an adverse analytical finding, not the percentage of athletes from the testing pool that return an adverse analytical finding, therefore, there is some discrepancy in this comparison. Yet even when considering this discrepancy, there remains a significant gap between athletes admitting to prohibited substance use and athletes sanctioned. This is reflected in multiple studies that demonstrate the testing is inconsistent as a deterrent to doping (Baudouin and Szymanski 2016; Overbye 2017). So, despite the prominence of testing in the anti-doping system, it is relatively ineffective as a tool. Additionally, the cost of testing relative to the number of adverse analytical findings is demonstrated to be extremely inefficient (Dvorak, Saugy and Pitsiladis 2014; Maennig 2014).

The technocratic system also relies on the ability to implement robust testing programs. Evidence has long suggested that inconsistencies exist between the quality of anti-doping programs between countries (e.g., Hanstad, Skille, and Loland 2010) and these disparities are still evident (Gray 2019; Houlihan and Hanstad 2019). Attempts have been made to address differences between nations and sports (Hanstad and Houlihan 2015). Yet the problem remains that not all anti-doping organizations have the necessary resources or the inclination to develop robust testing programs (Houlihan 2014). The result is that athletes can perceive the inequalities in testing undermining the anti-doping systems legitimacy (Efverström, Nader Ahmadi, Hoff, and Bäckström 2016). From a technocratic perspective, the system is only as strong as its weakest member. The inability to ensure that all anti-doping organizations have the requisite skills and resources to implement technological innovations is a significant shortcoming. Reflecting on Covid-19, it is unlikely that all anti-doping organizations globally will have the resources to quickly return to pre-crisis testing levels (O'Flynn 2020). If policy continues to privilege technological innovation and testing quality, and neglects ease of implementation, pursuing a technocratic system may only serve to increase disparities.

The last criticism discussed here in relation to the dependence on testing created by a technocratic system is the "arms race" mentality required (Henne 2014). As dopers continually find new performance enhancing methods and substances to avoid detection (Protti, Mandrioli, and Mercolini 2019), this nullifies the utility of existing

---

[1] A test that reveals the presence of a prohibited substance including those from athletes with a valid therapeutic use exemption.

tests demanding further investment. Micro-dosing, the practice of taking prohibited substances in a sufficiently small dosage to avoid biological accumulation whilst taking a sufficiently large enough dosage to elicit performance benefits is one such example. Evidence supports that micro-doses of recombinant human erythropoietin are sufficient to improve cardiovascular performance whilst minimizing the potential for detection (Sgrò et al. 2018). Gene-doping, the process of transferring "favorable" genetic material into the patient, is another example of a procedure that may be used to improve performance and requires a scientific response from the anti-doping system (Neuberger and Simon 2017). This is not to say that new promising testing methods are not being considered, for example, longitudinal metabolomics may help detect hormone misuse (Narduzzi et al. 2020). The issue is how long developments such as metabolomics will remain effective before new substances and methods emerge. Whilst anti-doping policy prioritizes testing (and processes to support testing) the "arms race" will continue.

The criticisms of testing quality, disparities in implementation and the perpetual nullification of tests can be contextualized by the reality that the reasons for prohibited substance use are sociological in nature. The application of technology and science to detect doping does not address the underlying social ecology (Smith et al. 2010). It is for the broader reasons that have just been outlined as well as the limitations of responses from anti-doping organizations to Covid-19, that practitioners should treat the pandemic as a focusing event to reassess the dependence on technology, not just current methods (Pitsiladis, Muniz-Pardos, Miller, and Verroken 2020; WADA 2020e). Testing will always be involved in anti-doping to some extent but an alternative multi-level approach to substance use in sport that diversifies responsibility across stakeholders can alleviate the reliance on technological innovation.

DIVERSIFYING RESPONSIBILITY FOR ANTI-DOPING

The extent to which there has been any radical change in anti-doping is questionable as WADA's policy still upholds the "basic principles of anti-doping established back in the 1960s" (Hunt, Dimeo, and Jedlicka 2012, 58). Evidence supports that anti-doping policy reform has been punctuated by key events such as Ben Johnson's positive test for stanozolol, the Festina Affair, and the Russian Olympic doping scandal (Brissonneau and Ohl 2010; Read, Skinner, Lock, and Houlihan 2019; Ritchie and Jackson 2014). These "focusing events" demonstrated policy deficiencies and provided opportunities to reassess the dominant policy paradigms (Ritchie and Jackson 2014). Covid-19 has also demonstrated policy deficiencies and served as a catalyst for discussion of new approaches (e.g., Pitsiladis, Muniz-Pardos, Miller, and Verroken 2020; WADA 2020e). It is the opinion of the author, though, that these discussions should be extended to examine the current technocratic model.

The current dependence on testing and technological innovation under a technocratic system has been acutely exposed by Covid-19. This is complicated by broader criticisms that testing is ineffective, inconsistent, and transitory. The technocratic system derives from the moral basis that doping threatens sport's integrity, the health of athletes, the notion of equal competition, and the Olympic ideals of the spirit of sport (Henne 2014; Kayser and Smith 2008). This manifests in WADA's vision of doping-free sport achieved by prohibition policy that morally defines unlawful behavior, detects via technocratic processes, and regulates with penalties (Skinner et al. 2017). Yet the failure of testing and the increased health risks posed by the prohibition approach undermine the current anti-doping system (Kayser and Tolleneer 2017). Covid-19 has served to further illustrate the enormous difficulties and unlikeliness of achieving doping-free sport under a prohibitive technocratic system that demands widespread, effective drug testing as well as scientific innovation. Given the aforementioned criticisms of the testing-based prohibition approach to anti-doping, alternative models and rationales for second generation anti-doping policies have emerged (Mazanov and Connor 2010). These alternatives include models based on medical ethics, corporate social responsibility and criminal frameworks each with its own strengths and weaknesses.

Legal arguments that doping constitutes fraud and should be criminalized to serve as a deterrent (Sumner 2017) still propagate the need for a rigorous technocratic system of surveillance and testing. Further, criminalizing doping raises serious concerns about the potential for miscarriages of justice if the science underpinning testing is not robust or competitors were framed. A corporate social responsibility approach advocates that the concerns of all relevant stakeholders about substance use in sport should be balanced and accommodated (Mazanov 2016). From this stance, it raises an interesting question for other approaches to substance use about which stakeholders should be prioritized and what views are privileged (e.g., athlete welfare versus commercial viability). However, it is limited by not explicitly stating how different stakeholders should be balanced or how substance use should be regulated only favoring "which regime best strikes a balance between the competing interests of the various stakeholders" (Mazanov 2016, 223). Arguments based on medical ethics assert that substance use is a social issue that transcends sport, so total suppression of doping via surveillance and testing is unachievable, therefore, social and physical harm reduction to athletes should take precedence (Savulescu, Foddy, and Clayton 2004; Smith and Stewart 2015). Testing still exists within this approach but to monitor the welfare of athletes and detect harmful substances. Criticisms of harm reduction suggest that it may force athletes (and junior athletes) into medically supervised doping and encourage athletes to use more dangerous substances or methods in pursuit of competitive advantage. The assumption that should certain substances and methods be permitted (within safe limits), all athletes and nations will have access to safe treatment conditions is also questionable (Towns and Gerrard 2014). These criticisms are valid, but unlike current policy where risky prohibited substance use still occurs, the reality of risks is considered, education and safeguarding support can be provided, and substance quality can be better guaranteed.

Criminalization, a corporate social responsibility approach, and harm reduction models all have strengths and weaknesses, but they are unable to escape the need for testing in some capacity. Therefore, there is merit in a responsibility diversification model of anti-doping that shifts the burden away from detection via technocratic processes. That is not to say that testing does not serve a purpose, but it should not be the central component.

The anti-doping literature is replete with suggestions other than testing to help deter athletes using prohibited substances including economic incentives (e.g., Lenten and Smith 2020), performance profiling (e.g., Hopker et al. 2018) and targeted education interventions (e.g., Sagoe et al. 2016). It is not within the scope of this chapter to consider all proposed strategies to improve anti-doping. Instead, this chapter argues for a strategic multi-level diversification of responsibility. Doping involves a network of stakeholders such as suppliers, physicians, teammates, managers, and officials (Bell, Ten Have, and Lauchs 2016). At present, anti-doping primarily depends on deterring and detecting athletes via testing and there is limited incentive for other key stakeholders to ensure athletes are protected. If the burden of responsibility was shifted away from athletes to sports teams and organizations (with sufficient oversight) there is incentive for these stakeholders to seriously engage in prevention and monitor their athletes. The premise being that the anti-doping system would be less dependent on testing as there would be greater motivation from teams and organizations to internally prevent their athletes from doping. Especially under the presence of other strategies such as increased intelligence and performance profiling enabled by a reduction in the dependence on testing.

At the athlete-level, Camporesi (2017) has suggested that stakeholders who hold power over athletes should be held responsible for any athletes using dangerous substances. The argument being that this would incentivize team owners, executives, and sponsors to ensure the safeguarding of their players. Precedent for this approach is provided by commercial fraud laws that holds financial officers responsible for fraud committed by their employees (Camporesi 2017). At an organizational-level, Maennig (2014) has suggested that responsibility for substance misuse should be shifted to national and international sports organizations through the threat of economic sanctions. If an organization is revealed through scientific or investigative methods to have a problem with athletes abusing substances, then they will face economic sanctions or even expulsion from the Olympics. The International Weightlifting Federation currently utilizes a similar premise by sanctioning national weightlifting federations if they exceed three positive tests within their nation in a calendar year. Therefore, there is an economic imperative for sports organizations to do everything within their power to support coaches and clubs preventing doping and educating athletes on the associated risks of substance misuse. These two methods have the indirect benefit that athletes can recognize if their sport or team suffers negative consequences due to their actions, their own economic income is jeopardized. This approach is however open to criticism about the justification of collective responsibility, but the presence of shared responsibility could foster further deterrence between athletes *if* managed correctly. At national and global levels, intelligence and investigations that target trafficking and distribution ensure that those responsible for supplying dangerous substances are held responsible and access to substances are restricted. These combined mechanisms create a system that places and connects responsibility on multiple stakeholders alleviating the dependence on athletes self-regulating their behavior.

The primary challenge that emerges is how to motivate stakeholders to fully support multi-level diversification of responsibility if they will bear accountability for athlete behavior. Previous scandals have suggested sports in the past have avoided looking for prohibited substance use or actively covered up doping for commercial reasons (Houlihan, Hanstad, Loland, and Waddington 2019). At present, monitoring stakeholder compliance with the World Anti-Doping Code predominantly operates at a descriptive level (Gray 2019; Houlihan, 2014), but the development of auditing by WADA's Compliance Task Force is a positive step in monitoring depth of compliance (WADA, 2020f). The presence of in-depth compliance monitoring by WADA should ensure organizations take their responsibilities seriously, especially now WADA has the capacity to apply graded sanctions for non-compliance with the World Anti-Doping Code. Owners, managers, and sponsors can be held responsible for athletes by national sports organizations, national sports organizations can be held accountable by international federations and Olympic bodies, which in turn can be monitored by WADA auditors.

Faced with the same challenge of minimal out-of-competition testing posed by Covid-19 a diversified responsibility approach should outperform the current technocratic detection system as the chain of responsibility reduces the burden on athletes to self-regulate their behavior. By linking athlete behavior to team owners, executives and sponsors as well as national and international sports organizations, there is greater incentive for these stakeholders to support and monitor athletes to prevent substance misuse. This reduces any "window of opportunity" as there are other mechanisms in place whilst testing is suspended. At present, responsibility for athlete behavior is not related to these influential stakeholders, therefore, there is little cause for these stakeholders to actively support anti-doping measures. Further, stakeholders should be more motivated to adopt other policies that aim to prevent doping by addressing the wider socio-cultural issues that may encourage substance use rather than simply trying to detect it. Phrased differently, in an environment where responsibility is shared rather than placed on the athlete there is greater incentive to invest resources to prevent doping in the first place rather than just detect it. This chain of responsibility is contingent, however, on rigorous compliance monitoring to ensure that coaches, clubs, and organizations do not simply try to hide doping behaviors.

CONCLUSION

In closing, Covid-19 has encouraged deep reflection on the status quo in many aspects of the sports industry and anti-doping should be no different. New models have been proposed which further entrench a technology driven approach, but this does not alleviate criticisms that Covid-19 is reflective of broader problems with a technocratic system. In this chapter, diversification of responsibility has been proposed as a new anti-doping model. Were the anti-doping system to be suspended regionally or globally again due to a resurgence of Covid-19 (or other geo-political factors), the absence of out-of-competition testing would not create a window of opportunity under a diversified responsibility model. This is because multi-level mechanisms would exist to persuade stakeholders throughout the network to ensure that athletes are not misusing substances rather than relying on detection via testing. Greater discussion is required about what the most effective mechanisms would be at all levels, but the fundamental idea of a chain of responsibility is key. It would be naïve to ignore the complex political environment that influences anti-doping policy. If WADA is to effectively regulate and audit all stakeholders, there is a need to ensure that they are transparent and accountable as an organization to maintain equality between Code signatories. Ultimately, Covid-19 has not created new problems, but exposed existing deficiencies. A diversified responsibility anti-doping model can address these shortcomings of the current technocratic dominant system.

REFERENCES

Athletics Integrity Unity. 2020. "Athletics Integrity Unit Update Regarding Covid-19." *Athletics Integrity Unit,* March 26, 2020. https://www.athleticsintegrity.org/downloads/pdfs/know-us/en/AIU-UPDATE-Update-regarding-Covid-19.pdf

Australian Anti-Doping Agency. 2020. "ASADA Refines Testing Program in Light of New Government Guidelines." *Australian Anti-Doping Agency*, March 24. 2020. https://www.asada.gov.au/news/asada-refines-testing-program-light-new-government-guidelines

Baudouin, Claire, and Stefan Szymanski. 2016. "Testing the Testers: Do More Tests Deter Athletes from Doping. "*International Journal of Sport Finance* 11 (4): 349-363.

BBC. 2020. "Doping in Sport: US Anti-Doping Head Fears Athletes Could 'Take Advantage' of Reduced Tests." *BBC*, March 27, 2020. https://www.bbc.co.uk/sport/52064293

Bell, Peter, Charlotte Ten Have, and Mark Lauchs. 2016. "A Case Study Analysis of a Sophisticated Sports Doping Network: Lance Armstrong and the USPS Team. "*International Journal of Law, Crime and Justice* 46: 57-68.

Benson, Daniel. 2019. "Ochowicz: No Red Flags in Denifl's Biological Passport." *Cycling News*, March 3, 2019. https://www.cyclingnews.com/news/ochowicz-no-red-flags-in-denifls-biological-passport/

Benson, Daniel. 2020. "Is There Now Free Rein on Doping?" *Cycling News,* May 8, 2020. https://www.cyclingnews.com/features/is-there-now-free-rein-on-doping/

Borry, Pascal, Timothy Caulfield, Xavier Estivill, Sigmund Loland, Michael McNamee, and Bartha Maria Knoppers. 2018. "Geolocalisation of athletes for out-of-competition drug testing: ethical considerations. Position statement by the WADA Ethics Panel. "*British Journal of Sports Medicine* 52 (7): 456-459.

Brissonneau, Christophe, and Fabien Ohl. 2010. "The Genesis and Effect of French Anti-Doping Policies in Cycling. "*International Journal of Sport Policy and Politic* 2 (2): 173-187.

Camporesi, Silvia. 2017. "An Alternative Solution to Lifting the Ban on Doping: Breaking the Payoff Matrix of Professional Sport by Shifting Liability Away from Athletes. "*Sport, Ethics and Philosophy* 11 (1): 109-118.

Devriendt, Thijs, Davit Chokoshvili, and Pascal Borry. 2019. "The Athlete Biological Passport: Challenges and Possibilities." *International Journal of Sport Policy and Politics* 11 (2): 315-324.

Duiven, Erik and Olivier de Hon. 2015. "The Dutch Elite Athlete and the Anti-Doping Policy." *Anti-Doping Authority Netherlands*, July 2015. https://www.dopingautoriteit.nl/media/files/2015/The_Dutch_elite_athlete_and_the_anti-doping_policy_2014-2015_international_summary_DEF.pdf.

Dvorak, Jiri, Martial Saugy, and Yannis P. Pitsiladis. 2014. "Challenges and Threats to Implementing the Fight Against Doping in Sport. "*British Journal of Sports Medicine* 48 (10): 807-809.

Efverström, Anna, Nader Ahmadi, David Hoff, and Åsa Bäckström. 2016. "Anti-doping and Legitimacy: An International Survey of Elite Athletes' Perceptions. "*International Journal of Sport Policy and Politics* 8 (3): 491-514.

Elbe, Anne-Marie, and Werner Pitsch. 2018. "Doping Prevalence Among Danish Elite Athletes. "*Performance Enhancement & Health* 6 (1): 28-32.

Ellingworth, James, 2020 "WADA Looks to Artificial Intelligence to Catch Dopers." *Associated Press*, May 26, 2020, https://apnews.com/3068308c761132a1485bb9c2848d130d.

Engelberg, Terry, Stephen Moston, and James Skinner. 2015. "The Final Frontier of Anti-Doping: A Study of Athletes Who Have Committed Doping Violations. "*Sport Management Review* 18 (2): 268-279.

Farrand, Stephen. 2020. "Only 5% of Anti-Doping Tests Carried Out Due to Lockdown." *Cycling News*, May 6, 2020. https://www.cyclingnews.com/news/only-5-of-anti-doping-tests-carried-out-due-to-lockdown/

Futterman, Matthew. 2020. "Coronavirus Pandemic Hobbles World Antidoping Efforts." *New York Times*, March 30, 2020. https://www.nytimes.com/2020/03/30/sports/olympics/coronavirus-doping-athletes-olympics.html

González, Juan Marcos, F. Reed Johnson, Matthew Fedoruk, Joshua Posner, and Larry Bowers. 2018. "Trading Health Risks for Glory: A Reformulation of the Goldman Dilemma. "*Sports Medicine* 48 (8): 1963-1969.

Gray, Stacie. 2019. "Achieving Compliance with the World Anti-Doping Code: Learning from the Implementation of Another International Agreement. "*International Journal of Sport Policy and Politics* 11 (2): 247-260.

Hanstad, Dag Vidar, Eivind Å. Skille, and Sigmund Loland. 2010. "Harmonization of Anti-Doping Work: Myth or Reality? "*Sport in Society* 13 (3): 418-430.

Hanstad, Dag, and Barrie Houlihan. 2015. "Strengthening Global Anti-Doping Policy Through Bilateral Collaboration: The Example of Norway and China. "*International Journal of Sport Policy and Politics* 7 (4): 587-604.

Henne, Kathryn. 2014. "The emergence of moral technopreneurialism in sport: Techniques in Anti-Doping Regulation, 1966–1976. "*The International Journal of the History of Sport* 31 (8): 884-901.

Hopker, James, Yorck O. Schumacher, Matthew Fedoruk, Jakob Mørkeberg, Stéphane Bermon, Sergei Iljukov, Reid Aikin, and Pierre-Edouard Sottas. 2018. "Athlete Performance Monitoring in Anti-Doping." *Frontiers in Physiology* 9: 1-4.

Houlihan, Barrie, and Dag Vidar Hanstad. 2019. "The Effectiveness of the World Anti-Doping Agency: Developing a Framework for Analysis. "*International Journal of Sport Policy and Politics* 11 (2): 203-217.

Houlihan, Barrie. 2014. "Achieving Compliance in International Anti-Doping Policy: An Analysis of the 2009 World Anti-Doping Code. "*Sport Management Review* 17 (3): 265-276.

Houlihan, Barrie, Dag Vidar Hanstad, Sigmund Loland, and Ivan Waddington. 2019. "The World Anti-Doping Agency at 20: Progress and Challenges. "*International Journal of Sport Policy and Politics* 11 (2): 193-201.

Hunt, Thomas M. 2011. *Drug Games: The International Olympic Committee and the Politics of Doping, 1960–2008*. Texas: University of Texas Press.

Hunt, Thomas M., Paul Dimeo, and Scott R. Jedlicka. 2012. "The Historical Roots of Today's Problems: A Critical Appraisal of the International Anti-Doping Movement. "*Performance Enhancement & Health* 1 (2): 55-60.

International Testing Agency. 2020. "ITA Update Concerning the Covid-19 Pandemic." *International Testing Agency*, March 18, 2020. https://ita.sport/2020/03/18/ita-update-concerning-the-covid-19-pandemic/

Kayser, Bengt, and Aaron CT Smith. 2008. "Globalisation of Anti-Doping: The Reverse Side of the Medal. "*British Medical Journal* 337 (7661): 85-87.

Kayser, Bengt, and Jan Tolleneer. 2017. "Ethics of a Relaxed Antidoping Rule Accompanied by Harm-Reduction Measures. "*Journal of Medical Ethics* 43 (5): 282-286.

Keating, Steve. 2020, "Interview: Coronavirus Will Not Be Opportunity for Drug Cheats Says WADA Chief." Reuters, March 27, 2020. https://uk.reuters.com/article/uk-health-coronavirus-doping-banka-inter/interview-coronavirus-will-not-be-opportunity-for-drug-cheats-says-wada-chief-idUKKBN21E340

Kirby, Kate, Aidan Moran, and Suzanne Guerin. 2011. "A Qualitative Analysis of the Experiences of Elite Athletes Who Have Admitted to Doping for Performance Enhancement. "*International Journal of Sport Policy and Politics* 3 (2): 205-224.

Lenten, Liam JA, and Aaron CT Smith. 2020 "Testing Conditional Superannuation as an Anti-Doping Policy Supplement for Safeguarding Athlete Health and Welfare. "*Performance Enhancement & Health* 7 (3-4): 100159.

Leventhal, Adam. 2020. "Lockdown Gives 'Window of Opportunity' for Footballers to Beat the Drug-Testers." *The Athletic*, April 20, 2020. https://theathletic.co.uk/1763540/2020/04/24/anti-doping-lockdown-ukad-drug-testing/

Maennig, Wolfgang. 2014. "Inefficiency of the Anti-Doping System: Cost Reduction Proposals. "*Substance Use & Misuse* 49 (9): 1201-1205.

Mahendru, Dhruv, J. Kumaravel, Vidya M. Mahalmani, and Bikash Medhi. 2020. "Athlete Biological Passport: Need and Challenges." *Indian Journal of Orthopaedics* 54: 64–270.

Marclay, François, Patrice Mangin, Pierre Margot, and Martial Saugy. 2013. "Perspectives for Forensic Intelligence in Anti-Doping: Thinking Outside of the Box." *Forensic Science International* 229 (1-3): 133-144.

Mazanov, Jason, and James Connor. 2010. "Rethinking the Management of Drugs in Sport. "*International Journal of Sport Policy and Politics* 2 (1): 49-63.

Mazanov, Jason. 2016. "Beyond Antidoping and Harm Minimisation: A Stakeholder-Corporate Social Responsibility Approach to Drug Control for Sport. "*Journal of Medical Ethics* 42 (4): 220-223.

Meier, Henk E., and Marcel Reinold. 2018. "Immunizing Inefficient Field Frames for Mitigating Social Problems: The Institutional Work Behind the Technocratic Antidoping System. "*SAGE Open* 8 (2). https://doi.org/10.1177/2158244018780954

Morgan, Liam. 2020. "CHINADA to resume testing in China after suspension due to coronavirus." *Inside the Games*, February 22, 2020. https://www.insidethegames.biz/articles/1090901/chinada-to-resume-testing-in-china

Narduzzi, Luca, Gaud Dervilly, Michel Audran, Bruno Le Bizec, and Corinne Buisson. 2020. "A Role for Metabolomics in the Antidoping Toolbox? "*Drug Testing and Analysis*. https://doi.org/10.1002/dta.2788

Nationale Anti-Doping Agentur. 2020. "Corona Virus (Sars-Cov-2): Update of Nada." *Nationale Anti-Doping Agentur*, May 18, 2020. https://www.nada.de/en/nada/news/news/newsdetail/news/detail/News/corona-virus-sars-cov-2-update-der-nada/

Nestler, Stefan. 2020. "Has the Coronavirus Opened the Door to Unchecked Doping?" *DW*, April 2, 2020. https://www.dw.com/en/has-the-coronavirus-opened-the-door-to-unchecked-doping/a-52991515

Neuberger, Elmo W. I. and Perikles Simon. 2017. "Gene and Cell Doping: The New Frontier-Beyond Myth or Reality." In *Acute Topics in Anti-Doping*, 62: 91-106.

Oelmaier, Tobias. 2020. "Doping: How Coronavirus is Affecting the War Against the Cheats." *DW*, May 28, 2020. https://www.dw.com/en/doping-how-coronavirus-is-affecting-the-war-against-the-cheats/a-53598537

O'Flynn, Paul. 2020. "WADA Says Lockdown Not Doping 'Golden Opportunity'." *RTE*, May 31, 2020. https://www.rte.ie/news/2020/0531/1143662-anti-doping/

Overbye, Marie. 2017. "Deterrence by Risk of Detection? An Inquiry into How Elite Athletes Perceive the Deterrent Effect of the Doping Testing Regime in Their Sport. "*Drugs: Education, Prevention and Policy* 24 (2): 206-219.

Park, Jin-Kyung. 2005. "Governing Doped Bodies: The World Anti-Doping Agency and the Global Culture of Surveillance." *Cultural Studies? Critical Methodologies* 5 (2): 174-188.

Pavitt, Michael. 2020. "Estonian Coach Admitted Coordinating Blood Doping FIS Decision Reveals." *Inside the Games*, April 9, 2020. https://www.insidethegames.biz/articles/1092994/alaver-blood-doping-aderlass-skiing.

Petrou, Michael and Margarita Pakhnotskaya. 2020. "Summary of the Key Findings from the T-DO Survey on the Impact of COVID-19 Pandemic on Anti-Doping Policy and Practice." *Council of Europe*, June 18, 2020. https://rm.coe.int/t-do-2020-19rev-covid-19-survey-results/16809efef6.

Pitsiladis, Yannis, Borja Muniz-Pardos, Mike Miller, and Michele Verroken. 2020 "Sport Integrity Opportunities in the Time of Coronavirus." *Sports Medicine*. https://doi.org/10.1007/s40279-020-01316-6.

Ponzetto, Federico, Norbert Baume, Carine Schweizer, Martial Saugy, and Tiia Kuuranne. 2019. "Steroidal Module of the Athlete Biological Passport." *Current Opinion in Endocrine and Metabolic Research* 9: 14-21.

Protti, Michele, Roberto Mandrioli, and Laura Mercolini. 2019 "Perspectives and Strategies for Anti-Doping Analysis." *Future Science* 11 (3): 149-152.

Read, Daniel, James Skinner, Daniel Lock, and Barrie Houlihan. 2019. "Legitimacy Driven Change at the World Anti-Doping Agency. "*International Journal of Sport Policy and Politics* 11 (2): 233-245.

Ritchie, Ian, and Greg Jackson. 2014. "Politics and 'Shock': Reactionary Anti-Doping Policy Objectives in Canadian and International Sport. "*International Journal of Sport Policy and Politics* 6 (2): 195-212.

Ryan, Barry, 2020. "Q&A: WADA President Witold Bańka on Testing During Lockdown." *Cycling News*, May 7, 2020. https://www.cyclingnews.com/features/qanda-wada-president-witold-banka-on-testing-during-lockdown/

Sagoe, Dominic, Geir Holden, Eirin Nygaard Karlsholm Rise, Therese Torgersen, Gøran Paulsen, Tron Krosshaug, Fredrik Lauritzen, and Ståle Pallesen. 2016. "Doping Prevention Through Anti-Doping Education and Practical Strength Training: The Hercules Program. "*Performance Enhancement & Health* 5 (1): 24-30.

Savulescu, Julian, Bennett Foddy, and Megan Clayton. 2004. "Why We Should Allow Performance Enhancing Drugs in Sport. "*British Journal of Sports Medicine* 38 (6): 666-670.

Sefiha, Ophir, and Nancy Reichman. 2016. "When Every Test is a Winner: Clean Cycling, Surveillance, and the New Preemptive Governance. "*Journal of Sport and Social Issues* 40 (3): 197-217.

Sgrò, Paolo, Massimiliano Sansone, Andrea Sansone, Francesco Romanelli, and Luigi Di Luigi. 2018. "Effects of Erythropoietin Abuse on Exercise Performance. "*The Physician and Sports Medicine* 46 (1): 105-115.

Skinner, James, Daniel Read, and Lisa A. Kihl. 2017. "Applying a Conceptual Model of Policy Regime Effectiveness to National and International Anti-Doping Policy in Sport." In *Corruption in Sport: Causes, Consequences, and Reform*, edited by Lisa Kihl, 62-78. Oxon: Routledge.

Smith, Aaron CT, and Bob Stewart. 2015. "Why the War on Drugs in Sport Will Never Be Won. "*Harm Reduction Journal* 12 (1). https://doi.org/10.1186/s12954-015-0087-5

Smith, Aaron CT, Bob Stewart, Sunny Oliver-Bennetts, Sharyn McDonald, Lynley Ingerson, Alastair Anderson, Geoff Dickson, Paul Emery, and Fiona Graetz. 2010. "Contextual Influences and Athlete Attitudes to Drugs in Sport. "*Sport Management Review* 13 (3): 181-197.

Sridhar, Shrivastha. 2020. "Coronavirus: Reduced Drug Testing 'A Gift' to Cheats in Sport, Says British Race Walker Tom Bosworth." *The Independent*, April 7, 2020. https://www.independent.co.uk/sport/general/athletics/coronavirus-sport-drug-testing-wada-world-anti-doping-agency-tom-bosworth-a9451616.html

Sumner, Claire. 2017. "The Spirit of Sport: The Case for Criminalisation of Doping in the UK. "*The International Sports Law Journal* 16 (3-4): 217-227.

The Independent. 2020. "Russian Anti-Doping Agency Suspends Testing Amid Coronavirus Outbreak." *The Independent*, March 27, 2020. https://www.independent.co.uk/sport/olympics/coronavirus-rusada-suspends-testing-athletes-olympics-russia-latest-a9430091.html

Thevis, Mario, Katja Walpurgis, and Andreas Thomas. 2020. "Analytical Approaches in Human Sports Drug Testing: Recent Advances, Challenges, and Solutions. "*Analytical Chemistry* 92 (1): 506–523.

Towns, Cindy R., and David F. Gerrard. 2014. "A Fool's Game: Blood Doping in Sport. "*Performance Enhancement & Health* 3 (1): 54-58.

U.K. Anti-Doping. 2020. "UKAD Statement on COVID-19 Procedures." U.K. Anti-Doping Agency, March 17, 2020. https://www.ukad.org.uk/news/ukad-statement-covid-19-procedures.

Ulrich, Rolf, Harrison G. Pope, Léa Cléret, Andrea Petróczi, Tamás Nepusz, Jay Schaffer, Gen Kanayama, R. Dawn Comstock, and Perikles Simon. 2018. "Doping in Two Elite Athletics Competitions Assessed by Randomized-Response Surveys. "*Sports Medicine* 48 (1): 211-219.

U.S. Anti-Doping Agency. 2020. "USADA Statement Regarding COVID-19 and Anti-Doping Testing Protocol with Video Message to Athletes from CEO Travis T. Tygart." U.S. Anti-Doping Agency, March 17, 2020. https://www.usada.org/statement/usada-statement-covid19-antidoping-protocol/.

WADA. 2019. "WADA Leads Exciting Collaboration on Dried-Blood-Spot Testing." World Anti-Doping Agency, October 3, 2019. https://www.wada-ama.org/en/media/news/2019-10/wada-leads-exciting-collaboration-on-dried-blood-spot-testing.

———. 2019b. "2018 Anti-Doping Testing Figures." World Anti-Doping Agency. Accessed July 7, 2020 https://www.wada-ama.org/sites/default/files/resources/files/2018_testing_figures_report.pdf.

———. 2019c. "World Anti-Doping Code." World Anti-Doping Agency, June 1, 2019. https://www.wada-ama.org/en/resources/the-code/world-anti-doping-code

———. 2020a. "COVID-19: Athlete Q&A." World Anti-Doping Agency, March 23, 2020. https://www.wada-ama.org/sites/default/files/resources/files/covid-19_qaforathletes_en_0.pdf

———. 2020b. "Covid-19: ADO Guidance for Resuming Testing." World Anti-Doping Agency, May 6, 2020. https://www.wada-ama.org/sites/default/files/resources/files/20200506_ado_guidance_resuming_testing_en.pdf
———. 2020c. "International Standard for Testing and Investigations." World Anti-Doping Agency, March 1, 2020. https://www.wada-ama.org/sites/default/files/resources/files/isti_march2019.pdf
———. 2020d. "WADA updates its COVID-19 guidance for Anti-Doping Organizations." World Anti-Doping Agency, March 20, 2020. https://www.wada-ama.org/sites/default/files/resources/files/20200320_covid-19_update_en.pdf
———. 2020e. "WADA updates its COVID-19 guidance for Anti-Doping Organizations." World Anti-Doping Agency, May 6, 2020. https://www.wada-ama.org/en/media/news/2020-05/wada-updates-its-covid-19-guidance-for-anti-doping-organizations
———. 2020f. "Audits." World Anti-Doping Agency. Accessed July 7, 2020 https://www.wada-ama.org/en/audits
Woolf, Jules, Jason Mazanov and James Connor. 2017. "The Goldman dilemma is Dead: What Elite Athletes Really Think About Doping, Winning, and Death. "*International Journal of Sport Policy and Politics* 9 (3) (2017): 453-467.

CHAPTER 3

Analyzing the "Position Paper on the Impact of the Covid-19 Crisis on the Sport Sector"

Mariann Bardocz-Bencsik, Niki Koutrou, and Rachel May

The Covid-19 pandemic hit Europe in early 2020. As with other sectors, sport was struck particularly hard by the measures imposed by different governments to contain the spread of this highly infectious, acute respiratory virus through enforcing social distancing measures within their respective national territory. No stakeholder in European sport remained unaffected. Small clubs and associations are non-profit by nature and thus do not typically have financial reserves. Closing their doors, and therefore losing their revenues, put them in an extremely difficult situation, as they still needed to pay their fixed costs. Professional sport clubs and elite athletes were also impacted heavily, as leagues, competitions, and regular training came to a halt as well.

Given the cross-border nature of the pandemic and its impacts on all sectors, it is fundamental to respond to it on a global level, in addition to national, regional, and local efforts. The "Position paper on the impact of the COVID-19 crisis on the sport sector" was the first response to the pandemic from the European sport sector. Position papers are written statements that describe a certain issue and present the opinion of the author(s) on that issue, often proposing concrete actions. As the above-mentioned position paper was a remarkably rapid response to the crisis, having been published in April 2020, and expresses the opinion of its forty-four institutional signatories in European sport, it is worth examining it closely. In order to achieve this, we will utilize Princen's typology of agenda-setting strategies in European Union (EU) policy processes. Additionally, the chapter will focus on the items of the action plan outlined in the position paper. By discussing these elements, we shed light on the concrete, innovative responses to the pandemic that were suggested by the signatories of the position paper.

INTRODUCTION TO EUROPEAN SPORTS POLICY

Ever since the establishment of the European single market in 1993, the EU and especially the Court of Justice of the European Union (CJEU) have shaped the environment in which sport operates on the continent. European sports policy has grown in significance in recent years, particularly driven by sport's role as an area of substantial economic activity accounting for 2.12% of the total GDP (€279.7 billion) within the EU in 2012 (European Commission 2018, 9). Traditionally, sport has enjoyed relative freedom and autonomy to self-regulate its activities, perceiving external regulation as a threat or unnecessary, unless it was related to funding requirements. Sport structures have shifted from a traditional pyramidal structure with governing bodies at the top, and athletes at the bottom without significant power to express their voice in strategic decisions. This situation has slowly been overturned with the application and development of EU sports law and policy, where in certain cases European sport stakeholders challenged the traditional authority of the sport governing bodies (Garcia and de Wolff 2018, 288).

Evolution of the EU's Sport Competence

The Treaty of Maastricht came into force in 1993, which meant a transition from an economy-focused community to one that integrates social, cultural, political, and economic aspects alike. With the Treaty, the EU added an article on culture to its legal structure for the first time and established a formal relationship between culture and other sectors of European policy (Culture Action Europe n.d.). While it was the Lisbon Treaty in 2009 that officially granted the EU explicit competencies in the field of sport, many of the most ground-breaking cases of the CJEU occurred prior to the adoption of the Treaty. Cycling pacers Bruno Walrave and Norbert Koch in 1974, football player Jean-Marc Bosman in 1995, and swimmers David Meca-Medina and Igor Majcen in 2006, all established the reality that sport must comply with EU law, whenever it constitutes an economic activity.

Walrave and Koch were two Dutch nationals working as motorcyclist pacers at cycling competitions. In 1970, the International Cycling Union changed its regulations and decided that pacers and cyclists at world championships needed to have the same nationality. Walrave and Koch considered this new regulation a threat to their livelihood and successfully argued in court that the regulation infringed EU law on free movement of workers and services (CJEU 1974).

Bosman, a footballer in the Belgian First Division, wanted to change clubs and play for a French team after his contract expired. However, the French club did not pay the Belgian club's transfer fee demand, and therefore the Belgian team would not release him. Bosman took the case to the CJEU and sued for restraint of trade. According to the court's decision, Bosman and all EU football players were given the right to a free transfer within the EU at the expiration of their contracts, based on their right to free movement as workers (CJEU 1995).

Long-distance swimmers Meca-Medina and Majcen both failed a post-competition doping test in 1999. The two athletes filed a case against the European Commission (EC), arguing that the doping control rules of the International Olympic Committee were not compatible with the EC rules on competition and freedom to provide services. Their long and complicated case resulted in the CJEU's decision that anti-doping rules cannot be considered solely as sporting rules, as they affect paid workers and shall be considered under the scope of the EC Treaty (CJEU 2006). These three cases helped bring sporting rules under EU law.

Article 6 of the Lisbon Treaty gave the EU the authority to carry out actions to support, coordinate, or supplement the action of the member states in a range of areas, which included sport. Article 165 of the Treaty on the Functioning of the European Union (TFEU) stated that, "The Union shall contribute to the promotion of European sporting issues, while taking account of the specific nature of sport, its structures based on voluntary activities and its social and educational function" (European Union n.d.).

After the adoption of the Treaty, the EC created a budget to prepare future EU actions in the field of sport, based on the initiative of the European Parliament. Between 2009 and 2014, eighty-eight projects were funded with a total amount of €37 million for projects tackling issues as doping, match-fixing, encouraging good governance, and volunteering in sport, among other topics (European Commission 2014, 3). In January 2011, the EC published its communication, "Developing the European Dimension in Sport," setting out the EC's view on how the provisions in Article 165 were to be implemented. In May 2011, the First Council Work Plan for Sport was adopted by the EU's sport ministers for the period of 2011-2014. The work plan declared the priorities of the EC in the field of sport to be: the integrity of sport, social values of sport, and the economic aspects of sport. This offered the emerging EU sports policy some form of strategic direction (Garcia and de Wolff 2018, 299).

While practices have changed since the adoption of the work plan, the main priorities have remained similar from the first work plan, over the second work plan (2014-2017) and the third work plan (2017-2020). The third one, adopted in 2017, outlined the three main priorities as: the integrity of sport; the economic dimension of sport, (in particular innovation in sport); and sport and society (Council of the European Union and the Representatives of the Governments of the Member States 2017).

The EU's intervening role in sport is primarily conducted in three key ways. First, when generic EU policies affect sport entities' activity. The aforementioned 1995 Bosman ruling by the CJEU is an illustrative example of EU legislative implications on the conduct of sport. Second, the EU intervenes in sport to achieve wider EU policy goals such as by using sport as a means to tackle social and economic deprivation in disadvantaged areas. Finally, the EU intervenes to fund sport for sport's sake, as a legitimate sphere of activity. For instance, it supports projects that aim to enhance opportunities for participation without any other social outcomes, such as supporting sport for people with disabilities. However, the EU is limited in its capacity to intervene in sport, as it does not hold any legal competence to do so, unless it is justified through alternative policy activities and soft law measures (Henry and Matthews 1998, 3).

Acknowledging the above-detailed wide range of legislations on an EU level, in 2018 the EC launched an initiative to raise sport's profile in policy agendas on the

European, national, regional, and local levels. The SHARE initiative (SportHub: Alliance for Regional Development in Europe) brought together a variety of stakeholders, including public authorities, sport organizations, higher education institutions, and representatives of the business sector across Europe who are engaged in highlighting sport's significance in regional development. SHARE makes sure that sport's role in regional development is considered as part of decision-making at all levels. One of SHARE's main activities is collecting best practices in a publicly accessible database, while it is also active in capacity-building activities, organizing events, and publishing policy papers (European Commission n.d. (a)).

Soon after the start of Covid-19's rapid spread across the European continent, various members of the SHARE initiative—led by the EU Office of the European Olympic Committees (EOC EU Office)—started working together on a position paper to reflect on the situation. The European Olympic Committees (EOC) is the umbrella body for fifty National Olympic Committees in Europe and its mission is to lead the continent in the global delivery of high-level sport and healthy lifestyles. Its EU Office is located in Brussels, the de facto capital of the EU and it is the representation of the EOC and other sport organizations to EU institutions. It carries out manifold activities, for instance, identifying, monitoring, and analyzing subjects relevant to sport at European level; it also manages EU sport-related projects and compiles position papers (European Olympic Committees EU Office 2020a).

BACKGROUND OF THE POSITION PAPER

The publication of the position paper on April 20, 2020, was the first coordinated response to the Covid-19 pandemic in European sport. It was published on the website of the EOC EU Office and the website of several signatories and on the same day it was sent to numerous high-profile EU-level politicians. These key figures included the President of the EC, Ursula von der Leyen; the EC Commissioner responsible for sport, Mariya Gabriel; the EC Commissioner responsible for cohesion and reforms, Elisa Ferreira; the President of the European Parliament, David Sassoli; and representatives of the Croatian EU Presidency (EOC EU Office 2020a). The position paper was signed by forty-four signatories who were encouraged to distribute the paper on their communication channels, including social media, and many of them did so. The list of signatories included numerous National Olympic Committees, sport federations, including the Union of European Football Associations (UEFA), the International Basketball Federation (FIBA), and European Athletics. One of the most popular social media items in this regard was the original tweet of the EOC EU Office that linked the publication of the paper to the then-upcoming meeting of the EU ministers of sport. That tweet was retweeted thirty-six times by July 10, 2020, possibly reaching tens of thousands of people (@EOCEUOffice, April 20, 2020).

The date of the publication—April 20—was considered early given that the World Health Organization (WHO) had declared the outbreak a Public Health Emergency of International Concern on January 30, 2020. At that time, Europe was not considered a focal point of the global situation, as Covid-19 cases started increasing within the EU only from February 21 onward (European Council 2020). Given that the position paper was published just fifty-nine days after this increase, the signatories' reaction was quick and highly efficient.

THE THEORY OF AGENDA-SETTING IN EU POLICY

Agenda-setting is the first step in policymaking, as it places an issue into policymakers' consideration. Agenda-setting is therefore a key strategy of political actors. The relevance of the position paper on the impact of Covid-19 on the sport sector can be understood through Princen's (2011) typology of agenda-setting strategies in EU policy processes. Princen developed a typology of strategies that political actors use to put issues on the EU agenda. The position paper advocates for sport's eligibility for support under generic or specific EU funding schemes directed to overcome the negative impacts of the pandemic. As such, analyzing it through this typology helps us understand the thought process of its initiators and signatories.

Princen's typology builds on two separate challenges in putting issues on the EU's policy agenda: gaining attention and building credibility; and two factors that actors can impact: venues and frames. This double division results in four types of agenda-setting strategies.

The first challenge, to gain attention, is common to all agenda-setting undertakings (*ibid.*, 928). At the time of the writing of the position paper, WHO already declared Covid-19 a Public Health Emergency of International Concern (World Health Organization 2020). As such, drawing the EU's attention to the issue was not a substantial challenge, since EU institutions were already addressing it. The second challenge, building credibility for the EU to deal with the issue, was a more complex one in the case of the sport sector, due to the EU's limited competence in sport (Garcia, de Wolff, and Yilmaz 2018, 34). This limited competence only permits the EU to support, coordinate, or complement the policy measures of national governments. The position paper therefore points towards the economic and social strengths of the sport industry and suggests that the sector could play a role in tackling the crisis caused by the pandemic. It draws attention to the fact that one-in-every-thirty-seven Europeans is employed in the sport sector and that sport can help alleviate the negative effects of the crisis on people's health, socialization, and overall wellbeing (Anonymous 2020).

The first one of the factors that the actors could impact during the pandemic was venues. These are distinct institutional spheres where policies are developed (Princen 2011, 929). For instance, it might make a difference whether economic policy-makers or environmental policymakers discuss policy issues around organizing sport events. Most likely they would approach the topic from different angles and emphasize different aspects. According to Princen, managing who takes part in the policy-making process depends on the attempts to direct the issue to venues that are the most receptive to them. In order to find the most receptive venues, the position paper suggested measures on both EU and national levels, and it was sent to the key figures in the European sports policy sphere, including the leaders of EU institutions.

The second factor the actors could impact was how their issue was defined, in other words, framed. The issue of taking action to mitigate the negative impacts of Covid-19 was framed in a way that it calls for action from both EU policy-makers and national governments, pointing towards the various negative impacts of the pandemic on the sport sector on both levels.

Princen suggests two strategies for agenda-setters in order to gain attention to the issue. The first is to guide it towards the most relevant venues to make supporters take action in his words, "mobilizing supporters" (*ibid.*, 929). The second is to frame these issues in a way that the supporters would be interested in taking action, in other words, "arousing interest" (*ibid.*, 929). The latter can be done by "big words" and "small steps" as well. Using big words means that the agenda-setters make a connection between their issue and some deeply-rooted European values, for instance, active civil society, solidarity and democracy. The "small steps" approach draws attention to some "technical" aspects of an issue and builds up support for policies gradually. Examples of small steps include conducting studies or organizing conferences.

Princen offers two other strategies for agenda-setters, to gain attention and build credibility. Building credibility is also related to the two factors of "venues" and "frames." As to venues, building credibility calls for a strategy of "capacity-building" at the EU-level, so the venues would be prepared to deal with the issue. When it comes to framing, the strategy is called "claiming authority." It means that the agenda-setters need to build a strong argument about why the issue needs European-level treatment (*ibid.*, 931). It can be done by either connecting the issue to existing EU-level policies or identifying common ground.

The initiators of the multi-stakeholder position paper used mixed strategies in calling relevant stakeholders to action in order to mitigate the negative impacts of Covid-19 on the sport sector. They used the strategy of "mobilizing supporters" by calling high-profile EU-level politicians and national governments to action. They also used the strategy of "arousing interest" by using the "big words approach," drawing on the key point why national and EU-level actions were both needed to fight the impacts of the pandemic. Finally, they also used the strategy of "claiming authority" by linking the issue to existing EU policies. The work of the European Commission-initiated SHARE network was important in advocating for sport's relevance in various policy areas, including innovation, research, and social cohesion.

INTRODUCTION TO THE SIGNATORIES

Among the forty-four signatories, there were fourteen member organizations of the SHARE initiative and thirty organizations that were not part of the network. The profile of the signatories varies in many ways. Some are single-sport organizations, some are multi-sport associations, while others advocate for physical activity in broader terms half are European or global umbrella organizations, while the other half work on a national level. Table 1 lists the signatories and shows the number of organizations they represent.

Table 1.1: Signatories of the Position Paper

Name of the organization	Also known as	SHARE initiative member	Level of operation	# of organizational members (full membership)
European Capitals and Cities of Sport Federation	ACES Europe	yes	European	n/a
Active Local Europe		yes	European	n/a
Association of Sport and Municipalities		yes	National	n/a
European Smart Specialisation Partnership on Sport & Vitality	ClusSport consortium	yes	European	n/a
Sports and Technology Cluster		yes	European	n/a
Croatian Olympic Committee	HOO	yes	National	n/a
European Non-Governmental Sports Organisation	ENGSO	yes	European	32
European Observatoire of Sport and Employment	EOSE	yes	European	30
European Olympic Committees EU Office	EOC EU Office	yes	European	n/a

Name of the organization	Also known as	SHARE initiative member	Level of operation	# of organizational members (full membership)
The European Platform of Sport Innovation	EPSI	yes	European	82
Federation of the European Sporting Goods Industry	FESI	yes	European	54
It's Great Out There		yes	European	24
Sport and Citizenship	Sport et Citoyenneté	yes	European	n/a
Union of European Football Associations	UEFA	yes	European	55
The Association for International Sport For All	TAFISA	no	Global	270
Austrian Federal Sports Organisation	Sport Austria	no	National	67
Belgian Olympic Interfederal Committee	BOIC	no	National	39
Czech Olympic Committee	COC	no	National	n/a
Dutch Olympic Committee*Dutch Sports Federation	NOC*NSF	no	National	77
EuropeActive		no	European	151
European Athletic Association	European Athletics	no	European	51
European Handball	EHF	no	European	50

Name of the organization	Also known as	SHARE initiative member	Level of operation	# of organizational members (full membership)
Federation				
European Outdoor Group	EOG	no	European	112
European Paralympic Committee	EPC	no	European	54
European Volleyball Confederation	CEV	no	European	56
Fare network	Football Against Racism in Europe	no	Global	127
German Football Association	DFB	no	National	27
German Olympic Sports Confederation	DOSB	no	National	101
Hellenic Olympic Committee		no	National	27
International Basketball Federation	FIBA	no	Global	213
Maltese Olympic Committee		no	National	n/a
National Olympic and Sports Committee of Luxemburg	COSL	no	National	61
Norwegian Olympic Committee and Confederation of Sports	NIF	no	National	11234

Name of the organization	Also known as	SHARE initiative member	Level of operation	# of organizational members (full membership)
National Olympic Committee and Sports Confederation of Denmark	DIF	no	National	62
National Olympic Committee of Austria		no	National	38
National Olympic Committee of Finland		no	National	90
National Olympic Committee of Italy	CONI	no	National	94
National Olympic Committee of Portugal	COP	no	National	64
Olympic Committee of Slovenia - Association of Sports Federations	OKS	no	National	39
Polish Olympic Committee		no	National	37
Romanian Olympic and Sports Committee	COSR	no	National	32
Rugby Europe		no	European	47
Slovak Olympic and Sports Committee	SOSV	no	National	36
Swedish Sports Confederation	RF	no	National	70

Source: Based on organizational websites (2020)

DISCUSSING THE ACTION PLAN OF THE POSITION PAPER

This section presents the arguments proposed by the respective sport stakeholders within the action plan of the position paper. The action plan stresses the importance of adopting a homogenous response to the Covid-19 crisis on both sport entities and sport personnel in the EU. To this end, the position paper treats all parts of the sport sectors equally, including the private, public, and voluntary sectors. The position paper not only highlights the need for innovative solutions to support and reconfigure sport and physical activity both at the top-down and bottom-up levels across the EU, but it also stresses the significant contribution of sport and physical activity to making societies and EU citizens more resilient (Anonymous 2020). The purpose of supporting the European sport sector is therefore two-fold: to both stimulate the sector's recovery and to allow sport to play a role in helping society recover from the effects of national Covid-19 measures. As discussed previously, this aligns with Princen's (2011) "arousing interest" agenda-setting strategy, whereas both national and EU strategies are needed to tackle an issue that surpasses geographical borders.

The signatories urged the EU and member states to redirect the European Structural and Investment Funds (ESIF) or other EU and national funding streams towards achieving this goal. ESIF encompass five funds and covers over half of the EU's funding. Its purpose is to invest in creating jobs and a sustainable and healthy European economy and environment (European Commission n.d. (b)). Advocating for the redirection of some ESIF sources and other funding streams to support the sport sector's recovery aims to "claim authority" by linking the issue and making it relevant to existing EU policies, as suggested by Princen's agenda-setting typology (*ibid.*, 936). Most importantly, the position paper calls for cooperation and dialogue at EU level by inviting member states to consider sport in their discussions, focusing on identifying joint solutions in addressing the consequences of the pandemic (Anonymous 2020). This action plan point aimed to "arouse interest" amongst both national and EU stakeholders by suggesting that sport activity cuts across borders. Consequently, European-level cooperation in sport and sport-related issues, such as doping, match-fixing, and lack of physical activity, is highly important (European Parliament 2019).

The paper specifies nine items to be included in any action plan, the design and implementation of which was being sought by the signatories. Six of the proposed actions focus on the financial structures around catalyzing recovery from the impacts of Covid-19, while three others call for innovative practices to mitigate the societal challenges caused by the pandemic (Anonymous 2020).

Action Plan Items Related to Funding

Six actions suggest financial solutions to combat the negative effects of Covid-19. These actions are:

- *Ensuring the sport sector is eligible [for] funds for the protection of jobs, employees and self-employed against the risk of dismissal and loss of income.*

- *Lightening the rules relating to state aid, as is already the case in other sectors, with a view to allowing tax breaks for entities and organizations that promote sport activities.*

- *Providing loans to ensure the liquidity of sport clubs and other associations through existing EU financial instruments (e.g. the European Investment Bank) or newly created instruments as a response to this crisis.*

- *Redirecting certain EU and national funding streams and notably the European Structural and Investment Funds towards actions promoting the wellbeing of citizens including through sport and physical activity.*

- *Setting up public and private solidarity funds for grassroots sport clubs and associations and their employees, including outsourced coaches and freelancers—self-employed persons.*

- *Creating new funding opportunities as innovative ways to promote sport and physical activity in times when people are restricted to their homes.*

The proposed funding-related measures call for the sport sector's eligibility to monetary solutions, such as funding streams, and amendments to rules of state aid and loans. According to the position paper, funding schemes that could support the recovery of the sport sector include the European initiatives Support to mitigate Unemployment Risks in an Emergency (SURE), the Coronavirus Response Investment Initiative (CRII), and the Coronavirus Response Investment Initiative Plus (CRII+) (Anonymous 2020). It also called for the set-up of new funding opportunities, both public and private funds, including those that promote an active home-based lifestyle. These action points are illustrative of the vulnerability felt in certain parts of the sport sector, particularly for the voluntary-based sport entities, in terms of funding. By effectively advocating for the wider implications of sporting activity, the position paper "claims authority" in arguing for European attention.

Non-Financial Elements of the Action Plan

Three actions suggest innovative, non-monetary practices to support the European society get back on track after Covid-19. These items are:

- *Stimulating innovation programs (industrial modernisation) for sport enterprises to address the current societal challenges.*

- *Helping schools and physical education teachers to continue training pupils through digital means that are effective and safe (and stimulate innovation), i.e. through funding, guidelines, best practice cases, internet price concessions.*

- *And ultimately, stimulating a healthy active lifestyle in the working population, both those working at home and at the office by introducing innovative solutions to stimulate physical activity.*

By explicitly mentioning schools and the "working population" the proposed action plan asks for sport to reach the majority of the population. Nonetheless, it also importantly includes a further call to be responsive to specific needs, which may be relevant for those who are not engaged in education or employment. Again, here these specific points ultimately aim to "arouse interest" by explicitly referring to the wider positive externalities associated with sporting activity.

The action plan explicitly and implicitly calls for innovation and a needs-based response that will adapt to a new normal. This aims to ensure that physically active lifestyles are accessible and commonplace despite the circumstances and possible restrictions. Innovative practices often assume a digitalization of communication processes, coaching or even participation. Nevertheless, it is important to acknowledge that the societal consequences of Covid-19 measures are likely to contribute to the rise of inequality and some innovations may create new barriers to participation. This suggestion also opposes the traditional nature of sport and of most voluntary-based clubs that often operate with limited human, physical or financial resources, and thus have limited capacity to introduce innovative sport participation strategies (Morgan 2013, 383).

The action plan of the position paper uses strategies of both "arousing interest" and "claiming authority" to enhance sport's legitimacy as an area that generates significant economic and social activity, and contributes to wider goals in relation to health and wellbeing, in order to advocate for a more central role for sport in accessing EU subsidies. The influential governing body of European football, UEFA, was among the signatories of the position paper, even though it had previously worked towards avoiding regulatory interventions by public authorities, such as EU institutions (García 2009, 274). UEFA, along with the other signatories, including the governing bodies of some of the most affluent sports at a European and international level, such as FIBA and the European Athletics Association, voiced its support within the position paper for more widespread actions to tackle the impacts of Covid-19. This further suggests the relevance of strategies that "mobilize supporters" in "appropriate venues" and achieving widespread partnerships for effective agenda-setting.

It is worth noting that the suggestions of the action plan are echoed by a document published by the Council of the EU in June. The "Conclusions of the Council and the Representatives of the Governments of the Member States meeting within the Council on the impact of the COVID-19 pandemic and the recovery of the sport sector" called for efforts on local, regional, national, and EU levels to mitigate the negative impacts of the virus, and suggests both monetary and non-monetary solutions, just like the position paper (Council of the EU 2020).

IMPLICATIONS, REFLECTIONS, AND LIMITATIONS

The chapter analyzes recent developments in EU sports policy by discussing contemporary responses to the Covid-19 crisis through the "Position paper on the impact of the COVID-19 crisis on the sport sector," which was jointly developed and supported by forty-four stakeholders in the field of sport. Agenda-setting was used as a conceptual framework to guide the analysis of the position paper. Agenda-setting is an important aspect in policy-making, as consideration of issues guides policymakers' decision-making (Princen 2011, 927). However, agenda-setting in the EU is not always straightforward as two challenges can emerge in the process. Firstly, gaining attention for the issue at stake can be an obstacle, and secondly, convincing various stakeholders that the EU is best placed to deal with the issue can also be difficult (*ibid.*, 928–929). The position paper illustrates collective solidarity, which is often reported as one of the positive non-sport social outcomes associated with sport participation (Coalter 2007, 19). This is broadly reflected through the quick response of various key national, European, and global sport stakeholders in acting as signatories of the position paper. They signed the paper in an effort to address the impact of the pandemic on sport and ensure a sustainable European sport sector. This was achieved through advocating for protecting sport jobs and income, safeguarding of sport participants at various levels, innovating in sport and physical activity to encourage alternative forms of participation, and redirecting funding streams at national and EU level to support sport organizations and reduce unemployment. The initiators of the position paper mobilized potential supporters and defined their issue in a way that appeals to a broader network of stakeholders. Both strategies are central to the agenda-setting process (Princen 2011, 929).

Despite this positive move, the boundaries between levels of responsibility in EU sports policy are often blurred. Across different EU member states, vastly different resources and organizational capacities are available to be enacted or leveraged to support a bottom-up approach to policy implementation. Inconsistencies in governmental policies or priorities in relation to sport may hinder the capacity of the sport sector in capturing the attention of policy-makers and lobbying for its sustainability at a national level (Garcia, de Wolff, and Yilmaz 2018, 32). The second challenge, building credibility for the EU to deal with the issue, is a more complex one in the case of the sport sector, due to the EU's limited competence in sport (*ibid.*, 34).

Another challenge for most countries is the lack of data and systematic and timely monitoring of the impacts and responses to various emerging issues at a national level (*ibid.*, 29). Therefore, the extent to which countries will actually develop detailed and consistent policies in relation to addressing the impact of Covid-19 on sport in their respective contexts is questionable. How these national efforts could therefore be translated into a consistent EU approach in tackling the issues emerging out of the pandemic, specifically in relation to sport, leading to actual policy adoption and implementation is also under debate. This suggests that sport in the EU is still a "vulnerable" policy area (Princen 2011, 939), and perhaps in order to promote sport matters effectively, arousing interest through mixing diverse strategies and issues and mobilizing appropriate supporters is the best way forward to place sport higher on the EU policy agenda-setting.

The position paper does this well by involving relevant actors and "venues," such as the members of the EU-initiated SHARE network, and by carefully articulating the need for wider, EU-coordinated efforts and actions to protect the sport sector; not just for sport's sake but also for its potential in contributing to the EU's wider economic and social goals, and by assisting in the efforts to "achieve a sustainable, healthy Europe" through bringing "sport and physical activity into the heart of all policies," as discussed within the document. Indeed, harmonization of policies in relation to ensuring a sustainable sport sector in response to the pandemic, would perhaps act as a catalyst for sport in achieving a wider recognition and a central role in EU policy affairs. Nonetheless, the long-term impact of the document in shaping the EU sports policy agenda remains to be seen.

REFERENCES

Anonymous. 2020. "Position Paper on the Impact of the COVID-19 Crisis on the Sport Sector." https://euoffice.eurolympic.org/files/position_paper_COVID-19%20final_revision.pdf.

Coalter, Fred. 2007. *A Wider Social Role for Sport: Who's Keeping the Score?* New York: Routledge.

Council of the European Union and the Representatives of the Governments of the Member States. 2017. "Resolution of the Council and of the Representatives of the Governments of the Member States, Meeting within the Council, on the European Union Work Plan for Sport (1 July 2017-31 December 2020)." https://eur-lex.europa.eu/legal-content/EN/TXT/?uri=CELEX%3A42017Y0615%2801%29.

Council of the European Union. 2020. "Conclusions of the Council and the Representatives of the Governments of the Member States Meeting within the Council on the Impact of the COVID19 Pandemic and the Recovery of the Sport Sector." https://www.consilium.europa.eu/media/44622/st08926-en20.pdf.

Court of Justice of the European Union. 1974. "B.N.O. Walrave and L.J.N. Koch v Association Union Cycliste Internationale, Koninklijke Nederlandsche Wielren Unie and Federación Española Ciclismo." https://eur-lex.europa.eu/legal-content/EN/TXT/?uri=CELEX%3A61974CJ0036.

———. 1995. "Union Royale Belge des Sociétés de Football Association ASBL v Jean-Marc Bosman, Royal Club Liégeois SA v Jean-Marc Bosman and Others and Union des Associations Européennes de Football (UEFA) v Jean-Marc Bosman." https://eur-lex.europa.eu/legal-content/EN/TXT/?uri=CELEX%3A61993CJ0415.

———. 2006. "David Meca-Medina and Igor Majcen v Commission of the European Communities." https://eur-lex.europa.eu/legal-content/EN/TXT/?uri=CELEX%3A62004CJ0519.

Culture Action Europe. n. d. "Advocacy Glossary." Accessed 15 July 2020. https://cultureactioneurope.org/files/2015/02/CAE-ADVOCACY-GLOSSARY-13.pdf.

European Commission. 2014. *Preparatory Actions and Special Events 2009-2013*. Luxembourg: Publications Office of the European Union.

———. 2018. *Study on the Economic Impact of Sport through Sport Satellite Accounts*. Luxembourg: Publications Office of the European Union.

———. n.d. (a) "SHARE Initiative." Accessed July 15, 2020. https://ec.europa.eu/sport/share-initiative_en.

———. n.d. (b) "European Structural and Investment Funds." Accessed September 18, 2020. https://ec.europa.eu/info/funding-tenders/funding-opportunities/funding-programmes/overview-funding-programmes/european-structural-and-investment-funds_en.

European Council. 2020. "Timeline – Council Actions on COVID-19." Accessed July 15, 2020. https://www.consilium.europa.eu/en/policies/coronavirus/timeline/.

European Olympic Committees. n.d. "Who We Are." Accessed July 15, 2020. https://www.eurolympic.org/who-we-are/.

European Olympic Committees EU Office. 2020a. "EOC EU Office Coordinates a Multi-stakeholder Covid-19 Position Paper Asking the EU to Support Sport Organisations." https://euoffice.eurolympic.org/blog/eoc-eu-office-coordinates-multi-stakeholder-covid-19-position-paper-asking-eu-support-sport.

European Olympic Committees EU Office (@EOCEUOffice). 2020b. "EU Sport Ministers will discuss tomorrow the drastic impact of #covid19 on #sport. @EU_Commission & Member States must ensure that sport is eligible for CRII and CRII+ & other support. Check the position paper signed by 43 sport organisations. More info: https://bit.ly/3bzWx4E." Tweet, April 20, 2020. https://twitter.com/EOCEUOffice/status/1252199382918803456.

European Parliament. 2019. "EU Sports Policy Going Faster, Aiming Higher, Reaching Further." https://www.europarl.europa.eu/RegData/etudes/BRIE/2019/640168/EPRS_BRI(2019)640168_EN.pdf.

European Union. n. d. "Treaty of Lisbon Amending the Treaty on European Union and the Treaty Establishing the European Community." Accessed July 15, 2020. https://eur-lex.europa.eu/legal-content/EN/TXT/?uri=uriserv:OJ.C_.2007.306.01.0001.01.ENG&toc=OJ:C:2007:306:TOC#d1e835-1-1.

García, Borja. 2009. "Sport Governance after the White Paper: The Demise of the European Model?" *International Journal of Sport Policy and Politics* 1 (3): 267–284.

García, Borja, and Mads de Wolff. 2018. "European Law and the Governance of Sport." In *Research Handbook on EU Sports Law and Policy*, edited by Jack Anderson, Richard Parrish, and Borja García, 287–306. Cheltenham: Edward Elgar Publishing.

Garcia, Borja, Mads de Wolff, and Serhat Yilmaz. 2018. "Issue Framing and Institutional Constraints in EU Agenda-setting: An Analysis of European Union Sport Policy." *Journal of Contemporary European Research* 14 (1): 23–39.

Henry, Ian Paul, and Nicola Matthews. 1998. "Sport, Policy and European Union: The Post-Maastricht Agenda." *Managing Leisure* 3 (1): 1–17.

Morgan, Haydn. 2013. "Sport Volunteering, Active Citizenship and Social Capital Enhancement: What Role in the 'Big Society'?" *International Journal of Sport Policy and Politics* 5 (3): 381–395.

Princen, Sebastiaan. 2011. "Agenda-setting Strategies in EU Policy Processes." *Journal of European Public Policy* 18 (7): 927–943.

World Health Organization. 2020. "COVID 19 Public Health Emergency of International Concern (PHEIC) Global Research and Innovation Forum: towards a Research Roadmap." https://www.who.int/publications/m/item/covid-19-public-health-emergency-of-international-concern-(pheic)-global-research-and-innovation-forum.

CHAPTER 4

Containing the Virus, Killing Sports Journalism: How Rugby League in Australia Muscled its Way out of Lockdown

Tracey Lee Holmes

It should not come as a shock that a nation as obsessed with sport as Australia has a robust, if not over inflated, sports media. Traditional newspapers, news websites, subscription television, and free-to-air channels have had their own coverage of sport boosted by huge growth in media sites owned by sports themselves. Websites such as afl.com.au and nrl.com.au provide daily stories and athlete interviews for Australia's two biggest football codes, Australian Rules Football (AFL) and National Rugby League (NRL). Content is created for fans of the game but is also used by mainstream media allowing the sports themselves a level of control over the daily news narrative. When Covid-19 forced a nationwide sports hiatus, with the exception of horseracing, which had approval by various state governments to continue, the NRL had played only two of the scheduled twenty-five rounds of the 2020 season; the AFL had played only one of twenty-two.

Sport delivers television networks their highest rating programs year-on-year. It is why in 2015 television rights deals earned the NRL AU$1.8 billion over four years and the AFL AU$2.5 billion over six years. The bulk of both deals came from Foxtel, partly owned by Rupert Murdoch's News Corp (Mason and Stensholt 2015; Walter 2015). With a pandemic-induced nationwide shutdown, no football meant no games to broadcast; no football on television meant declining audiences; and audience drop offs meant less advertising dollars. The sports-media bubble did not so much deflate as burst. Overnight.

Contracts that promised a full round of football each week were breached, lawyers from both sides interpreted the meaning of "force majeure," while the seemingly ever-upward spiraling sports entertainment industry had suddenly gone into reverse. By March, Australia's highest profile sports stood down around 80% of their staff, an option open to employers during an emergency whereby, without being held responsible, they can withhold pay and instruct employees not to come to work. Some employees remained on 20% of their salaries, while others were encouraged to sign up for the government's emergency "Job Keeper" program, which guaranteed a flat fortnightly payment of AU$1500. The sports media's staple diet of match previews, analysis, and reviews dried up.

On April 9 came the news Foxtel made 200 workers redundant with another 140 stood down. Sports governing bodies kept checking their bank accounts to see whether the latest quarterly payments from the broadcaster had been made. The AFL and the NRL both began emergency meetings with state and territory governments eager to get sign-off on special bio-security details designed to stop the spread of the virus while getting the football economy back in gear before the sports collapsed financially (7News 2020; Pengilly 2020).

Anybody who stood in the way of sports' return by asking legitimate questions about the risk to health, forced flu injections, and leaving families behind for months to live in a bubble, were ridiculed and described as "holding the game to ransom" by journalists, reporters, pundits, and presenters whose own jobs depended on the game's survival.

This chapter explores how reporters at Australia's pay TV sports channel, Fox Sports, and to a lesser extent their colleagues at the free-to-air Nine Network, lost their ability to "report" and became part of the PR machine for the rugby league–a sport that began muscling its way back onto the field before the lockdown was over.

SPORT AND PAY TV: A MARRIAGE OF CONVENIENCE

Fox Sports is a network of television channels formerly owned by Rupert Murdoch's News Corp. It is broadcast on the pay television platform, Foxtel, a joint partnership between News Corp and Australia's largest telco, Telstra. In March 2018, Fox Sports and Foxtel merged into a single entity with News Corp owning a 65% majority stake (AAP 2018).

Australia's most popular sports, such as Australian Rules, rugby league, soccer, and cricket, as well as many other second-tier sports, are all broadcast on the Fox Sports network. Foxtel also owns the rights for many of the same sports on its "Kayo" service, a streaming service designed for those who consume sport on their smart phones that provides access at a much cheaper monthly subscription fee. The top tier leagues have all benefited from the annual multi-million-dollar rights fees paid by Foxtel to each governing body. Year-on-year sport dominates the top twenty most watched programs across all Foxtel channels with the NRL competition featuring more often than any other sport. Even in 2019, a year featuring high rating quadrennial events such as the Ashes Cricket series (test matches played between traditional rivals England and Australia) and the Rugby World Cup, it was the NRL that claimed eight of the top twenty watched programs on Foxtel, ahead of cricket with five of the top twenty (Knox 2020).

The NRL is governed by the Australian Rugby League Commission (ARLC, or "the Commission"). It is a winter competition that runs from March to September each year. There are sixteen teams in the men's competition. There is also a women's competition, referred to as "the NRLW," with four teams involved in a four-week competition. For the purposes of this chapter, only the men's competition is discussed as its season had already begun when the Covid-19 pandemic hit.

THE VIRUS ARRIVES

On January 25, 2020, Australia recorded its first four cases of Covid-19. It took forty-six days for Australia to confirm its first one hundred cases, but only four more days after that the number doubled (Ting 2020).

In the meantime, the NRL's 2020 season kicked off on March 12 with a match between the Parramatta Eels and the Canterbury Bulldogs at Bankwest Stadium in front of 21,363 fans. It was the same day the United States basketball league, the National Basketball Association, became the first professional sports league in the world to postpone its season (ESPN 2020).

Before the NRL's opening match, the NRL CEO Todd Greenberg spoke to free-to-air broadcaster Channel 9, highlighting the health of the players as the NRL's major concern,

> Well we're keeping a close eye on everything as you can imagine. I mean the primary responsibility is the health and safety of our players, so we've put some steps in place immediately for this weekend to ensure that we put the players first. There'll be a lot less activity in and around our players primarily to protect them because we want to see all the games go ahead as planned. (NRL.com 2020)

The following day, on March 13, the Australian Prime Minister Scott Morrison banned the gathering of more than 500 people at outdoor events. The NRL announced that the upcoming second round of competition would be played in empty stadiums with no fans allowed (Sporting News 2020). It would be only a matter of days before the sport had to face the inevitable—it was not only unsafe to continue, but it would be irresponsible to try.

WHAT NEWS? NOTHING TO SEE HERE

Four days before the NRL decided it was going into a pandemic-induced hiatus, Foxtel announced it was firing up to twenty of its news staff. A spokesperson suggested it was "not about the Corona virus" but more to do with "the very soft advertising market" (Cheik-Hussein 2020). Head of Fox Sports Peter Campbell, said the company was refocusing on delivering programs centered on its "marquee" sports, including the NRL, and as a result there would be less "news programming." He explained,

> Customer viewing now peaks in the morning and evening with low daytime viewership, therefore we are going to focus on delivering live sports news and the channel's marquee programs, including *AFL Tonight, NRL Tonight* and *Cricket AM*, during those peak periods. Unfortunately, less live

sports news programming will mean a number of redundancies from the Fox Sports News team. (Media Week 2020)

This announcement came only eight weeks after an earlier batch of redundancies were made at Fox Sports (Robinson 2020), and it would take only three weeks more for the news to get worse. On April 9, a further 200 staff at Fox Sports were made redundant and 140 others were stood down. Foxtel CEO, Patrick Delaney, predicted the Australian sports landscape was about to shift,

> What the team at Fox Sports have all done to reinvent our programming so our customers stick with us has been extraordinary. And the ratings tell us customers are engaged with our classic matches, documentaries, pop-up channels and live shows, and value what we are producing. However, we need to be prepared for a scenario in sport where season starts are delayed further (due to Covid-19). It is clear all codes are struggling with significant financial challenges and we should anticipate that the future shape of sport in Australia will be very different. (Blackiston 2020)

On the back of an AU$417 million calendar-year loss by parent company Foxtel, there were rumblings that more staff would be axed before the pandemic eased. ABC Business Reporter Andrew Robertson explained that Fox Sports streaming service Kayo had dropped from 408,000 paying subscribers on March 31 to 272,000 by May 2 (Robertson 2020).

The demise of news and numerous other sport-specific programs at Fox Sport was tragic for those who lost their jobs during a pandemic-led economic recession, but the impact was felt beyond the network itself. With its constant stream of half-hourly sports news programs cut from its schedule, except in the limited prime-time mornings and evenings, other sports media around the country lost one of their own vital sports-news sources. The sports reporters presenting the programs that filled the void became cheerleaders to "bring back the game" lest they be next in line for the exit door. The survival of the Fox Sports Network depended on sport being played. The "news" of sport was relegated to the bench of Australia's all-sports network as public relations and flag waving took its place.

A FORCE TO BE RECKONED WITH

On March 23, with just two rounds of the NRL's 2020 season played, the Chairman of the Australian Rugby League Commission (ARLC) Peter V'Landys called a media conference. Flanked by the NRL's CEO Todd Greenberg, the Chairman announced the competition was being suspended. He predicted a "financial crisis" for the game and from the outset made it clear his sole focus was to get the game back on the field as soon as possible. He explained,

Due to the rapid rate of infection we can no longer guarantee the safety of our players to continue to play. We are going to look at every available option open to us over the next week or so as to how we can recommence the season—be it in other areas, be it in northern Queensland—all the options are still on the table. We have a world-renowned pandemic expert and they are very, very, concerned at the rapid rate of this infection and as I said we will and always consider the health of our players before anything else. (Walsh 2020)

The NRL CEO, Todd Greenberg, who until then had been the game's official spokesperson rather than the Commission chairman, added it was a "deeply sad day but one of the most responsible days in the game's history" (Walsh 2020). His own history as CEO would be short-lived. Like many of the Fox Sports reporters who had interviewed him during his seven years as CEO, he too would be gone before the next month was out.

By this time, Australia had closed its borders to all but returning citizens and residents. Non-essential businesses were ordered to close from March 25 and Australians were prevented from travelling overseas. Globally, more than 350,000 people had been infected and the lives of 15,346 had been taken (The Guardian 2020). Fox Sports, though, were among the earliest converts to what was starting to resemble a "movement" led by a man who would later be dubbed "St Peter." Those in the Australian media familiar with how Peter V'Landys operated regarded him as a "can do" man, not interested in hurdles or excuses, only interested in "how to." Despite concerns from the Rugby League Players Association (RLPA), health authorities, and government officials, V'Landys made it evident he was singularly focused on setting a date for the return of the game. By sticking a stake in the ground and declaring it could be done, he flipped the challenge—no longer was it about the rugby league proving how it could be done, he was challenging the disbelievers to prove to him why it could not be. It was a tactical ploy the media quickly adopted. For example, an article in the *Sydney Morning Herald*, written by its chief rugby league reporter, headlined, "When V'Landys decides upon a course of action, there is no stopping him. And he doesn't care who he upsets" (Proszenko, 2020).

Under his chairmanship, V'Landys described the ARL Commission in the NRL's 2019 Annual Report as a body active in finding solutions to problems, although nobody could have foreseen the coming challenges posed by Covid-19 at the start of the new year, "Our Commission is a can-doc Commission and no challenge will ever be taken off the table in season 2020," he commented (V'Landys 2019).

Even the harshest critic would have to admit there was some truth to the description. As well as being chair of the ARLC, V'Landys was the fulltime CEO of Racing NSW and one of its board members. Horseracing was the only sport in the country that was not suspended during the Covid-19 pandemic. In a country full of gamblers, where Australians wager more and lose more than any other people in the world, V'Landys took a punt: without any other detail he named a date for the NRL's return. It would be May 28. On the day it was announced AAP reported,

> It's hoped teams will be allowed to train from May 4 but while the NRL has been bullish about getting back to normal service as soon as possible, primarily to limit the catastrophic financial fallout of the season being interrupted, there have been few specific details about how the league plans to carry on. (AAP 2020)

While serious health and biosecurity questions had not yet been answered, let alone asked, Fox Sports went straight into celebration mode. "We're creating history," the headline screamed, "Legends, fans hail V'Landys as NRL sets return date." The Fox Sports online story that night read, "The NRL is back and you can put it in your diary. Put some cold ones in the fridge, and get thinking about whether you'll be watching it with pizza, a Chinese takeaway, or why not both? May 28 is the date" (Burgess 2020).

Former player turned Fox Sports presenter Sam Burgess led the charge on the evening programs with unquestioning support,

> I do think there's going be so many things to dissect and talk about, but we need to jump on board right now and support it. We're creating history, what we are doing right now will live on for hundreds of years... In my opinion the decisions should be strong and authentic and we should all get behind it. Whatever we do the Australian public will remember it forever so will the fans, players and administrators. (Burgess 2020)

To deliver on his promise, V'Landys had to get sign-off from the various state and territory governments where the elite competition would be played. He employed his own bio-security expert and frequently declared in interviews that the advice he was getting was the best. With ten of the sixteen teams in the NRL competition based in Australia's largest state, NSW, getting the approval of its Premier, Gladys Berejiklian, was key. But she was not convinced elite sport should be played. She explained that "We are in a pandemic. It's life and death. You might forego your own safety, but to compromise someone else's safety, that's inexcusable" (Marks 2020).

State border closures, and international border restrictions in the case of the New Zealand Warriors team, posed unique challenges. The concerns of players and the fears of their families had to be managed, even cajoled, as did the public's initial perception that the sport was seeking favorable treatment while the rest of society was heading into lockdown. Government authorities in Queensland, the Australian Capital Territory (known as the ACT), Victoria, and New Zealand all had to be convinced that the league could come up with a plan that would satisfy their chief medical experts. Queensland Premier, Anastasia Palaszczuk, was also calling for more details than just a start date, "I'm saying to the NRL, send the detailed plan, send all of your health information, send how it's all going to work" (AAP 2020).

V'Landys held an ace card in his negotiations with the various state governments. With the economy already spluttering and heading towards recession, he knew how much the game contributed to government budgets through gambling. Australians spent AU$219 billion in the 2017-2018 financial year, according to the Australian Gambling Statistics Report (Queensland Government Statisticians Office 2019). Betting on horseracing totalled AU$25.8 billion, while betting on other sport added up to AU$11.6 billion. The NSW government alone received AU$2.3 billion in tax revenue for the 2017-2018 year (Roth 2020). The NRL's 2019 Annual Report states its own income from "sponsorship and wagering" was worth AU$84 million (2019, 138). NRL insiders say five years ago gambling accounted for AU$2.3 million in revenue, in 2019 that had increased to almost AU$30 million.

An innovation committee was formed by Peter V'Landys, and subsequently dubbed "Project Apollo." Rugby league great Wayne Pearce, also an ARL Commissioner and a media favorite, was put in charge of a carefully selected group that included the NRL's Chief Corporate Affairs Officer Liz Deegan (a former News Corp executive who joined the NRL in August 2019) and the NRL's Chief Commercial Officer Andrew Abdo (who was only weeks away from becoming the acting CEO.) The CEO of the players union, Clint Newton, was also appointed. Those with the best understanding of the two most important components of the game, the broadcasters and the players, were put in charge of finding the solutions under Pearce's captaincy. According to Pearce,

> There's actually ten work streams in place, so it's a really complicated exercise and those work streams, hopefully, will converge in the next seven days and that will give us a lot more detail about all aspects of the program and that includes competition structure, the actual specific protocols we need to put in place and a whole lot of other stuff. (Pearce 2020)

Both Pearce and V'Landys were experienced media operators. A strategy that resembled a political election campaign unfolded from the start. Each day there were announcements and updates either from Project Apollo or the Commission Chairman. Despite his day job at Racing NSW, V'Landys made frequent appearances on Fox Sports programs and was available for a growing number of soft interviews with both News Corp papers (whose journalists are regular Fox Sports guests) and with Nine Newspapers, owned by Nine Entertainment Co, the NRL's free-to-air broadcast partner. There was a near total absence of critical questions put to the Chairman and no one offered an expert counter view. The pace set by the ARLC Chairman meant most in the media had no time to analyze or question but were kept busy chasing the man in charge.

Without knowing his days in the job were numbered, NRL CEO Todd Greenberg was also reminding the public, through the media, that pushing for a return in the middle of a pandemic was not a case of one set of rules for the game and another set of rules for everyone else. It was all about "the people." He explained that,

This is a very big industry and employs thousands of people all across the game inside and outside and some people feel that we only focus on the players, but we understand that the guy selling hotdogs at Leichhardt Oval on the weekend is hurting as much for his small business as those across the rest of our industry. Peter and I feel a huge sense of obligation and duty together in getting games back to unlock the rugby league industry and make sure people are back earning their incomes, and the fans get what they want most, which is footy on the weekends. (Whaley 2020)

Meanwhile 95% of "the people" who worked for the NRL, and many staff members at clubs, had been stood down. Some were put on the government "Jobkeeper" program while others were eventually let go completely. This part of the story received scant media coverage. A narrative was starting to play out; while the rest of the community had to abide by strict lockdown regulations, it was in the community's interest that rugby league should be allowed to resume. According to Pearce,

> The reason we are getting back on the paddock is because we believe that we need to set an example to the community. The economy is bleeding, our industry is bleeding, we've got thousands of our people joining the unemployment lines in recent weeks like hundreds of thousands of other people and we want to give them a sense of hope. (Pearce 2020)

IN UNCERTAIN TIMES, PLAYERS SEEK CLARITY

Immediately after the competition was suspended, negotiations between the NRL, clubs, and players began. Naturally, the game's CEO was central to such discussions. Without knowing when the game would be back, when the next instalment of broadcast fees would be paid, and when the bank balance would hit negative territory, Todd Greenberg needed to be frugal. Based on a worst-case scenario, the players were offered one month's salary. It was rejected out of hand. The players, as partners in the game, needed more certainty than that.

On March 31, the RLPA issued a list of ten demands it sought from the NRL including financial clarity, the right to independently audit NRL finances, and direct involvement in talks with broadcasters over the game's rescheduling and the competition structure (Chammas 2020). With almost daily negotiations ongoing for a full month, gains that had been made in getting government approval to restart the competition were threatened by the lack of a deal with the players. RLPA CEO Clint Newton was standing firm, despite the media painting the situation as "a pay dispute" carrying negative overtones at a time when unemployment rates continued to rise around the nation. He explained,

> We haven't got a firm pay offer from the NRL because that is still being worked through with the broadcasters. There is no player revolt, there is no

pay dispute because there are no figures and no numbers available to work through (Marks 2020).

Around this time, a significant change occurred in Australia's infection rate. With gatherings of only two people allowed, borders closed to foreign visitors, and Australians arriving home heading straight into fourteen days of quarantine, infections acquired from overseas began to drop. There was certainly hope the virus had been contained, avoiding the huge numbers of infections and deaths being witnessed in Italy and the United States. But there was also an awkward fear; a reluctance to assume the stereotypical "she'll be right, mate" attitude Australians are known for. Australian streets were empty. There was no traffic during peak times and the lights remained switched off in many of the Central Business District high-rise office towers.

NRL player frustrations were also building. They were expected to keep fit and train as much as possible at home while waiting to find out if they were going to continue to be paid. There were rumors some clubs would fold completely. Even players with multi-year contracts in place had no reason to be confident they would be honored. Government action, with the support of all major banks, allowed mortgage-deferral for some homeowners whose employment was affected, while those who rented were told they might qualify for rent relief. The RLPA and the NRL had agreed to initial terms in early April with players forfeiting five months of their twelve-month salaries if the competition could not resume. They were guaranteed pay for two months (RLPA, 2020). But once the resumption of competition looked likely, and the broadcast deals were re-negotiated, a new player deal was struck.

Players were originally told it was likely they would all be sent to a hub—a secure, quarantine bubble, away from partners and children. This raised concerns not just for their own welfare but also for that of their family members left behind. In an interview for this chapter, the Chair of the RLPA, Deidre Anderson, explained how the situation turned once that requirement was dropped,

> That was a significant change. Behind the scenes there were a significant amount of issues that were unresolved. There were an enormous amount of wellbeing issues and family related issues around the lockdown. We weren't "holding them to ransom", the players were just saying "unless a, b, c and d, are resolved we can't agree to any of this." I think that's what's been left out of this whole equation, the players were never holding the NRL to ransom for money, never. It was reported on a number of occasions that that was the case. (Anderson 2020)

With the exception of the New Zealand Warriors, which had to leave families behind and re-locate to regional NSW in Australia to quarantine before the competition restarted, others were told they could stay at home but had to commit to remaining isolated when not at training or playing on match day. Although this ended up being revised a number of times as the pandemic entered a second wave, it was the breakthrough that was needed. A competition restart date of May 28 was confirmed.

BROADCASTERS DESPERATE FOR PRODUCT, PLAY HARDBALL

If the competition did not resume, the NRL was in danger of not getting its next quarterly payment from its broadcast partners, Foxtel and Nine, due on April 1, 2020. The broadcasters saw the suspension of competition as an opportunity to renegotiate their contracts, downwards. Stories appeared questioning the financial mismanagement of the game. On March 30, nine told its shareholders it would save AU$130 million if the 2020 season was canceled (Godde 2020), sparking fear the broadcaster may walk away from the game altogether.

A week later, a Nine spokesman accused the NRL of financial "mismanagement" and "squandering millions of dollars from broadcast rights deals" over many years (Logue 2020). Interestingly, despite suggesting it had been happening for years, the broadcasters had not complained about it previously. It became a major talking point on all Fox Sports programs. Subsequently Greenberg was shut out of meetings with both Nine and Fox Sports. On April 20, Nine CEO Hugh Marks went on the record praising V'Landys as "a man who wants to get things done" (Williamson 2020).

By that evening Greenberg was no longer the NRL's CEO. The news broke on the Nine Network that he had "fallen on his sword" (Glover 2020). V'Landys held meetings at his Racing NSW office with the CEOs of both broadcasters, taking a leading role in negotiations to redraw their rights contracts. Nine newspaper, *The Financial Review*, reported a detailed timeline of meetings resulting in a May deal that ended "two decades of unsustainable broadcast rights inflation" and a combined AU$150 million reduction on the previous deal negotiated by Greenberg (Mason 2020). But it gave the game certainty. V'Landys gave details in an exclusive interview, again, with broadcast partner Nine, where he described the negotiations as "brutal" (De Silva 2020). While appearing at odds publicly, in private the negotiations guaranteed a win-win situation for the broadcasters and the NRL. The game was back in action and the NRL could pay its bills, while the broadcasters retained their product at a discounted fee. V'Landys availability almost exclusively to right-holders, with non-paying media frozen out, also meant another slice of the rugby league pie was handed over to private interests, despite many believing rugby league to be a public game.

SPORTS JOURNALISM: FEARLESS AND INDEPENDENT, OR LEADING THE CHEERING?

While fulfilling his duties as CEO of Racing NSW throughout the turbulent months of the NRL's competition suspension, V'Landys was available almost daily for the game's broadcast partners Nine and Fox Sports. As chairman of the ARLC he was a frequent interviewee on numerous NRL panel-discussion programs. He was congratulated, cheered, and celebrated. Nine continued to "break" its own news throughout the suspension with details of negotiations they were a party to.

News Corp (Foxtel's majority shareholder) and Nine Entertainment (owners of the Nine television network) also control most of Australia's print media. It is the racing industry that helps keep papers in print. V'Landys day job put him at the heart of a racing industry that spends an estimated AU$28 million a year on advertising (Meade 2019). With Australians amongst the biggest gamblers in the world, state governments have also developed a soft spot for an industry that can be counted on for millions in tax revenue each year.

The relationships between the gambling industry, the media, state governments, and sports like horseracing and rugby league are multi-layered and intertwined. V'Landys knows, more than most, which string to pull for maximum effect. No wonder he has been dubbed St. Peter. Fox Sport even had its presenters sing "Hallelujah" for its station promotion celebrating the return of the competition.

V'Landys pulled off a remarkable competition comeback in the midst of a global pandemic, making rugby league the first sport in Australia to do so. He did it with the help of his media friends who appeared incredibly willing to give him a mostly free ride and governments who benefit from the huge amounts gambled on sport.

If anything, the return of rugby league during Australia's Covid-19 shutdown reveals how the power and influence of politics, big business, and professional sport intersect. When fans talk of "our game," they either ignore, or are ignorant to, those who actually own it and how it is controlled. Narratives are created behind closed doors and promoted publicly through an interdependent media with vested interests. Alternative narratives and critics are frozen out and the public remains mostly unaware of how they are being influenced and used in a multibillion-dollar industry.

As for sports journalism, which has always struggled to be afforded the same credibility as other specialist reporting commissions, this episode has done little to enhance its reputation. History will show the game of rugby league defied the odds and made a successful comeback before any other sport in Australia. No doubt the fans were happy, even though they could only watch from home. The players were back doing what they were paid to do although the atmosphere was a little different. Fake crowd noise was played on speakers around empty venues to replicate the cheering and jeering usually provided by fans. The NRL became the model for other sports looking at resuming their own competitions. Broadcasters got themselves a better deal and while governments maintained strict protocols for the general public, making exemptions for sport guaranteed at least one part of state revenue would continue to flow while other areas of the economy stagnated or went into decline. After all, being locked at home with live sport on the TV screens and little else to do, online gambling provided the perfect distraction. It seems everyone was a winner in this game, except the sports journalists.

REFERENCES

AAP. 2018. "Foxtel and Fox Sports Complete Merger." *SBS Online*, April 3, 2018. https://www.sbs.com.au/news/foxtel-and-fox-sports-complete-merger.

———. 2020. "Queensland Premier's Blunt Demand for NRL Restart." *Ballina Shire Advocate,* April 23, 2020. https://www.ballinaadvocate.com.au/news/premiers-blunt-demand-for-nrl restart/4001021/.

ABC/AAP. 2020. "NRL Announces Suspension of 2020 Season Due to Coronavirus Pandemic." *ABC News Online*, March 23, 2020. https://www.abc.net.au/news/2020-03-23/nrl-announces-suspension-of-2020-season-due-to-coronavirus/12082158.

Anderson, Deidre. 2020. Chairperson, Rugby League Players Association. Phone interview by author. July 12, 2020.

Blackiston, Hannah. 2020. "Foxtel Cuts 200 Jobs, Stands Down 140 Team Members as it Accelerates Transformation." *Mumbrella Online*, April 9, 2020. https://mumbrella.com.au/foxtel-cuts-200-jobs-stands-down-140-team-members-as-it-accelerates-transformation-624248.

Burgess, Sam. 2020. "'We're Creating History': Legends, Fans Hail V'Landys as NRL Sets Return Date." *Fox Sports Online,* April 9, 2020. https://www.foxsports.com.au/nrl/nrl-2020-return-day-may-28-peter-vlandys-wayne-pearce-coronavirus-covid19/news-story/d53c8fd96f674ff825ad7fdde638bd75.

Chammas, Michael. 2020. "The 10 Commandments: What NRL Players Want Before Accepting Pay Cut." *Sydney Morning Herald*, March 30, 2020. http://www.smh.com.au/sport/nrl/the-10-commandments-what-nrl-players-want-before-accepting-a-pay-cut-20200329-p54f3g.html.

Cheik-Hussein, Mariam. 2020. "Fox Sports Cuts Jobs in 'Weak' Advertising Market, Not Linked to Coronavirus.' *Ad News,* March 19, 2020. https://www.adnews.com.au/news/fox-sports-cuts-jobs-in-weak-advertising-market-not-linked-to-coronavirus.

De Silva, Chris. 2020. "V'Landys Opens up on 'Brutal' Nine Negotiations." *Nine's Wide World of Sport*, April 22, 2020. https://wwos.nine.com.au/nrl/peter-v-landys-opens-up-on-brutal-negotiations-with-nine-hugh-marks-and-todd-greenberg-exit/6e13082f-2d47-483a-89db-38f56b36e0ce.

ESPN. 2020. "NBA Suspends Season Until Further Notice After Player Tests Positive for the Coronavirus." *ESPN Online*, March 12, 2020. https://www.espn.com.au/nba/story/_/id/28887560/nba-suspends-season-further-notice-player-tests-positive-coronavirus.

Glover, Ben. 2020. "Todd Greenberg Stands Down as NRL CEO as Pressure Takes its Toll." *Nine's Wide World of Sport,* April 20, 2020. https://wwos.nine.com.au/nrl/todd-greenberg-stood-down-as-nrl-boss/4d14ffb3-39a0-4c6f-bb6b-2f3a184b4468.

Godde, Callum 2020. "NRL Virus Crisis from Shutdown to Return." *Newcastle Herald*, May 27, 2020. https://www.newcastleherald.com.au/story/6771514/nrl-virus-crisis-from-shutdown-to-return/.

Knox, David. 2020. "2019 Ratings: The Final Word." *tvtonight.com.au*, February 1, 2020. https://tvtonight.com.au/2020/02/2019-ratings-the-final-word.html.

Logue, Matt. 2020. "Nine Network Slams NRL and its Handling of the Game Over Many Years." *Daily Telegraph*, April 9. https://www.theaustralian.com.au/sport/nrl/nine-network-slams-nrl-and-its-handling-of-the-game-over-many-years/news-story/1b36fb79ac5798d36def294ee8554d10.

Marks, David. 2020. "NRL Season Restart Under a Cloud as Players Raise Pay, Biosecurity Concerns during Coronavirus Shutdown." *ABC News Online,* April 30, 2020. https://www.abc.net.au/news/2020-04-30/coronavirus-nrl-players-raise-pay-concerns/12202404.

Mason, Max. 2020. "How COVID-19 Created Sustainable Rugby League for NRL, Nine and Foxtel." *The Financial Review*, May 29, 2020. https://www.afr.com/companies/media-and-marketing/how-covid-19-created-sustainable-rugby-league-for-nrl-nine-and-foxtel-20200529-p54xra.

Mason, Max, and John Stensholt. 2015. "AFL Signs $2.5 Billion Broadcast Deal." *The Sydney Morning Herald,* August 18, 2015. https://www.smh.com.au/business/companies/afl-to-announce-2b-broadcast-deal-20150818-gj1ppz.html/ cited August 10, 2020.

Meade, Amanda. 2019. "Tone Deaf? How News Corp Remains in Thrall to the Melbourne Cup." *The Guardian,* November 4, 2019. https://www.theguardian.com/australia-news/2019/nov/04/a-sure-thing-how-australias-love-of-gambling-keeps-horse-racing-alive.

Media Week. 2020. "Fox Sports and Sky News Cut Staff at Fox Sports News." *Media Week Online,* March 18, 2020. https://www.mediaweek.com.au/fox-sports-and-sky-news-cut-staff-at-fox-sports-news/.

NRL. 2019. "Annual Report." https://www.nrl.com/siteassets/about/annual-reports/nrl_annualreport_2019.pdf.

———. 2020. "Greenberg Addresses Coronavirus Threat." March 12, 2020. https://www.nrl.com/news/2020/03/12/greenberg-addresses-coronavirus-threat/.

Pearce, Wayne. 2020. Interview on "The Ticket Podcast." *ABC NewsRadio,* April 12, 2020. https://podcasts.apple.com/au/podcast/the-ticket-podcast/id898138253.

Pengilly, Adam. 2020. "NRL to Check Every Player's Home, Promote Use of Phone Tracing App." *The Sydney Morning Herald,* April 26, 2020. https://www.smh.com.au/sport/nrl/nrl-to-check-every-player-s-home-promote-use-of-phone-tracing-app-20200426-p54nap.html.

Problem Gambling. 2020. "Gambling in Australia.' *ProblemGambling.net.au.* 2020. Cited July 3, 2020. http://www.problemgambling.net.au/ausgambling.html.

Proszenko, Adrian. 2020. "Peter V'Landys, One of the Most Influential Figures in Australian Sport." *The Sydney Morning Herald,* April 16, 2020. https://www.smh.com.au/sport/nrl/peter-v-landys-one-of-the-most-influential-figures-in-australian-sport-20200416-p54kiw.html

Queensland Government Statisticians Office. 2019. "Australian Gambling Statistics Report." Queensland Treasury. 35th Edition. Part 2.1, summary table A.

Robertson, Andrew. 2020. "Coronavirus Losses May Force Newscorp and Rupert Murdoch to Rethink the Foxtel Business Model." *ABC News Online,* May 10, 2020. https://www.abc.net.au/news/2020-05-10/coronavirus-challenges-may-force-foxtel-murdoch-to-rethink-model/12231094.

Robinson, Georgina. 2020. "Tip of the Iceberg: Other Sports Braced for Cuts at Fox Sports." *The Sydney Morning Herald,* January 1, 2020. https://www.smh.com.au/sport/rugby-union/top-rugby-host-sacked-on-eve-ofsuper-rugby-launch-20200123-p53tyi.html.

Roth, Lenny. 2020. "Gambling: An Update." *NSW Parliamentary Research Service.* Accessed July 6, 2020. https://www.parliament.nsw.gov.au/researchpapers/Documents/Gambling_an%0update.pdf.

Sporting News. 2020. "Coronavirus: NRL Announces Round Two Fan Shutout Following Government's Mass Crowd Ban." *Sporting News Website,* March 13, 2020. https://www.sportingnews.com/au/league/news/nrl-2020-north-queensland-cowboys-brisbane-broncos-rugby-league/18oql4vbitfgc1mlok0tpfokvi.

The Guardian. 2020. "Coronavirus Latest: 23 March at a Glance.' *The Guardian* March 23, 2020. https://www.theguardian.com/world/2020/mar/23/coronavirus-at-a-glance-23-mar-evening.

Ting, Inga, and Alex Palmer. 2020. "One Hundred Days of the Coronavirus Crisis." *ABC News Online,* May 5, 2020. https://www.abc.net.au/news/2020-05-04/charting-100-days-of-the-coronavirus-crisis-in-australia/12197884?nw=0.

V'Landys, Peter. 2019. In *NRL 2019 Annual Report.* https://www.nrl.com/siteassets/about/annual-reports/nrl_annualreport_2019.pdf.

Whaley, Pamela. 2020. "No 'Bad Ideas' for NRL's Apollo Project." *Canberra Times,* April 3, 2020. https://www.canberratimes.com.au/story/6710116/no-bad-ideas-for-nrls-apollo-project/?cs=14280

Walsh, Dan, and Alicia Newton. 2020. "NRL Suspends Competition Due to Coronavirus Pandemic." *NRL.com,* March 23, 2020. https://www.nrl.com/news/2020/03/23/nrl-suspends-competition-due-to-coronavirus-pandemic/.

Walter, Brad. 2015. "How Rupert Murdoch Helped NRL Hit $2 Billion Jackpot." *The Sydney Morning Herald,* November 27, 2015. nrl/how-rupert-murdoch-helped-nrl-hit-2-billion-tv-rights-jackpot-20151126-gl8zod.html#ixzz3sgY04Ios/ cited August 10, 2020.

Williamson, Nathan. 2020. "NRL Coronavirus: Nine CEO Hugh Marks Reaffirms the Network's Commitment to the Sport." *Sporting News,* April 20, 2020. https://www.sportingnews.com/au/league/news/nrl-coronavirus-nine-ceo-hugh-marks-return-peter-vlandys-rugby-league/2sqkyi3lxolz1u2yl4rpo3qed.

7News. 2020. "National Cabinet Meeting to Make Decisions on AFL and NRL Restart Plans." *7NEWS.com.au,* May 1, 2020. https://7news.com.au/sport/afl/federal-cabinet-meeting-to-make-decisions-on-afl-and-nrl-restart-plans-c-1010132.

CHAPTER 5

Covid-19 and the Instrumental Use of Sport: What Does the Future Hold for Sport-for-Development Organizations?

Haydn Morgan, Jeremy Hapeta, Rochelle Stewart-Withers, and Justin Coleman

INTRODUCTION

The global spread of Covid-19 has had severe health implications for nearly all countries and created significant economic challenges to the sport sector, with mega-events and professional sport across the world postponed or canceled, and recreational/community sport suspended in line with World Health Organization guidelines in relation to mass gatherings (Parnell et al. 2020). However, given the broader symbolic and cultural resonance of sport on wider society, the impact of Covid-19 on the sport sector was felt far beyond the highly commercialized elite-end of the spectrum. Since the turn of the millennium, sport has become an increasingly mainstream feature of policy and development agendas across the world and noted as an implement through which a breadth of social issues may be addressed (Guilianotti 2011; McGee 2018). Indeed, evidence indicates that sport can be used as a tool to empower certain populations and communities, enhance physical and mental health, and act as an enabler of social inclusion (Hartmann and Kwauk 2011; Sherry et al. 2015; Hermens et al. 2017; Morgan et al. 2019). Therefore, the impact of Covid-19 on "sport-for-development" (SfD) organizations, whose purpose is to utilize sport as an instrument to engage vulnerable populations and address a breadth of social imperatives, is an important consideration in the post-pandemic sporting environment (Collison et al. 2018).

As a further concern, in many countries, SfD provision is absorbed by charitable or voluntary organizations, which, in recent years, have plugged the deficits created by retreating State provision (Morgan 2013). Recent projections have indicated that, as a result of the pandemic, the charity sector in the United Kingdom could lose approximately £3.7 billion in as little as three months (Perraudin 2020) and that of the 166,000 registered charities in the United Kingdom (NCVO 2019), one in ten could disappear before the end of 2020 (Butler 2020) leaving approximately 900,000 people vulnerable to unemployment (NCVO 2019). Consequently, these potentially catastrophic forecasts for the charitable sector in relation to their pivotal role as providers of key social services raises questions as to how plausible it is for charitable organizations that utilize sport as a tool to support vulnerable populations to continue their SfD mission. Moreover, the effects of the pandemic may force governments to reconsider their position in relation to social welfare provision, placing further economic pressure on already unprecedentedly challenged public purses.

In this chapter we examine the response to the Covid-19 pandemic by SfD organizations in the United Kingdom and Aotearoa New Zealand—two countries whose governments have responded to the pandemic with vastly contrasting approaches. Specifically, we draw upon conversations with practitioners in the SfD sector from both countries to provide commentary on the key challenges to sustainability facing this sector of the sport industry as well as consider the opportunities that may be presented in the period following lockdown. While SfD organizations have demonstrated resilience and an appetite to implement alternative means to continue their engagement work during lockdown, uncertainty surrounding future funding presents a significant challenge to the sustainability and survival of these organizations.

Background and Context: Covid-19 in the United Kingdom and Aotearoa New Zealand

The U.K. governmental response to Covid-19 progressed from advice around handwashing and social distancing in early March 2020, to an announcement on March 23 of stricter lockdown measures instructing the public to only leave their home for a small number of purposes (including for half an hour of exercise per day). These lockdown measures, which included the closing of all non-essential shops and the suspension of social gatherings, remained in place until May 13, after which a series of steps designed to loosen these restrictions and reopen society were announced (The Health Foundation 2020). It should be noted that the recovery strategy only applied to England, with devolved parts of the United Kingdom (Wales, Scotland, and Northern Ireland) adopting their own strategies to ease lockdown.

The response of the U.K. government has not been without its critics, principally because of the high transmission rate of Covid-19 in the United Kingdom and the significant number of related deaths. Indeed, it has been reported that the introduction of the lockdown measures a week earlier than implemented would have reduced the death toll by at least a half (Stewart and Sample 2020) and that a rushed recovery strategy could lead to a second wave of infections and a further peak in fatalities (Booth, Stewart and Partington 2020). Such criticism has been delivered amidst several concerning forecasts regarding the outlook for the U.K. economy. For example, the Organisation for Economic Cooperation and Development (OECD) has estimated that the U.K. economy may shrink by as much as 14% in 2020 and is set to be the hardest hit economy among OECD nations. Relatedly, while there has been widespread approval for the government's prompt introduction of the Job Retention

Scheme (OECD 2020), unemployment projections have ranged between 7.3% (HM Treasury 2020) and 11% (KPMG 2020) by the end of 2020.

In contrast, across the globe, New Zealand's response to Covid-19 has been viewed as an enormous success (Cousins 2020; Jones 2020). Considered to be the strictest set of restrictions worldwide, the goal was to lock down early and aim for elimination of the virus (Baker et al. 2020; Cousins 2020). When the first Covid-19 related death was reported outside of China in mid-March, New Zealand sought to close its borders to foreign travellers who were arriving from countries that had reported high infection rates, and restrictions were placed on any returning New Zealanders with symptoms. Within days, the border was closed to all non-citizens and returning residents.

On March 21, Prime Minister Jacinda Ardern introduced a four-stage Covid-19 alert system, thus outlining the immediate risk and communicating clearly what was expected of New Zealand's five million population (McGuire et al. 2020). On March 25, Alert Level 4 (the highest level in the system) was declared, and all New Zealanders, by law, were required to stay at home (Baker, et al. 2020), unless accessing essential services or exercising locally. At this point, New Zealand had 102 recorded cases, and no deaths, by comparison the United Kingdom had 6,500 cases and 330 deaths by the time lockdown was implemented (Jones 2020). While in lockdown New Zealand was able to develop and implement an extensive testing and contact tracing system and on June 8, with no new community transmissions in seventeen days and all Covid-19 patients considered recovered, the New Zealand government announced the country would move back to Alert Level 1, removing all remaining restrictions except border controls (Anderson 2020). While some cases of Covid-19 were detected in August, which led to a raising of the alert level, the virus has remained largely contained.

The "go hard, go early" approach (Jones 2020) and the cautious manner by which New Zealand shifted from Alert Level 4 back to Level 1 drew some criticism, with opposition Members of Parliament, the media, some in the private sector, and those opposed to the New Zealand government's welfare spending and relief packages particularly vocal. Indeed, the national economy is hugely dependent on both the tourism and hospitality sectors (Henrickson 2020), and in economic downturn it is the most vulnerable who are affected most deeply (Barber et al. 2020). However, in general there has been overwhelming support for the approach taken by the Labour-lead New Zealand government, with 91.6% indicating that the Level 4 "stay at home" order was the correct decision (Lynch 2020).

While political commentators have debated the potential benefits and limitations of these two approaches, they offer deeply contrasting positions on how best to manage the health, social, and economic imperatives that are impacted by Covid-19. Consequently, we now offer commentary on how the emphasis and timing of these contrasting government actions impacted on the response of SfD organizations during lockdown, focusing upon the challenges and opportunities that face this sector as a result of the pandemic.

Sport-for-Development in the U.K.: Response, Challenges and Opportunities

Anecdotal evidence from practitioners involved in U.K. sport-for-development policy and practice indicates that the response to the Covid-19 pandemic has reinforced the resilience and sense of unity of the personnel in the sector. As such, and where resource has allowed, organizations appear to have reacted strongly to maintain front-line services for marginalized or vulnerable people and rallied together with other delivery partners to ensure continuity of provision. The motivation to respond in this fashion underlines the passion exhibited by many in the sector to help others and "give back" to society (Morgan and Bush 2016; Morgan et al. 2019; Nols et al. 2019). This is perhaps unsurprising, given that many in this sector have themselves overcome personal hardship or trauma (Spaaij and Jeanes 2012; Morgan and Parker 2017). This life experience often provides the basis for becoming engaged in this sector in the first place and fosters the resilience to maintain services in the face of adversity.

However, despite this very admirable response, there is a growing sense that some practitioners experienced increased levels of fatigue as work became more intense due to the pandemic. Anecdotal evidence indicates that adjustments to working patterns and practices brought about by increased digital engagement for meetings with colleagues and interactions with project participants had a negative health impact on practitioners, both physical and mental. Practitioners reported increased sedentary behavior and longer working hours as a result of government instructions about home-working, leading to considerable concern around employee well-being and how long practitioners could sustain their current levels of work intensity. In addition, the reactive response to the pandemic meant that organizations were doing limited pro-active planning for the medium- and longer-term. As will be explained below, there is a tendency for SfD organizations to focus on the short-term. However, the impact of the pandemic was long lasting on health, wider society and the economy (OECD 2020), meaning that strategic responses will, at some point, need to be mindful of longer-term strategies to remain sustainable and prepare for both "a marathon" and "a sprint" simultaneously.

Uppermost within the threats to sustainability is the limited amount of financial support that may be available or granted to SfD projects and organizations. As noted, it is reported that the charity sector in the United Kingdom faced a £10 billion shortfall caused by soaring demand for services and lost fundraising income, with one in ten U.K. charities facing the prospect of bankruptcy before the end of 2020 (Butler 2020). As one example, the 2020 London Marathon was postponed, with a replacement event scheduled for October but restricted to elite competitors only (Ingle 2020). As the largest annual fundraising event in the United Kingdom, with £66.4 million raised for charities in 2019 (Ingle 2020) this, and other canceled mass participation events, meant an important revenue source for SfD organizations temporarily disappeared. While the U.K. government pledged £750 million to support frontline charities, this is expected to be prioritized for charities who directly support people adversely affected by Covid-19 (Perraudin 2020). Therefore, these severe financial challenges emerged at a juncture when the communities that the charity sector support are in most need of their services.

A further factor that may exacerbate financial sustainability is the widespread practice of SfD organizations to operate on a short-term, project-focused basis (Kelly 2011; Morgan and Costas Batlle 2019). Many organizations lack the financial reserves to survive without the frequent funding of new projects, or extensions to funding arrangements for existing projects. A critical issue is that re-investment into existing projects is often contingent on meeting pre-determined indicators of success (Collins 2010; Morgan and Costas Batlle 2019), which became more of a challenge when social distancing restrictions forced SfD organizations to prioritize the servicing of existing project participants. Therefore, with opportunities limited to engage new participants and boost project attendance numbers, an additional threat to the financial sustainability of many organizations was created, especially for organizations and charities that are highly specialized or have a comparatively narrow focus to their provision.

An accompanying concern is the impact that financial constraints in the SfD sector will have on human resource capacity. While the government Job Retention Scheme has helped to secure jobs in the short term and save important funds for organizations in the SfD sector, there is growing concern that the furloughing of staff could act as a "waiting room" for redundancy (Partington 2020). Anecdotally, there is already evidence that SfD practitioners have sought to diversify their incomes during lockdown, undertaking short-term employment in industries associated with the "gig economy" for example, which is directly reducing their capacity to contribute to the operating environment of SfD projects. Ironically, with approximately 9.3 million jobs in the United Kingdom furloughed under the Job Retention Scheme (Statistica, 2020), the U.K. has seen an uptake in volunteering since lockdown (Butler, 2020). While this has not necessarily been related to volunteering in sport-based projects, there is potential for SfD organizations to tap into the renewed interest in volunteering and recruit from this surge of new volunteers.

Despite these clear challenges to financial sustainability, the unity of response to the pandemic has generated opportunities for new partnerships to be constructed involving both SfD and more "mainstream" organizations from the public, private, and third sectors. Importantly, the necessity to respond to the pandemic through the pooling of resources and expertise has brought together organizations that, until now, have never sought to understand the overlaps in their provision. Again, anecdotal evidence reveals that new (and importantly, different) partners have been engaged by SfD organizations and that this has enabled fresh conversations and novel solutions to be considered in how to use sport and physical activity for development purposes. In a sector that is renowned for its routinized inertia in relation to partner selection (Slack and Parent 2006), whereby the same partners are engaged irrespective of the contingencies of the task or context, the pandemic has encouraged SfD organization to reassess their partner complementarity (Parent and Harvey 2009). As such, it would appear that configurations of partners are shifting in order to optimize organizational survival (Lindsey et al. 2019) with some organizations remaining open to sharing resource, knowledge, and expertise, while others have become more strategic and single-minded in their approach to partnership.

Additional threats emerged during lockdown that further challenged the impact and efficacy of SfD provision at the delivery level. Uppermost in these threats is the impact that social distancing measures have had on maintaining relationships with vulnerable and "at-risk" groups. As has been noted elsewhere, the deployment of sport as a tool to address social issues and engage marginalized groups is a laborious and non-linear process (Hartmann and Kwauk 2011), requiring frequent and consistent connection with the leaders and facilitators of sport-based programs (Morgan and Bush 2016; Parker et al. 2018). Strong relationships between the leaders of sport-based programs and their participants are essential (Coalter 2013; Morgan and Parker 2017), and the pandemic impeded the fostering of these relationships. While the anecdotal evidence suggests that practitioners found novel methods to remain connected with the participants of their programs, in particular as the government eased restrictions on geographical movement and the use of outdoor space, there was deep-rooted concern that new connections were not being formed at a time when, arguably, they were needed most. It is reported that in the U.K., health and social problems increased at a rapid rate among young people, with mental health problems a particular area of concern (Campbell 2020). Research has documented how vulnerable or "hard-to-reach" youth are specifically difficult to locate and engage (Hartmann and Kwauk 2011) leading to a genuine unease about the number of (young) people who could be (or need to be) supported through sport and physical activity programs who were not being identified.

However, and more optimistically, it was evident that engagement in sport and physical activity was of upmost importance during the pandemic in terms of impacting mental and physical health (Jimenez-Pavon et al. 2020; Sport England 2020). With daily exercise being among the permitted activities announced by the government at the start of lockdown, Sport England (2020) reports that physical activity levels increased after the outbreak of Covid-19, in particular among younger adults, higher socio-economic groups, and in rural communities. These findings present challenges as to how to (re-)engage individuals who are not in these demographic groups, and continued restrictions on social proximity will require practitioners to re-examine how sports can be undertaken safely (Evans et al. 2020). Nevertheless, the increased uptake of exercise during lockdown presents a clear opportunity for practitioners to develop innovative ways to use physical space and continue to encourage sport and physical activity as a remedy to social issues. It would appear that increased levels of physical activity, in concert with the additional time that individuals were afforded by lockdown, has enabled the public to re-engage with their communities and reconsider their own connection with physical space. People explored their communities with a different perspective, and this re-connection has, arguably, enabled them to identify more strongly with their locales than before lockdown. As a result of this heightened engagement with, and awareness of, the local community, there is potential to uncover where the needs of the community are most pressing. Aligned with the concept of community consciousness (Henderson and Thomas 2013; Morgan and Bush 2016), this enhanced appreciation of community needs may translate into solutions to local issues being generated from the "bottom-up," and present SfD practitioners with the insights to better identify where and how they may enact a role in addressing community issues.

The many difficulties created by the Covid-19 pandemic presented an unlikely opportunity for advocates of sport-for-development to re-think the role of sport and physical activity as a "cross-cutting tool" and demonstrate its worth and value in contributing to government agendas and policies post-pandemic. Arguably, as the government looks for solutions to the longer-term health, social, and economic challenges, at least there is a tangible opportunity for the SfD sector to use their collective voice to advocate and influence future government planning to address the uncertainties of the future.

Sport-for-Development in Aotearoa New Zealand: Response, Challenges and Opportunities

Johnstone and George (2020) argue that sport showcases human achievement and unites the nation, which other scholars have explored in relation to national identity (Dickson 2007) and wider social cohesion in New Zealand (Spoonley and Taiapa 2009). Given the prominence of sport in New Zealand society, it is perhaps unsurprising that sport has been identified as a key sector through which the government planned its response to Covid-19. Whilst some themes were consistent with trends seen in U.K. SfD organizations, anecdotal evidence reveals some nuanced distinctions for the SfD sector within New Zealand due to the different ways these governments dealt with the pandemic.

As in the United Kingdom, indications suggest that physical activity levels increased within New Zealand during Level 4 lockdown and that individuals re-connected positively with their local communities during this period. Walking was identified as a major contributor to increased levels of physical activity, and there is anecdotal evidence that time spent being active supported increased wellbeing and whanau (family) cohesion. While there is an assumption that adults in high-deprivation communities do not fully comprehend the value of physical activity, opportunity exists for walking to be utilized as a tool to encourage additional or sustained levels of physical activity engagement or further participation in sport. Furthermore, as individuals re-connected with their community spaces, the lockdown period highlighted the stark differences between and within communities, to further highlight the need for these differences to be accounted for through locally-generated solutions.

Financial impacts were also evident in New Zealand, where the funding of organizations that support vulnerable groups was significantly affected by Covid-19. While many of these organizations continued operating as essential services throughout lockdown, such as by providing food parcels, others closed all or significant parts of their activities and operations due to shortfalls in funding and resources (BDO New Zealand 2020). The Rising Foundation, for instance, a not-for profit non-governmental organization working with young people in lower socio-economic areas in South Auckland, noted that it needed to raise $1 million (NZ) annually to deliver services around mentoring, helping participants gain driver licences, and providing them with employment experience opportunities (Biddle 2020). Prior to the pandemic, New Zealand already faced issues in relation to high rates of food insecurity and family violence, a housing crisis, rising addiction, and un/under-employment. It is thus argued that these issues have only been exacerbated by Covid-19 (Henrickson 2020). With reference to unemployment, the most significant impact was for those between 20-24 years of age, which was up 70%, followed by a 63% increase for those in between 25-29 years of age (Philanthropy New Zealand 2020), with Māori disproportionately affected (Barber et al. 2020; Henrickson 2020).

With many organizations reliant on charitable financial support, large reductions to the revenues of philanthropic organizations due to the cancellation or postponement of major fundraising events, had inevitable knock-on effects (BDO New Zealand 2020; Biddle 2020). In addition, gambling based revenue from the NZ Lotteries Commission contributes hugely to the community in the areas of sport, the arts, and social welfare (NZ Government n.d). However, due to the closure of pubs and bars during lockdown, other gambling-based revenues decreased markedly, such as those from gaming machines (BDO New Zealand 2020). The Minister of Racing and Internal Affairs, alongside the Minister for the Community and Voluntary Sector, evaluated the gambling framework to consider changing the mechanisms for contributions made to community and sporting groups via these means (Philanthropy New Zealand 2020).

To address these financial shortfalls, the New Zealand government was quick to act with support packages. For example, to counter an anticipated increase in demand for social services during and after lockdown, the government announced that social sector organizations and community groups that work to feed and shelter the homeless, support those with disabilities, and help keep families safe from violence would receive an additional $27 million (NZ), effective immediately to enable them to work through the Covid-19 lockdown and its consequences (Sepuloni 2020).

More broadly, the government announced the "Wellbeing Budget 2020: Rebuilding Together," which included a $50 billion (NZ) Covid-19 Response and Recovery Fund (New Zealand Treasury 2020), of which $265 million was allocated to the sport sector. Despite being nicknamed the "Sport Recovery Package," there appeared to be an aspirational intent to utilize the $265 million for purposes beyond surviving and reviving the sport sector, post-pandemic. Anecdotal evidence indicates that the funding boost was targeted at the community-level for thriving and flourishing in sport, with the Minister for Sport and Recreation (also the Minister of Finance) Grant Robertson, stating: "all levels of the [sport] sector have been affected by Covid-19 and this funding is focused on making sure the sector continues to thrive, while also ensuring New Zealanders can continue to maintain their wellbeing through physical activity" (Johnstone and George 2020). The additional funding presents a major opportunity to re-start and strengthen SfD work, after the lockdown. Furthermore, while the Sport Recovery Package equated to approximately $53 (NZ) per person on average, the funding was targeted towards priority groups, which also saw community sport initiatives receive a significant amount. Sport New Zealand's (SNZ) Chief Executive, Peter Miskimmin, stated that these funds were dedicated to addressing accessibility and other barriers or issues facing "communities of need" (Johnstone and George, 2020), particularly within lower socio-economic, high deprivation areas, which outlines the potential for SfD organizations to benefit from the Sport Recovery Package.

One such SfD organization that benefited from the package was the Sir John Walker "Find Your Fields of Dreams" (FYFOD) Foundation. The FYFOD foundation offers eight programs, including "Community Swim," which funds free transport and access to swimming lessons for lower socio-economic schools in South Auckland. The aim is to teach children life skills, such as confidence and water safety. This is usually funded by Auckland City Council, gaming foundations, trusts, and private businesses. However, as noted, in the post-Covid-19 environment these revenue streams were depleted. The announcement that the government pledged funds for such programs was therefore positive news for SfD organizations. However, there was also concern that this funding may not reach its intended recipients, leading to calls for a review into how sport and recreation is serviced, especially in Auckland. In an interview on Television New Zealand's One News bulletin, Rick Pickard, General Manager of FYFOD, stated that he "would love to see everyone involved in sport, particularly in the upper management of sport, actually come out to the coal face and see what is happening and what is needed."

Such views highlight the importance of coherent strategic direction in ensuring that the impact of the Sport Recovery Package is not wasted and funding streams flow into front-line delivery services. SNZ implemented a new strategy prior to Covid-19, and indications are that the pandemic should not impede endeavours to realize this strategy. Central to the implementation of the strategy is the need to incorporate a diversity of worldviews, where "other" standpoints and voices are recognized. As such, there is an increased emphasis on female and indigenous (Māori) involvement in setting strategic priorities and outcomes. Consistent with elements of thought diversification, the clarity provided by the Living Standards Framework (LSF) provided SNZ with a "Southern Cross" reference point (see Figure 1). In New Zealand, the Ministry of Health draws on renowned Māori scholar, Emeritus Professor Sir Mason Durie's "Southern Cross" model of indigenous Health Promotion—Te Pae Māhutonga (Durie 1999) in order to navigate the myriad pathways towards holistic wellbeing. The bi-culturally inspired "journey" that SNZ embarked on has seen it become more inclusive of other realities and perhaps more responsive to alternative lived experiences. Consequently, the LSF's twelve domains, which aspire to develop multiple wellbeing priorities, allowed SNZ to reflect upon how it, as an organization, can contribute towards enhancing wellbeing and help the government to meet their wellbeing agenda.

Figure 1: The Treasury's Living Standards Framework

The Treasury's Living Standards Framework

To help us achieve our vision of working towards higher living standards for New Zealanders, we developed the Living Standards Framework. Our Living Standards Framework provides us with a shared understanding of what helps achieve higher living standards to support intergenerational wellbeing.

Our work is focussed on promoting higher living standards and greater intergenerational wellbeing for New Zealanders. These require the country's Four Capitals – human, social, natural and financial/physical – to each be strong in their own right and to work well together.

The Four Capitals (natural, human, social, and financial and physical) are the assets that generate wellbeing now and into the future

Looking after intergenerational wellbeing means maintaining, nourishing, and growing the capitals

- Natural Capital: All aspects of the natural environment that support life and human activity. Includes land, soil, water, plants and animals, minerals and energy resources.
- Human Capital: The capabilities and capacities of people to engage in work, study, recreation, and social activities. Includes skills, knowledge, physical and mental health.
- Social Capital: The norms, rules and institutions that influence the way in which people live and work together and experience a sense of belonging. Includes trust, reciprocity, the rule of law, cultural and community identity, traditions and customs, common values and interests.
- Financial and Physical Capital: Financial and human-made (produced) physical assets, usually closely associated with supporting material living conditions. Includes factories, equipment, houses, roads, buildings, hospitals, financial securities.

The 12 Domains of current wellbeing reflect our current understanding of the things that contribute to how New Zealanders experience wellbeing
- Civic engagement and governance
- Cultural identity
- Environment
- Health
- Housing
- Income and consumption
- Jobs and earnings
- Knowledge and skills
- Time use
- Safety and security
- Social connections
- Subjective wellbeing

Resilience prompts us to consider how resilient the Four Capitals are in the face of change, shocks, and unexpected events

Source: New Zealand Treasury, 2018.

The adoption of the LSF as their reference point enabled SNZ to return to the more inclusive and wider-reaching approach that was started prior to Covid-19 and ensure that the opportunity to re-set and re-consider the broader impact of sport as a developmental tool was not lost. Indeed, an expressed threat to re-starting sport in New Zealand post-Covid-19 was the idea that the act of simply re-starting sport would see a regression back to the "default" traditional mental models and potentially threaten the significant progress made pre-Covid-19. Thus, there was a fear that the "opportunity of a lifetime" for social change and a shift of health and economic priorities could be lost and that, instead of significant and sustainable change, the sport sector could simply revert to the status quo and return to "normal" modes of operating. Perhaps, in this regard, Covid-19 may well have done New Zealand an unintended favour and forced everyone to re-think the way that we administer and govern organized sport in contemporary Aotearoa New Zealand society.

Conclusion

The Covid-19 pandemic had a significant social and economic impact on the area of sport for development. As well as interrupting the critical work undertaken by SfD organizations to engage and support marginalized populations, the pandemic exposed several risks for the sustainability and survival of these organizations. Primarily, these relate to the shortfall in funding in the months and years beyond Covid-19. While the financial picture in New Zealand appeared more promising than the United Kingdom, both countries may experience the reduction or termination of certain SfD projects and/or organizations, alongside unavoidable job losses, leaving the sector and more importantly, the recipients of SfD work more vulnerable.

However, the uncertainty of financial and human resources was not restricted to the SfD sector and impacted in similar ways on elite and recreational sport. This will lead to the various sectors of the sport industry competing for the same limited funds from government, commercial, and charitable agencies, meaning that the future sustainability of sporting organizations may turn into an "arm-wrestle" of cautious strategizing, self-promotion, and political lobbying to secure future financial support. Debates about where the focus and direction of government policy and financial support for sport should be have raged for decades (Hylton 2013), and centered around whether that focus should be on supporting sport for sport's sake, or be allocated to organizations and projects that use sport as a "cross-cutting" developmental tool (Collins 2010). However, the severity and intensity of the pandemic has brought such debates into even sharper focus and could make relationships between various sporting stakeholders more isolated and strained, as each one argues for resources.

For SfD organizations, their lower public profile and weaker lobbying position—comparative to the more mainstream stakeholders in the sport sector—means that proponents of the instrumental value of sport will need to be both precise and united in expressing their advocacy for sport's role in addressing societal problems. In both the United Kingdom and New Zealand, the reported increase in physical activity levels and the deeper engagement that individuals have had with their communities during the lockdown period presented a critical and opportune moment to demonstrate the value of sport as a tool for development. While our commentary has only been able to reflect on these two countries, these important similarities may serve as a foundation for other countries to petition for the potential for sport to make a substantial contribution to individual health and wellbeing, but also to social and economic recovery in the post Covid-19 era.

REFERENCES

Anderson, Charles. 2020. "Ardern: New Zealand has 'Won Battle' against Community Transmission of Covid-19." *The Guardian*, April 27, 2020. https://www.theguardian.com/world/2020/apr/27/new-zealand-prepares-to-lift-strict-lockdown-after-eliminating-coronavirus.

Baker. Michael, G., Amanda Kvalsvig, Ayesha J Verrall, Lucy Telfar-Barnard and Nick Wilson. 2020. "Editorial: New Zealand's Elimination Strategy for the COVID-19 Pandemic and What is Required to Make it Work." *New Zealand Medical Journal* 133 (1512): 10-14. https://assets-global.website-files.com/5e332a62c703f653182faf47/5e868bb63837 6249c360942f_Baker%20FINAL.pdf.

Biddle, D-L. (2020, April 15). Coronavirus: Small charities, non-profits, at risk during Covid-19 pandemic. *Stuff NZ*, https://www.stuff.co.nz/national/health/coronavirus/121010867/coronavirus-small-charities-nonprofits-at-risk-during-covid19-pandemic.

Booth, Robert, Heather Stewart and Richard Partington. 2020. "'Turning the Tide': PM set 12-Week Target then 40,000 People Died." *The Guardian*, June 11, 2020, p.1.

Butler, Patrick. 2020. "Coronavirus Leaves One in 10 UK Charities Facing Bankruptcy this Year." *The Guardian*, June 9, 2020. https://www.theguardian.com/world/2020/jun/09/coronavirus-leaves-one-in-10-uk-charities-facing-bankruptcy-this-year.

Campbell, Denis. 2020. "One in Four Youths with Mental Health Issues Cannot get Help during Lockdown." *The Guardian*, May 14, 2020. https://www.theguardian.com/society/ 2020/may/14/one-in-four-youths-cant-get-mental-health-support-amid-covid-19-crisis.

Coalter, Fred. 2013. "'There is Loads of Relationships Here': Developing a Programme Theory for Sport-for-Change Programmes." *International Review for the Sociology of Sport* 48 (5): 594–612. https://doi.org/10.1177%2F1012690212446143.

Collins, Michael. 2010. "From 'Sport for Good' to 'Sport for Sport's Sake' Not a Good Move for Sports Development in England? *International Journal of Sport Policy and Politics* 2 (3): 367–379. https://doi.org/10.1080/19406940.2010.519342.

Cousins, Sophie. 2020. "World Report: New Zealand Eliminates COVID-19." *The Lancet* 395 (10235): 1474. https://doi.org/10.1016/S0140-6736(20)31097-7.

Dickson, Geoff. 2007. *National Identity: An Annotated Bibliography*. Auckland: New Zealand Tourism Research Institute.

Durie, Mason. 1999. "Te Pae Māhutonga: A Model for Māori Health Promotion." *Health Promotion Forum of New Zealand Newsletter* 49 (2).

Evans, Adam, Joanna Blackwell, Paddy Dolan, Josef Fahlen, Remko Hoekman, Verena Lenneis, Gareth McNally, Maureen Smith and Laura Wilcock. 2020. "Sport in the Face of the COVID-19 Pandemic: Towards an Agenda for Research in the Sociology of Sport." *European Journal for Sport and Society*. https://doi.org/10.1080/16138171.2020.1765100.

Guilianotti, Richard. 2011. "The Sport, Development and Peace Sector: A Model of Four Social Policy Domains." *Journal of Social Policy* 40 (4): 757-776. https://doi.org/10.1017/ S0047279410000930.

Hartmann, Douglas and Christina Kwauk. 2011. "Sport and Development: An Overview, Critique, and Reconstruction." *Journal of Sport and Social Issues* 35 (3): 284-305. https://doi.org/ 10.1177%2F0193723511416986.

Henderson, Paul and David Thomas. 2013. *Skills in Neighbourhood Work*, 4th ed. London: Routledge.

Hermens, Niels, Sabina Super, Kirsten Verkooijen and Maria Koelen. 2017. "A Systematic Review of Life Skill Development through Sports Programs Serving Socially Vulnerable Youth." *Research Quarterly for Exercise and Sport* 88 (4): 408-424. https://doi.org/10.1080/02701367.2017. 1355527.

HM Treasury. 2020. "Forecasts for the UK Economy: A Comparison of Independent Forecasts," no. 394 (May). London: HM Treasury.

Hylton, Kevin (ed.). 2013. *Sport Development: Policy, Process and Practice*. London: Routledge.

Ingle, Sean. 2020. "London Marathon Becomes Elite-Only Race Running Laps in St James's Park." *The Guardian*, August 6, 2020. https://www.theguardian.com/sport/2020/aug/06/london-marathon-becomes-elite-only-race-running-laps-st-james-park.

Jimenez-Pavon, David, Ana Carbonell-Baeza and Carl Levie. 2020. Physical Exercise as Therapy to Fight against the Mental and Physical Consequences of COVID-19 Quarantine: Special Focus in Older People. *Progress in Cardiovascular Diseases*. https://dx.doi.org/10.1016%2Fj.pcad.2020.03.009.

Johnstone, Duncan and Zoe George. 2020. "Government Details $80m Sport Recovery." *Stuff*, July 7, 2020. https://www.stuff.co.nz/sport/other-sports/122055691/ government-details-80m-sport-recovery.

Jones, Anna. 2020. "Coronavirus: How New Zealand went 'Hard and Early' to Beat Covid-19." *BBC News*, July 10, 2020. https://www.bbc.com/news/world-asia-53274085.

Kelly, Laura. 2011. "'Social Inclusion' through Sports-Based Interventions?" *Critical Social Policy* 3 (1): 126–150.

KPMG. 2020. *Hard Times: UK Economic Outlook*. London: KPMG.

Lindsey, Iain, Tim Chapman and Oliver Dudfield. 2019. "Configuring Relationships between State and Non-State Actors: A New Conceptual Approach for Sport and Development." *International Journal of Sport Policy and Politics*. https://doi.org/10.1080/19406940.2019.1676812.

Lynch, Jenna. 2020. "NewsHub Reid Research Poll: Overwhelming Number of Kiwis back Government's Lockdown Decisions." *Newshub*, May 15, 2020. https://www.newshub.co.nz/home/politics/2020/05/newshub-reid-research-poll-overwhelming-number-of-kiwis-back-governments-lockdown-decision.html.

McGee, Darragh. 2018. "Youth, Re-inventive Institutions and the Moral Politics of Future-Making in Postcolonial Africa." *Sociology* 53 (1): 156-173. https://doi.org/10.1177%2F0038038518772773.

McGuire, David, James E. A. Cunningham, Kae Reynolds and Gerri Matthews Smith. 2020. "Beating the Virus: An Examination of the Crisis Communication Approach taken by New Zealand Prime Minister Jacinda Ardern during the Covid-19 Pandemic." *Human Resource Development International*. https://doi.org/10.1080/13678868.2020.1779543.

Morgan, Haydn. 2013. "Sport Volunteering, Active Citizenship and Social Capital Enhancement: What Role in the 'Big Society'?" *International Journal of Sport Policy and Politics* 5 (4): 381-395. https://doi.org/10.1080/19406940.2013.764542.

Morgan, Haydn and Anthony Bush. 2016. "Sports Coach as Transformative Leader: Arresting School Disengagement through Community Sport-Based Initiatives." *Sport, Education and Society* 21 (5): 759-777. https://doi.org/10.1080/13573322.2014.935319.

Morgan, Haydn and Ioannis Costas Batlle. 2019. "'It's Borderline Hypocrisy': Recruitment Practices in Youth Sport-Based Interventions." *Journal of Sport for Development* 13 (7): 1-14.

Morgan, Haydn and Andrew Parker. 2017. "Generating Recognition, Acceptance and Social Inclusion in Marginalised Youth Populations: The Potential of Sports-Based Interventions." *Journal of Youth Studies* 20 (8): 1028-1043. https://doi.org/10.1080/ 13676261.2017.1305100.

Morgan, Haydn, Andrew Parker, Rosie Meek, and Jon Cryer. 2019. "Participation in Sport as a Mechanism to Transform the Lives of Young People within the Criminal Justice System: An Academic Exploration of a Theory of Change." *Sport, Education and Society*. https://doi.org/10.1080/13573322.2019.1674274.

NCVO. 2019. *UK Civil Society Almanac 2019*. London: The National Council for Voluntary Organisations.

New Zealand Government. 2020. *COVID-19 Alert System*. https://covid19.govt.nz/covid-19/covid-19-alert-system/alert-system-overview/.

New Zealand Treasury. 2018. "The Treasury Approach to the Living Standards Framework." Accessed July 8, 2020. https://treasury.govt.nz/publications/tp/treasury-approach-living-standards-framework-html.

New Zealand Treasury. 2020. "Wellbeing Budget 2020: Rebuilding Together." Accessed July 8, 2020. https://www.treasury.govt.nz/publications/ wellbeing-budget/ wellbeing-budget-2020.

Nols, Zeno, Reinhard Haudenhuyse, Ramon Spaaij and Marc Theeboom, M. 2019. "Social Change through an Urban Sport for Development Initiative? Investigating Critical Pedagogy through the Voices of Young People." *Sport, Education and Society* 24 (7): 727-741. https://doi.org/10.1080/13573322.2018.1459536.

OECD. 2020. *OECD Economic Outlook* 2020, no. 1 (June). doi.org/10.1787/0d1d1e2e-en.

Parent, Milena and Jean Harvey. 2009. "Towards a Management Model for Sport and Physical Activity Community-Based Partnerships." *European Sport Management Quarterly* 9 (1): 23-45.

Parnell, Daniel, Paul Widdop, P., Alex Bond and Rob Wilson. 2020. "COVID-19, Networks and Sport." *Managing Sport and Leisure*. https://doi.org/10.1080/23750472.2020.1750100.

Parker, Andrew, Haydn Morgan, Samaya Farooq, Ben Moreland and Andy Pitchford. 2018. "Sporting Intervention and Social Change: Football, Marginalised Youth and Citizenship Development. *Sport, Education and Society* 24 (3): 298-310. https://doi.org/ 10.1080/13573322.2017.1353493.

Partington, Richard. 2020. "Extend Coronavirus Wage Subsidies or Risk Delayed Redundancies, Firms Warn." *The Guardian*, April 29, 2020. https://www.theguardian.com/business/2020/apr/29/extend-coronavirus-wage-subsidies-or-risk-delayed-redundancies-firms-warn.

Perraudin, Frances. 2020. "Rishi Sunak Heeds Calls to Help Charities with £750m Extra Funding." *The Guardian*, April 8, 2020. https://www.theguardian.com/politics/2020/apr/08/rishi-sunak-heeds-calls-to-help-charities-with-750m-extra-funding.

Sherry, Emma, Nico Schulenkorf and Laurence Chalip. 2015. "Managing Sport for Social Change: The State of Play." *Sport Management Review* 18: 1-5. https://doi.org/10.1016/ j.smr.2014.12.001.

Slack, Trevor and Milena Parent. 2006. *Understanding Sport Organisations"* 2nd ed. Champaign, IL: Human Kinetics.

Spaaij, Ramon and Ruth Jeanes. 2012. "Education for Social Change? A Freirean Critique of Sport for Development and Peace." *Physical Education and Sport Pedagogy* 18 (4): 442-457. https://doi.org/10.1080/17408989.2012.690378.

Sport England. 2020. "Coronavirus: The Story so Far." Accessed 12 June 2020. https://www.sportengland.org/know-your-audience/demographic-knowledge/coronavirus#the_story_so_far.

Spoonley, Paul and Catherine Taiapa. 2009. *Sport and Cultural Diversity: Responding to the Sports and Leisure Needs of Immigrants and Ethnic Minorities in Auckland.* A report for the Auckland Regional Physical Activity and Sport Strategy. Massey University.

Statistica. 2020. "Number of Jobs Furloughed under the Job Retention Scheme in the United Kingdom between April 20 and June 28, 2020." Accessed 8 July 2020. https://www.statista.com/statistics/1116638/uk-number-of-people-on-furlough/.

Stewart, Heather and Ian Sample. 2020. "'Thousands of Lives' Could have been Saved by Earlier Lockdown." *The Guardian*, June 11, 2020. https://www.theguardian.com/world/2020/jun/10/uk-coronavirus-lockdown-20000-lives-boris-johnson-neil-ferguson.

Television New Zealand's One News. 2020. "Calls for Review into Auckland Sport and Recreation Funding." *TVNZ*, July 10, 2020. https://www.tvnz.co.nz/one-news/sport/other/calls-review-into-auckland-sport-and-recreation-funding.

The Health Foundation. 2020. "Covid-19 Policy Tracker." Accessed June 12, 2020. https://www.health.org.uk/news-and-comment/charts-and-infographics/covid-19-policy-tracker.

Wade, Amelia. 2020. "Covid 19 Coronavirus: Lockdown to Lift Jacinda Ardern says New Zealand to Move to Level 3 from 11.59pm next Monday." *New Zealand Herald,* April 20, 2020. https://www.nzherald.co.nz/nz/ news/article.cfm?c_id=1&objectid=12326157.

CHAPTER 6

Time Out: How is the Media Industry Using the Covid-19 Lockdown to Rethink its Coverage of Women and Sport?

Gina S. Comeau and Barbara Ravel

INTRODUCTION

The Covid-19 lockdown provided sport journalists with a unique opportunity to rethink the media coverage of women's sport. Historically, women have been underrepresented in traditional media, with a number of issues raised pertaining to the gendered pattern of coverage (Goodyear-Grant 2013). More specifically, coverage of women's sports and female athletes was practically non-existent in both print and broadcast media in much of the twentieth century, and men's professional sports still receive the majority of media attention today. When women's sport was covered, female athletes were often sexualized, trivialized, and/or infantilized (Bruce 2016; Crossman, Vincent and Speed 2007). In other words, the coverage was fraught with issues relating to visibility and to quality. Post-2000 (and particularly post-2010) studies find that while change has occurred, concerns persist in relation to both the quantity and quality of coverage (Black and Fielding-Loyd 2019; Cooky, Messner and Musso 2018; Ravel and Gareau 2016). Social media researchers note more positive tendencies with challenging gender stereotypes in sport (e.g., Pegoraro, Comeau and Frederick 2018).

In many fields, such as economics and public policy, external shocks have been shown to disrupt dominant ideas and systems (Golob 2003). Could the Covid-19 pandemic act as such a shock to the gendered nature of sport and its coverage? The Covid-19 health crisis has disrupted sports on a global scale, with a significant number of regional, national, and international sporting events postponed or canceled and the majority of training facilities closed. The shutdown of sports provided a number of unique opportunities to bring about change in both the quality and quantity of sports media coverage. With no live sports to cover, media outlets could provide equal coverage of canceled events and their impact on male and female athletes; it could profile women's sports and past games; it could feature female athletes; it could train reporters and newscasters on recognizing gender bias (among other biases) in the media. In an opinion piece written in May 2020, Canadian Women & Sport argued that the Covid-19 crisis provided a unique opportunity for gender equity but also expresses concern that the opposite could happen, and women might be left behind (Canadian Women & Sport 2020).

This chapter examines print media coverage of sports during the first few months of the Covid-19 outbreak, from mid-January 2020 until the end of April 2020. While the primary aim is the framing of women's sport and female athletes, a secondary interest is to understand which sports, athletes, and stories were normalized and at whose expense during the crisis. A feminist framing lens is used to make sense of the media content—more specifically, media coverage of women's sport during the first few months of the sports lockdown as represented in three presses in Canada, France, and the United States. The overarching objective is to uncover the tendencies in sport media coverage during the first few months of the Covid-19 health crisis.

The chapter seeks to uncover whether the media industry used the dearth of live sports as an opportunity to change the gender-biased media coverage of women's sport and female athletes or whether it left women behind, thus reinforcing gendered patterns of media coverage. It argues that newspapers did not use the Covid-19 crisis as an opportunity to address inequities in the media coverage of sports but mostly maintained the status quo, normalizing sports as male; in some cases, media coverage magnified sport inequalities. This chapter begins by reviewing the broader literature on media and sport and subsequently turns its lens towards the feminist scholarship on gender, media, and sport. The second section outlines the study's research methods. The third presents the study's findings in the following three categories: legitimate and mainstream sports, gendered patterns, and crisis patterns.

GENDERED PATTERNS OF SPORTS COVERAGE

Female athletes and women's sports have made significant gains on a number of fronts in recent decades, with increased sporting opportunities for women and girls at the recreational, competitive, collegiate, and professional levels. Despite these increases, media representations of women's sports and female athletes pale in comparison to coverage of men's sports and male athletes. Numerous studies have identified gendered patterns of coverage of female athletes in a specific sport (Black and Fielding-Loyd 2019; Ravel and Gareau 2016), in multisport events (Antunovic 2016), in women's sports in general (Bruce 2016), and in various types of media such as newsprint (Crossman, Vincent and Speed 2007), television (Cooky, Messner and Musto 2018), and social media (Tofelleti, Pegararo and Comeau 2019). While social media show how fans and athletes are challenging these gender norms, the majority of studies note the promotion of heteronormativity and femininity as well as the frequent trivialization of female athletes in both English- and French-speaking countries in print media and sports news websites (Coche 2015).

Bruce (2016) estimates that 10% of print media coverage is of women's sports across various countries (362). Similar results have been found in subsequent studies. For example, Hovden and von der Lippe show that representation is also stalled at 10% in Nordic states, which are generally considered advanced in terms of gender equality (2017). The exception to the rule is during major international sport events, where media scholars have found a more equitable representation of sports. Scholars such as Antunovic have noted that female athletes consistently receive more coverage during the Olympic Games than at other times (2016, 1559). A similar increase was documented in a cross-national study undertaken by Crossman, Vincent and Speed (2007). They found that 42.5% of articles during the Wimbledon Tournament focused on female competitors (2007, 36). Petty and Pope (2019) have noted improvements in the visibility of female athletes as well as task-relevant coverage during the 2015 FIFA Women's World Cup. While these instances indicate a positive trend, particularly during the Olympics, Villalon and Weiller-Abels have found the increased coverage remains fraught with issues such as framing female athletes as wives, girlfriends, and mothers, gender marking, and comparing female athletes to their male counterparts (2018, 1139). These exceptions of increased coverage during major international events are, in part, explained by nationalism (Antunovic 2016).

In numerous countries—such as the United Kingdom, the United States, Australia, Canada, and France to name a few—everyday coverage continually contributes to making women's sports invisible and presenting male athletes as superior to their female counterparts (for example, see Gee and Leberman 2011; Gody-Pressland 2014; Coche 2015; Villalon and Weiller-Abels 2018). Gendered portrayals of female athletes imply that their value is somehow lesser than their male counterparts (Villalon and Weiller-Abels 2018). So not only is newsprint and broadcast media dominated by men's sports, the majority of that coverage is mostly of professional team sports (Hovden and von der Lippe 2017). Wensing and Bruce begin their 2003 study with the affirmation that the media constructs sport as a "male domain" and values professional male sport above all else (387). The valuing of men's sports and commercialism further devalues women's sports, determining what is news and what is newsworthiness (Antunovic 2016).

The male as norm also means more resources are given to produce men's sports media content and less to women's sports (Villalon and Weiller-Abels 2018). The framing of women's sports as lesser has led to what Musto, Cooky, and Messner (2017) have aptly labelled gender-bland sexism, which contributes to maintaining gendered patterns of coverage,

> This "bland" language normalizes a hierarchy between men's and women's sports while simultaneously avoiding charges of overt sexism; sexism in sport is not codified as an assessment of each individual athlete's merit and talent. Consequently, gender-bland sexism reinforces gender boundaries and hierarchies, presenting a fictitious view of inherent male superiority in a way that is subtler and more difficult to detect than before. (578)

The authors demonstrate that sportscasters describe men's games with interest and excitement and that the coverage is filled with dominating language whereas, the opposite was found in coverage of women's sports. Dominant language was found to rarely be used when covering women's sport (*ibid*, 587). The idea presented is that this leads to "bland" and unexciting coverage of women's sporting abilities, which gives the impression that women's sports are not interesting and inferior to men's sports and constructs males as superior athletes (*ibid*).

RESEARCH METHODS

The authors performed a content analysis of three newspapers—*The Globe and Mail*, *The New York Times,* and *Le Monde*—during the first few months of the Covid-19 health crisis, from January 18 to April 26, 2020. This includes weekend edition coverage that coincides with the period examined in this edited collection. Newspapers were selected by circulation and availability. In Canada, *The Globe and Mail* is the most widely distributed broadsheet, and in the United States, *The New York Times*, according to Agility Research & Strategy, ranks third in distribution but first in reaching "opinion leaders" (2020a,b). As for *Le Monde*, it is ranked second in terms of distribution in France but first in online paid access (Statista 2020). Given the limited timeframe to complete this topical study, the authors selected the weekend editions of each newspaper given their more substantial coverage. The majority of weekend editions are larger than their weekday editions, partly due to reader time constraints during the week. *The Globe and Mail* attributes this to readers having more time to read on weekends, with more readers consuming online editions during weekdays and more reading the Saturday print edition (2019). For example, *The Globe and Mail* weekday print editions reached 899,000 readers and weekend editions reached 1.6 million readers and 6.65 million readers weekly, print and online combined (Globe & Mail 2019). As a result, weekday editions tend to be shorter and weekend editions larger, offering more in-depth coverage and often providing highlights of the week. The authors used Statista and Agility to identify the highest distribution per country. In total, there were 342 sport articles published in the three newspapers during this eleven-week period.

The researchers used primarily qualitative research methods along with basic quantitative methods to explore sports coverage during the first few months of the health crisis. They sought to understand sports media coverage in terms of quantity and quality during this period. The first method involved quantifying the number of sports articles written during the stated period and codifying these into one of five categories: men's, women's, gender-neutral, primarily male with some female athlete coverage, and primarily female with some male athlete coverage. The second method was guided by the researchers' desire to understand potential changes in type of coverage and involved categorizing the articles by sport and exploring the constructions and framing of female athletes. Previous feminist research on the topic informed the categories: dominant versus lackluster, gender markers, comparisons to male athletes, unrelated topics, and femininity. Lastly, albeit not the primary objective of this study, the authors also coded all other articles, seeking to identify if other inequities found within sport were covered during the eleven-week period.

Findings

Legitimate and Mainstream

The findings echo what much of the sport media research has identified in terms of gendered patterns of coverage. Even during a global health crisis with a dearth of live sports, sports media still constructed sports as a "male domain" in Canada, the United States, and France and as such presented men's sports and male athletes as legitimate. The vast majority of articles examined provided the researchers with an idea as to what constitutes mainstream sports in major newspapers: male and professional. Professional men's sports teams thus remain at the top of the sport pyramid and, as such, mainstream. Although types of professional sports varied cross-nationally with hockey receiving the most coverage in Canada, basketball in the United States, and soccer in France, the sports that received the most coverage in each country was a men's professional team sport. Professional men's teams were also in second and third place in both the United States and Canada, with American football in second place in both countries and baseball and football (soccer) finding their way into third place. France was slightly different with coverage of biathlon, an individual professional sport which includes men's and women's events, and rugby in third place. With the exception of biathlon in France, the three most covered sports in each country were professional and male. Even though biathlon included coverage of female athletes, the majority of cross-national coverage in the three countries was still dedicated to male athletes playing football (100%), baseball (100%), hockey (97%), basketball (96%) or soccer (93%), giving the impression that women do not play these sports and thus rendering them invisible, as only 3% of hockey articles, 4% of basketball articles, 7% of soccer articles, and 0% of football and baseball articles examined featured females athletes in the examined period.

In terms of overall coverage of sports in Canada, France, and the United States, coverage from mid-January to the end of April averaged 10%, supporting recent research. The average coverage of men's sports was 75%, with the remainder of articles either gender-neutral or discussing both men's and women's sport in which case coverage was inequitably distributed to favor men's sports. The invisibility of female athletes was even more striking on some days where there was no coverage of women's sports and female athletes—such as on February 9, March 8, March 29, and April 1 in *Le Monde*, on February 8, February 29, and April 18 in *The Globe and Mail*, and lastly on February 16 in *The New York Times*—reinforcing sport as a male domain. The three newspapers favored men's sports, with slight variances in percentage. *The Globe and Mail* had the fewest articles dedicated to women's sports compared to men's—8% versus 79%—with the remainder of articles either gender-neutral or mentioning both men's and women's sports, but overall favoring the former. *Le Monde* had the highest percentage of articles dedicated to women's sports (15%) and the lowest coverage of men's sports (72%).

Gendered Patterns

Conventional hyperfeminine norms were observed mostly in *The Globe and Mail* and *The New York Times*; gender-bland sexism was present in all three newspapers. Women were frequently presented as wives, girlfriends, and mothers in regular articles and when men's families were mentioned, it was generally in a profile piece and not consistently, as with female athletes. One example is an article published on March 7 titled "Bujold Hopes to Cap Comeback from Baby with Trip to Olympics" and begins with words of wisdom she would tell her child; the first two paragraphs continue to describe Bujold as a mother versus outlining her athletic prowess or her experience as an Olympian and eleven-time national champion. Rather the focus is on how having a baby has fulfilled her and helped her "refine her focus" (Ewing 2020). This kind of framing is found in numerous examples and central to storylines even when the athlete is not a mother. An interview article covering Maria Sharopova's retirement from tennis, featured in *The New York Times*, focused on the possibility of her having children and mentioned other female players who had children, as well as on her family life as a child, rather than on her career as an athlete (Clarey 2020, L3). The article centers first on her role as a potential future mother, as a daughter, and then as an athlete. Despite significant athletic accomplishments, the majority of the first part of the article is on her other roles. In all articles examined where the female athlete is presented as a wife and/or girlfriend, it is as a heterosexual one, reinforcing heteronormativity.

Confirming Musto, Cooky, and Messner's findings (2017), numerous examples of gender-bland sexism were found in the newspapers. The most striking instance was featured in *The Globe and Mail*. Two articles were both printed on the same day (January 25), on the same page (S3), each featuring professional athletes, one male and one female, who had both obtained the same golf score, 10- under 62. The female golfer score is described as such, "Madelene Sagstrom birdied seven of the first nine holes and shot a 10-under 62 on Friday to take the second-round lead in the Gainbridge LPGA" (Associated Press 2020b). The male golfer's score is described with much more enthusiasm and admiration, "Ryan Palmer had a round as magnificent as the weather at Torrey Pines, making 11 birdies for 10-under 6 on the North Course" (2020a). It is hard to find fault with the first article on women's sport, which is actually longer than the one covering the male golfer. Yet, it is also one of few articles profiling female athletes on that day and lacks excitement despite the female athlete's similar results. Contributing to lackluster framing of women's sport is the tendency to use more quotations, in the same newspaper, when describing events rather than the reporter analyzing or describing them. It illustrates "respectful" coverage and normalizes sport as a male domain.

Female athletes were often also indirectly framed as frail, with a greater focus on their injuries compared to men's injuries. Examples include a short tennis tournament article that mentions an absent player's injury three times and twice for another absent player, rather than using those words to describe tournament play (Canadian Press

2020) and in longer articles more serious injuries are less frequently mentioned if the athlete is male (Davidson 2020). It was also noted that often more words were dedicated to women's injuries than men's injuries in articles of a similar length on the same day, when there are already fewer articles dedicated to women's sports (Associated Press 2020b; Ewing 2020). The slight dramatization of injuries and childbirth cannot be characterized as the overt sexism found in past medicalized discourses that were framed to keep women from playing sports (Petty and Pope 2019; Musto, Cooky and Messner 2017) but rather give the impression that female athletes are inferior. This was more frequent in *The Globe and Mail* coverage. There is a tendency to normalize injuries when a male athlete is injured, giving the impression that injuries are normal and part of the game, whereas when a female athlete is injured or gives birth, it is dramatized (see Ewing 2020 and Brady 2020 for contrasting examples). Representations emphasizing the toughness of male athletes and the frailty of female ones give the impression that women get injured more easily and that it is harder for them to heal—rather than framing injuries as part of being an athlete. The rules are different.

Crisis Patterns

The first few weeks of sport coverage during the Covid-19 health crisis reflect normal gendered patterns of coverage, with many stories emphasizing heteronormative femininity and normalizing sport as a male domain. These patterns continued throughout the examined period, but as more sporting events were postponed and canceled, there were fewer live sports to cover, leaving a number of slots open to cover sports differently. The stories from mid-March onward highlight editorial choices made by the three newspapers—whether that was to cover sports differently, address inequities and other problems in the field of sport, offer less coverage, or provide no coverage. The stories covered and those not covered are very telling as they magnify existing inequities in sports. As mentioned in the previous section, gendered patterns were present throughout the examined period and new crisis patterns emerged in the second half. There was less coverage of women's sports despite there being no sports for men or women and coverage became more inclusive of other sports (i.e., non-professional and individual). The print media's definition of sport seemed to expand. As more and more events closed and the health crisis was declared a pandemic, rather than being more inclusive of women's sports or minorities, both *The Globe & Mail* and *The New York Times* chose to write about obscure men's sports, computer-simulated baseball tournaments, cheating in chess tournaments, fitness routines, recreational sports, and knucklehead culture, to name a few. Most general articles on the impact of Covid-19 on sports referred to men's sports, and not only the traditionally favored team sports. Stories of what to watch during the Covid-19 pandemic and laments on the lack of sports once again referred to men's sports, perpetuating the myth of sport as male, professional, and mainstream.

The choices made are telling of how female athletes, athletes with disabilities, and LGBTQ athletes are further othered during times of crisis.

Newspapers chose to feature retired athletes, more often than not male, rather than redress sport inequities. For example, *The New York Times* featured an Olympian equestrian athlete who was injured in a 2019 riding accident (Macur 2020). The article focused on the tragedy of the incident and the impact of Covid-19 on his rehabilitation plan. While the authors are not criticizing the choice to feature a former athlete who was injured years ago, they do question the lack of coverage of Paralympian athletes and sports. Newspapers could have covered a number of stories pertaining to Paralympian athletes and sports, such as how the health crisis modified the training plans and access to facilities for Paralympian athletes. Interestingly, the Macur (2020) article followed current Paralympians media frames by focusing on the disability, tragedy, and unrelated factors (English et al. 2020, 8), despite the fact that there was no discussion of competing again. The only mention of Paralympic sports was in one article referencing the Olympics and Paralympics, highlighting the sparsity of coverage of athletes with disabilities and its restriction to international events.

Crisis patterns diverged between newspapers, with *The New York Times* addressing some of the major problems of sports, such as abuses, cheating, and doping, more than the other newspapers. However, *The New York Times* failed to feature any gender equity issues but did include some limited coverage on the impact of Covid-19 on former female athletes (i.e., Longman 2020). This publication also had two stories that mentioned the lack of diversity in sports and racism in sport; both articles failed to engage with the topic but fare better than the other two publications, which included no coverage. In the period examined, all three newspapers had their lowest average coverage of female athletes in April 2020, with all three having less than 10% of articles dedicated to women and sport. The highest percentage was in *The New York Times* (8.7%), the second highest was in *The Globe and Mail* (6.7%) and the least highest was in *Le Monde* (0%), bearing in mind that *Le Monde* had no sport coverage on some days. Not only did *The New York Times* fare better in featuring female athletes, it also had more articles covering men's sports that also included some mini coverage of women's sport (22% of April articles) versus what was found in *The Globe and Mail* (3% of April articles). While a small snapshot in time, these numbers are alarming as they are lower than average and in three countries that are considered to be progressive in terms of gender issues.

Concluding Thoughts

The purpose of this study is to first provide a cross-national examination of sports coverage during the first few months of the global health crisis. As the health crisis developed into a pandemic, thereby producing a dearth of live sports, coverage of live sports became more challenging for media. The sport section became smaller in all three newspapers during some weeks. There was no coverage in *Le Monde* on some days and the sport section was merged with other sections in *The Globe and Mail*. The lack of live sports provided an opportunity for print media to reconsider the framing of female athletes and sports and reduce gender biases in terms of both quantity and quality of coverage, but our research shows that these patterns did not change during the global health crisis. At the time of this writing, the world is still in the midst of the Covid-19 pandemic and there is still opportunity to change gendered patterns of sport coverage; however, this first glimpse offers little hope. As more data becomes available, future studies will provide a clearer picture of media coverage during world crises.

This chapter is a cautionary tale. As with many other equity battles, it is possible to lose gender gains in sports coverage. The researchers fear that the pandemic could potentially setback years of progress in women's sport coverage or, even worse, negatively impact all aspects of women's sport. Questions remain as to whether underlying patterns of inequity were only magnified during times of crises or actually worsened. The last few weeks of collected data indicate a downward pattern. As Musto, Cooky, and Messner (2017) point out, gender-bland sexism, similar to color-blind racism, makes it "more difficult to see" and as such is more challenging to address (592). In addition, editorial choices as to which stories to cover and which aspects of the story to emphasize all contribute to how language is used, which in turn plays a key role in maintaining gender biases. To summarize, sport media failed when given an opportunity to resolve a number of issues relating to sport in society and indicate that the health crisis did not act as an exogenous shock to inequities in print media. With a number of sporting events canceled, there were opportunities for newspapers to cover issues relating to racism in sport during Black History Month in February or to sexism in sport on International Women's Day, which is celebrated on March 8. Rather than focus on promoting female athletes on March 8, *Le Monde* had zero coverage of women's sport on that day. It is important to not limit coverage of racism and sexism in sport to specific events. These observations do provide opportunities to commemorate people, events, success and racial and gender barriers in greater detail particularly if they avoid representations that hinder anti-racism efforts (Phia and Adams 2016). This leads the researchers to question whether the same trend continued into June, which is Pride Month and whether sport media covered athlete activism supporting Black Lives Matter in May and June and, if so, how were these black and LGBTQ athletes represented in print media.

The health crisis afforded opportunities to engage critically with how the shutdown impacted female and male athletes differently. For example, how the salary gap impacted home training environments. In other words, articles could address the impact on all athletes and how that impact differs. It is important to note that this chapter examines print media during the first few months of the crisis; an examination of televised media that replayed many past sporting events and relied on nostalgia to keep fans watching (Gammon and Ramshaw 2020) might have rendered different results. Nostalgia was not a significant theme in this study. A number of questions remain unanswered as the crisis continues. What will be the broader implications of the health crisis, with limited resources, and the continued construction of sport as male, and the othering of women, racialized minorities, and athletes with disabilities?

REFERENCES

Agility PR Solutions. 2020a. "Top 10 Canadian Newspapers." Accessed January 14, 2020. https://www.agilitypr.com/resources/top-media-outlets/top-10-canadian-print-outlets/.

———. 2020b. "Top 10 U.S. Newspapers by Circulation." Accessed March 6, 2020. https://www.agilitypr.com/resources/top-media-outlets/top-10-daily-american-newspapers/.

Antunovic, Dunja. 2016. "'You Had to Cover Nadia Comaneci': 'Points of Change' in Coverage of Women's Sport." *The International Journal of the History of Sport* 33 (13): 1551-1573.

Antunovic, Dunja, and Andrew D. Linden. 2015. "Disrupting Dominant Discourses: # HERESPROOF of Interest in Women's Sports." *Feminist Media Studies* 15 (1): 157-159.

Associated Press. 2020a. "Palmer Surpasses Snedeker At Torrey Pines." *Globe & Mail*, January 25, 2020. Gale Academic OneFile.

———. 2020b. "Sagstrom takes Lead at Gainbridge LPGA." *Globe & Mail*, January 25, 2020. Gale Academic OneFile.

Black, Jack, and Beth Fielding-Lloyd. 2019. "Re-Establishing the 'Outsiders': English Press Coverage of the 2015 FIFA Women's World Cup." *International Review for the Sociology of Sport* 54 (3): 282-301.

Brady, Rachel. 2020. "Healthy Powell has Hot Hand against Wizards." *Globe & Mail*, January 18, 2020. Gale Academic OneFile.

Bruce, Toni. 2016. "New Rules for New Times: Sportswomen and Media Representation in the Third Wave." *Sex Roles* 74 (7-8): 361-376.

Canadian Press. "Canada Drops First Two Rubbers to Switzerland at Fed Cup Qualifier." *Globe & Mail*, February 8, 2020. Gale Academic OneFile.

Canadian Women & Sport. 2020. "Crisis Presents an Opportunity to Rethink Gender Equity in Sport." May 26, 2020. https://womenandsport.ca/crisis-presents-an-opportunity-to-rethink-gender-equity-in-sport.

Coche, Roxanne. 2015. "The Amount of Women's Sports Coverage on International Sports News Websites' Home Pages: Content Analysis of the Top Two Sites from Canada, France, Great Britain and the United States." *Electronic News* 9 (4): 223-241.

Cooky, Cheryl, Michael A. Messner, and Michela Musto. 2015. "'It's Dude Time!' A Quarter Century of Excluding Women's Sports in Televised News and Highlight Shows." *Communication & Sport* 3 (3): 261-287.

Crossman, Jane, John Vincent, and Harriet Speed. 2007. "The Times They are A-Changin' Gender Comparisons in Three National Newspapers of the 2004 Wimbledon Championships." *International Review for the Sociology of Sport* 42 (1): 27-41.

Davidson, Neil. 2020. "Wolfpack in Tough, as They Face Defending Champs." *Globe & Mail*, February 29, 2020. Gale Academic OneFile.

English, Peter, Bridie Kean, Simone Pearce, Timothy Peters, Katy Kirby, and Angela Calder. 2020. "'Masters of Your Fate and the Captains of Your Soul': Media Representations of the 2018 Invictus Games." *Sport in Society*, https://doi.org/10.1080/17430437.2020.1738394

Ewing, Lori. 2020. "Bujold Hopes to Cap Comeback from Baby with Trip to Olympics." *Globe & Mail*, March 7, 2020. Gale Academic OneFile.

Gammon, Sean and Gregory Ramshaw. 2020. "Distancing from the Present: Nostalgia and Leisure in Lockdown." *Leisure Science: An Interdisciplinary Journal* https://doi.org/10.1080/01490400.2020.1773993.

Gee, Bridget L. and Sarah I. Leberman. 2011. "Sports Media Making in France: How They Choose What We Get to See and Read." *International Journal of Sport Communication* 4 (3): 321-343.

Godoy-Pressland, Amy. 2014. "'Nothing to Report': A Semi-Longitudinal Investigation of the Print Media Coverage of Sportswomen in British Sunday Newspapers." *Media, Culture & Society* 36 (5): 595-609.

Golob, Stephanie R. 2003. "Beyond the Policy Frontier: Canada, Mexico and Canada, and the Ideological Origins of NAFTA'" *World Politics* 55 (3): 361-398.

Goodyear-Grant, Elizabeth. 2013. *Gendered News: Media Coverage and Electoral Politics in Canada*. Vancouver: UBC Press.

Longman, Jere. 2020. "Pioneer in Women's Game Faces Different Type of Opponent" *The New York Times*, April 5, 2020. Gale Academic OneFile.

Macur, Juliet. 2020. "After a Fall, an Equestrian Tries to Get Up." *The New York Times*, April 19, 2020. Gale Academic OneFile.

Musto, Michela, Cheryl Cooky and Michael A. Messner. 2017. ""From Fizzle to Sizzle!" Televised Sports News and the Production of Gender-Bland Sexism." *Gender & Society* 31 (5): 573-596.

Pegoraro, Ann, Gina S. Comeau and Evan L. Frederick. 2018. "#SheBelieves: The Use of Instagram to Frame the US Women's Soccer Team during #FIFAWWC." *Sport in Society* 21 (7): 1063-1077.

Petty, Kate and Stacey Pope. 2019. "A New Age for Media Coverage of Women's Sport? An Analysis of English Media Coverage of the 2015 FIFA Women's World Cup." *Sociology* 53 (3): 486-502.

Ravel, Barbara, and Marc Gareau. 2016. "'French Football Needs more Women like Adriana'? Examining the Media Coverage of France's Women's National Football Team for the 2011 World Cup and the 2012 Olympic Games." *International Review for the Sociology of Sport* 51 (7): 833-847.

Salter, Phia S. and Glenn Adams. 2016. "On the Intentionality of Cultural Products: Representations of Black History as Psychological Affordances." *Frontiers in Psychology* https://doi.org/10.3389/fpsyg.2016.01166.

Staff. 2020. "Globe Weekend Edition is the Most Read Saturday Newspaper in Canada." *Globe and Mail*, May 2, 2019. https://www.theglobeandmail.com/business/article-globe-weekend-edition-is-the-most-read-saturday-newspaper-in-canada/.

Statista. 2020. "National Daily Newspaper: Most Popular Newspapers France 2019." Books and Publishing. January 20, 2020. https://www.statista.com/statistics/784974/paid-circulation-volume-national-dailies-by-publication-france/.

Toffoletti, Kim, Ann Pegoraro, and Gina S. Comeau. "Self-Representations of Women's Sport Fandom on Instagram at the 2015 FIFA Women's World Cup." *Communication & Sport* https://doi.org/10.1177/2167479519893332

Villalon, Christina and Karen Weiller-Abels. 2018. "NBC's Televised Media Portrayals of Female Athletes in the 2016 Rio Summer Olympic Games: A Critical Feminist View." *Sport in Society* 21 (8): 1137-1157.

Wensing, Emma H. and Toni Bruce. 2003. "Bending the Rules: Media Representations of Gender during an International Sporting Event." *International Review for the Sociology of Sport* 38 (4): 387-396.

Sport Participants

CHAPTER 7

Working out Covid-19: Being a Les Mills Instructor and Managing Health in Times of Quarantine

Karin Andersson, Ulrike Vogl, and Jesper Andreasson

INTRODUCTION

When the World Health Organization (WHO) declared the Covid-19 disease a pandemic, a large amount of the world's population was confined by curfews and other restrictions of movement. Unsurprisingly, during the lockdowns exercising at home employing (online) on-demand services was soon identified as a productive measure to counter the increasing levels of physical inactivity (PI) that followed quarantine-habitus. One of the suppliers for such online workout routines is the New Zealand-based *Les Mills International* (LMI), which is licensing and branding certain "exercise-to-music programs" (referred to as exertainment, a portmanteau of "exercise" and "entertainment"). Currently, LMI is the world's biggest provider of standardized fitness workouts, known for training programs such as Bodypump™, Bodyattack™, and CXWORX™.

Preceding the Covid-19 pandemic, LMI's exercise routines were taught in more than one hundred countries by approximately 130,000 instructors. Their workouts are to be understood as social events known as "exertainment"—working out together—therefore, group fitness instructors may face severe professional consequences due the immediate closure of gyms as well as social distancing.

In this chapter, we will provide insights into how group fitness instructors understood their roles as fitness professionals during the Covid-19 pandemic. We will not only touch on how they continue to live out their "instructorhood" in new and alternative ways, but also how they tried to manage health during the Covid-19 crisis. In doing so, we consider differences due to socio-economic status (e.g., LMI full-time instructors vs. instructors with their main job outside the fitness industry), living situation (living alone or with other family members or friends, with or without children), and national context as lockdowns were implemented differently depending on each country's rules, varying from government recommendations and partial travel restrictions in Finland to a virtual curfew in Israel and Jordan.

The chapter builds upon data gathered during April 2020. Four focus-group interviews with altogether ten participants in clusters of two to four people were conducted. The participants are *LMI* instructors, active in six different countries: Austria, Belgium, Finland, Israel, Jordan, and the United States. Participants were invited to participate on a voluntary basis after having filled out an online questionnaire concerning being a LMI instructor.[1] The benefit of using focus groups is that they provide a possibility for participants to engage in processes of "sharing and comparing," which ideally "provide insights into both what participants think and why they think the way they do" (Morgan and Hoffman 2018, 250). Due to the international compositions of the focus groups as well as Covid-19 restrictions, the semi-structured discussions were conducted by the investigator online, via Skype. The conversations varied between sixty and ninety minutes in length. The primary investigator (K. Andersson) is herself an active Les Mills instructor and currently conducts an ethnographic Ph.D. study investigating the Les Mills community. Dr. Vogl has also received training as a Les Mills instructor but has never practiced the profession. Dr. Andreasson has published research on the Les Mills community but is not himself an instructor. The authors have carefully reflected on their situatedness to avoid biased conclusions.

BACKGROUND: LES MILLS AND ON-DEMAND FITNESS

LMI explicitly presents itself as a global tribe, propagating an altruistic motto—for a fitter planet (Les Mills 2020). During the Covid-19 crisis, LMI appealed to the idea of global connectedness, for instance, by launching a social media campaign called #LesMillsUnited. The purpose of the campaign was to keep instructors and their clients motivated at home. Instructors were asked to film themselves executing a physical exercise that is contained within a program they teach and then to upload the short clip onto social media, encouraging viewers to perform the exercise themselves. Additionally, many instructors were encouraged to make use of virtual platforms (e.g., Zoom, Facebook, Instagram) to maintain contact with fitness clients.

The *ad hoc* philosophy of striving for a "fitter planet" can be interpreted as foregrounding personal health, potentially for people all around the globe (although access is restricted to people who enjoy a membership in a fitness center). Being the world's most profitable producer of standardized fitness routines, LMI assert to take a stand against the alleged threat of physical inactivity, which was declared a pandemic in 2012 (Hall et al. 2020, 1). However, based on medical research highlighting correlations between obesity, nutrition, and fatal diseases, fitness has been construed as a powerful remedy against illness since the 1960s (see Cooper 1968). As the Covid-19-related restrictions have significantly confined people's possibilities to

---

1 The authors acknowledge that there are many alternatives to Les Mills' workout programs. The decision to investigate this particular community was to receive input from fitness professionals teaching the same programs but in different countries. Since Les Mills has its own educational system, the respondents share some knowledge of program structures, and will have been sent the same Covid-19 campaign material no matter where in the world they reside. Hence, their status as Les Mills instructors ensure some common ground where everyone could express their opinions on specific topics.

exercise (Chen et al. 2020, 103), LMI can presently frame their online on-demand services as seemingly desirable solutions (or last resorts) in times of restricted mobility. Additionally, since the outbreak of Covid-19, the discourse on health is predominantly situated within what Rushton and Williams (2012) refer to as a paradigm of "security"—the threat of illness, or even death, through Covid-19. According to Luzi and Radaelli (2020, 4), "physical exercise emerges as a cornerstone, as a preventive measure to improve host defense against influenza viral infection and other metabolic diseases in obese subjects" (see also Chen et al. 2020, 103; Jiménez-Pavón et al. 2020).

The link between physical inactivity, obesity, and illness serves as a justification for the fitness industry, including LMI, to offer training programs, claiming an active role in disease prevention. Conversely, in their #LesMillsUnited campaign, LMI forbade the words pandemic, corona, and Covid-19, as it was supposed to be a "positive vibes only" crusade. In the end, there are clear economic interests at stake: the Covid-19 related lockdowns could affect LMI (and the fitness industry in general) negatively. As fitness centers closed, people looked for alternatives, e.g., running outdoors and taking extensive walks. There are no studies yet that have investigated how the aftermath of Covid-19 could come to affect physical activity, but researchers have looked at how a natural catastrophe can have a negative impact. In 2011, a severe tsunami and hurricane hit east Japan and researchers found that a decrease in physical activity could be noticed as long as three years after the incident (Okazaki, Suzuki, and Sakamoto 2015, 722). Hall et al. (2020) foreshadow that Covid-19 will have a similar effect. Preliminary results from an online survey in Flanders (Scheerder et al. 2020) suggest that people consider themselves to have more time to move since the lockdown. Of the already active respondents, 36% reported moving more, 23% less, and 41% the same. Noticeably, of those who were not very active (i.e., exercise less than once a week), 58% reported moving more, whereas 30% within this group do not move at all. The biggest obstacles found to prevent physical exercise were: sport infrastructure closed (50%), no friends to train with (30%), and fear of infection when doing sports (12%). Therefore, keeping clients hooked was, unsurprisingly, a recurring theme in our group discussions between LMI instructors, which we will return to shortly.

In addition to their focus on personal health, LMI represents ideals contained in what Crawford (1980) referred to as an ideology of healthism. This paradigm constitutes health as consisting of a fit body that, in turn, translates into cultural capital. Healthism, which developed throughout the 1970s, marks a shift towards an individualization of health. Tolvhed and Hakola (2018) point out that the ideology implies that individuals can choose to prevent illness by living (allegedly) healthily. As a consequence, a toned body is perceived as a reflection of self-control and a "healthy" inner world of the subject, whereas the "unhealthy" body is read as a moral and aesthetic personal failure (2018, 192). Seen from this perspective, being part of a global fitness community that strives for "a fitter planet" is a matter of personal choice. Clients who choose LMI workouts to stay healthy and fit make allegedly responsible choices for themselves and the state. They are taught by instructors who are encouraged to act as role models, which in the words of Jackie Mills (one of the owners) are "someone who is positive and is also a great teacher" (Andreasson and Johansson 2014).

RESULTS

Relocating Instructorhood?

Clearly, the Covid-19 pandemic disrupted instructors' abilities to pursue their professional duties (and identities) in gyms. Instead of going to their workplaces to meet clients, socialize, teach, and inspire, many of the participants were largely confined to their respective homes in different countries. Only one of the participants, (Pekka, 48 years old) who lives in Helsinki, Finland, still teaches face-to-face classes. Pekka has taught LMI programs for ten years, is licensed in six programs, and also functions as a tribe coach—a local program specialist who should contribute extra support to fellow instructors within a certain region and for a certain program). He described how gyms in Finland were given the choice to remain open and conveys the following concerning the Covid-19 situation and being an instructor:

> As long as the government doesn't force us to stop, I will continue my classes, but I have been cautious about what I post on social media. I have made my mind up; I want to go on as normal as possible.

Even though social isolation is voluntary in Finland, Pekka is aware that coming together for group fitness activities could be considered controversial and upsetting. Keeping everyday life and instructorhood as intact as possible, as Pekka aimed to do, was not a consensus among the mainly isolated participants.

One solution to deal with the Covid-19 situation, has been to reorganize all communication into a virtual mode in order to maintain social distancing. Joy, a Brazilian woman in her early thirties living in Washington D.C. in the U.S., for example, reported that her facility had to close and that her gym instead offers workouts online. She also explained that she tried to keep in contact with many other instructors via group chats, since it made her feel less lonely. This seemingly straightforward rearranging and relocating of instructorhood was also mirrored in a range of other interviews. Yet, some of the participants felt disadvantaged by the necessity of online communication. For instance, Glen, a part-time instructor in his thirties who teaches LMI classes at a university in North Carolina, U.S., described himself as not being very "high-tech." He said that "so much information is being shared by LMI and instructors that it gets confusing as to what is official."

Although most participants were not actively teaching classes during the pandemic, all except two still stated that they felt as if they had a meaningful function to fill. Diana, a presenter (an advanced instructor who has gone through various extra training to represent LMI officially on a national level) and longtime instructor, currently pregnant and residing in Israel narrated, "I went from being on stage teaching to now just socializing and motivating. I really try to keep the community alive." Her statement signaled a clear shift; a transition from leading a group of exercisers to being a different sort of forerunner. Both the professional function and environment had transitioned. Melissa, a middle-aged instructor with a background as a professional dancer based in Vienna, Austria, continued,

> We are fitness leaders, and we have a role in society to fill right now. We chose this and it's a natural instinct of our instructors to wanna help.

The imperatives seem to align with a sense of altruism derived from LMI's official motto—for a fitter planet—indicating a general wish for increased global health—a purpose that each instructor may choose to embody and act out on differently. Significantly, some participants seemed to consider the pandemic a time where their commitment to LMI's overarching values were put to the test. For example, Glen made it a high priority to be inclusive. To enable clients the possibility to continue exercising from home, he was streaming classes from his own living room. He narrated,

> We tried the first viral Bodypump class this week. Anyone who didn't have equipment was told to wear a weighted backpack, some bottles of Gatorade or cans of soup, whatever really. (Glen)

Although it is possible to purchase LMI's gear online, Glen showed awareness that not everyone will have done so, or possibly do not have the financial means of doing so. He further explained that his self-confidence while giving online classes improved each time, although it felt unusual to teach in front of a webcam. This mindset was mirrored in Joy's narrative who confessed that teaching in front of the computer cannot compare to face-to-face classes as it lacks connection with the customers. She therefore attempted to create "togetherness" and inclusion by using a chat function, asking where people are from and if they are motivated to move—admittedly mostly to motivate herself. She summarized, "It is mentally draining and physically exhausting to teach the virtual workouts."

Simultaneously, there were instructors who felt less inclined or even lacking the means of relocating their routines. Linda, a Vienna-based twenty-seven-year-old psychology student, explained, "It feels like I stopped being an instructor five weeks ago, since I can't teach." She recounted that only very few instructors at her local gym in Vienna were asked to give online classes—she was not one of them. Thus, not all instructors were given the possibility to move into the virtual arena of group fitness.

As shown in this section, there are various ways our participants performed and navigated their instructorhood during the Covid-19 lockdown. Firstly, it was evident that rules and recommendations concerning social distancing heavily impacted the respondents' possibilities to interact with clients, which is normally a prerequisite to teach a group fitness class. For instance, in Finland, Pekka had the possibility to teach classes face to face, whereas the Viennese instructors were limited by a five-people-together rule, and Diana in Israel was on an even stricter curfew. Further, the restrictions resulted in a spatial relocation from the professional sphere of the gym to the private home, which inevitably put some trainers residing in smaller dwellings at a disadvantage. Contextually, teaching was given a new platform and medium—the internet. In addition, the virtual sphere was also used as a tool to nurture the relationship with colleagues and to stay connected to the wider fitness community, which will be discussed in the following section.

Reconceptualizing the Meanings of a Fitness Community and Instructorhood

As argued by psychologists, in a crisis we tend to increase our prerogatives over things within our reach, such as our bodies, nutrition, and daily routines (Luzi and Radaelli 2020, 4). In the midst of crude restrictions, therefore, fitness, training, and the upkeeping of instructorhood may provide a sense of belonging to a fitness community. At the same time, social isolation may increase a sense of detachment from fellow community members, such as co-instructors and clients. Klaus commented,

> I really miss going to the fitness studio. Having a talk before and after class. This time has made me realize that LM is like school with friends and workouts—it is its own microcosmos—its own universe. (Klaus)

Klaus compared LMI to a school, implicitly highlighting its didactic and socializing nature. Based on an earlier statement, "I am just lazy at home," he seemed to need the spatial and social setting to perform the physical labor; similar to a school where one receives clear instructions. Joy agreed and highlighted some lockdown revelations,

> Corona reveals the power of group fitness. We are all doing the same thing. That makes you realize how big the tribe[2] really is and how many people we reach every day.

---

2 LMI refers to themselves as a global tribe. Coming from New Zealand, they used to foreground Maori culture, which is potentially problematic, since they are not Maori descendants. Within our discussions, Glen was the only participant who pointed this out and said that he does not find it politically correct that LMI refers to themselves as a tribe, and that it could be interpreted as offensive. In light of the Black Lives Matter movement, LMI officially decided to desist in referring to themselves as a tribe in July 2020.

As the consuming of exercise routines transferred to on-screen activities, Joy noted that this did not provide the same satisfaction as performing the workouts together in real life. Diana also touched upon the social dimensions of individual fitness, "the current situation shows us that it's not just about the workout. Anyone can do LM on-demand now, but it's not the same. It's hard to imagine a life without LM."

Losing the power of the group and feelings of belonging, several of the participants reflected the essence of instructorhood. Pekka, for example, explained that he believed that the imposed Covid-19 break will ignite deep reflection among LMI instructors, generally, causing some to appreciate their classes more sincerely, and others to leave the fitness business permanently. He himself regularly joined with colleagues for walks, keeping an advised one-meter distance, and reported to observe mainly two ways in which instructors in Helsinki made sense of the current situation: either as a time for self-improvement or self-pity. Accordingly, Melissa said that, "corona is a perfect time to think about what kind of instructor you wanna come back as and prepare for that time."

Moving away from the isolated personal experience of being physically present in the gym, one respondent emphasized the current importance of the global LMI community. Jamal asserted, "As fitness leaders we have to do something to members as well, if you think about the cause—for a fitter planet—that means we need to move and make people move. It's not about salary, I do it to encourage." Combining a feeling of collective belonging with exercising dutiful control both over his own and other people's bodies, Jamal understood the Covid-19 era as a period where one should live and spread LMI's values. Underlining that he did not do it for financial gain contributed to a utilitarian and almost altruistic sense of purpose.

Present in the same group and commenting on the same topic, Melissa exclaimed, "Lockdown is a powerful tool to get people into fitness." Although both respondents seemed to be in full agreement with one another, they subconsciously represented two genuinely different standpoints. Jamal was speaking of spreading an ideological message of movement promoting health, whereas Melissa discussed the lockdown as a forceful marketing strategy for selling fitness. Although these endeavors seemed to contradict one another, both instructors seemed convinced that both actions were equally necessary—fitness is for everyone but comes at a price.

This section highlighted different ways instructors articulated and felt belonging towards the LMI community. Those instructors who reported being active in LMI's social media groups generally seemed to feel empowered by the idea of being a part of something global, whereas other respondents who claimed to miss their own participants and gym expressed micro-environmental belonging.

Bodily Capital and Aesthetics During Covid-19

In this section we will focus on how interviewees negotiated their possibilities of maintaining their individual physical standards during quarantine. Following "stay-at-home-regulations," home-workouts were rapidly being offered by gyms, individual trainers, and even mainstream television. Daily exercise remained seemingly important during lockdown and has proven positive physiological and mental benefits (Chen et al. 2020, 104). Nevertheless, to a fitness professional a well-kept and fit body is a trademark of credibility, and thoughts regarding returning to teaching caused both excitement and anxiety in respondents. Klaus had to take the governmental measurements in Austria very seriously to avoid anyone in his family contracting the virus. He conveyed that he was not active on chat forums for either local or global instructors, but only stayed in touch with befriended colleagues. Teaching virtual classes was not something he considered doing, "It's called group fitness for a reason—staring into a camera would be too weird for me. I won't do any virtual classes, and frankly, seeing the posts demotivates me and makes me feel bad I don't work out more."

Klaus clearly expressed uneasiness concerning not performing as much exercise as accustomed, and later in the interview mentioned that he eats carelessly and had gained weight. Before the outbreak of the pandemic, he taught LMI's Bodyattack program once a week, a cardio routine that he described as very advanced and physically demanding, "It will be really hard going back to teaching classes after this long break of doing basically nothing."

Participating in the same group discussion, Diana agreed and added, "I am six months pregnant so my fitness will not get better, but I still feel pressured to work out, to keep fit to when I have to start teaching again, but I always feel this pressure. I wouldn't say that it started with the virus, but this situation makes it worse." Similar to Klaus, Diana lacked motivation to exercise at home, since her main impetus to train was the feeling of working out in a group—experiencing movement and music together—being "exertained."

In contrast to Klaus and Diana's experiences, most other participants reported engaging in more physical activity during lockdown than they used to before it began. For instance, apart from teaching some face-to-face classes each week, Pekka had also begun a new strength program for himself to "get fitter," since he had more time to invest in training. "Getting stronger for the time after the pandemic, I decided that instead of lying on the sofa and feeling sorry for the world, this is my time to focus on myself, do my outmost to better myself as an instructor." Empowered by an industrious and individualized mindset, Pekka said that he was trialing new programs from LMI that he had wanted to try before. Convinced by the benefits of his recently invented strength program, he concluded that the pandemic offered great opportunities to improve ones' own competence and ability as a fitness professional, but also offered time to reflect critically upon oneself.

Conversely, although the U.S.-based trainers Glen and Daisy exercises frequently during lockdown, they did not intend to improve their physiques, but stated that fitness is supposed to be stress-relieving. Glen narrated, "wellness should be more important than fitness," implying that feeling healthy should excel aesthetics. Daisy concurred and deemed exercise a therapeutic tool, "I do not feel pressured. I got into fitness because of a depression I had, and fitness changed my life and became my medicine. Everyone will be coming back from the same thing. Me struggling will be authentic. If it doesn't look hard it doesn't push the participants either." Clearly, being out of breath in front of her class when she returns to the gym is not something that Daisy dreads but rather embraces. In fact, she explained that her exhaustion will possibly increase the credibility of her own commitment to the exercise routine.

Admittedly, depending on if an instructor is a full-time trainer or not, ideas concerning the body seemed to differ. When asked if staying fit was a priority to the full-time trainer Jamal, he exclaimed, "I have to work out. This is my job. When everything goes back to normal, I have to keep my fitness level. We need to be as sharp as possible going back to normality, since we are teaching demanding programs and people expect to see top fitness with perfect technique." To Jamal, his personal physique did not appear to be a matter of choice, but rather a professional prerequisite achieved by dedication and discipline. Jamal further stated that he was teaching classes in front of his computer in his living room and that "it is awkward when the family is watching." Reading between the lines, having this mindset could cause tremendous pressure on the individual, not merely to find possibilities of maintaining a perfect physique (in a state of complete lockdown, as in Jordan), but also to ensure a steady financial income.

This section has shown that regardless if exercise is described as a coping strategy during difficult times, a necessity, or as pure leisure, it evidently remains a part of life during quarantine. In summary, the severity of lockdown measures and if a trainer worked full-time within the fitness industry are the factors that seemingly had the most impact on how instructorhood was negotiated. For example, Pekka, residing in Finland where lockdown was voluntary, decided to "go on as normal" and trains more, whereas Diana, living in Israel with a curfew, decided to "dress up to go grocery shopping." Similarly, Jamal, a full-time coach on strict lockdown in Jordan, narrated that it is not an option for him to lose his conditioned physique, while Klaus, an enthusiastic part-time instructor in Vienna, revealed that he will not work out again until he can return to the gym.

DISCUSSION AND CONCLUSION

This chapter dealt with how the lifestyle of group fitness instructors have changed, both professionally and personally, due to the Covid-19 virus. Since physical exercise with LMI remains a high priority to the interviewees, the pandemic does not seem to challenge core ideals. All but two participants reported doing LMI classes on a regular basis from home, and several even perform an excess of LMI workouts since they have more spare time.

Keeping a fit physique turned out to have different motivations. Two respondents claimed to exercise to rid themselves of stress, one full-time trainer asserted that it is his job to be extraordinary fit, and one instructor stated she would continue since she was professionally obliged to do so. The remaining took an almost impartial stance, conveying the message that the workout routines are simply a part of everyday life.

This reveals willingness or an urge to maintain a certain fitness level, aesthetic look, bodily capital, or an ounce of "normality" even in quarantine. To gain a deeper understanding of this outcome, one would need to trace the motivation for teaching LMI fitness in the first place. According to a survey conducted in 2019 where teaching imperatives of LMI instructors based in Austria were explored, one of the driving forces for giving classes turned out to be "working on a strong and fit self" (K. Andersson and U. Vogl, unpublished data), which the investigators connected to neoliberal exercising strategies where a lean body functions as bodily capital, superior to an allegedly unhealthy undefined physique. Concurrently, working on improving ones' physique could be interpreted as a substitute for other entrepreneurial projects that the pandemic prevents pursuing.

The aforementioned study also revealed clusters of interrelated ideas indicating that an LMI instructor should always appear a role model: an "authentic," fit, and inspiring persona. Building on these results, this chapter also illustrated that the pandemic has not significantly altered fundamental teaching or exercise motivations, but rather strengthened them. The participants conveyed differing views and understandings of how LMI dealt with the Covid-19 situation, but most agreed that the #LesMillsUnited campaign, discussed in the introduction, did not motivate them to train, but, indeed, increased personal belonging towards the global LMI community. This is a continuous goal of LMI, as each instructor is also a paying customer for program choreographies. Accordingly, one respondent said that "lockdown is a powerful tool to get people into fitness," which implied a fine line between forging the fitter planet—"helping" people to healthy lifestyles—and selling the LMI concept.

If standardized fitness concerns generating a healthier mankind, selling a product, or possibly both, is not a new question *per se*. However, in the light of the Covid-19 pandemic, we find ourselves at the intersections of capitalism, global health, and personal wellbeing, causing unprecedented moral dilemmas. It is noteworthy, for example, that none of the participants expressed concern about the pandemic and its fatalities. Omission is a powerful tool; what is not being said can be understood as equally interesting as to what was said (Gee 2018, 4).

To conclude, it is worth considering that the pandemic could destabilize the base of healthism as an ideology, which does not seem to have readily available answers for a crisis of this magnitude. Since general wellbeing has long been taken for granted, the idea of health has had the possibility of developing in various directions and taking health to new extremes. For instance, pre-pandemic the use of steroids was becoming more frequent among hobby exercisers, as well as participation in marathons, triathlons, and other demanding extreme sports (Andreasson and Johansson 2019). Presently, when a large amount of the world's population might fear for their (actual) wellbeing, it is likely that health will be discussed in other dimensions again—health as the absence of disease rather than as an expression of aesthetics, extraordinary strength, or slenderness. Further research could investigate the status of the lean body during and after a health-crisis, as well as how a pandemic like Covid-19 might mobilize new definitions of personal health to hobby exercisers—can Covid-19 possibly ignite a more lasting reevaluation of individual health?

REFERENCES

Andreasson, Jesper, and Johansson, Thomas. 2014. *The Global Gym. Gender, Health and Pedagogies.* Basingstoke: Palgrave Macmillan.

———. 2019. *Extreme Sports, Extreme Bodies: Gender, Identities and Bodies in Motion.* Cham: Palgrave Macmillan.

Chen, Peijie, Lijuan Mao, George P. Nassis, Peter Harmer, Barbara E. Ainsworth, and Fuzhong Li. 2020. "Coronavirus Disease (COVID-19): The Need to maintain regular Physical Activity while taking Precautions." *Journal of Sport and Health Science* 9 (2): 103–104. https://doi.org/10.1016/j.jshs.2020.02.001

Cooper, Kenneth. 1968. *Aerobics.* New York: Bantham Books.

Crawford, Robert. 1980. "Healthism and the Medicalization of Everyday Life." *International Journal of Health Services* 10 (3): 365–388. 10.29397/reciis.v13i1.1775

Gee, James Paul. 2018. *Introducing Discourse Analysis. From Grammar to Society.* Abingdon, Oxon, New York, NY: Routledge.

Hall Grenita, Carl J. Lavie, Deepika R. Laddu, Ross Arena, and Shane A. Philips. 2020. "A Tale of two Pandemics: How will COVID-19 and Global Trends in Physical Inactivity and Sedentary Behavior affect one another?" *Progress in Cardiovascular Diseases.* https://doi.org/10.1016/j.pcad.2020.04.005.

Jiménez-Pavón, David, and Carbonell-Baeza, Ana, and Lavie, Carl J. 2020. "Physical Exercise as Therapy to fight against the Mental and Physical Consequences of COVID-19 Quarantine: Special Focus in older People." *Progress in cardiovascular diseases* 63 (3): 1-3. https://doi.org/10.1016/j.pcad.2020.03.009.

Les Mills International. Accessed July 1, 2020. https://www.lesmills.com.

Les Mills International. 2020. "Our Tribe." Accessed June 1, 2020. https://www.lesmills.com/fit-planet/our-tribe/.

Luzi, Livio, and Maria Grazia Radaelli. 2020. "Influenza and Obesity: Its Odd Relationship and the Lessons for COVID-19 Pandemic." *Acta Diabetologica* 57: 759-764. https://doi.org/10.1007/s00592-020-01522-8.

Morgan, David L, and Kim Hoffman. 2018. "Focus Groups." In *the SAGE Handbook of Qualitative Data Collection,* edited by Uwe Flic, 250–263. Los Angeles: SAGE.

Okazaki Kanzo, Koya Suzuki, Yusuru Sakamoto, and Keiji Sasaki. 2015. "Physical Activity and Sedentary Behavior among Children and Adolescents living in an Area affected by the 2011 Great East Japan Earthquake and Tsunami for 3 Years." *Preventive Medicine Reports* 2: 720-724.

Rushton, Simon, David Owain Williams. 2012. "Frames, Paradigms and Power: Global Health Policy-Making under Neoliberalism." *Global Society* 26 (2): 147–167. https://doi.org/10.1080/13600826.2012.656266.

Scheerder, Jeroen, Annick Willem, Veerle de Bosscher, Erik Thibaut, and Margot Ricour. 2020. "Sporten in Tijden van Crisis. Profiel van de Corona-Sporter." Presentation at KU Leuven, UGent, VUB. Accessed June 11, 2020. https://kics.sport.vlaanderen/wetenschappelijkonderzoek/Documents/200411_onderzoek_Coronasporter.pdf.

Tolvhed, Helena, and Outi Hakola. 2018. "The Individualization of Health in Late Modernity." In *Conceptualising Public Health: Historical and Contemporary Struggles Over Key Concepts,* edited by Johannes Kananen, Sophy Bergenheim, and Merle Wessel, 190-203. Oxford: Routledge.

CHAPTER 8

Swolecial Distancing: Gym Closures and the Quarantine Workout

Broderick D.V. Chow

SYMPATHY FOR THE SWOLE

On March 20, 2020 when U.K. Prime Minister Boris Johnson announced the closure of all pubs, clubs, cafes, restaurants, bars and gyms, I was searching for kettlebells on Amazon. My own London gym had been closed for two days already. A member had tested positive for Covid-19, and despite deep cleaning the writing was on the wall. The closure was barely necessary. As the pandemic intensified, attendance at the gym had dropped off sharply. It was me, the worried personal trainers, and a few other Olympic weightlifters.[1] The cavernous underground space in Farringdon, normally sweaty and noisy, was cold and silent.

I ordered a sixteen-kilogram kettlebell and an eight-kilogram one, and some resistance bands. Scarcity and panic buying made dumbbells and Olympic bars unaffordable luxuries, like flour and toilet paper. Instagram was my enemy. My fists clenched whenever I saw the home gym set-ups of weightlifter friends, a combined jealousy at their continued ability to lift and the fact they live in a property big enough to have a garage or gazebo (in London? Come on). I figured I would get by for a couple weeks on home workouts. But those early workouts felt horrible. I came to sport and physical culture in my thirties so I won't pretend I'm Lu Xiaojun—the Chinese weightlifter and gold medallist at the 2012 summer Olympic Games—but I can (or could) snatch 90kg, clean 105kg, back squat 150kg, deadlift 180kg. I can confidently say I am the strongest person at the small university where I teach. I grunted and sweated my way through squats, lunges, and kettlebell swings but those kettlebells felt like I was pressing soup tins.

In these uncertain times, it is hard to convince anyone to have sympathy for the swole. Ours is hardly the most pressing concern in the face of a public health

---

[1] I refer to the sport of Olympic weightlifting, in which athletes train to lift a one-rep maximum in two lifts, the snatch and the clean and jerk, as distinct from weight training or resistance training. I have been Olympic lifting for six years and coaching for three.

emergency and a global socioeconomic and political crisis. "Can't you just go running?" a friend asked me, and as the cloud of red mist cleared from my eyes, I realised he was correct. What could be less essential right now than building hypertrophic muscle or gratuitous strength? Even the language of "gainz" is antithetical to Covid-19's discourses of scarcity, limits, and communal good.

Essential and Inessential Exercise

This chapter considers the relationships between exercise, disease, and inequality, which the Covid-19 pandemic has made starkly clear. I theorize the disruption to fitness practices and the quarantine home workout in relation to the discourse of "essential" activity, which I argue reveals a tension in the cultural meaning of fitness and physical culture. The idea of "essential" exercise is one of the most contested aspects of the current crisis. From March 26 to May 11, 2020, U.K. government guidelines permitted "one form of exercise a day, for example a run, walk, or cycle— alone or with members of your household" (Johnson 2020a). As sportswriter Jonathan Liew suggested, this "feels less like a permission and more like an imperative" (Liew 2020). Liew optimistically extols the value of "small sport" being discovered in this time: an individual's relationship to their body and activity that is motivated by pleasure and personal satisfaction (*ibid.*). But this "imperative" functions in an authoritarian way, too. People have been forced out of parks for moving too slowly, as if walking were not exercise, as if rest and recovery were not central to fitness. Councils have warned citizens that parks are open for "exercise only" (Bromley Council 2020).

The idea that running or walking in the park is the only essential use of (urban) public green space raises questions of inequality, access, and privatization. Writing on the closure of Brockwell Park on April 5, 2020, after 3,000 people used it to sunbathe (that is, to be *idle*), journalist Lynsey Hanley connected the discourse of the essential to nineteenth-century questions of contagion and the work of Victorian reformers who campaigned for urban parks as a way of improving the health of the working poor (Hanley 2020). Gothic literature scholar Emma Liggins argued that urban public and private space in the nineteenth century was intrinsically linked to class inequality, which in turn characterised the responses to epidemics by authorities in these times (Liggins 2020).

When government shuts down gyms while simultaneously declaring outdoor space for exercise only, two discursive framings of physical culture and fitness emerged. On the one hand, physical activity is a public health imperative, meaning exercise is an activity essential to individual and public health. Pre-Covid-19 guidance by the U.K.'s Chief Medical Officers (September 2019) emphasized the "protective effect of physical activity on a range of many chronic conditions including coronary heart disease, obesity and Type 2 diabetes, mental health problems and social isolation" while simultaneously underlining the risks of inactivity (Dept of Health and Social Care 2019). Thus, in the initial stages of the pandemic, exercise (once a day, close to home) was one of the only legitimate reasons to leave the house. On the other hand, "fitness" also has cultural and aesthetic qualities supplementary to what might be considered essential physical activity. Expressed in forms like bodybuilding, strength sports, and CrossFit, fitness practices are highly inessential, an unnecessary or extreme addition to the normal functioning of the body (as evidenced by the very concept of hypertrophy in physical culture—the enlargement of muscle tissue).

The tension between essential and inessential exercise is threaded through the history of physical culture, from the nineteenth century onwards, and in this chapter, I turn to this history to make sense of our pandemic present. My analysis builds upon historical research on physical culture and exercise, including biographical and autobiographical accounts, and puts this research into dialogue with theoretical ideas in theater and performance studies. Physical culture, I argue, proposes an ideology that individualizes responsibility for one's health and wellbeing, which, in a highly class-stratified society, creates significant inequalities of access. In the first section, I look at the "exercise cure" for another strange epidemic—neurasthenia—as an example that demonstrates how essential exercise is not just a physiological but an ideological imperative. However, physical culture was hardly austere or pious but exceedingly theatrical and flamboyant, reliant on acts of elaborate showmanship to communicate the gospel of health and fitness. This suggests that there are other values that individuals find in fitness outside of its health benefits. In the second section, I discuss the "inessential" but simultaneously invaluable aspects of fitness by comparing home workout performances on social media and livestreaming to the theatrical performances of physical culture pioneers. The chapter concludes with a hopeful recommendation for redistribution of access to inessential "leisure" activities in the post-pandemic era.

ESSENTIAL EXERCISE

The quarantine workout and the discourse of "essential exercise" is tied deeply to questions of individual responsibility and resilience. While in the U.K. the government's response to the pandemic has been colloquially called a "lockdown," the policing of such orders requires a careful balance of between individual responsibility and trust in government (Connolly 2020). An article by Katarina Giritli Nygren and Anna Olofsson concerning Sweden's minimal lockdown restrictions in the early stages of the pandemic notes how the approach of recommendations, rather than prohibitions, targeted the "self-regulating individual in terms of not only trust but also solidarity" (Nygren and Olofsson 2020, 4). While Sweden's approach of leaving shops and restaurants open seemed comparatively *laissez-faire*, the U.K. government's individual guidance relied on the same form of individualism: "you **must** stay at home. You should not meet friends or relatives who do not live in your home. You may only leave for home for very limited purposes [...]" (Johnson 2020b). The second-person address and imperative (you *must*, you *should*, you *may*) was placed alongside a call to take responsibility for not overwhelming a beloved system of social welfare (the National Health Service): "If too many people become seriously unwell at one time, the NHS will be unable to cope." Thus, Home Secretary Priti Patel's non-apology for government mismanagement of Personal Protective Equipment (PPE) for the NHS ("I'm sorry if people feel there have been failings") (Parveen 2020) and Health Secretary Matt Hancock's call for NHS workers not to "overuse" PPE (Stewart and Campbell 2020), must be read as part of this larger structure of individualization.

Fitness is also a significant public health imperative that individualizes responsibility for one's health. A report on the seventieth anniversary of the founding of the NHS by the King's Fund exploring the relationship between the NHS and the public found that "there was strong support [among their representative sample] for the idea of individuals taking more responsibility for their health [...] by moderating unhealthy behaviors such as excessive alcohol consumption and doing regular exercise" in order to reduce strain on the service (Burkitt et al. 2018, 16). Public Health England's 2016 guidance, "Health matters: getting every adult active every day" while not mentioning fitness, sets out a clear individual and communal moral imperative for physical activity: "Increasing physical activity has the potential to improve the physical and mental health and wellbeing of individuals, families, communities and the nation as a whole" (Public Health England 2016).

Jennifer Smith Maguire's *Fit for Consumption* considered such individual moral imperatives through history, interviews, ethnography, and analysis of fitness publications. "Participation in the fitness field," she wrote, "is bound up with producing subjectivities that are fit to consume, in that they locate the production of meaning, identity and relationships with others in the processes of consumption" (Maguire 2007, 192). Thus, because it is tied to consumer capitalism, fitness individualizes a social problem (health) and reproduces a "class-based stratification of health and health risks" (Maguire 2007, 204). A similar class-based stratification appears when we look back to fitness in the nineteenth century, especially in its relation to another sort of "pandemic."

Neuraesthenia and the Exercise Cure

The late-nineteenth century saw the outbreak of another strange disease. Identified by physician George M. Beard in 1880 as neurasthenia (literally, weak nerves), the disease, like Covid-19, had a wildly varied aetiology of symptoms, including "blurred vision, indigestion, restlessness, backache, constipation, disorientation, headache, throat irritation, colds, dizziness, loss of appetite, palpitations, and spitting up blood" (Rotunda 1993, 186). Like Covid-19, it seemed to affect men far more than women. In fact, neurasthenia could be thought of as "masculine" form of hysteria, hence French psychologist Jean-Michel Charcot's name for it, *hysterie virile* (Mosse 1996, 85). As in the case of hysteria, today neurasthenia is primarily thought of as a social and political phenomenon, rather than a physiological disorder. But at the time, this primarily middle-class disease was thought to be caused by too much "brain work" (Rotunda 1993, 187).

Unlike Covid-19, which is directly attributable to a virus called severe acute respiratory syndrome coronavirus 2 (SARS-CoV-2), neurasthenia is less a physiological phenomenon than a discursive one, a "zone of intensity," which dance scholar Kélina Gotman defined as "a complex of ideas and events, a temporary holding zone in which concepts in formation overlap with one another" (Gotman 2017, 2). The U.S. American historian David G. Schuster argued that the concept of neurasthenia captured a disjuncture between the Victorian manly ideal of will and control, and "political, social and personal realities" (Schuster 2011, 86). While nineteenth-century men valued control, wage labour and market instability meant that the reality of their lives seemed out of control, producing an individualized diagnosis: neurasthenia, weak nerves, weak *will* (Schuster 2011, 86-7). Neurasthenia was class-based as well as gendered. Emerging in parallel with the disorder, Taylorist Scientific Management and industrial automation was creating and building a bourgeois managerial middle class, so neurasthenia confirmed a hierarchy of labour—mental work, as opposed to manual labour, was so difficult it could literally make you sick.

The cure for neurasthenia was exercise: outdoor hikes, virilizing activities, and physical culture. If neurasthenia was a disease of weak nerves and will, it followed that the will could be trained through "manly" activities (another moral imperative that, as we will see, is repeated in twentieth-century fitness culture). According to Nicholas Turse, the exercise cure was thought to "foster survival instincts, primitivism, competition, aggression, and muscle-building" that would enable the male neurasthenic to return to and survive the "civilized world" (Turse 1999, 35). A vivid example of the exercise cure is provided in Theodore Dreiser's unfinished autobiographical novel *An Amateur Laborer*. Dreiser fell prey to neurasthenia after the failure of his second novel, *Sister Carrie*, and his brother Paul sent him to the sanatorium of retired wrestler and physical culturist William Muldoon in the pastoral landscape of rural New York State. With exercise, fresh air, and discipline, Dreiser recovered. At Muldoon's sanatorium, even showers were timed and disciplined: "Ten seconds in which to jump under the spray and get myself thoroughly wet, twenty seconds in which to jump out and soap myself over, ten seconds to get back under again and rinse all the soap off and twenty seconds in which to retch and dry the skin" (Dreiser 1904[1983], 73-4). Under Muldoon's regime, showers were like CrossFit WODs.

Dreiser's auto-fiction crystallized the relationship between class, labour, gender, and exercise. His neurasthenia was brought on by sudden, enforced idleness—the kind we are seeing during Covid-19 with the rise of unemployment and furlough schemes. He wrote: "I found myself bereft of the power of earning a living with my mind and was compelled to turn to my hands. These had never been trained in any labor" (Dreiser 1904[1983], 4). Unlike the essential workers with whom he shared long queues for day-to-day employment, Dreiser's writer was an imposter: "People did not like my appearance. They seemed to take it for granted that I was physically unable to do anything and passed me by" (Dreiser 1904[1983], 27). But despite this precarious opening, Dreiser was saved by his class, the familial safety net of his brother, a successful songwriter. The sanatorium run by Muldoon cost a small fortune and Dreiser despised his fellow boarders, though it was also a kind of self-hatred. Later, upon leaving, cured, Dreiser decided to become an essential worker, and picked up work on the railroads. But this kind of work was not freeing nor like the vitality of throwing medicine balls with Muldoon. "There was something too of the relentless and indifferent that characterizes nature's grosser mood," he wrote "of the slow, grinding force of a machine that has you in its grip, crushing you, and does not know it is, and could not stop, if it would" (Dreiser 1904[1983], 111). And crucially, "real," productive labour, was destructive to his body (Travis 2008, 43).

The influence of neurasthenia on British, American, and European fitness culture was significant. Turse argued that neurasthenia was crucial to the rise of weight training as a mainstream practice. He suggested that the socio-political-economic conditions that had produced a crisis in the manly ideal correspond to the rise of an aesthetic ideal produced, importantly, in one's leisure time (Turse 1999, 36-38). Bodybuilding was not the only technology neurasthenics used to augment their masculine energy—Carolyn Thomas de la Peña's *The Body Electric* documented the "strange machines" and quack cures like "radium waters" that emerged during this period, a sort of wellness industry *avant la lettre* (de la Peña, 1999, 14).

In bodybuilding pioneer Eugen Sandow's book *Life is Movement*, he wrote about being struck by a bout of neurasthenia as a result of too much mental labour while setting up his schools of physical culture in the early 1900s. Thus, the co-development of fitness culture and neurasthenia in the late nineteenth and early twentieth centuries marked exercise as "essential" at the intersection of class and gender. But it is important also to note how such discourse of the "essential" was highly ideological. As the entrepreneurial and managerial middle-class grew, so too did activities that mythologized a "lost" masculine ideal, which were only made possible by the increased leisure time that such class inequalities afforded. Fitness was essential to avoid disease—not heart disease or Type 2 diabetes, but the neurasthenic threat of lost manhood. We see the influence of neurasthenia in the discourses of fitness practices such as CrossFit, which communicates an ideology of individual resilience. As J.C. Herz wrote, CrossFit's vision of the world says that "life, the universe, could swerve in unexpected ways and make daunting physical demands, [so] that your survival or success might at any moment hinge on your ability to move your body and some kind of heavy load over distance quickly" (Herz 2015, 1). But just as Dreiser found, unless you are an essential worker, such capacities are rarely put to use in modern life.

Biopolitics of Slow Death

Under lockdown, the allotment of daily essential exercise and the quarantine home workout are *not* for those whose work is deemed essential. Those in health and social care, food supply, essential public services, utilities, public safe, education and childcare, and transport, simply do not have the time or capacity to do burpees in their living rooms. From a performance studies perspective the quarantine workout may be read as a *performance* of failure and recovery, an individual drama in which the body fails and recovers. This performance is what Lauren Berlant called a "melodrama of the care of the monadic [individual, bounded] self," linked to a larger biopolitics of the administration and management of life itself (Berlant 2007, 758). Reading historically in relation to another drama of failure and recovery (from neurasthenia) makes stark the divide between those populations for whom recovery (in the form of monetary bailouts, Universal Credit, furlough, etc.) no matter how inadequate might still be forthcoming, and majority Black and brown populations whose essential labor sustains the survival of the body politic as a whole but whose actual bodies are offered up to a regime of neoliberal "slow death" (Berlant 2007). "Slow death" refers to the endemic, as opposed to epidemic or pandemic conditions of debility and structural inequality under capitalism, which, as Cedric J. Robinson proposed, is always a *racial capitalism* (Robinson, 1983). The disproportionate impact of Covid-19 on Black, Asian, and minority ethnic (BAME) populations in the United Kingdom, as in other countries, thus evidences Fiona Godlee's claim in the *British Medical Journal* that racism is "the other pandemic" (Godlee 2020, 369), but which, more accurately, has been endemic to the formation of capitalism under coloniality. Fitness's performance of individual resilience and self-management then, might frame how we understand CrossFit CEO Greg Glassman's racist tweets on June 8, 2020 (see Gorman and Taylor 2020). Furthermore, fitness's discourses of individual responsibility and resilience call on the subject of "hyper-accelerated capitalist life" to "always be optimizing" (Tolentino 2019). But as Jasbir Puar argued, "in neoliberal, biomedical, and biotechnological terms, the body is *always debilitated* in relation to its ever expanding potentiality" (Puar 2011, 153, emphasis added). But who has access to such potentiality—in other words, who can recover from debility—is determined by a larger structure of race, gender, and class. Under the Covid-19 lockdown, those structures and divisions have become all too stark.

INESSENTIAL EXERCISE

If the discourse of essential exercise reveals fitness to be a performance of failure and recovery that is marked by racial, class-based, and gendered inequalities, the historical connection of theater and fitness enables us to view fitness as *inessential*, excessive, a luxury, showy, and even annoying—or, in other words *theatrical*—opening up possibilities for individual agency and resistance.

Joe Wicks and the Quarantine Workout

The closure of gyms left personal trainers and fitness coaches scrambling to adapt to lockdown conditions and a lack of space and equipment in order to survive. Many personal trainers are self-employed and were therefore only eligible for the government's complicated Self-Employment Income Support Scheme. The vast majority took to Instagram, providing filmed home workouts for free as a brand-building activity and creating online coaching programs. Guardian journalist Amelia Hill has noted how such online activities have actually been more profitable than in-person training sessions for some coaches (Hill 2020). By far the most successful face of the quarantine workout is British fitness coach Joe Wicks, also known as The Body Coach. Already a minor celebrity as a result of his Lean in 15 meal and workout books (which began on his Instagram account), at the start of the pandemic Wicks began streaming 30-minute live workouts on YouTube under the series "P.E. with Joe," Monday to Friday at 9 AM. In June these were scaled back to three times per week. By this time each workout was amassing a huge number of views (at time of writing, the most recent livestream, July 6, 2020, was viewed by 278,524 people). The sessions were initially aimed at children, hence the name of the series, but a few weeks into the pandemic it was clear Wicks was popular with adults too. It is not difficult to see why. Wicks is an engaging and positive personality, constantly chatting to the audience throughout the thirty minutes. He is handsome and funny. YouTube revenue earned from these livestreams has been donated to the NHS and he has a gentle sense of patriotism ("together we can help keep the nation moving") (Wicks 2020). Watching his videos as a coach myself, you notice that his physical ability is not necessarily the best (his burpees are performed with a distinctively rounded back). But what has made him a national treasure in these uncertain times is his affable personality and the way he connects to his audience. P.E. with Joe uses the livestream chat function to build community. Viewers say hello to Joe and each other, and like a great radio DJ, Joe says hello right back.

The Theatricality of Fitness

Long before Covid-19, personal trainers, fitness professionals, and bodybuilders had already been using Instagram and YouTube to build up their personal brands. These visual-dominant forms of social media (in contrast to the micro-blogging of Twitter) directly connect back to the performances of early physical culturists in the late nineteenth and early twentieth centuries. Perhaps the most famous of these early fitness pioneers was the early bodybuilder Eugen Sandow. Like Wicks, Sandow was not the strongest or most physically capable. But he was the best at performing an ideal. By the time of Sandow's debut in England in the 1880s, physical culture performances including strongman and wrestling were a highly popular act in the Music Hall and vaudeville theaters. Sandow's gimmick was combining above-average physical strength and ability with extraordinary physical development. He was not just strong, he *looked* strong.

The importance of Sandow's look reveals what I am calling the *theatrical* nature of fitness. Derived from the Greek word for "seeing place," theater, as distinct from drama or performance, relates strongly to the visual. This visual dominance has also led it to be connected to ideas of fakery and illusion. Thus, theatricality has historically been accompanied by a philosophical anti-theatricalism that dislikes theater for being "showy, deceptive, exaggerated, artificial, or affected" (Postlewait and Davis 2003, 5). Theater is suspect because, according to Martin Puchner, it uses "human performers as signifying material in the service of a mimetic project" (Puchner 2002, 5). In others, theater's spectacle deceives its audience.

Certainly, there was an element of this in Sandow's performances. His debut on the New York stage was as a bit of stage magic in a musical comedy called *Adonis* (1893) about a statue brought to life. At the play's finale, Henry E. Dixey, playing Adonis, climbed back atop a pedestal, striking a pose. The curtain fell, and then as the audience applauded, rose again on the body of Sandow, striking the same pose as Dixey. His muscular body itself was the spectacle (see Kasson 2001, 24-25). By June of that same year, Sandow was the headliner of Florenz Ziegfeld's Follies tour across the Northeast United States. In these performances he posed, performed feats of strength, and lectured on physical culture, as part of a variety show that included music, magic, comedians, dancers, and acrobats. In such performances, he was billed as "The Strongest Athlete on Earth" or "The Perfect Man." Sandow's theatrical performances were not unique to him, but part of a larger constellation. The connection of theater and performance to physical culture is undeniable when we look at the archive. These shows could be small scale (such as weightlifting displays and lecture performances at local clubs) or large (including Sandow, wrestling shows, and strongman turns) and encompassed both male and female performers.[2]

Physical culturists used theater and performance like fitness professionals use Instagram today, in order to spread the gospel of health, fitness, and strength. But this connection of fitness and theater, I suggest, goes beyond a historical curiosity. On a conceptual level, the fact that fitness was spread through theatrical acts reveals that it is also a form of performance that goes beyond the normative, essential dictates of health. What motivated audiences to take up physical culture after witnessing a Sandow performance was not a fear of disease but desire to look (to perform) a similar way. In other words, the theatricality of fitness actually reveals its inessential nature—it is a practice in excess of the everyday essential. This is most obvious in forms like bodybuilding, in which the body is developed and enhanced to hyperbolic proportions, but its impetus or motivation trickles down to everyday gym culture. It isn't essential to be swole. Which is why in the quarantine videos of bodybuilders like Eric Janicki (@ericjanickifitness on Instagram) there is an obvious theatricality. Despite Janicki having an affably normal persona on video like Wicks (one video begins with him tripping over a series of low agility hurdles), his hyper-muscular physique and extremely well-equipped garage gym set up shows a devotion to self-making far beyond the everyday.

---

[2] My forthcoming monograph, *Dynamic Tensions: Performing Fitness, Physical Culture, and Masculinity* investigates this interdisciplinary history.

Removing fitness from the discourse of the essential, however, shows a value that goes beyond health. Indeed, fitness practices like bodybuilding can, in extreme forms, be extremely detrimental to one's health. Like the theater, another inessential industry under threat of collapse in the U.K., fitness is valuable because it is *culture*, providing the space for individual expression and agency. When I do weightlifting and bodybuilding in the gym, in the months ago that increasingly feel like a lifetime ago, I work on perfecting gestures and patterns of movement as detailed or fine as a *pas-de-chat* in ballet or the placement of a sung note. To build biceps, chest, and quads, I must mindfully *express* biceps, chest, and quads. By practicing such movements, I find myself as part of a community, ensemble, or assembly of others, just as readers of Sandow's magazine across the globe did in the early twentieth century or Wicks's viewers do today. None of this is essential. But like the theater, which provides space for people to assemble in the service of watching and being watched, it is worth saving.

Conclusion: The Redistribution of Swole

In this chapter I have argued that fitness has historically been discursively framed as both essential (a necessary part of public health) and inessential (a culture of theatricality, swoleness, and extraordinary bodies). The tension between these two framings is starkly revealed by the Covid-19 pandemic, when political guidance on essential exercise outdoors (walking, running, biking) obscures the inaccessibility, both through lockdown and class inequality, of inessential practices of fitness such as bodybuilding and weightlifting. But whereas the discourse of essential exercise under lockdown reveals a biopolitics of inequality, debility, and an endemic "slow death" of Black and brown bodies, the inessential nature of fitness, or, in its nineteenth-century coinage "physical culture" reminds us that it is indeed a *culture*, composed of acts of performance that are valuable simply because they are expressive and enriching. These "swolecial" performances are a form of self-making by which subjects can negotiate their embodied relationships to society, politics, and economics, and find an important sense of community with others. Like the theatrical fitness performers of the nineteenth and early twentieth centuries, online workout celebrities like Joe Wicks understand the value of fitness to provide an inessential physical practice through which to connect with others.

After submitting the first draft of this chapter, gyms in England and Wales reopened on July 25, and I began training again. In order to be able to participate in fitness culture again, I have reorganized my working life—working early in the morning and late in the evening in order to take time in the quietest part of the day to go train. I am privileged to do this by an academic position that enables me to organize my working hours in this way and my ability to work from home. Soon, though, I found there was no need to do this, because there was barely anyone in my Central London gym, even at "peak" hours. Training in a cavernous, near empty facility makes the inequality of access to the inessential luxury of fitness culture very stark.

In a crisis, it is difficult to make an argument for any practice that might seem inessential. As I have argued in this chapter, however, we can look to history to uncover the ideological functions that discourses of the essential serve and the class relations they reveal. After Covid-19, we must therefore not return to "normal," but instead explore a redistribution of access to the inessential activities of fitness—not just bodybuilding, but all those theatrical forms of fitness that align with enjoyment, expression, and culture. Ensuring access to swole must be along lines of radical equality—which means first and foremost that, in the post-Covid-19 world, we must eliminate the class-based and racialized divisions that currently organize labor and leisure.

REFERENCES

Berlant, Lauren. 2007. "Slow Death (Sovereignty, Obesity, Lateral Agency)." *Critical Inquiry.* 33 (4): 54-780.

Bromley Council. 2020. "Parks and Greenspace Visitors Need to Follow Guidelines." Accessed July 14, 2020. https://www.bromley.gov.uk/news/article/1563/parks_and_greenspace_visitors_need_to_follow_guidelines.

Burkitt, Rachel et al. 2018. "The Public and the NHS." The King's Fund. June 2018. https://www.kingsfund.org.uk/sites/default/files/2018-06/The_public_and_the_NHS_report_0.pdf

Connolly, John. 2020. "Public Attitudes and the Management of the COVID-19 Crisis: The Importance of Personal Responsibility." London School of Economics (blog). May 1, 2020. https://blogs.lse.ac.uk/politicsandpolicy/personal-responsibility-covid-19/

de la Peña. 2005. *The Body Electric: How Strange Machines Built the Modern American.* New York City: NYU Press.

Department of Health and Social Care. 2019. "UK Chief Medical Officers' Physical Activity Guidelines." Accessed July 14, 2020. https://assets.publishing.service.gov.uk/government/uploads/system/uploads/attachment_data/file/832868/uk-chief-medical-officers-physical-activity-guidelines.pdf

Dreiser, Theodore. 1904[1983]. *An Amateur Laborer.* Philadelphia: University of Pennsylvania Press.

Godlee, Fiona. 2020. "Racism: The Other Pandemic." *The British Medical Journal.* 369. https://www.bmj.com/content/369/bmj.m2303.

Gorman, Alyx and Josh Taylor. 2020. "CrossFit CEO Greg Glassman Resigns After Offensive George Floyd and Coronavirus Tweets." *The Guardian,* June 10, 2020. https://www.theguardian.com/us-news/2020/jun/10/greg-glassman-crossfit-ceo-resigns-george-floyd-protest-coronavirus-tweets-conspiracy-theories/.

Gotman, Kelina. 2017. *Choreomania: Dance and Disorder.* Oxford: OUP.

Hanley, Lynsey. 2020. "Lockdown Has Laid Bare Britain's Class Divide." *The Guardian,* April 7, 2020. https://www.theguardian.com/commentisfree/2020/apr/07/lockdown-britain-victorian-class-divide.

Herz, J.C. 2014. *Learning to Breathe Fire: The Rise of CrossFit and the Primal Future of Fitness.* New York, Three Rivers Press.

Hill, Amelia. 2020. "'I'm More Successful Online': Personal Trainers Adapt to Lockdown Routine." *The Guardian,* July 10, 2020. https://www.theguardian.com/world/2020/jul/10/im-more-successful-online-personal-trainers-adapt-lockdown-routine.

Johnson, Boris. 2020a. "Prime Minister's Statement on Coronavirus (COVID-19): 23 March 2020." *Gov.uk,* March 23, 2020. Accessed July 14, 2020. https://www.gov.uk/government/speeches/pm-address-to-the-nation-on-coronavirus-23-march-2020

———. 2020b. "Prime Minister's Letter to the Nation on Coronavirus." *Gov.uk,* March 28, 2020. Accessed July 14, 2020. https://assets.publishing.service.gov.uk/government/uploads/system/uploads/attachment_data/file/876876/CCS155_CCS0320349160-003_PM_letter_to_nation_on_coronavirus_Accessible.pdf.

Joseph, Jonathan. 2013. "Resilience as Embedded Neoliberalism: A Governmentality Approach." *Resilience: International Policies, Practices, and Discourses* 1 (1): 38-52.

Kasson, John F. 2001. *Houdini, Tarzan and the Perfect Man: The White Male Body and the Challenge of Modernity in America.* New York: Hill and Wang.

Liew, Jonathan. 2020. "The Pleasures of Small Sport Can Help Us All Through Coronavirus Lockdown." *The Guardian,* March 30, 2020. https://www.theguardian.com/sport/2020/mar/30/small-sport-coronavirus-lockdown-olympic-legacy.

Liggins, Emma. 2020. "Coronavirus: What Can We Learn from Victorian Attitudes to Contagion?" Manchester Metropolitan University. May 15, 2020. Accessed July 14, 2020. https://www.mmu.ac.uk/news-and-events/news/story/12325/.

Maguire, Jennifer Smith. 2007. *Fit for Consumption: Sociology and the Business of Fitness*. London: Routledge.

Mosse, George L. 1996. *The Image of Man: The Creation of Modern Masculinity*. Oxford: OUP.

Nygren, Katarina Giritli & Anna Olofsson. 2020. "Managing the Covid-19 Pandemic Through Individual Responsibility: The Consequences of a World Risk Society and Enhanced Ethopolitics." *Journal of Risk Research*. https://doi.org/10.1080/13669877.2020.1756382.

Parveen, Nazia. 2020. "Priti Patel Says 'Sorry if People Feel There Have Been Failings' Over PPE." *The Guardian*. April 11, 2020. https://www.theguardian.com/world/2020/apr/11/priti-patel-says-sorry-if-people-feel-there-have-been-failings-over-ppe.

Postlewait, Thomas, and Tracy C. Davis. 2003. "Theatricality: An Introduction." In *Theatricality*, edited by Thomas Postlewait and Tracy C. Davis, 1-39. Cambridge: Cambridge University Press.

Puar, Jasbir. 2011. "Coda: The Cost of Getting Better: Suicide, Sensation, Switchpoints", *GLQ*, 18 (1): 149-158.

Puchner, Martin. 2002. *Stage Fright: Modernism, Anti-Theatricality, and Drama*. Baltimore: Johns Hopkins University Press.

Public Health England. 2016. "Health Matters: Getting Every Adult Active Every Day." July 19, 2016. Accessed July 14, 2020. https://www.gov.uk/government/publications/health-matters-getting-every-adult-active-every-day/health-matters-getting-every-adult-active-every-day.

Robinson, Cedric J. [1983]2019. *On Racial Capitalism, Black Internationalism, and Cultures of Resistance*. Ed. Quan, H.L.T. London: Pluto Press.

Rotundo, E. Anthony. 1993. *American Manhood: Transformations in Masculinity from the Revolution to the Modern Era*. New York: Basic Books.

Schuster, David G. 2011. *Neurasthenic Nation: America's Search for Health, Happiness, and Comfort, 1869-1920*. New Brunswick: Rutgers University.

Stewart, Heather and Dennis Campbell. 2020. "NHS Workers Angered at Hancock's Warning Not to Overuse PPE." *The Guardian*. April 10, 2020. https://www.theguardian.com/society/2020/apr/10/matt-hancock-urges-public-not-to-overuse-ppe.

Tolentino, Jia. 2019. "Athleisure, Barre snd Kale: The Tyranny of the Ideal Woman." *The Guardian*. August 2, 2019. https://www.theguardian.com/news/2019/aug/02/athleisure-barre-kale-tyranny-ideal-woman-labour.

Travis, Jennifer. 2008. "Injury's Accountant: Theodore Dreiser and the Railroad", *Studies in American Naturalism* 3 (1): 42-60.

Turse, Nicholas. 1999. "Prometheus Unbound: The Technology of Bodybuilding in the Nervous Age." *Past Imperfect* 8: pp. 33-61.

Wicks, Joe. 2020. "P.E. with Joe." The Body Coach. March 2020. Accessed July 14, 2020. https://www.thebodycoach.com/blog/pe-with-joe-1254.html

CHAPTER 9

Havocking a Dream: The Impact on Athletes of the Suspension of Tokyo 2020

Marjorie Enya and Katia Rubio

"Fellow athletes let me start with the good news first: we will all be able to celebrate the Olympic Games Tokyo 2020 even if it's only in 2021" (IOC 2020a). With these words, the International Olympic Committee (IOC) President Thomas Bach opened his message to athletes, which accompanied the joint statement from the IOC and the Tokyo 2020 Organizing Committee about the decision to postpone the Olympic Games. By the time this decision was communicated, on March 24, 2020, the IOC had already suffered heavy criticism for its delay in reaching a decision (Ingle 2020), with many prominent athletes acting as the most ferocious critics of this delay (Keh et al. 2020).

The way the IOC handled its communication strategy leading up to the decision to postpone Tokyo 2020 was seen as disconnected from the grim reality taking place around the world as the Covid-19 pandemic took shape (Almeida et al. 2020). In the period leading up to the announcement, sport media covered the impact of the Covid-19 crisis by assembling commentary from a variety of stakeholders; however, almost every piece of news published in the following month was about the financial, political, and logistical challenges arising from the postponement of the Olympics. Athletes speaking up on their social media platforms, or in traditional media, may have been one of the most important driving forces to accelerate the decision to postpone the Olympic Games (Keh et al. 2020). Nevertheless, when the attention shifted to the economic and logistical impact of the postponement, the perspectives of athletes began to be pushed out of the frame. It is too soon to project and analyze the extent and weight that this postponement will have on the Tokyo 2020 Olympic enterprise (Enya et al. 2020), but that does not stop speculations on that particular front from dominating much of the public discourse about the decision. The intent of this chapter is to shift the focus to a different direction.

This chapter aims to explore the impact of the postponement of the Tokyo 2020 Olympic Games on athletes, by addressing it as more than a shift in timelines and schedules, but a dramatic event that has many profound effects. Many studies have shown that participating in the Olympic Games is the greatest ambition for high performance athletes, considered to be the pinnacle of their athletic careers (Debois et

133

al. 2012). In spite of the IOC's reassuring tone and positive rhetoric in discussing the postponement of Tokyo 2020, the reality is that for many athletes, this change means the practical impossibility to fulfill this dream (Macur et al. 2020). This impossibility stems from a number of circumstances that are oftentimes made invisible by claims that athletic achievements depend solely on one's determination, discipline, and talent.

Immediately after the decision to postpone Tokyo 2020 was made public, athletes' reactions from around the world were gathered by media outlets (Reuters 2020a), exposing many of the nuances and complexities that the Covid-19 crisis created for their lives. This chapter does not suggest that it would have been safe and responsible for the Games to proceed on the originally planned date, but that more attention needs to be directed at the emotional and psychological effects this had on athletes. For athletes like Steele Johnson, U.S. Olympic silver medalist in diving, the immediate concern was the financial viability of dedicating another year to training, despite a significantly low income; for others, the concern was related to other career aspirations that had to be put on hold for another year (Klosok and Church 2020); for those who had made family plans based on Tokyo 2020's original date, this had a significant impact on their plans to get pregnant (UOL 2020); for Paralympic athletes with a degenerative disease, one year can mean unpredictable effects on their classification at the time of the Games (Fraga 2020); this list of issues arising from this ripple effect is endless, and in many ways the disruption caused by the decision resulted in significant stress and losses for the athletes. In this sense, approaching the effects of the postponement of the Tokyo 2020 Olympic Games on athletes as a grief response can help inform a more humanized approach to what they have experienced.

ON GRIEF

While there are many types of grief, and academic researchers have not reached a consensus on how to conceptualize it, the baseline concept that will be adopted for the purpose of this analysis considers grief as the intense emotional response set off by a loss (Rubin 1999). One of the most relevant theoretical approaches for the conceptualization of grief is the attachment theory (Bowlby 1961), which suggests humans have a tendency to create strong emotional bonds with others, from which stems an intense emotional reaction in the event of a separation. As such, the "self" can be considered an attachment object. Research on athletes' emotional responses to injuries supports understanding their experience of such events as a loss of "self," as occurrences that prevent them from carrying on many self-defining activities, such as training towards excellence, and interacting with peers and coaches. As a state of deprivation, loss can be either a real event or a symbolic one (Peretz 1970), in the sense that deprivation may represent a potential future loss. In the case of high-performance athletes, it can be a loss of status, a financial loss, or even the loss of control over one's situation. Symbolic losses are also influenced by the intensity of emotional investment one has made in the matter that is perceived to be lost. In simple terms, the more intense, deep, and long our emotional investment, the more the threat of losing it will have an impact on us, thus generating a grief response. Considering that athletes dedicate years to improving their performance to peak at exactly the right time, and change their whole lifestyles to accommodate their athletic pursuits, the potential future loss of their Olympic dream because of the global pandemic likely created a grief response.

Most clinical studies about grief processes deal with the loss of a significant other through observation of bereaved subjects. The pervasiveness of the process of grief has been an object of great interest to clinical researchers, which led to a myriad of different frameworks and approaches to make sense of the different manifestations observed in grieving subjects. However, the most common approach to grief responses used to understand athletes' manifestations when confronted with a detachment from their athletic selves is Kübler-Ross' five-stage model (Kübler-Ross 1969). According to Kübler-Ross, even though the process is not linear (Bugen 1977) and not everyone goes through every one of the stages, this paradigm can be a valuable tool in understanding a person's behavior during a grieving period.

For the purpose of this chapter, what matters is not the applicability of different grief stages frameworks, but having an approach that acknowledges the magnitude of this event for athletes as a perceived loss, or a *de facto* loss. At first sight, having the possibility to participate in the Olympic Games in a future date may give the impression that the postponement does not represent a loss *per se*, in which case the impact on athletes could be seen as manageable through routine adaptation and an exercise of re-organizing their preparation with a different date in mind. However, previous research about the psychological effects arising from other events that prevent athletes from training and competing, such as injuries, point out that even disturbances of a smaller scale (such as a short term injury) can cause severe distress on high performance athletes (Evans and Hardy 1995). In the case of the Covid-19 crisis, the projected impact is even more severe considering the unprecedented nature of this situation, which makes it impossible to foresee its expected duration (unlike the case of most injuries), and its universal pervasiveness.

The list of issues arising for athletes from the Covid-19 crisis is lengthy, underscoring that the pandemic incurred manifold losses that were perceived at each athlete's individual, personal, level. Even within the same team, the effects of the pandemic were incredibly different for each athlete. The next sections will address some of those perceived losses for athletes, reinforcing the argument that a careful approach to the effects of the pandemic on them must start with a mindful appreciation of each athlete's circumstances.

A LOSS OF SELF

In order to understand the magnitude of the impact that postponing the Olympics had on athletes, and to underscore that this experience can be perceived as a loss, it is important to understand that, for athletes, the practice of sport is not only an activity or labor, but a key constituent of their identity. Olympic athletes are highly skilled individuals who perform in competitions that emulate a heroic imagery. The characteristics embodied by athletes, such as resilience, strength, grit, and endurance, are highly praised by contemporary societies, which value ascensions and victories. For society at large, the mythical heroic imagery justifies a competitive attitude, and in sport this reference is additionally strengthened by many people's understanding that winning is the greatest possible outcome of sport. Olympic athletes, as quasi mythical creatures, are publicly recognized and occupy a certain space in people's imagery, with mass media as the greatest facilitator of this process (Rubio 2001 and 2019). The sudden suspension of all sports activities due to the Covid-19 crisis was not only an estrangement from what one does, but an estrangement from what one is.

The concept of identity, within the field of cultural studies, defines one's "self" as a result of one's interactions with others and society. This interactionist approach does not exclude the existence of one's core essence, but understands that this very essence is formed and modified through a continuous dialogue with society, culture, and the many identitary components they offer (Hall 2006). This decentralization of "self" opens the possibility for one to embody a multitude of identities, each one defined and consolidated not only based on affiliations and similarities, but especially on one's differences to others: *I am what the other is not* (Han 2017). This understanding is particularly relevant for high performance athletes' grip on their own identities as something that stems from their differentiation from society at large. They are exceptional not only for their level of athletic skills, but also for their commitment to a lifestyle that requires exceptional discipline and sacrifices. As Covid-19 eliminated athletes' opportunities to nourish this sense of differentiated self, their loss is two-fold: not only were they unable to perform their athletic selves in training and competition, it was also impossible for them to continue to nourish their athletic selves based on what usually sets them apart in terms of routines and habits. The U.S. canoeist Casey Eichfeld, for example, still managed to get out on the water to train, but said that it was the other twenty hours of the day in which he was at home that gave him a glimpse into what retirement will look like (Washington Post 2020).

LOSING ONE'S CONTROL OVER THE CONTROLLABLES

A key aspect of an athlete's preparation is discerning what is within one's control and what is not, always striving to decrease the number of elements that fall into the latter category (Jackson, Dover and Mayocchi 1998). Routines and consistency are *sine qua non* for excellent athletic performance, as is perfectionism for sports like gymnastics, synchronized swimming, and diving (Kamyar 2018). Research shows, however, that perfectionism in athletes is primarily maladaptive and renders individuals more vulnerable to negative outcomes if they experience personal failures (Flett and Hewitt 2005). As Covid-19 disrupted every sport training program, many Olympic athletes scrambled to assemble pieces of equipment and put together some form of training environment compliant with shelter-in-place orders. Social media platforms were flooded with images of athletes' creative solutions to try to partially emulate some of their regular training sessions. However, even that sometimes comic relief underscored the unpleasant reality that most training structures were inimitable and simply unavailable during the Covid-19 crisis, and that many athletes' housing conditions were unable to incorporate any form of training structure. For example, Haley Anderson, who is a U.S. open water swimmer, started using bottles as weights as she could not gain access to any swimming pool. Artistic swimmers who did not have access to a swimming pool struggled even more, as much of their performance depends on synchrony with their teammates (Washington Post 2020).

High performance athletes' daily training environments are not just a relevant piece of infrastructure that enables performance, it is also where most of athletes' social interactions commonly take place, and where they find important elements of their support network. During the Covid-19 crisis, many programs tried to maintain some form of online routine, but the spontaneity of normal interactions could not be replicated in online sessions, and athletes' support staff end up losing many relevant non-verbal cues to identify if and when their intervention was necessary. Moreover, the financial impact of the pandemic on some sports governing bodies meant losing some of that support altogether, as many roles had to be made redundant and many staff members furloughed (Reid 2020), without even the chance to say goodbye in person to the athletes with whom they had fostered close relationships.

Losing access to a daily training environment was about more than having to deal with sub-par training conditions. It was a loss of control over something that thus far had belonged to the realm of controllables, and an at least partial estrangement from key constituents of their immediate support network. Each athlete's reaction to that was unique. Framing athletes' reactions to Covid-19 as a grief process highlights that there was a wide range of possible responses, and that while the crisis was essentially collective, the impact it had on each athlete was unique and informed by a multitude of factors, including but not limited to culture, gender, sport *ethos*, career phase, race, and availability of resources. For instance, a survey conducted by the National Collegiate Athletic Association about well-being status during the pandemic demonstrated that family and personal responsibilities were cited as a barrier to training much more frequently by Black and Latino participants than by White student-athletes (40% and 27%, respectively) (NCAA 2020). This is not to add to the stereotyped portrayal of Black and Latino student athletes as coming from disadvantaged socioeconomic backgrounds compared to their White counterparts, but rather to recognize that, in general, Black and Latino communities were more widely and severely impacted by the pandemic (Oppel Jr. et al. 2020).

A LOOMING INVOLUNTARY CAREER TRANSITION

Perhaps the most dramatic impact of the Covid-19 crisis will be for those athletes who, for a variety of reasons, are not be able to continue. Studies of the end of an athlete's career gained increased importance and visibility since the end of the 1980s, particularly as that decade marked the end of the amateur phase in the Olympic Movement. It is a complex, multidimensional, and individual process (Lavallee 2005).

According to Lavallee (1997), adaptation to athletic career transition is defined by the intersection of three groups of factors: the athlete's characteristics (such as age, health conditions, and psychological traits), the athlete's perception about the transition (such as available resources and causes for retirement), and characteristics of the athlete's environment pre- and post-retirement (quality of family, social, and institutional support, ability to maintain one's social and financial status). For instance, the degree to which an athlete is attached to her or his athletic identity is an important factor for one's adjustment to post-athletic career (Grove, Lavallee, and Gordon 1997), as athletes who develop a stronger, and somewhat exclusive athletic identity tend to struggle more to adapt to a life outside of sport (Sinclair and Orlick 1993). The reason for retirement tends to play a key role in the athlete's adaptation to a life outside of sport, particularly whether the decision to retire was voluntary or not (Taylor and Ogilvie 1994).

There has been evidence that involuntary, unforeseen causes for retirement are most likely to cause emotional distress (Brandão et al. 2000). This is what many high-performance athletes initiating a career transition amidst the Covid-19 crisis will potentially be going through. An example of this were the many athletes who faced severe financial strains regarding dedicating themselves to sport, and in many cases adding one year to that was not a feasible option for them and their families (Macur et al. 2020). The social distancing measures and lockdown policies put in place to help contain the spread of the virus also impacted the livelihood of those athletes whose income depended at least partially on event appearances. It is likely that some of them will also have to forego their athletic aspirations in order to make up for that lost income.

While the career transition process by itself does not necessarily equal a problematic period, or traumatic phase in one's life (Coakley 1983), it is possible to presume that there will be additional hardship for athletes who strove for a spot in their country's Olympic delegation and then faced the possibility of initiating a career transition (BBC 2020) without fulfilling this dream due to circumstances completely outside of their control. Chinese badminton player Lin Dan, for instance, was hoping to end his career with a third Olympic gold in Tokyo but acknowledged that this had become impossible with the postponement of the Games. He announced his retirement in July, stating that at thirty-seven years old, his physical pain and fitness levels made it impossible for him to go on for another year (ESPN 2020). One of the most dramatic cases of career termination deriving from the pandemic was the England Rugby Football Union's (RFU) decision to terminate their rugby sevens program altogether (Reuters 2020b). On August 7, the RFU told their group of Olympic hopefuls that their contracts would not be renewed, meaning that after the end of the month they would be unemployed and potentially no longer in contention to join Team Great Britain by the time the Games actually take place. It is worth mentioning that Team Great Britain won a silver medal in the men's rugby sevens event in Rio 2016, suggesting that not even those with a solid athletic performance, in a country where their sport was extremely popular, were safe in their athletic careers.

GRIEF: A PROCESS THAT TAKES TIME IN THE AGE OF ACCELERATION

The "great pause" imposed by Covid-19 is considered by many as an opportunity to redefine the future we want to create, as throughout history pandemics have arguably worked as a magnifying glass for society's flaws and problematic systems (Harari 2020). Sport is a phenomenon that is not detached from broader social issues, and the Covid-19 crisis may have pushed the world of sport to reflect on the fragilities of the sports industry, and on the value of sport beyond the entertainment spectacle. The Olympic industry's immediate response to the crisis, however, seems to have fallen short in acknowledging and embracing the vulnerability and the humanity of those around whom the sports universe should revolve: the athletes.

Scholar Heather Reid (2017) has explained that the world of sport has been increasingly dominated by what she calls an efficiency ethos, that is, a set of values that privileges a quantitative understanding of athletic performance and sport. This ethos in sport is relevant because it influences the way we behave in, interpret, and explain sport, and informs how much value the sporting community will place on each aspect of sport. In an efficiency ethos setting, sport is explained and valued based on objective, quantifiable measures, in an effort to eliminate all subjectivity. In that sense, the Olympic Movement could be a space in which a different ethos could be fostered so as to counterbalance the many shortcomings of the efficiency ethos,

> The problem with the prevailing Efficiency Ethos is that it narrows down the goals and values of sport to the point of dehumanizing the practice. The Olympic Ethos counterbalances the Efficiency Ethos by reintegrating a historically humanistic philosophy of sport into the goods to be preserved and exalted within sporting communities. (Reid 2020, 416)

In a data-obsessed world, athletic performances and even athletes themselves, are reduced to a quantified self, a mass of accurately collected data that is, however, destitute of a narrative. This failure to acknowledge athletes as whole human beings who function within unique broader contexts stands in the way of grasping the magnitude of the aftermath of the Covid-19 crisis in their lives.

Shortly after the announcement of the Tokyo 2020 postponement, the IOC launched a social media campaign called "Stay Active, Stay Healthy" (IOC 2020b), in which athletes were asked to share tips on how to remain fit and strong. The rhetoric of the campaign was one of unwavering motivation, highlighting the benefits of sport and physical activity to one's overall well-being. The rhetoric was problematic as it glossed over of the stark inequalities that made it impossible for a considerable number of people (Olympic athletes and hopefuls included) to access the resources necessary to stay active while at home. Moreover, the IOC failed to acknowledge that many athletes themselves were experiencing significant losses in different areas of their lives. The storm was in some ways similar across the globe, but athletes navigated it on very different boats.

Experiencing losses in a world that has little or no space for negativity and nuance is all the more complicated when social interactions have been forcibly pushed to social media. Research has shown a link between time spent on social media and increased symptoms of anxiety and depression (Andreassen et al. 2016; Lin et al. 2016). One of the sources for anxiety related to social media use is the fact that social media has become a space for the disclosure of unrealistic portrayals of reality, which leaves viewers with a constant impression that everyone else's life is happier or more interesting (Shensa et al. 2016). As elite athletes are increasingly scrutinized on social media (Hanton et al. 2005), the impact of this is likely to be even more stressful for them not only as they were scrutinized, but as they saw how other athletes adapted to the circumstances imposed by Covid-19. In that sense, it is fair to presume that the content curation of sports institutions that disclosed only the videos of athletes best adapted to carry on training was not helpful for athletes coping with this situation under harsher conditions. Moreover, this constantly positive narrative alienated those athletes to whom the pandemic meant the end of their careers. Changing the online narratives (especially the official ones) to include less manicured realities in this moment could be significant not only to avoid the alienation of athletes with fewer resources available, but also to alleviate the pressure on elite athletes who are constantly pushed to perform and behave as role models (Harris 1994). Reading the impact of the losses athletes faced through a lens of grief would help inform the building of a more humanized narrative about their experiences through the Covid-19 crisis. This lens prioritizes the understanding of the nature and significance of those losses for each athlete, instead of focusing on the general inspirational narrative that can be projected from the experiences of the few athletes least impacted by the crisis. It also exposes the absurdity of expectations that are oftentimes bestowed upon athletes in this moment of struggle; dealing with grieving subjects requires solidarity and empathy, not pressure to accelerate or invisibilize their healing process.

USING THE LENS OF GRIEF TO SUPPORT ATHLETES' MENTAL HEALTH

In a survey conducted by the IOC across the Athlete365 community of athletes, entourage members, and other stakeholders (IOC 2020c) in May 2020, over 50% of athletes stated that finding ways to train and keeping their motivation were the two the biggest challenges they faced during the Covid-19 crisis, followed by their difficulty with managing their mental health and their sporting career. Long before the pandemic, on May 15, 2019, the IOC published a consensus statement on mental health in the *British Journal of Sport Medicine*, which was a result of a thorough review of recent scientific literature about mental health among elite athletes. The creation of the multinational work group that produced this paper is in itself a strong indication that the IOC has been giving increasing attention to mental health issues among athletes, and exploring ways to minimize the negative impacts that the sport environment could have on one's mental health. The consensus statement provides thirteen future directions for research in this field. This chapter addresses a couple of the key issues mentioned in the paper, such as the need to empower athletes' support networks with relevant information to foster environments that are conducive to athletes' mental well-being, and to enhance the understanding of sport as a subculture within society. Nevertheless, even though topics related to mental health have been increasingly present in conversations about sport, the stigma around the topic and confusion on the terms used to talk about it still persist (Reardon et al. 2019). The toll this pandemic had on athletes' mental health is something that must be followed and addressed carefully, and framing their losses as something able to trigger grief responses may help inform an approach that is thorough and empathetic, without the unrealistic expectation that athletes should be able to pick up from where they left off once sports activities resume. Seeing athletes as grieving subjects after relevant losses is a way of acknowledging the need for a period of adjustment back into their routines as they move on.

Mental health is essentially qualitative, but the sports world has been consistent and increasingly dominated by a quantitative ethos in which sport can be reduced to its quantifiable aspects: records, medal count, figures in the sports business. Improving sport culture around mental health, then, depends not only on raising awareness around the existence of mental health issues, but is also conditional to a different approach to the value of efficiency, as there are processes that cannot be optimized in its name, and need to follow a pace of their own. This is the area in which a grief process approach to athletes' socioemotional responses to the Covid-19 crisis is perhaps most valuable. Although grief has also been subject to a certain sanitization (that is, an expectation of what grief should look like, how long it should last, and which grief is legitimate or not), the pervasiveness of its effects and its ubiquitousness in human experience make it arguably one of the few aspects of modern life in which there is still a certain tolerance for people to linger, contemplate, and process things at their own pace.

There is a certain eagerness to inaugurate the new normal (Asonye 2020), and sports play an important role in re-establishing that sense of normalcy (Bergeron 2020). However, the severity of the impacts of the Covid-19 crisis on athletes means their transition back into training will have to factor in not only their losses in terms of strength and conditioning, but also the mental toll the pandemic had on them (Keh 2020). Framing those losses as something of a magnitude able to trigger a grief response is a way to recognize that their impact is felt at the individual level, and that they carry manifold implications that must be considered when helping athletes heal from this crisis. As Isadora Cerullo, an Olympic athlete herself, stated,

> The health and well-being of the athletes, and the future of the Olympic Games depends on discarding romanticized notions of overcoming

adversities and adopting a holistic view and practical approach to athletes' experiences. (Cerullo 2020)

The past years have seen tremendous progress in sports governing bodies governance structures to make athletes be heard (Chappelet 2020); this crisis could be a starting point for a shift in sport culture to also make sure athletes feel *seen*, not only observed or watched, and not only when they are competing, at their best.

REFERENCES

Almeida, William D., Rovilson Freitas, Edilene Mendonça, and Katia Rubio. 2020. "Following the Agenda of Others: IOC Communication in the Olympic Postponement." *Olimpianos Journal of Olympic Studies* 4 (1): 64-83 https://doi.org/10.30937/2526-6314.v4.id96.

Andreassen, Cecilie Schou, Joel Billieux, Mark D. Griffiths, Daria Kuss, Zsolt Demetrovics, Elvis Mazzoni, and Stale Pallesen. 2016. "The Relationship between Addictive Use of Social Media and Video Games and Symptoms of Psychiatric Disorders: A Large-scale Cross-sectional Study." *Psychology of Addictive Behaviors* 30 (2): 252e262. https://doi.apa.org/doi/10.1037/adb0000160.

Asonye, Chime. 2020. "There's Nothing New about the 'New Normal.' Here's Why." *World Economic Forum*, June 5, 2020. https://www.weforum.org/agenda/2020/06/theres-nothing-new-about-this-new-normal-heres-why/.

BBC. 2020. "Tokyo 2020: How Athletes Reacted to Olympic Games Postponement." *BBC*, March 24, 2020. https://www.bbc.com/sport/olympics/52027542

Bergeron, Tom. 2020. "Hope. And a Sense of Normalcy: Why Sports Matter in a Crisis." *Roi-NJ*, May 21, 2020. https://www.roi-nj.com/2020/05/21/opinion/hope-and-a-sense-of-normalcy-why-sports-matters-in-a-crisis/.

Bowlby, John. 1961. "Process of Mourning." *International Journal of Psychoanalysis* 42: 315-340.

Brandão, Maria Regina Ferreira, Maria Christina Akel, Samuel do Amaral Andrade, Maria Aparecida Nery Guiselini, Luis de Andrade Martini, and Marisa Agresta Nastás. 2000. "Causas e Consequências da Transição de Carreira Esportiva: Uma Revisão de Literatura." *Revista Brasileira de Ciência e Movimento* 2020 8 (1): 49-58 http://dx.doi.org/10.18511/rbcm.v8i1.355.

Bugen, Larry A. 1977. "Human Grief: A Model for Prediction and Prevention." *American Journal of Orthopsychiatry* 1977 (47): 196-206. https://doi.org/10.1111/j.1939-0025.1977.tb00975.x.

Cerullo, Isadora. 2020. "Impact and Meaning of the Postponement of Tokyo 2020 from an Athlete Perspective." *Olimpianos Journal of Olympic Studies* 4 (1): 28-36. https://doi.org/10.30937/2526-6314.v4.id94.

Chappelet, Jean-Loup. 2020. "The Unstoppable Rise of Athlete Power in the Olympic System." *Sport in Society* 23: 1-15. https://doi.org/10.1080/17430437.2020.1748817.

Coakley, Jay J. 1983. "Leaving Competitive Sport: Retirement or Rebirth?" *Quest: Human Kinetics* 35: 1-11. https://doi.org/10.1080/00336297.1983.10483777.

Debois, Nadine, Aurélie Ledon, Cécile Argiolas, Elizabeth Rosnet. 2012. "A Lifespan Perspective on Transitions During a Top Sports Career: A Case of an Elite Female Fencer." *Psychology of Sport and Exercise* 5: 660-668. https://doi.org/10.1016/j.psychsport.2012.04.010.

Enya, Marjorie, Mateus Nagime, and Dominik Gusia. 2020. "Postponing the Tokyo 2020 Olympic Games: Stress-testing Governance in the Olympic System and Limitations to Agenda 2020." *Olimpianos Journal of Olympic Studies* 1: 49-63. https://doi.org/10.30937/2526-6314.v4.id90.

ESPN. 2020. "Badminton Great Lin Dan Retires after 2 Olympic Golds and Five World Titles." *ESPN*, July 4, 2020. https://www.espn.com/badminton/story/_/id/29407759/badminton-great-lin-dan-retires-2-olympic-golds-five-world-titles.

Evans, Lynne, and Hardy Lew. 1995. "Sport Injury and Grief Responses: A Review." *Journal of Sport and Exercise Psychology* 17: 227-245.

Flett, Gordon L., and Paul L. Hewitt. 2005. "The Perils of Perfectionism in Sports and Exercise." *Current Directions in Psychological Science* 14: 14-18, https://doi.org/10.1111/j.0963-7214.2005.00326.x.

Fraga, João. 2020. "Andrew Parsons vê Paradesporto de alto Rendimento Excludente." *Olimpíada Todo Dia*, August 24, 2020. http://www.olimpiadatododia.com.br/paralimpicos/260403-andrew-parsons-defende-exclusao-de-paratletas-em-nome-da-ciencia/.

Grove, J. Robert, David Lavallee, and Sandy Gordon. 1997. "Coping with Retirement from Sport: The Influence of Athletic Identity." *Journal of Applied Sport Psychology* 2, 191-203. https://doi.org/10.1080/10413209708406481.

Hall, Stuart. 2006. *A Identidade Cultural na Pós-Modernidade*. Rio de Janeiro: DP&A.

Han Byung-Chul. 2017. *The Scent of Time: A Philosophical Essay in the Art of Lingering*. Kindle.

Hanton, Sheldon, David Fletcher, and Guy Coughlan. 2005. "Stress in Elite Sport Performers: A Comparative Study of Competitive and Organizational Stressors." *Journal of Sports Science* 23: 1129–41.

Harari, Yuval Noah. 2020. "The World after Coronavirus." *Financial Times*, March 20, 2020. https://www.ft.com/content/19d90308-6858-11ea-a3c9-1fe6fedcca75.

Harris, Janet C. 1994. *Athletes and the American Hero Dilemma*. Champaign: Human Kinetics.

Ingle, Sean. 2020. "Athletes across Globe call for Olympic Postponement as Countries Pull Out." *The Guardian*, March 23, 2020. https://www.theguardian.com/sport/2020/mar/23/athletes-across-the-globe-call-for-olympic-postponement-as-countries-pull-out.

IOC. 2020a. "Joint statement from the International Olympic Committee and the Tokyo 2020 Organizing Committee." Accessed June 20, 2020.https://www.olympic.org/news/joint-statement-from-the-international-olympic-committee-and-the-tokyo-2020-organising-committee.

———.2020b. "Olympic Highlights 29-06-2020." Accessed June 29, 2020. https://www.olympic.org/news/olympic-highlights-29-06-2020.

———.2020c. "Understanding your Challenges". Accessed August 25, 2020. https://www.olympic.org/athlete365/voice/understanding-your-challenges/.

Jackson, Susan A., Jeremy Dover, and Lisa Mayocchi. 1998. "Life after Winning Gold: Experiences of Australian Olympic Gold Medallists." *The Sport Psychologist* 12 (2): 119-136. https://doi.org/10.1123/tsp.12.2.119.

Kamyar, Royan 2018. "What I learned: Over 50 Olympic Athletes Daily Routines." *Owaves,* March 21, 2018. https://owaves.com/what-i-learned-from-researching-50-olympians/.

Keh, Andrew. 2020. "These Athletes Had the Coronavirus. Will They ever Be the Same?" *New York Times*, May 29, 2020. https://www.nytimes.com/2020/05/29/sports/coronavirus-survivors-athletes.html.

Keh, Andrew, Matt Futterman, Tariq Panja and Motoko Rich. 2020. "An Olympic Showdown: The Rising Clamor to Postpone the Tokyo Summer Games." *New York Times*, March 21, 2020. https://www.nytimes.com/2020/03/21/sports/olympics/tokyo-olympics-coronavirus-cancel.html?auth=login-email&login=email.

Klosok, Alesk, and Ben Church. 2020. "Athletes Come to Terms with 'Heartbreaking' Tokyo 2020 Postponement." *CNN*, March 25, 2020. https://www.cnn.com/2020/03/25/sport/athletes-reaction-tokyo-2020-olympics-postpone-spt-intl/index.html.

Kübler-Ross, Elisabeth. 1969. *On Death and Dying*. London: Tavistock.

———. 1975. *Death: The Final Stage of Growth*. London: Prentice Hall.

Lavallee, David, Sandy Gordon, and J. Robert Grove. 1997. "Retirement from Sport and the Loss of Athletic Identity." *Journal of Personal & Interpersonal Loss* 2 (2): 129-147 https://doi.org/10.1080/10811449708414411.

Lavallee, David. 2005. "The Effect of a Life Development Intervention on Sports Career Transition Adjustment." *Sport Psychology* 19: 193-202. https://doi.org/10.1123/tsp.19.2.193.

Lin, Liu yi, Jaime E. Sidani, Ariel Shensa, Ana Radovic, Elizabeth Miller, Jason B. Colditz, Beth L. Hoffman, Leila M. Giles, and Brian A. Primack. 2016. "Association between Social Media Use and Depression among U.S. Young Adults." *Depression and Anxiety* 33 (4): 323-331. https://doi.org/10.1002/da.22466.

Macur, Juliet, Karen Crouse, Andrew Keh, Matthew Futterman. 2020. "Olympians Have another Year to Prepare for Tokyo. It's a Blessing and a Curse." *New York Times*, March 24, 2020. https://www.nytimes.com/2020/03/24/sports/olympics/coronavirus-olympics-athletes-reaction.html.

NCAA: National College Athletic Association (2020). "Survey Shows Student-Athletes Grappling with Mental Health Issues." *NCAA*, May 22, 2020. http://www.ncaa.org/about/resources/media-center/news/survey-shows-student-athletes-grappling-mental-health-issues.

Oppel, Richard A., Robert Gebeloff, K.K., Rebecca Lai, Will Wright and Mitch Smith 2020. "The Fullest Look Yet at the Racial Inequality of the Virus." *New York Times*, July 5, 2020. https://www.nytimes.com/interactive/2020/07/05/us/coronavirus-latinos-african-americans-cdc-data.html.

Peretz, David. 1970. "Development, Object-Relationships and Loss." In *Loss and Grief: Psychological Management in Medical Practice*, edited by Bernard Schoenberg, Arthur Carr, David Peretz, and Austin Kutscher, 3-19. New York: Columbia University.

Reardon, Claudia L., Brian Hainline, Cindy Miller Aron, David Baron, Antonia L. Baum, Abhinav Bindra, Richard Budgett. et. al. 2019. "Mental Health in Elite Athletes: International Olympic Committee Consensus Statement." *British Journal of Sports Medicine* 53: 667-699. http://dx.doi.org/10.1136/bjsports-2019-100715.

Reid, Heather L. 2017. "Why Olympia Matters for Modern Sport." *Journal of the Philosophy of Sport* 44 (2), 159-173. https://doi.org/10.1080/00948705.2017.1327323.

Reid, Heather L. 2020. *Olympic Philosophy: The Ideas and Ideals behind the Ancient and Modern Olympic Games*. Sioux City: Parnassos Press.

Reid, Scott M. 2020. "US Olympic and Paralympic Committee Announces Layoffs, Furloughs." *The Orange County Register*, May 21, 2020. https://www.ocregister.com/2020/05/21/usopc-announces-layoffs-furloughs/

Reuters. 2020a. "Reaction to Postponement of the Tokyo 2020 Olympics." *Reuters*, March 25, 2020. https://www.reuters.com/article/us-health-coronavirus-olympics-reaction/reaction-to-postponement-of-the-tokyo-2020-olympics-idUSKBN21C0PZ.

———. 2020b. "RFU Scraps Sevens Programme due to COVID-19 Fallout." *Reuters*, August 7, 2020. https://www.reuters.com/article/rugby-sevens-england/rugby-rfu-scraps-sevens-programme-due-to-covid-19-fallout-telegraph-idUSL4N2F92AN.

Rubin, Simon Shimshon. 1999. "The Two-Track Model of Bereavement: Overview, Retrospect, and Prospect." *Death Studies* 23 (8): 681–714.

Rubio, Katia. 2001. *O atleta e o mito do herói*. São Paulo: Casa do Psicólogo.

———. 2019. "Identidade Heroica e Narrativas Biográficas: a Memória do Esporte por Atletas Olímpicos." *Olimpianos Journal of Olympic Studies* 3: 1–24 https://doi.org/10.30937/2526-6314.v3.id85.

Shensa, Ariel, Jaime E Sidani, Liu Yi Lin, Nicholas D Bowman, and Brian A Primack. 2016. "Social Media Use and Perceived Emotional Support among US Young Adults." *Journal of Community Health* 41 (33: 541-549. https://doi.org/10.1007/s10900-015-0128-8.

Sinclair, Dana A., and Terry Orlick. 1993. "Positive Transitions from High-Performance Sport." *The Sport Psychologist* 7: 138–150. https://doi.org/10.1123/tsp.7.2.138.

Taylor, Jim, and Bruce C. Ogilvie. 1994. "A Conceptual Model of Adaptation to Retirement among Athletes." *Journal of Applied Sport Psychology* 6: 1-20 https://doi.org/10.1080/10413209408406462.

UOL. 2020. "Adiamento de Tóquio-2020 afeta Planos de Gravidez de Atletas." *Universo Online*, May 27, 2020. https://www.uol.com.br/esporte/videos/2020/05/27/olimpiada-adiada-afeta-plano-de-gravidez-de-jogadoras-da-selecao-de-volei.htm.

Washington Post. 2020. "How US Olympians Are Training at Home." *Washington Post*, May 12, 2020. https://www.washingtonpost.com/sports/2020/04/14/olympic-athletes-training-home-workouts/?arc404=true.

CHAPTER 10

Interruption of Training, Sedentary Behavior, Resilience, and Mood State Among Female Catchball Players During the Covid-19 Social Isolation Period

Hilla Davidov

INTRODUCTION

From the beginning of March 2020, the Israel National Catchball Federation canceled its training due to governmental restrictions put in place during the Covid-19 pandemic (i.e., social distancing, self-isolation, and other measures). Similar restrictions were required by other Catchball federations around the world. The aim of this study was to examine the individual activity behavioral patterns, resilience, and mood state among female Catchball players during the period of March to May 2020.

Catchball is a social-impact start-up initiated in Israel combining sports with social activity. It is aimed at encouraging women to participate in physical activity and build leadership skills, as well as empowering participants to support the unification of their local community.

Survey participants were 178 female Catchball players. The target group discontinued training due to current Covid-19 regulations. The study group completed a Hebrew language version of the following self-report questionnaire: The Multidimensional Mood State MDMQ and Connor-Davidson Resilience Scale (CD-RISC-10). The scale demonstrated to have good internal consistency (Cronbach's alpha = 0.88 in both MDMQ & CD-RISC-10). Additional questions about behavioral profiles prior to and during the period of social isolation (e.g., being physically active, rest phases such as sleep, eating, and sedentary behavior) were included in the survey. Similar questionnaires were conducted in English with Catchball players in Canada, the United States, Romania, and Kenya.

Data processing included the ANOVA statistical method and LSD post hoc tests to analyze the differences between nation's means in the sample group, and Path Analysis to evaluate the relationships between mood states and resilience.

All participants reported exercising more times per week than before the lockdown, excepting Kenya; however, there was a shorter duration per bout of training during the Covid-19 social isolation period compared to before. There were changes in behavioral patterns reported during the Covid-19 social isolation period, indicating more "screen time," more hours sleeping, more food consumption, and accompanying weight changes. The resilience score and Mood State (Positive and Negative) was similar among national groups.

Israeli Covid-19 Implications

The outbreak of Covid-19 in Israel came to light in February 2020. Towards the end of February, the first patients began to appear in Israel, initially arriving mainly via inbound flights from Europe (Wikipedia 2020). The first verified patient report in Israel was recorded on February 27, 2020. Strategies for addressing the outbreak included Ministry of Health guidelines designed to prevent the disease from spreading, including social distancing, as well as isolation at home for those who had been in proximity of Covid patients, or who were returning from countries where Covid-19 was prevalent. This resulted in the elimination of mass events and provision of hospital care to those requiring medical assistance. In the sport sector, activity was totally stopped. The number of flights to and from Israel was gradually reduced in order to mitigate further imported cases of the virus. As the epidemic intensified, additional government ministries were required to take reactive measures, including the Prime Minister's Office, the Ministry of Finance to address economic problems created by the epidemic, and the Ministry of Defense, which was involved in integrating the Israel Defense Force (IDF) to provide medical care for those in need.

A survey conducted by the national Central Bureau of Statistics (CBS) painted a complex picture regarding Israeli societal resilience following two months of successful response to the measures implemented, but, on the flip side, the significant public health accomplishment exacted a heavy toll on the economy and society. The landscape indicates a growing sense of stress, loneliness, and, above all, profound anxiety concerning the implications for the economic situation. At the same time, it seems that a large majority of Israelis adapted rapidly to the serious challenges imposed by the sanitary guidelines aimed at restricting viral spread. This was reflected in the broad compliance with the lockdown instructions, the high level of trust in the government, and, to a greater extent, in the local authorities. Given these findings, it is clear that along with the need to track morbidity and testing rates, there is a need to track the social and economic ramifications of the pandemic. Such monitoring would be relevant in possible future crises as well (Elran and Even 2020, 1). This study will focus on the social impacts of the lockdown period by examining individual activity behavioral patterns, resilience, and mood state among female Catchball players during the period of Covid-19 social isolation. To curb the spread of the disease on a global scale, various national governments advocated for social distancing measures with varying degrees of enforcement, ranging from unenforced recommendations to quarantine and business closures. For this particular study, it is to be noted that comparable social distancing measures were effectively in place across the countries included in this study.

About Catchball

Catchball is a team ball game that is similar to volleyball. The game is played by two teams of six players on a volleyball court and with volleyball net. The main difference between Catchball and Volleyball is that in Catchball, players must catch the ball with both hands before they can pass it on (hence the name "Catchball"). The ball is put in play with a serve thrown over the net to the opponents. The rally continues until the ball is grounded on the playing court, goes "out" or a team fails to return it properly. The game has two sets of up to twenty-five points. If two sets are not decisive, a third set of up to fifteen points is played.

The International Catchball Federation (ICF) was founded in 2018 and is registered in Switzerland. Today there are more than twenty countries that promote Catchball. Regarding the five countries in this research, Israel has 4,475 players divided into 365 teams, Romania has one hundred players divided into nine teams, Canada has one hundred players divided into six teams, the U.S. has seventy players across five teams and Kenya has twenty-eight teams with a total of 350 players. While in Israel the players have 6.82 years (average) of training, in the other countries experience is much lower at 0.88 (first year, Kenya and Romania), two years (U.S.) and 2.94 years (Canada), as shown in Table 1.1.

Table 1.1: Variation between nations

		Mean		
Country	*Numbers*	*Age*	*Average years playing Catchball*	*Days in social isolation*
ISR	119	45.4	6.82	40.22
U.S.	26	46.12	2	49.32
CAN	17	52.06	2.94	57.12
KEN	8	28	0.88	29.71
ROM	8	43.29	0.88	40.63
Total	178	45.28 Range: 19-77	5.21 Range: Less than a year-31	42.88 Range: 0-84

Source: Author

Physical Activity, Health, and Resilience

Physical activity is an important determinant of health and is likely affected by social distancing measures, as prolonged confinement at home may lead to increased sedentary behavior, such as prolonged sitting (Owen 2010, 1140). Examples of sedentary activities include working at a computer, zoom meetings, watching television, playing games, and using mobile devices. These activities reduce regular physical activity (hence lower energy expenditure) and can lead to increased caloric intake (boredom, plenty of free time, and available food throughout the day) that can consequently lead to weight gain.

Home confinement is a fundamental safety step to limit infections from spreading widely. However, prolonged home confinement can lead to a sedentary lifestyle known to result in a range of chronic health conditions. Maintaining regular physical activity and exercise routines in a safe home environment is an important strategy for healthy living during the Covid-19 pandemic (Chen 2020, 103).

The current crisis urges us to address priorities linked to health, resilience, and physical fitness. Sport and physical activity contribute to making societies more resilient. Sport, then, is a tool to tackle the Covid-19 pandemic and may contribute to rebuilding societies during and after the crisis. Exercising and participating in sports, with emphasis on group/community exercise, are important components in returning to a daily routine, readjusting, promoting community resilience, and support well-functioning citizens of our communities.

Catchball, Physical, and Psychological Empowerment

Catchball leagues provide women and adolescent girls with the opportunity to participate in a team sport and to develop an enjoyable, healthy pastime that elevates the spirit while improving their wellbeing and self-esteem.

A 2019 study showed significantly higher results on fitness components and specific physical performance among Catchball players than non-players. In addition, there was a positive effect on aerobic fitness and related measures, such as blood pressure and resting heart rate. (Meckel et al. 2019, 1).

Another study in 2020 study showed that participation in group physical activity is associated with an increase in social capital and a more active and healthier lifestyle. Participants reported improvement in their physical, emotional, and social health, better eating habits, and an increase in exercise frequency over time. Participants also reported an increase in social capital, which is, strengthening relationships with others, receiving and providing support, and helping others versus the outcomes of the control group (Tesler 2020).

In addition, Catchball is known to have a strong unifying impact on the player community. In a survey conducted in early March 2020 with 463 players from Israel, 93.8% reported that they are in contact with team players and 85.7% reported a lack of physical activity and communal gatherings during the social isolation period (Davidov 2020, 1).

The majority of female Catchball players are mothers and working women who have limited leisure time. The ability to take time off from being a Mum, the feeling of doing something for oneself (Mums' own voices), and how they negotiate being physically active alongside the role expectations associated with being a mother (Walsh et al. 2018, 1) are essential to gender parity through sport. Women do benefit from team sports and the accompanying physical and psychological empowerment, as well as develop team loyalty, giving them a sense of belonging (Paul and Blank 2015, 1). To be a part of a Catchball team contributes to strengthening social cohesion and expanding social connections in a geographical area. Today, social interaction becomes more and more dependent on the Internet. However, through Catchball-related interactions there is a regular basis for community social gatherings.

Women participating in Catchball demonstrated feelings of empowerment and self-determination when they spoke about sport providing them with "me time." Creating space for this time and claiming the right to have something for themselves was important to all the women (Batey 2014, 34). Perceptions of competence were enhanced through their sport involvement and being a member of a sports team was particularly important because these mothers gained enhanced feelings of relatedness and a sense of belonging (Batey 2014, 35).

Image 1: Israel Catchball Association

Source: Liav Peled

Definitions

In April 2020, a report was published by the Israel Ministry of Culture & Sport regarding the significance of sport in its contribution to health and social resilience of the country's residents (Sharabi 2020, 1). Given this report's determination of the positive impact of participation in a team sport (health and social aspects) (Sharabi 2020, 7), it might be reasonable to hypothesize that the interruption of training would have substantial effects on individual activity behavioral patterns, resilience, and mood state among female Catchball players. This study was focused on three self-reported questionnaires regarding those concepts. As such, it is necessary to define each of these concepts.

Sedentary Behavior

Sedentary behavior is any waking behavior characterized by an energy expenditure ≤1.5 metabolic equivalents (METs) while in a sitting, reclining, or lying posture. In general this means that any time a person is sitting or lying down they are engaging in sedentary behavior. Common sedentary behaviors include screen time (e.g., television viewing, video game playing, computer use), driving automobiles, and reading (Tremblay 2017, 2).

Resilience

The human capacity to face and overcome challenges is strengthened by experiences of adversity (Grotberg 1997, 1). Resilience is defined by "the success (positive developmental outcomes) of the (coping) process involved (given the circumstance)" (Leipold and Greve 2009, 41). It emphasizes that the cultural context within which individuals live, coupled with structural factors such as unequal power dynamics and social inequalities, are key determinants in supporting or undermining individual and community resilience.

Mood State

Mood is a set of feelings, ephemeral in nature, varying in intensity and duration, and usually involving more than one emotion (Lane and Terry 2000, 7). Physical activity is an effective influencer of mood states (Lepamaki 2006, 312). The current mental state of an individual can be differentiated from other mental properties and is characterized as follows: Mood state is a current inner experience and inner perception of an individual (i.e., experientially represented) and not the individual's observable behavior (Steyer et al. 1997, 4).

Methodology

Study Participants

Survey participants were 178 female Catchball players: 119 from Israel, twenty-six from the U.S., seventeen from Canada, eight from Romania, and eight from Kenya. Those countries were chosen based on voluntary coach approval and residents having more than three weeks of social isolation. Further criteria were that each country needed to have at least five teams, fifty players, and have active Catchball training for more than six months before the training was paused in each country.

The questionnaires were distributed to each local Federation representative via the Google forms application. Questionnaires were disseminated by the representative of each federation to all listed players via mobile text message. Participation was based on voluntary self-selection. Only in Kenya was Internet access limited for some of the players who were in remote regions. All study participants were required to provide informed consent before participating in the study. All survey responses were anonymized. Table 1.1 shows the variation between nations across a few parameters, such as: numbers of participants, age, years of experience in Catchball training, and days in social isolation.

The average age was 45.28 years, with a range of 19 to 77 years. The average time playing Catchball was 5.21 years (since 2015, range 2005 to 2020). In terms of work-related activities, 58.42% continued working during the social isolation/quarantine period (41.57% from home and 16.85% at their normal workplace). Additionally, 26.40% stopped working, while 15.17% did not work before and during the social isolation/quarantine period. The average days in social isolation/quarantine was 42.88 days (range: 0-84 days).

Study Design

The Israel Catchball players completed a Hebrew language version the Multidimensional Mood State MDMQ and Connor-Davidson Resilience Scale (CD-RISC-10). Additional questions about behavioral profiles prior to and during the social isolation period (e.g., being physically active, rest phases such as sleeping, eating, and sedentary behavior) were included in the survey. Similar questionnaires were conducted in English with Catchball players from: U.S., Canada, Romania, and Kenya.

Data processing included ANOVA statistical method and LSD post hoc test to analyze the differences between nation's means, and Path Analysis to evaluate the relationships between mood states and resilience. Additional questions about behavioral profiles (sedentary behavior) prior to and during the social isolation period were included in the survey. Chi-squared (x^2) was used to evaluate the differences in eating habits and weight changes between nations. A Pearson test was conducted to evaluate the correlation between screen time before and during the Covid-19 social isolation period.

Resilience CD-RISC-10

The Connor–Davidson Resilience Scale (CD-RISC) has been demonstrated to be a valid and reliable tool (Wang 2010, 499). The CD-Risc-10 was used to assess participants' resilience levels. The ten-item scale is comprised of ten of the original twenty-five items from the CD-RISC-25 scale. In subsequent studies utilizing independent samples, some instability was revealed in the 25 items factor structure. This led to the recognition of an abridged 10-item version, the CD-RISC-10. The remaining ten items were thought to be a better reflection of the ability to bounce back from the variety of challenges that can arise in life (Riopel 2020). Each item was rated on a five-point Likert scale from zero ("not true at all") to four ("true nearly all the time"). Total scores were obtained by summing all responses and ranged from 0 to 40, with higher scores reflecting greater resilience (Wang 2010, 501). Cronbach's alpha for internal consistency of this questionnaire was previously determined to vary between 0.88 and 0.97 (Davidson 2020, 108).

Mood State MDMQ

The MDMQ questionnaire was used to assess participants' Mood State, using the short version with twelve items. The MDMQ is an English version of the Multidimensional Mood State Questionnaire (twenty-four items). The original version is in German and has been published by Hogrefe Publishers (Steyer et al. 1997). The questionnaire contains the items, the dimension measured by the item, and the coding directions (+ and -). The coding scheme is simply to invert the negative items (1 to 6, 2 to 5, 3 to 4, 4 to 3, 5 to 2 and 6 to 1) and then take the sum of all items of the same scale: good-bad, awake-tired, calm-nervous. As opposed to the German version with five answer categories, the English version has six answer categories that are also labeled. This new version aims to have less skewed distribution patterns as compared to the original form. The short forms are balanced with four items (two positive and two negative) of each of the three scales in every short version. Cronbach's alpha for internal consistency of this questionnaire was previously determined, for the three MDBF scales, to vary between 0.87 and 0.97 (Steyer et al. 1994, 320-328).

RESULTS

Sedentary Behavior

Most participants reported more exercise during the Covid-19 social isolation period than before, with the exception of Kenya, as shown in Figure 1. All participants, again excepting those from Kenya, also reported a higher frequency of exercise per week but shorter in duration during Covid-19 social isolation than before, as shown in Figure 2. Additionally, only 25.21% declared performing exercise such as yoga, meditation, breathing exercise, or mindfulness. Differences between nations are shown in Table 1.2.

Table 1.2: Yoga/Meditation/Breathing exercise/Mindfulness during Social isolation

Country	Participant	Numbers	%
ISR	119	10	8.4
U.S.	26	6	23.07
CAN	17	8	47.05
KEN	8	1	12.5
ROM	8	5	62.5
Total	178	20	25.21

Source: Author

Figure 1: Training, times per week, before and during Covid-19 social isolation among nations

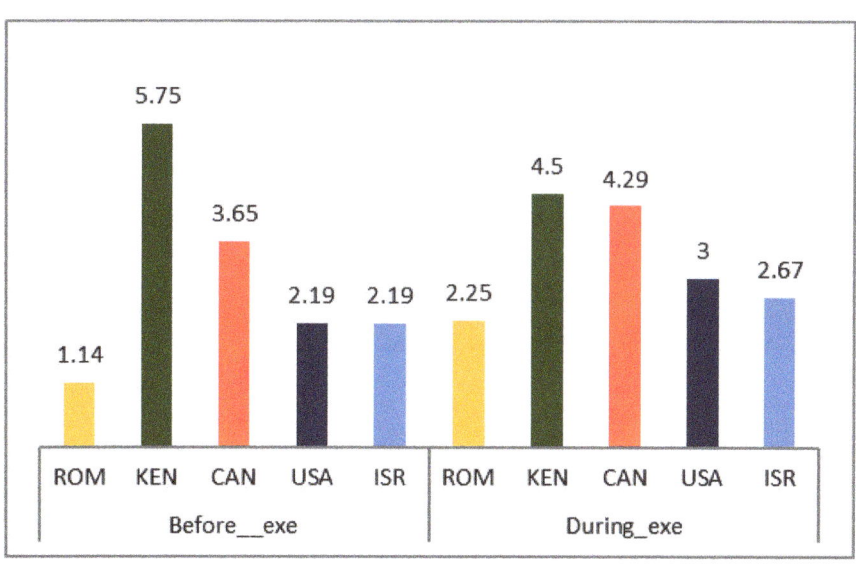

Source: Author

Figure 2: Training, duration of training (minutes) prior to and during Covid-19 social isolation among nations

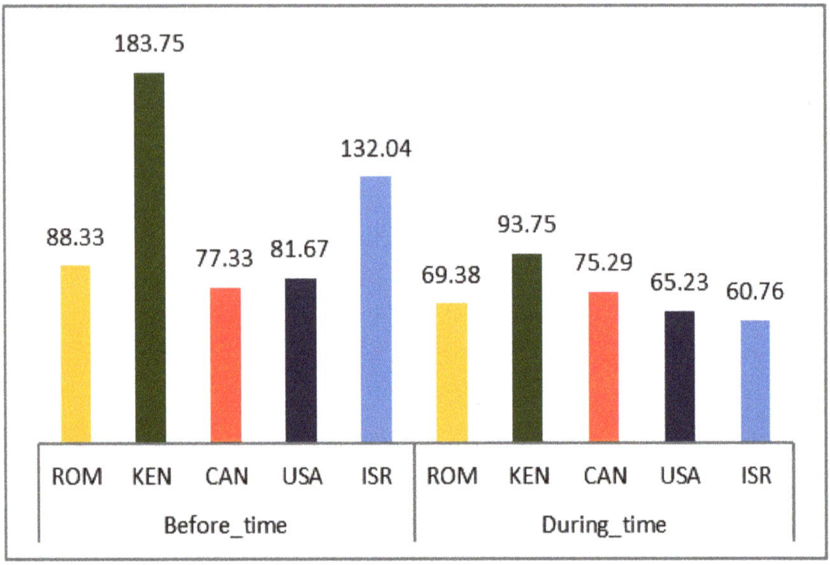

	ROM	KEN	CAN	USA	ISR
Before_time	88.33	183.75	77.33	81.67	132.04
During_time	69.38	93.75	75.29	65.23	60.76

Source: Author

Prior to Covid-19 social isolation, one-way ANOVA test among nations of Catchball training frequency (times per week): $F_{(4, 172)} = 23.95$, $p = .001$. A significant difference between nations was found on this variable. During Covid-19 social isolation, one-way ANOVA test among nations of alternative training frequency (times per week): $F_{(4, 173)} = 3.20$, $p = .014$. A significant difference between nations was found on this variable.

Prior to Covid-19 social isolation, one-way ANOVA test among nations on duration of Catchball training: $F_{(4, 167)} = 6.67$, $p = .001$. A significant difference between nations was found on this variable. During Covid-19 social isolation, one-way ANOVA test among nations on duration of training (alternative for Catchball training): $F_{(4, 167)} = 0.526$, $p = .717$. A significant difference between nations was not found on this variable.

Common sedentary behaviors were higher during Covid-19 social isolation than before, as shown in Figure 3. Before social isolation 6.70% reported no screen time at all. Figure 3 shows a decrease by 1-2 hours screen time from 40.11% of total participants before the social isolation period to 17.42% during. On the other hand, an increase in screen time was shown for 3-4, 5-6, and 7+ hours per day during Covid-19 social isolation.

The Pearson test found a positive correlation r = 0.59, p = .001 between before and during Covid-19 social isolation screen time. Those who had more screen time before Covid-19 social isolation also had more screen time during Covid-19 social isolation.

Figure 3: Screen time, hours per day, before and during Covid-19 social isolation

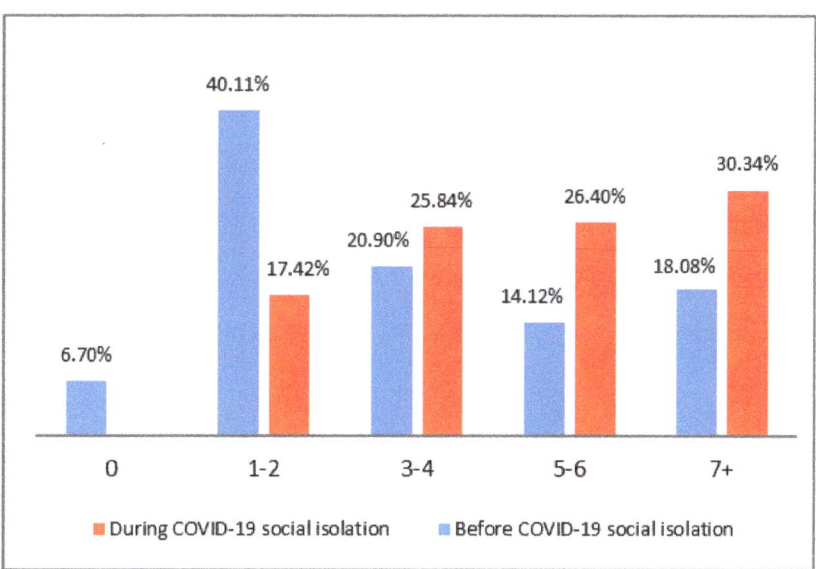

Source: Author

During the Covid-19 social isolation period, the duration of sleeping hours per night was higher than before the social isolation period across all nations, as shown in Figure 4. Regarding eating behaviors, the results, as shown in Figure 5 were: 48.31% of total participants felt they were eating more than usual, 41.57% eating as usual, and 10.11% less than usual during Covid-19 social isolation. In order to further examine whether there is a relationship between country and eating behavior, chi-squared (x^2) test was conducted and significant differences between nations were not found x^2 $(df = 8) = 4.24, p = .83$, as shown in Figure 6.

Figure 4: Sleeping hours per night, prior to and during Covid-19 social isolation among nations

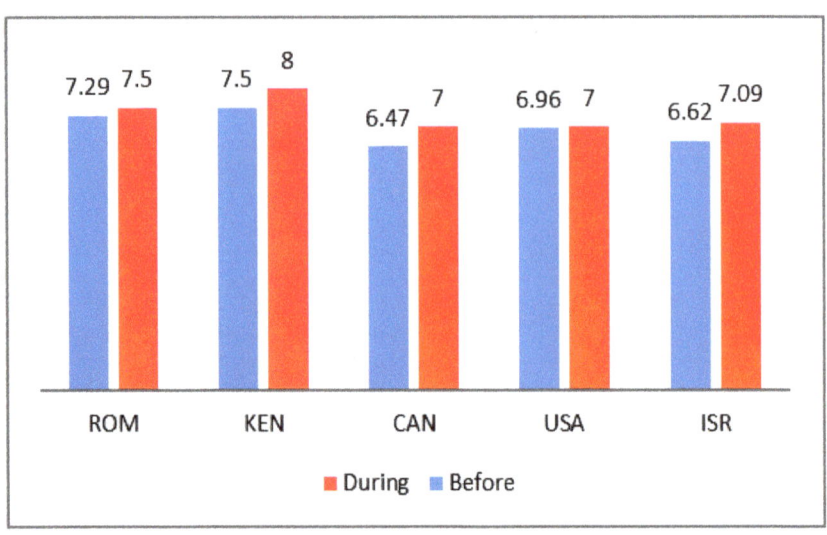

Source: Author

Figure 5: Eating behavior during Covid-19 social isolation

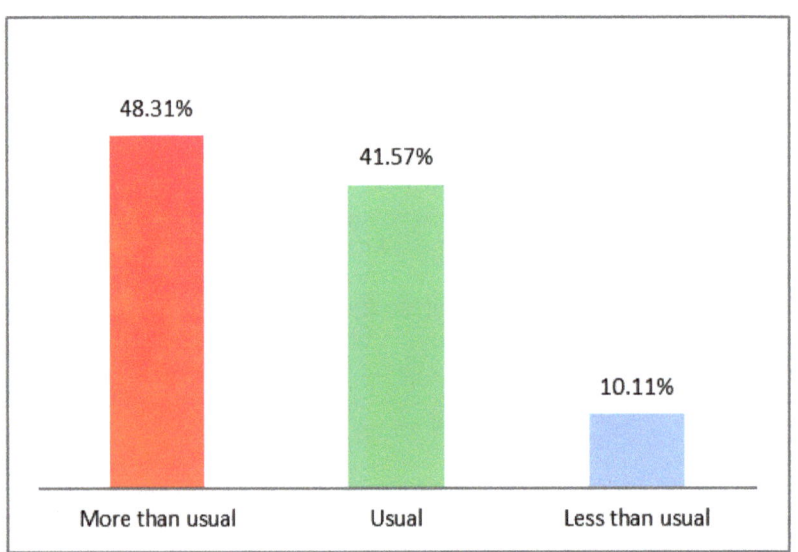

Source: Author

Figure 6: Eating behavior during Covid-19 social isolation among nations

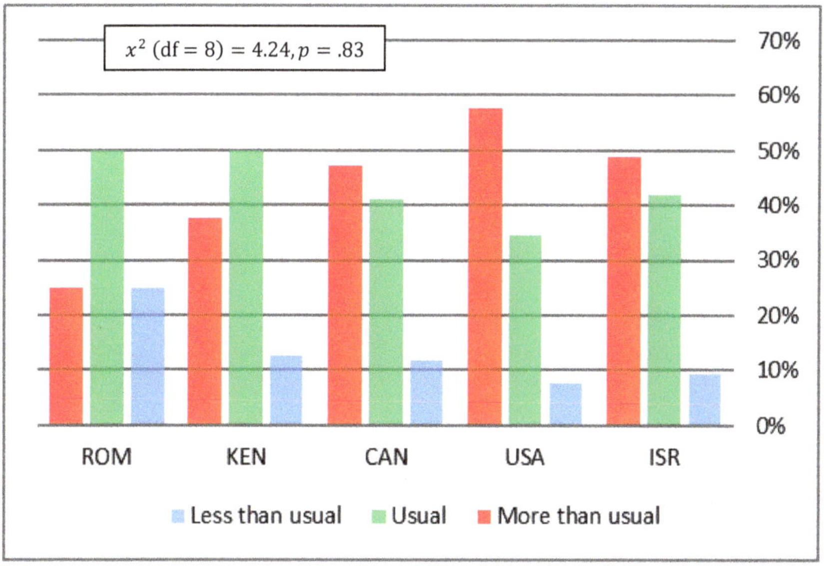

x^2 (df = 8) = 4.24, p = .83

Source: Author

The participants were asked about weight changes during the Covid-19 social isolation period. The results, as shown in Figure 7 were: 39.33% of total participants reported weight gain, 39.33% reported weight did not change, 10.67% reported losing weight, and 10.67% did not know. In order to examine whether there is a relationship between country and weight changes, chi- squared (x^2) test was conducted and significant differences between nations were not found x^2 $(df = 8) = 4.24, p = .83$, as shown in Figure 8.

Figure 7: Weight changes during Covid-19 social isolation

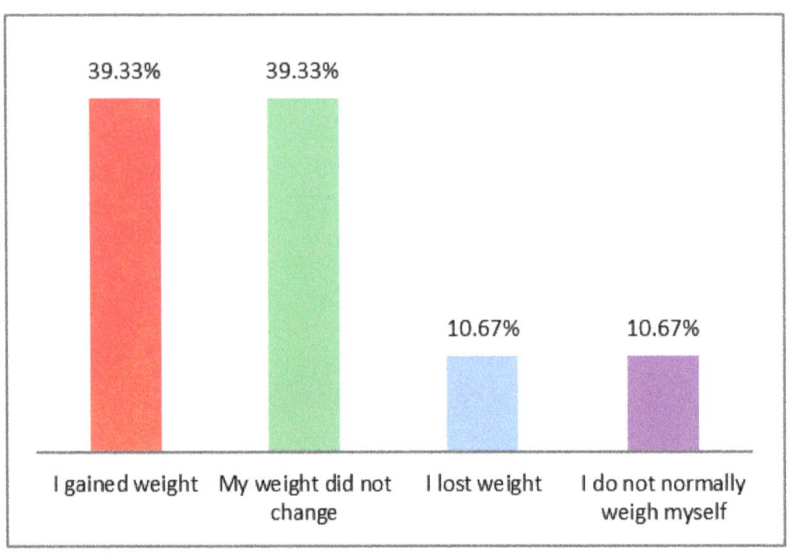

Source: Author

Figure 8: Eating behavior during Covid-19 social isolation among nations

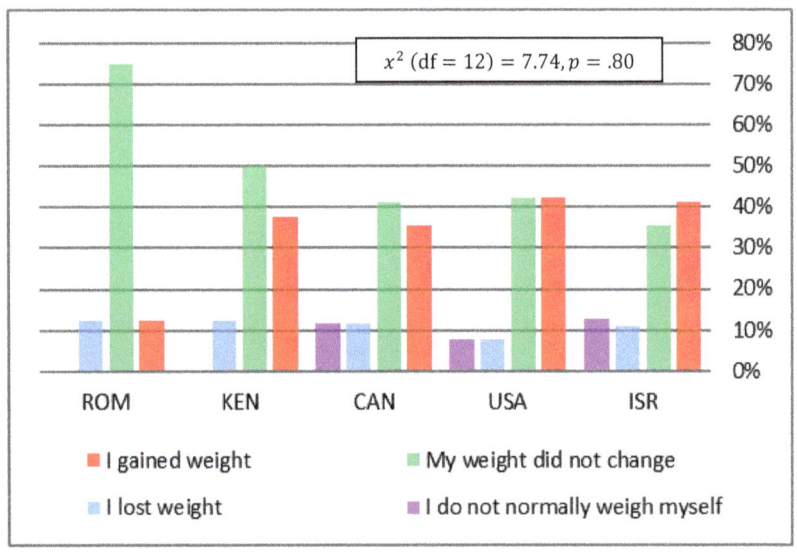

Source: Author

Resilience CD-RISC-10

The CD-RISC-10 scale demonstrated good internal consistency (Cronbach's alpha = 0.88). No significant difference was found between nations related to the quality of Resilience. Romania and Canada tended to have higher resilience scores than other participating nations, shown as a percentage of the maximum score (40) in Figure 9. The one-way ANOVA test among nations on Resilience showed $F (4, 169) = 1.09$, $p = .363$.

Figure 9: Resilience mean and percentage of the maximum score for each nation
Scale 0-40

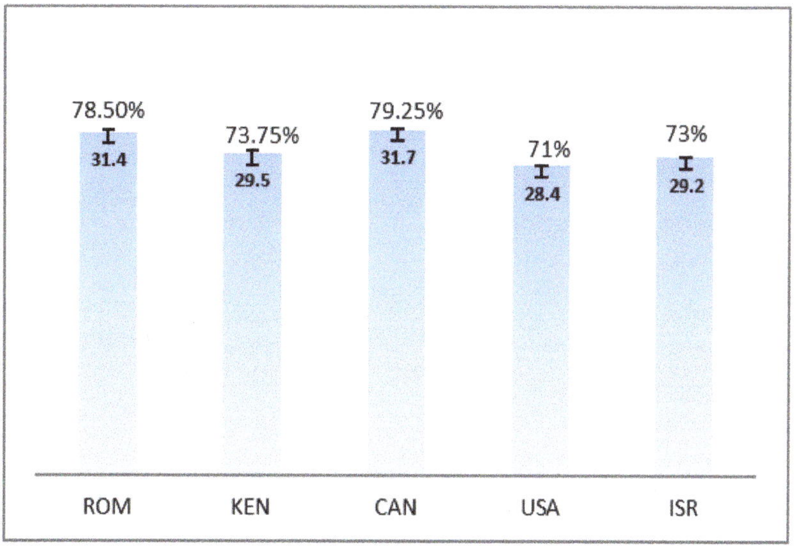

ROM	KEN	CAN	USA	ISR
78.50% / 31.4	73.75% / 29.5	79.25% / 31.7	71% / 28.4	73% / 29.2

Source: Author

Mood State MDMQ

The MDMQ scale demonstrated good internal consistency (Cronbach's alpha = 0.88). The Mood State means (Positive and Negative) of the maximum score for each nation were similar. The intensity of emotions in the U.S. was lower as compared to other nations. Descriptively, the U.S. Mood State mean (Positive and Negative) was the lowest, as shown in Figure 10. The Israel Mood State mean (Positive and Negative) of the maximum score was higher compared to all other nations, as shown in Figure 11.

Time Out

Figure 10: Mood State mean (Positive and Negative) ± SE of the maximum score for each nation, scale: 1-6

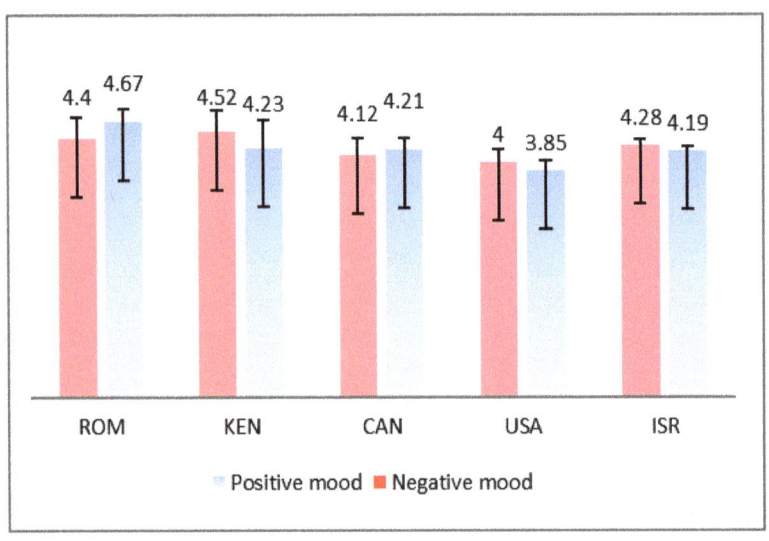

Source: Author

Figure 11: Mood State mean (Positive and Negative) of the maximum score for Israel as compared to other nations, scale: 1-6

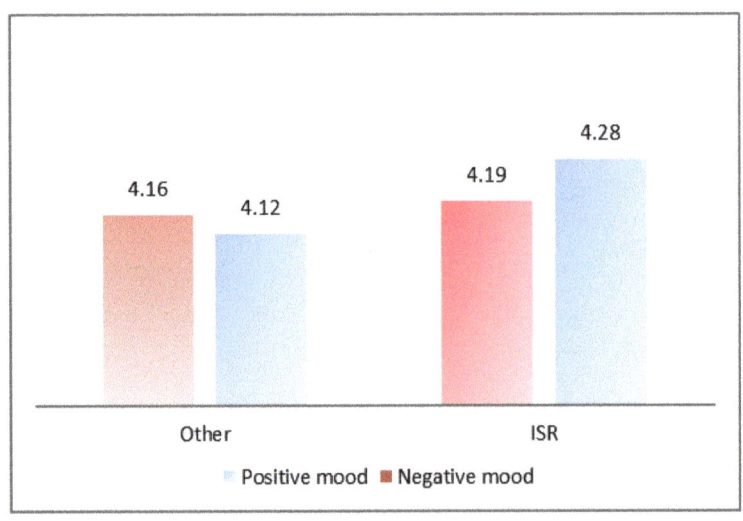

Source: Author

The one-way ANOVA test among nations on Negative Mood resulted in: $F (4, 173) = 0.72$, $p = .58$, LSD post hoc test not significant $f = 0.72$. The one-way ANOVA test among nations on Positive Mood showed: $F (4, 173) = 2.18$, $p = .072$. Israel-U.S. and U.S.-Romania, and each nation pair is significantly different from each other on Positive mood. Israel is different from the U.S. $p = .032$ and the U.S. is different from Romania $p = .007$. LSD post hoc test revealed significant ($p < .05$) differences between Israel and U.S. ($\Delta = 0.35$), U.S. and Romania ($\Delta = 0.82$) Mood State MDMQ.

DISCUSSION

Sedentary Behavior

More exercise during Covid-19 social isolation was reported by all participants with the exception of those from Kenya. This might be related to the fact that Kenyan participants typically have a higher training load and/or that the return to their village settings in order to be with their families decreased their training duration. These results are compatible with other studies of students from Italy (Di Renzo et al. 2020) and Spain (López-Bueno et al. 2020) where participants generally reported an increase in activity during lockdown (Ingram, Maciejewski, and Hand 2020, 7).

During Covid-19 social isolation the duration of alternative training (non-Catchball) was reduced. All participants reported higher exercise frequency per week, but shorter duration per training bout. The Catchball players from Kenya reported the highest frequency both before (almost 5.75 times a week) and during (4.5) the Covid-19 social isolation period, while Romania was the lowest before (1.14) and during (2.25) the social isolation period. Significant differences existed between nations in training frequency before and during the social isolation period, as well as in the duration of training before Covid-19 social isolation. There was no significant difference between nations regarding the duration per training during Covid-19 social isolation. The majority of participants had more free time in their home radius and, as they were normally physically active, they may have sought out other activities to maintain their fitness levels. Moreover, with the interruption of Catchball training due to stay-at-home restrictions, players could establish their own exercise schedule. Therefore, in place of having a concentrated training session they could opt for a more flexible exercise program during the course of the day, such as going for a walk in the morning and doing pilates in the evening. This allowed participants to create a tailor-made activity structure to stay fit.

Physical activities used as an alternative for Catchball training included running, walking, swimming, biking, pilates, strength training, and free weights. Only 25.21% of the total participants reported exercises such as yoga, meditation, breathing exercise, or mindfulness. Those were significantly more popular in Romania (62.5%) and Canada (47.05%), somewhat popular in the U.S. (23.07%), but very low in Kenya (12.5%) and Israel (8.4%), as shown in Table 1.2. The variation in social distancing measures with varying degrees of enforcement among nations was also likely influenced by socio-economic inequalities between regions and disparities in the ability to engage in or access recreational physical activity.

Those who reported more screen time before the Covid-19 social isolation period also had more screen time during the Covid-19 social isolation period. During social isolation no participant reported no screen time at all. However, there was a large shift towards more screen time reported at rates of four hours (25.84%), six hours (26.40%), and more than seven hours (30.34%) per day. Hours sleeping per night were also reported higher during Covid-19 social isolation at seven to eight hours, compared with 6.47-7.5 hours before the Covid-19 social isolation period. The increases in both screen time and sleeping hours during lockdown may reflect an increase in free time available due to the interruption of formalized Catchball training and social life in general outside of home activities.

As related to eating patterns, 48.31% reported that their consumption pattern was higher than usual, 41.57% reported no change, and 10.11% consumed less than usual during the Covid-19 social isolation period. Between nations, U.S. Catchball players reported eating more than usual at the highest rate (57.70%), while Romanian players were lowest at 25%.

Regarding weight management during the Covid-19 social isolation period, 39.33% of the total participants reported gaining weight while 39.33% reported no weight change. Interestingly, the main motives reported for physical activity in women are health and weight loss (Galili et al. 2011, 149). Between nations, U.S. (42.30%) and ISR (41.20%) showed the highest percentage of players who gained weight while Romania reported the lowest (12.50%). As the world attempts to curtail the Covid-19 pandemic, many may feel increasingly stressed, which can lead to emotional eating. When a stressful situation of this magnitude arises, people often experience substantial changes to their eating behaviors. These emotionally-based changes in eating behavior range from overeating to binge eating to severe caloric restriction (Warren 2020, 1). It is noteworthy that in this sample group of women weight management is likely a priority. This means that some of them already succeed maintaining a weight balance in spite of discontinued Catchball training, possibly through performing alternative physical training in their home radius.

Resilience CD-RISC-10

A significant difference between nations was not found regarding Resilience. Canada (31.7 = 79.25%) and Romania (31.4 = 78.50%) had higher resilience scores compared to other nations. However, all other nations demonstrated a resilience score exceeding 71%, which is almost in the fourth quarter. World studies show that participation in group/neighborhood physical activity is significantly associated with increases in community resilience and health measurements, such as well-being, life satisfaction, and happiness (Sharabi 2020, 7). Physical fitness is also associated with many traits and attributes required for resilience (Deuster and Silverman 2013, 28). This is significant to the findings reported above, as physical activity patterns increased for almost all participants (with the exception of Kenyan athletes) during this period. When physical fitness is balanced with a healthy diet and restorative sleep it can be a pathway to health and resilience (Deuster and Silverman 2013, 28).

Group activities, such as Catchball, allow participants to interact socially, strengthen social values, create social circles, establish community trust, gain social support and promote social engagement during the lockdown. In a time of crisis such as the current Covid-19 pandemic, belonging to the Catchball community can have significant benefits through its social networking channels, sense of community belonging, and the use of digital technology. Social encounter became virtual and may have served as a substitute for social interaction between team players during the lockdown period.

Mood State MDMQ

The Mood State mean (Positive and Negative) of the maximum score for all nations was similar. During social isolation there was more time with the family and potentially more free time for those who stopped working. However, it was also a time of future uncertainty, economic concern, and social remoteness that could easily change positive into negative mood. The intensity of emotions in the U.S. and Canada was lower than in Israel, Romania, and Kenya. Descriptively, the U.S. Mood State mean (Positive and Negative) was the lowest. The Israel Mood State mean (Positive and Negative) was higher compared to all other nations' scores in total. As mentioned above, physical activity has an effective influence on mood states and people may feel happier when involved in social activity, such as Catchball, and stopping this activity might have an effect on mood state. Differences in mood state between nations were not significant, though this might be related to the fact that activity profiles in general were higher and that could have prevented a measurable swing in mood state. It is important to note that in spite of the conclusions drawn in this study, a causal relationship between mood state and individual activity behavioral patterns has not been established yet. Follow-up studies would be beneficial in this respect.

LIMITATIONS

Several limitations to this study should be noted. Firstly, is the potential sampling bias due to the reliance on smartphones, application ownership, and Internet access. Secondly, there was a difference between the Israeli players who had more Catchball experience and players from other nations who had substantially less. Thirdly, the wide range in number of participants per nation makes a reliable comparison very difficult. Physical activity worldwide has increased (in frequency) but the training duration has decreased during the Covid-19 pandemic, with regional variability and different levels of lockdown (difference in time frame of social isolation in country and between countries). Within-region trends may reflect social distancing measures and changes in adherence to the rules and, as such, more formal analytic studies are required. Fourthly, no assessment of activity intensity was measured for the alternative training during the social isolation period. Finally, this study did not include a control group (non-active women), is recommended to include in future studies.

CONCLUSIONS

This study aimed to investigate individual activity behavioral patterns, resilience, and mood state among female Catchball players during the period of Covid-19 social isolation from March to May 2020. Official measures that restricted people's movements during the Covid-19 crisis did not necessarily mean that physical activity was limited or that all forms of exercise were eliminated entirely. Engaging in sports is a social, values-based, and educational tool whose influence encompasses all circles from the individual to the community, to the society as a whole. The effect of social distancing measures on overall physical activity, an important determinant of health, should be considered, particularly if prolonged social distancing is required.

The importance of this study is about the imbalance between restrictions imposed on the public as part of the Covid-19 pandemic and maintaining an active and healthy lifestyle. Regular and frequent physical activity, including routine exercise in a safe home environment, has been referenced as an important strategy for healthy living (i.e. mental and physical health), strengthening individual and community resilience to successfully meet the challenges of the current global pandemic.

Limiting the spread of Covid-19 by regulatory measures may cause unprecedented changes to daily routines, such as increasing sedentary behaviors. It could be argued that staying at home, while a safe means of preventing viral spread, can have unintended negative consequences in the form of a reduction in physical activity levels. Therefore, there is a strong rationale for promoting engaging in physical activity at home in order to stay healthy, to maintain fitness levels. Further, promoting eating, screen time, and sleeping behavior routines to support the immune system function may also be warranted in such a precarious environment. It should be noted that especially in a community that plays Catchball with an awareness of the importance of physical activity, it is important to maintain or improve active routines and to find exercise alternatives within mandated limits.

Catchball is a social impact sport, combining physical activity and collective assembly through sport. During the Covid-19 isolation period the gap between an active lifestyle and social interaction was exacerbated due to required distancing measures. In order to reduce future disparities during Covid-19 and beyond, it would is recommended to identify alternative solutions to maintain social interaction. For example, using digital communication channels, associated activities such as a Coach-driven joint fitness session, as well as shared dialogue through Zoom, Skype, and Microsoft Team sessions during the required stay-at-home mandate.

This study helps further a discussion on the negative collateral damage that social distancing measures may instigate or have on the Catchball community, as well as within the general population. Therefore, a national roadmap that helps support achievement of health-related standards through a physically active lifestyle, including ongoing social interaction through modern technology, should be part of global post-Covid-19 recovery plans. The various programs in the field of physical activity and sport in the community should be designed to help promote accessibility and resilience among different populations to convey the power of physical activity in promoting healthy lifestyles.

Acknowledgements

I would like to thank Professor Stephan Wassong, Professor Gershon Tenenbaum, Professor Shira Tibon, Dr. April Henning, and Mrs. Elizabeth Sluyter-Mathew for their support and comments.

REFERENCES

Batey, Jo, and Helen Owton. 2014. "Team Mums: Team Sport Experiences of Athletic Mothers." *Women in Sport and Physical Activity Journal* 22 (1): 30-36.

Brown, Stanly, P. 2001. *Introduction to Exercise Science*. Baltimore: Lippincott Williams and Wilkins.

Chen, Peijie, Lijuan Mao, George P. Nassis, Peter Harmer, Barbara E. Ainsworth, and Fuzhong Li. 2020. "Coronavirus Disease (COVID-19): The Need to Maintain Regular Physical Activity While Taking Precautions." *Journal of Sport and Health Science* 9 (4): 103-104.

Davidov, Hilla. 2020. "Catchball-Corona Questioner Report." *Israel Catchball Federation*. Unpublished.

Davidson, Jonathan R.T. 2020. "Connor-Davidson Resilience Scale (CD-RISC) Manual." Unpublished. Accessed May 4, 2020. www.cd-risc.com.

Deuster, Patricia and Marni N. Silverman. 2013. "Physical Fitness: A Pathway to Health and Resilience." *The Army Medical Department Journal*: 24-36.

Elran, Meir, and Shmuel Even. 2020. "Civilian Resilience in Israel and the COVID-19 Pandemic: Analysis of a CBS Survey." INSS Insight no. 1318. Accessed May 17, 2020. inss.org.il/publication/coronavirus-survey/.

Galili, Yair, Ilan Tamir, Yoav Meckel, and Alon Elyakim. 2011. "Get Up and Go: Changes in Physical Activities' Practices in Israel 1992-2008." *Social Issues in Israel* 12: 140-161.

Grotberg, Edith, H. 1997. "The International Resilience Research Project." Paper presented at the Annual Convention of the International Council of Psychologist.

Ingram, Joanne, Greg Maciejewski, and Christopher J. Hand. 2020. "Changes in Diet, Sleep, and Physical Activity Are Associated with Differences in Negative Mood During COVID-19 Lockdown." *Frontiers in Psychology* 11: Article 588604.

Lane, Andrew M, and Peter C. Terry. 2000. "The Nature of Mood: Development of a Conceptual Model with a Focus on Depression." *Journal of Applied Sport Psychology* 12 (1): 16-33.

Leipold, Bernhard, and Werner Greve. 2009. Resilience: "A Conceptual Bridge Between Coping and Development." *European Psychologist* 14 (1): 40-50.

Leppamaki, Sami. 2006. "The Effect of Exercise and Light on Mood." Ph.D. diss., University of Helsinki.

Owen, Neville, Phillip B. Sparling, Geneviève N. Healy, David W. Dunstan, and Charles E. Matthews. 2010. "Sedentary Behavior: Emerging Evidence for a New Health Risk." *Mayo Clinic Proceedings* 85 (12): 1138-1141.

Sharabi, Yossi. "The Culture and Sports Strategy to Cope with the Corona Crisis." *Ministry of Culture and Sport, Israel*. 1-17

Steyer, Rolf, Peter Schwenkmezger, Peter Notz, and Michael Eid. 1994. "Testtheoretisce Analysen des Mehrdimensionalen Befindlichkeitsfragebogens (MDBF)." *Diagnostica* 40 (4): 320-328.

Steyer, Rolf, Peter Schwenkmezger, Peter Notz, and Michael Eid. 1997. *Der Mehrdimensionale Befindlichkeitsfragebogen (MDBF)*. Göttingen: Hogrefe.

Tesler, Riki, Orna Baron, Shiran Bord, and Danny Moran. "Participation in the Mamanet Catchball League as a Health Promoter Through Social Capital." Accessed July 7, 2020. https://www.mamanet.org.il/viewArticle.asp?id=4215.

Tremblay, Mark S., Salomé Aubert, Joel D. Barnes, Travis J. Saunders, Valerie Carson, Amy E. Latimer-Cheung, Sebastien FM Chastin, Teatske M. Altenburg, and Mai J. Chinapaw. 2017. "Sedentary Behavior Research Network (SBRN) Terminology Consensus Project Process and Outcome." *International Journal of Behavioral Nutrition and Physical Activity* 14 (75): 1-17.

Walsh, Barbara, Eleanor M. Whittaker, Colum Cronin, and Amy E. Whitehead. 2018. "'Net Mums': A Narrative Account of Participants' Experiences Within a Netball Intervention. "*Qualitative Research in Sport, Exercise and Health* 10 (5): 604-619.

Wang, Li, Zhanbiao Shi, Yuqing Zhang, and Zhen Zhang. 2010. "Psychometric Properties of the 10-Item Connor-Davidson Resilience Scale in Chinese Earthquake Victims." *Psychiatry and Clinical Neurosciences* 64 (5): 499-504.

Warren, Cortney S. 2020. "How to Curb Emotional Eating During the COVID-19 Pandemic." Psychology Today. Accessed September 17, 2020. https://www.psychologytoday.com/us/blog/naked-truth/202003/how-curb-emotional-eating-during-the-covid-19-pandemic.

Wikipedia. "Outbreak of the Corona Virus in Israel." Accessed September 17, 2020. https://he.wikipedia.org/wiki/התפרצות_נגיף_הקורונה_בישראל.

PositivePsychology.com. "The Connor Davidson + Brief Resilience Scales." Accessed May 4, 2020. https://positivepsychology.com/connor-davidson-brief-resilience-scale/.

CHAPTER 11

Africa's International Sports Icons as Role Models and Activists During the Covid-19 Lockdown

Cecil G.S Tafireyi

INTRODUCTION

As the Covid-19 pandemic took its global toll, African international sports icons, notably Didier Drogba, Mohammed Salah, Samuel Etoo, Siya Kolisi, and Caster Semenya, served as role models and activists (Hotakie 2020). They had previously assumed these roles on the international stage as "ambassadors" and in a more national context in response to different political and humanitarian issues. In response to the Covid-19 pandemic, they had to take on critical roles ranging from provision of resources and food, to responding to discourses on Africa and relaying health messages to the general masses about Covid-19.

The impact of these global sport icons has been felt in different ways but mostly in the way people respond to the advice in return to their admiration of the icons. History has shown that sports in Africa have a direct influence on politics (Wright 1978, 362), as sport icons take advantage of their popularity and massive admiration to send messages to politicians. On the other hand, politicians have also used sports icons to send messages of health advice and politics, among others, even before the Covid-19 pandemic and lockdowns.

Despite some of the individual athletes not being officially appointed as ambassadors, they have taken it upon themselves to represent the African continent on political issues as well. The debate and discourse around the much-needed global vaccine to enable the globe to get back to "normal" went "offside" after the suggestion by some French doctors to test the Covid-19 vaccine on the African continent because of its poor health facilities and, hence, its vulnerability to Covid-19. International sports icons reacted politically by condemning such "racist utterances," further expounding that Africa is not a testing ground for vaccines (Kohler 2020).

It appears the sports icons are cognizant of the power sport lends their voices, as well as the monetary influence their sporting prowess brings to African economies and health facilities, particularly amidst political instability and pandemics like Covid-19. What is more interesting is the fact that the focus has always been on sport organizations as establishments, such as the role of IAAF and other sport organizations (Lapchick 1979; Booth 1998; Krieger 2017), but global sports icons are not known collectively as powerful opinion makers in Africa. This chapter elaborates the roles, activism, and responses of African international sports icons in the wake of the Covid-19 pandemic and their "admired" role model statuses.

METHODOLOGY

A narrative review of literature was employed in order to link the information already known on sport and politics in Africa to the trends during the Covid-19 lockdown. The latest information on African sport personalities with global status was primarily found on online news websites and in YouTube interviews with the athletes. Electronic media platforms, especially online news websites, were the most relevant at this point, as they were a major source of primary information due to Covid-19 lockdowns. The focus was mainly on the verifiable information that was said by the global sports icons themselves, from different news agencies around the world and not just in Africa. To verify the information, the focus was on more than one news website that confirmed the same text.

Text selection was based on the credibility of the source, specifically articles that reported verifiable information and not just editorial. The credibility of the sources was based on the outlet's reputation and trustworthiness. For instance, CNN and the BBC are generally trusted to report verifiable facts. Information from organizational websites such as CAF and FIFA, among others, was also regarded as credible and verifiable. It was important to consider verifiable primary information, what was said by the athletes, and confirmed by one or more news sources. The triangulation of academic literature and information on electronic media platforms was thus important in understanding the roles played by the African sports icons in response to the Covid-19 pandemic. The segmentation/group identification approach of social media text was also employed. In this approach "researchers can actively engage with social media data as an additional source that complements and augments existing qualitative research" (Social Media Research Group 2016, 11). The limitation of the methodology used was that generalizing the picture was not possible, but only individual examples could be given.

OVERVIEW OF THE COVID-19 PANDEMIC ON THE AFRICAN CONTINENT

Infections

The African continent confirmed its first case of Covid-19 in Egypt on February 14, 2020. Two weeks later, Sub-Saharan Africa reported the first case in Nigeria on February 27, 2020 (ITC 2020; World Bank 2020). As of April 18, 2020, Africa CDC reported 19,895 confirmed cases, including 1,017 deaths and 4,642 recoveries, from fifty-two African countries, while two countries (Comoros and Lesotho) were still virus-free (Financial Times 2020). During the same period, specifically by April 28, 2020, the US had recorded close to one million cases with 56,000 deaths (Internet world stats 2020). The United Kingdom recorded 103,093 cases by April 17, 2020; Russia 13,584; Germany 137,698; Italy 168,941; Spain 184,948; and France 165,027 (*ibid.*). It was not clear why Africa had recorded very low Covid-19 infections by April 2020, in sharp contrast with expectations from people and scientists around the world, but a quicker response was regarded as one of the contributing factors (OECD 2020).

Lockdowns

The whole African continent-imposed lockdowns to curb the spread of the Covid-19 pandemic. Many experts had anticipated high infection rates and more devastating consequences on the African continent due to the prevalence of underlying conditions such as Tuberculosis and AIDS among its populace (OECD 2020). However, a quicker imposition of restrictions and adherence to safety regulations, as dictated by the World Health Organization (WHO), helped Africa to slow down the spread of the pandemic. African governments reacted faster than elsewhere to impose travel restrictions and close borders to minimize contagion (OECD 2020). South Africa, for example, introduced an articulated response, comprising eight overlapping stages, including a strict lockdown and major economic mitigation measures to assist the affected population (OECD 2020). Due to economic threats, including severe hardships and strained food security of the lockdown restrictions, most African countries contemplated easing the restrictions from the month of July onwards (Hotakie 2020). African countries individually dealt with the pandemic, with more infections being recorded in Sub-Saharan Africa than in Saharan. At the same time "the one size fits all" WHO response to Covid-19 did not appear tenable in Africa, especially with regards to the total lockdown of economies (OECD 2020).

The Effect on Sport

All African countries individually stopped sport gatherings from March 2020, as soon as the lockdown restrictions were imposed. Though there was a strict following of WHO guidelines, the autonomy rested on the respective African sovereign governments to respond according to their localized situations. In football, there was a unanimous decision by the Confederation of African Football (CAF) to stop all football games. CAF President Ahmad Ahmad reiterated that, "I invite everyone to be very careful and wait for the situation to normalize. But beyond that, I do not want football to be a source of destabilization for the precautionary measures taken by the various governments to deal with the pandemic" (Hotakie 2020). The clear distinction of boundaries between sport and politics in Africa has always been heavily pronounced by sport and political organizations, respectively. All formal and non-formal sports were banned, and on April 30, 2020, all sporting events remained banned. The Eswatini Minister of Health, speaking on behalf of the government, described the possible return of normal sport and football as miraculous, especially in 2020 (Jele 2020). The Minister's statement could have been influenced by the limited capacity of Eswatini to deal with the Covid-19 pandemic, especially if sports like football were to continue unabated. Eswatini had declared a state of emergency in addition to the lockdown citing an inability to deal with the Covid-19 pandemic.

In South Africa, rugby players reportedly took salary cuts in order to cushion their clubs (Ray 2020). Poorer leagues, like those found in smaller countries including Lesotho and Eswatini, could not afford to keep paying their players and support staff, but received FIFA loans and grants to help cushion them against revenue loss (Jele 2020). Top marathon athletes in Kenya had to cut their training programs by more than 50% due to lockdown restrictions. Kenyan athlete Albert Korir said, "I went from 200 to 50 kilometres a week, so I am worried, when you start active training again you might get injuries" (Hotakie 2020). The Covid-19 lockdowns and restrictions thus posed serious threats to sport training, development, and performances. A huge technical risk was that some athletes faced a career "crash" if the pandemic lockdowns lasted beyond expected time frames, due to the principle of reversibility in sport training.

BACKGROUND OF ROLE MODELING/LEADERSHIP AND ACTIVISM

The ability of global sport persons in Africa to assume ambassadorial roles is the new "normal" in sport, especially as more football players started playing in lucrative European top-flight leagues, including the English Premier League, La Liga, and the Bundesliga. Some authors branded the exodus of African football players to the top leagues in the world as a "muscle drain" (Raffaele 2006, 2) and exploitation, but with little regard for the impact these players have on the African continent. These sports icons are widely celebrated and admired by many Africans, as they give a different perception and representation of Africans and hope to those who dream of coming out of poverty. On the other hand, familiarity and admiration of some African sports icons have led to political careers.

Understanding the background of the role modeling and activism of the African sports icons is mainly possible through differentiating the nature of their contributions. For instance, there are athletes who took political careers and others that were involved in humanitarian activities, role modeling, leadership, and activism but without official political positions. The "non-political" group of athletes including Dider Drogba, Mohammed Salah, Sadio Mane, and Samuel Etoo, have arguably donated to and spearheaded more humanitarian projects than those who took political positions.

Former global sports icons in Africa, such as Kirsty Coventry, George Weah, and Lamine Diack—a former French national champion in the long jump—have actively taken political roles. Coventry is the current Minister of Sports and Culture in Zimbabwe, Weah is the current President of Liberia, and Diack is the former Mayor of the Senegalese capital Dakar. Weah's election as President of Liberia in January 2018 was the first peaceful handover of power since the end of the Liberian civil war. It was anticipated that Weah would bring peace and stability as people equated his achievements in sport to politics (Elizabeth and Geraldine 2019).

The extent to which these individuals have participated in national politics, can also be related to the impact these global icons make on the African continent, through mostly "self-appointed" ambassadorial activities, leadership, and activism. With seven gold medals, Coventry is one of the most decorated Olympians in Africa, whilst Weah won the African player of the year three times and also boasts of being the only native African player to win the Ballon d'Or. The Ivory Coast international and former Chelsea football player, Didier Drogba, has in many instances intervened in the country's politics, much to the appreciation of the masses and oppressed. In fact, Drogba was selected for the Global Humanitarian award in 2011 (Scott-Elliot 2011).

In narrating how he managed to spearhead talks to end a civil war in Ivory Coast, Drogba asserted, "I knew that we could bring a lot of people together. More than politicians. The country is divided because of politicians; we are playing football, we are running behind a ball, and we managed to bring people together" (Scott-Elliot 2011). Here, sport and diplomacy had a direct impact in helping end a civil war in Africa. For a country in the midst of political crisis, Drogba became a symbol of hope for national cohesion (Künzler and Poli 2012, 208; Njororai 2014, 866). The African global sports icons have thus continued with this activism and role modeling for the benefit of the African people. Their contributions to the Covid-19 pandemic attest to their unwavering support for the African continent.

LATEST CONTRIBUTIONS OF THE GLOBAL ICONS

The powerful roles and ambassadorial activities of current and former athletes have continued throughout all "crisis" situations, and the Covid-19 pandemic has again brought to the fore such admirable qualities of global sports icons. Sadio Mane, Didier Drogba, Samuel Eto'o, Siya Kolisi, and Mohamed Salah all made some contributions to their respective countries in the form of money, facilities, and also strict warnings to abide by the WHO regulations. African sports icons were very successful on the international stage and in many instances would echo their sentiments from abroad. The Covid-19 pandemic presented a platform for the sports icons to implement their contributions to their home areas from March 2020 onwards.

In the sport of athletics, 800-meter Olympic champion Caster Semenya echoed sentiments about safe and hygienic ways of preventing the spread of the Covid-19 disease (Semenya 2020). She also jokingly said, "So Mr Ramaphosa (president) went there with the dab thing, that's not my thing. It's either I salute and then hello, bye. Dab from a distance. That gap, the gap that I hit in the 800m, 5-10m" (Semenya 2020). She was referring to social distancing and preferring not to dab when greeting, but to salute and greet from a distance. Semenya seemed to be pushing for her preferred ways of greeting, though the dab was recommended by WHO then. Similar health advice on Covid-19 was given by Mohamed Salah, Egypt international and Liverpool F.C. football player, who wished his home village-Nagrig health and safety and urged residents to avoid large gatherings and to stay committed to following health guidance regarding Covid-19 (Al-Masry 2020). Whilst the efforts of the sports icons are highly recommended and emulated, they are not without challenges. Semenya and Salah seemed to be aware of the ignorance of the African people in response to pandemics like Covid-19, and that may explain the emotions attached to the health messages.

Drogba handed out masks at the cathedral of Abidjan with the warning, "my sisters, my brothers, I ask you to take the matter very seriously, we tend to be too light about our reactions to the situation" (AFP 2020). Such a strong statement also exposed how Drogba was aware of social, political, and health matters in Ivory Coast and most probably across the African continent. Samuel Eto'o urged African communities to adhere strictly to precautionary measures. He echoed, "My African brothers and sisters! Covid-19 has taken over our lives. With malice, arrogance and without notice. It knows neither race, religion nor political parties. It kills the rich and the poor. Even in countries where research is done well, the consequences are disastrous. Unpredictable" (AFP 2020). In this statement, Eto'o appears to be addressing the misconceptions and conspiracy theories that were going around on various social media platforms about the Covid-19 pandemic, with regards to who is susceptible and vulnerable to infection.

In terms of activism, during the Covid-19 pandemic lockdown, the most politically motivated reactions were perhaps made by Samuel Eto'o and Didier Drogba in response to the discourse on testing some vaccines on the African continent. Two French professors, Jean-Paul Mira and Camille Locht, unilaterally agreed to an idea they thought was academically profound and scientifically logical. Professor Jean-Paul Mira, head of the intensive care unit at the Cochin Hospital in Paris, said, "If I can be provocative, shouldn't we do this study in Africa where there are no masks, no treatment, no resuscitation?" Whilst these statements were considered racist, ignorant, and inconsiderate in various media platforms, what was worse was comparing the vulnerability of the African continent to that of prostitutes (Bird 2020). There was also a very strong contrast and irony, as during that time Africa had very few cases as compared to that of France, the US, and China, hence not enough people to test the vaccine. Africans, on the other hand, could have been very skeptical of vaccines due to previous unethical practices (Weyzig and Schipper 2008) and conspiracy theories that went around during the Covid-19 lockdowns. Given the above background, hostile responses from Africa were obviously imminent, though expected more from politicians than sport stars.

In response, Eto'o was more direct and provocative whilst Drogba diplomatically stated, "It is inconceivable that we continue to accept this. I strongly denounce these serious, racist and contemptuous remarks!" Drogba further narrated, "Help us save lives in Africa and stop the spread of this virus which is destabilising the whole world, instead of considering us as guinea pigs. It is absurd!" (Bird 2020). The impact of the responses by the sports icons, recorded under the title "Africans react to French doctors' vaccines," was described as a "retraction" of the implications of the utterances by French doctors (Bird 2020). The retraction by Mira read, "I want to present all my apologies to those who were hurt, shocked and felt insulted by the remarks that I clumsily expressed on LCI this week." Two interesting insights exist here. First, the media branded the response by the African footballers as an African reaction, as if to suggest that the stars are ambassadors for the continent. Second, the apology made by Mira was done in realization of the reactions made by the sports icons, rubber-stamping their influence and "ambassadorial" status.

Although active and retired global football players are usually on the frontline in humanitarian aid and ambassadorial activities, notable contributions were evident from other global sports icons as well. These include, of late, the only native black African captain to win the World Rugby Cup, Siya Kolisi, the limelight of which was affected by the Covid-19 pandemic. Kolisi launched the Kolisi Foundation with his wife and distributed food hampers to the vulnerable people in the South African communities. Knowing pretty well how he is celebrated and respected, he not only provided food humpers, but also gave advice like his fellow sports icons. He reiterated,

> With the food packages that we drop off, we are adding messages in the local dialect of Xhosa, because this is predominately for the Xhosa areas. We put in instructions there for the masks all in Xhosa on how to put it on. But the most important is this: if you want people to stay home, tell them why. You can't just tell someone to stay home and not give them anything. (Christina 2020)

His statement pointed out the need for health authorities and the government to educate the nation on why they were being asked to stay at home during lockdowns rather than imposing on them. Kolisi gave a different perspective of responsibility and representation, as he focused on a tribe (XOSA) in South Africa who are vulnerable and needed further assistance in terms of knowledge breakdown and food provision

IMPACT OF THE ROLE MODELING

The level and impact of role modeling has shifted over time. For example, Diack had a strong impact on diplomacy (Booth 1988, 188), whilst footballers such as Eto'o, Drogba, and Salah, among others, have donated more tangible infrastructure (Taiwo 2020). However, Diack's role is a classic case of how sports persons can also utilize their influence to promote their individual interests (Booth 1988, 188). The African "solidarity ticket: can thus be used for various reasons, including to launch a future political career, as George Weah and others did.

In response to the Covid-19 pandemic, sports icons have impacted their nations in different ways. CAF president Ahmad highlighted the spontaneous solidarity shown by the African football family during the Covid-19 lockdown (Hotakie 2020). It is important to note that he is among the few high-profile sport leaders to brand a group of athletes from different African countries as a family whilst referring to their role in the Covid-19 pandemic, and also to acknowledging their roles and collective responsibilities. The global sports icons, though acknowledged and respected for their role modeling and ambassadorial activities, face a daunting and potentially dangerous task if they go against the expectations of the African governments.

Countries with global sports icons, such as Egypt, Ivory Coast, Senegal, South Africa, and Cameroon, among others, have benefited directly from the funding of various initiatives, such as provision of health facilities and food for vulnerable communities. It is difficult to measure directly the impact of their advice and responses directed towards lifestyle changes to fight Covid-19. What can be objectively measured at the moment are the financial contributions that these global sports icons have made to their respective countries and the magnitude of such donations. The Samuel Eto'o relief aid targeted 100,000 people, whilst Salah aimed to help an estimated 10,000 people in his home village in Egypt.

Like most African global football players, Salah was reportedly funding the construction of a medical clinic, youth center, and a school, as well as donating money to support local families in 2018 (Hambly 2020). Drogba donated a hospital in Ivory Coast to the government to help with screening for Covid-19, a move that was described by the mayor of Abidjan as an act of patriotism (Taiwo 2020). Due to the shortage of health facilities, a donation of a hospital in most African countries is of huge significance, hence the appreciation of Drogba's donation by the mayor of Abidjan. As highlighted earlier, it is also not the first time Drogba was involved in trying to contribute to the solutions of problems affecting Ivory Coast. Liverpool forward Sadio Mane made a donation of €45,000 to the national committee fighting against Covid-19 in his home country of Senegal (Carddick 2020). Mane also shared a video on social media, asking his compatriots to take Covid-19 "extremely seriously" (Carddick 2020). It appears that Mane, Salah, Drogba, and Eto'o were all cognizant of the fact that fellow compatriots were mostly likely to undermine the Covid-19 guidance, thus risking their lives, hence the strong cautions. All in all, their contributions were in three major areas; health advice and caution, resources to fight Covid-19, and, to a lesser extent, responding to discourses internationally.

Conclusions

In conclusion, the African global sports icons notably in Ivory Coast, Cameroon, Senegal, Egypt, and South Africa have assumed ambassadorial responsibilities, representing Africa and their nations in different political and economic dispensations. A few of them have also echoed sentiments in response to the testing of the Covid-19 vaccine on the African continent. Cognizant of their influence on politics and the health of the continent, the stars have continued to echo sentiments that give direction to policy on different matters and provide resources for infrastructure and/or health aid.

The Covid-19 pandemic brought another opportunity for the global sports icons to react and respond politically, socially, and by other humanitarian means. Global sports icons including Eto'o, Drogba, Semenya, and Koloisi were actively involved in disseminating important Covid-19 information and distributing aid to vulnerable communities. This rubber stamps once more the undeniable and solid relationship between sport and politics (Wright 1978, 362), but with a focus on African global sports personalities as role models in the Covid-19 lockdown.

As a result, the masses have and continue to benefit from the generosity and ambassadorial responsibilities of African athletes, especially regarding the Covid-19 pandemic. It is worth noting that the sports icons assumed those roles without necessarily having to be appointed by their respective governments. Some of the contributions were very impactful and attracted comments and admiration from politicians and the general public.

It is of paramount importance to highlight the distinction between the sports icons, especially football players and other athletes, in all situations including the Covid-19 pandemic. Football players in Africa have taken it upon themselves to take part in the development of their respective countries, characteristically starting with their hometowns. They have continued to focus on their hometowns again during the Covid-19 pandemic. Other athletes have followed suit, but with a concentration on foundations that have smaller magnitudes in comparison but have not shied away from using their voices to influence opinion making. The sports icons continued to use the same humanitarian foundations to mobilize health resources in response to the Covid-19 pandemic. Not much has been reported on the contributions of successful Kenyan and Ethiopian athletes respectively.

The chapter focused mainly on social media and online news texts and therefore may be limited in giving a generalized picture of the roles of African sports icons. However, this chapter is important for future references on the subject of African sports icons as role models and activists in different dispensations on the continent.

REFERENCES

AFP. 2020. "African Football Stars Make Donations to Fight Against Coronavirus." Ahram online. March 26, 2020. http://english.ahram.org.eg/NewsPrint/366068.aspx.

Al-Masry, Ali Youm. 2020. "Mohamed Salah Donates Thousands of Tons of Food to his Hometown." *Egypt Independent*, April 17, 2020. https://egyptindependent.com/mohamed-salah-donates-thousands-oftons-of-food-to-his-hometown/.

Bird, Jeorge. 2020. "'You're just S***!': Samuel Etoo and Didier Drogba Lead Crusade against 'Racist' Professors' Plan to Test Coronavirus Vaccine in Africa as Chelsea Legend Accuses Them of Treating People Like Guinea Pigs." *Mail online*, April 3, 2020. https://www.dailymail.co.uk/sport/sportsnews/article8184149/Samuel-Etoo-Didier-Drogba-slam-racist-professors-plan-testcoronavirus-vaccine-Africa.html.

Booth, Douglas. 1998. *The Race Game: Sport and Politics in South Africa*. London, Frank Cass.

Caddick, Geoff. 2020. "Coronavirus: Sadio Mane Makes Donation to Senegal Health." BBC Sport. March 17, 2020. https://www.bbc.com/sport/amp/football/51930624.

Christina, Macfarlane. 2020. "'There is Nothing Worse than Hunger,' Says South Africa Hero Siya Kolisi of Helping Townships during Lockdown." CNN Sports. April 18, 2020 .https://edition.cnn.com/2020/04/28/sport/siya-kolisi-south-africacoronavirus-spt-intl-cmd/index.html.

Elizabeth, Donnelly and Geraldine, O'Mahony. 2019. "A Conflicted Leader: George Weah's First Year in Liberia." Chatham House. January 28, 2019. https://www.chathamhouse.org/expert/comment/conflicted-leader-georgeweah-s-first-year-liberia.

Financial Times. 2020. "What Coronavirus Tests Does the World Need to Track the Pandemic?" *Financial Times*, April 9, 2020. https://www.ft.com/content/0faf8e7a-d966-44a5-b4ee-8213841da688.

Hambly, Matt. 2020. "Mohamed Salah Donates Food to his Hometown amidst Coronavirus." *GQ Middle East*, April 19, 2020. https://www.gqmiddleeast.com/Mohamed-Salah-Donates-To-HometownNagrig-Egypt-Coronavirus.

Hotakie, Alima. 2020. "Coronavirus: Kenyan Marathon Runners Struggle to Maintain Competitive Edge." Deutsche Welle, May 1, 2020. https://www.dw.com/en/coronaviruskenyan-marathon-runners-struggle-to-maintain-competitive-edge/a53298098.

Internet World Stats. 2020. "Country Corona Virus Report; Based on the United Nations Country List, and Covid-19 Data as of August 9, 2020." Internet World Stats. August 9, 2020. https://www.internetworldstats.com/list3.htm.

ITC. 2020. "Tracking of COVID-19 Temporary Trade Measures." Retrieved April 30, 2020. https://macmap.org/fr/covid19.

Jele, Sanele. 2020. "EFA Eligible for E9.9m FIFA Loan." *Times of Eswatini*, April. July 14, 2020. http://www.times.co.sz/sports/129095-efa-eligible-for-e9-9mfifa-loan.html.

Kohler, Lorenz. 2020. "Drogba Slams Racist Covid-19 Comments." KICKOFF, April 3, 2020. https://www.kickoff.com/news/articles/worldnews/categories/news/international/didier-drogba-samuel-eto-o-slamcomments-that-covid-19-vaccine-must-be-tested-on-africans/676258.

Krieger, Jörg. 2017. "We Don't Want to be Pushed by Outsiders; The International Association of Athletics Federations Attempts to Re-admit South Africa to the Global Athletics stage." *South Africa Journal for Research in Sport, Physical Education and Recreation* 39 (1/2): 169-186.

Künzler, Daniel, and Raffaele Poli. 2012. "The African Footballer as Visual Object and Figure of Success: Didier Drogba and Social Meaning." *Soccer & Society* 13 (2): 207–221.

Lapchick, Richard. 1970. "The Olympic Movement and Racism: An Analysis in Historical Perspective." *Africa Today* 17 (6): 17-27.

Njororai, Wycliffe. 2009. "Colonial Legacy, Minorities and Association Football in Kenya." *Soccer & Society* 10 (6): 866-882.

OECD. 2020. "Africa's Response to COVID-19: What Roles for Trade, Manufacturing and Intellectual Property?" OECD. June 23, 2020. http://www.oecd.org/coronavirus/policy-responses/africa-s-response-tocovid-19-what-roles-for-trade-manufacturing-and-intellectual-property73d0dfaf/.

Raffaele, Poli. 2006. "Migrations and Trade of African Football Players: Historic, Geographical and Cultural Aspects." *Afrika Spectrum* 41 (3): 393-414.

Ray, Craig. 2020. "SA Rugby Set for Pay Cuts." *Daily Maverick*, April 6, 2020. https://www.dailymaverick.co.za/article/2020-04-06-sa-rugby-set-for-paycuts/.

Scott-Elliot, Robin. 2011. "Drogba Heals the Wounds of Civil War in Homeland." *Independent*, December 14, 2011. https://www.independent.co.uk/sport/football/news-andcomment/drogba-heals-the-wounds-of-civil-war-in-homeland-6276549.html.

Semenya, Caster. 2020. ''Caster Semenya's Tips for Preventing the Spread of Covid-19." Discovery Channel, March 20, 2020. https://www.youtube.com/watch?v=ExfKb_NG2Cc.

Social Media Research Group. 2016. *Using Social Media for Social Research: An Introduction*. London: Government Social Research. https://assets.publishing.service.gov.uk/government/uploads/system/uploads/attachment_data/file/524750/GSR_Social_Media_Research_Guidance_-_Using_social_media_for_social_research.pdf.

Taiwo, Taiye. 2020. "Coronavirus: Drogba Donates Hospital for Screening in Ivory Coast." Goal, April 13, 2020. https://www.goal.com/enng/news/coronavirus-drogba-donates-hospital-for-screening-inivory/1ijtj3hw3ddsc1o5opca65i00d.

CHAPTER 12

A Unique and Special Solution for a Unique and Special Time: Training Professional Football Referees Virtually

Yuya Kiuchi, Bill Dittmar, and Scott Matteson

INTRODUCTION

With the outbreak of Covid-19, almost all major sport leagues and events suspended their activities. The professional football league in the United States, known as Major League Soccer (MLS), was no exception. After two weekends of matches in late February and early March 2020, MLS canceled all games for the foreseeable future. The lockdown affected not only players, coaches, and fans, but referees as well. At the MLS level, twenty-six referees, forty-six assistant referees, ten video assistant referees, and nine assistant video assistant referees serve on league games week after week. During normal times, these officials undergo regular training. For example, referees attend approximately twenty training meetings every year, in addition to mandatory fitness tests and other events. Every two weeks, they travel to either Dallas, Texas, or Minneapolis, Minnesota, to attend a training session. With the lockdown, the Professional Referee Organization (PRO), the organization in charge of MLS referees, faced the challenge of having to conduct all of its referee training online.

MLS referee training sessions include video analyses, small group discussions, physical training, and other educational opportunities. Prior to the shutdown, referee training was a combination of face-to-face and technology-mediated remote learning. Referees and their mentors—sometimes called assessors or coaches—previously used both asynchronous educational tools and synchronous video and phone conference tools to review their match performance, discuss interpretations of the Laws of the Game, or go over player and game management. This meant that integrating technology into its training was not new for PRO. Making a complete shift from a hybrid format of training to fully online training, however, was different. As Howard Webb, the PRO General Manager and the 2010 World Cup Final referee, commented, PRO had to offer quality training without compromising value and relevance, in the absence of any face-to-face meetings (Webb 2020).

Ample research exists on how to conduct effective referee training remotely or using technology. Referees in Israel participated in a referee decision simulator experiment to show the efficacy of training that combined a treadmill and a tablet to recreate a match-like situation (Samuel et al. 2019). Video-based training has also proven to improve the accuracy of referee and assistant referee decisions (Schweizer et al. 2011; Armenteros et al. 2018). Gulec et al. (2018) has suggested that future referee training could take place in a three-dimensional virtual environment. Ali Kizilt's (2011) work showed that referee fitness could be improved via distance physical education. Studies have also shown that online training is deemed to be just as efficient and effective as face-to-face learning without being detrimental to student- -in this case referee--performance, as long as proper course framework, means of communication, and responsibility of tasks are considered (Etherington et al. 2017; Soffer and Nachmias 2018; Jung and Rha 2000). For the chosen format to be successful, PRO had to carefully consider its approach and determine what would be the best for its members.

Although PRO's immediate plan was to hold its training on Zoom or another conference call system, within several days after the suspension of the league, it decided instead to utilize VirBELA, a 3-D avatar-based virtual reality collaborative platform. The platform turned out to be a useful tool, not only during the time of emergency, but possibly for the post-pandemic period. Furthermore, VirBELA allowed PRO to realize tangible training benefits such as high-quality technical training and intangible benefits including continued sense of support and community among its referees. Although the effectiveness of training on VirBELA will not become clear until MLS is fully back to its normal operation and the referee performance is evaluated, PRO instructor and referee experiences hint that virtual training has potential to be a part of formal referee training even in the post-pandemic period. PRO members' experiences also suggest the strengths and weaknesses of a synchronous 3-D virtual reality software for sport official training.

MOVING THE CLASSROOM TO VIRBELA

PRO's online training needs were two-fold. Tangible needs included the ability to show videos, offer breakout sessions, and provide other features to replicate the in-person training environment. Intangible needs were the ability to address the sense of uncertainties among referees. Continuing the sense of community, ensuring referees felt supported by PRO, and other psychological and emotional supports were important components of its online training.

Mark Geiger, the Director of Senior Match Officials, a former FIFA referee, and a two-time FIFA World Cup referee, stated that what made PRO's training unique was its quality, which has been proven by the large representation of PRO officials at both Men's and Women's FIFA World Cups in 2018 and 2019 (Geiger 2020). As PRO explored online platform options for its training immediately after the lockdown, Zoom and RingCentral were possible candidates to replace face-to-face camps because of PRO staff's familiarity with the systems. Geiger and his colleagues, however, knew that these platforms would not achieve anything close to the experience of having a face-to-face training session. Online training needs to generate instructional worth for the participants (Gregory et al. 2015). Geiger commented, "One of my biggest concerns was how we were going to keep the officials engaged, how we were going to provide education, what platform we were going to use, and how we were going to keep this going" (Geiger 2020). Webb characterized the conundrum as "unique and special" by stating that "the unique and special time needed a unique and special solution" (Webb 2020). PRO was willing to adopt a new tool if it properly met the organization's tangible and intangible needs.

It was in this context of the pandemic's "unique and special" time that PRO decided to test VirBELA. On March 16, 2020, four days after MLS announced that it would suspend its season for thirty days, Bill Dittmar met with Howard Webb and his team to discuss the transition into VirBELA. Dittmar, who was an assistant referee for nineteen years, had used the software to teach adult learners including the NAVY SEALs and other special operators, which give him confidence that the system would be a suitable replacement for PRO during the lockdown. As PRO had to quickly come up with a countermeasure, Dittmar's input was timely.

Although some organizations may not be open to adapting a new unfamiliar system (Fernandez 2017), Geiger explained that as soon as he made his avatar and started moving in the VirBELA environment, he knew the experience was different from Zoom and its equivalents. He explained that he "instantly saw a real benefit to having these camps again, while we were not going to be physically in the same space. But with avatars, we would be able to be there, and have those debates and those dialogues, and training sessions. We saw that they would be replicated in VirBELA that we would not be able to get from the Zoom or RingCentral meetings" (Geiger 2020). As MLS made an additional announcement on March 19 to further extend the season suspension, nine PRO staff members and Steve Taylor, the Executive Director of the Professional Soccer Referees Association, sat in an initial onboarding training to familiarize themselves with the system.

The following fourteen days were busy with onboarding and curriculum development. Seven additional referees were onboarded on March 20. Webb, Geiger, and Dittmar kept in close contact to prepare for the first referee camp on VirBELA scheduled for April 6 to 8. By March 28, not only had all PRO staff members and directors been onboarded, their virtual offices had been set up. Less than a week before the first camp, on April 2, Alan Black, PRO's Head of Coaching, Education, and Evaluation, and Geiger were formally trained as presenters on VirBELA. In the meantime, PRO staff generated course materials for its first camp on VirBELA as creating well-conceived training required an instructional design that took technology, delivery modes, instructors, learners (referees), and other resources into consideration (Genc and Tinmaz 2016; Yang 2017; Jan and Vlachopoulos 2018). Furthermore, creating challenging, thought-provoking content would improve training's educational value (Carpenter and Pease 2012).

From the beginning, referees found VirBELA easy to use and felt as if they were with other referees at a camp. Rubiel Vazquez, one of the MLS referees and also a FIFA referee, commented that once he created his avatar and explored the virtual environment, he felt that the software was "straightforward and self-explanatory" (Vazquez 2020). Chico Grajeda, an MLS referee with sixteen years of experience in the league, noted the initial encounter with VirBELA was easy and straightforward, although he admitted he was "not the most technically gifted person." Grajeda remembers that after making his own avatar, he logged on to VirBELA several days before the first VirBELA camp. Both Dittmar and Paul Scott, another retired MLS assistant referee, happened to be on VirBELA. Grajeda shared this experience by stating, "You get to see them. You know it's virtual. But that guy looks like Bill. The other guy looks like Paul. We ended up spending probably an hour together on campus, just chatting. It felt like we were together" (Grajeda 2020). This sense of togetherness demonstrated the intangible needs of PRO that VirBELA was able to offer as compared to a video conferencing system.

REFEREE TRAINING ON VIRBELA

Interaction in a virtual learning environment lends itself to a more dynamic training. Learners are originators of their own education, as they can move about and access various forms of educational resources (Nunes et al. 2018). In addition, learners tend to enjoy classes, have increased engagement, and are more attentive in virtual learning environments than in a more traditional setting (Wrzesein and Raya 2010). Despite these theoretical promises, as PRO held its first virtual camp between April 6 and 8, 2020, Geiger admitted he did not know what to expect. Webb and Geiger did not know how engaged referees would be or how much they would talk (Geiger 2020). This was a crucial concern for the success of the training because collaborative learning enables learners, in this case referees, to shift from a passive role to a more active role in their own educational experiences (Svendsen and Mondahl 2013). In addition, each stakeholder needs to be highly proactive in the learning environment and provide insight into how the experience can provide for improved learning opportunities (Wagner, Hassanien, and Head 2008). The quality of personal interaction was key to successful training for PRO.

On VirBELA, PRO was able to provide its learners with the ability to move about, explore, increase engagement, and have a sense of belonging and space. Despite a few challenges on VirBELA, which will be noted below, PRO staff and referees found the software easy to use and navigate, and felt they were in a space with their peers. Geiger remembers when he entered his VirBELA office for the first time, he had to sit his avatar down. He said, "I felt that [my avatar] was actually there and was going to get tired if it had to stand the whole time." Geiger continued, "so it had this feeling of being there" (Geiger 2020). Grajeda's earlier comment echoes Geiger's observation. VirBELA was able to meet both the tangible and intangible needs that PRO had identified as it transitioned from face-to-face to fully virtual.

Engagement, Interaction, and Space

VirBELA enabled PRO to recreate PRO's own space. Each PRO referee created an avatar and attended sessions in a passcode protected virtual office floor. Referees moved their avatars using their keyboard and mouse, similar to how one moves in an online game environment. In this virtual space, PRO rented seven virtual offices and access to a large conference room that seated sixty-five people. Each office had a name sign outside. Inside each office was a picture that each office occupant put on a wall, allowing referees to see familiar faces. The hallway that connected the offices and the training room featured a few group pictures of referees, again, showing familiar faces. The training room had a sign that read, "Professional Referee Organization Training Room." With all the pictures in offices and the hallway, PRO-specific signs, and presentation materials with PRO logos, the virtual space looked like it belonged to PRO and its referees. All these small but important features created "a sense of ownership of a physical space" (Webb 2020). This observation is consistent with scholarship on environmental customization, suggesting that it stimulates learners to gain different perspectives and insights than in a generic environment (Dickey 2005).

The sense of space also contributes to a sense of being together. In a virtual world, participants would not have to move their heads to look at the person speaking to hear others better as the sound is transmitted through the earpiece. However, referees have been caught turning their avatar head to the speaker, as they would in real life. The dynamics among referees were also generally consistent. Grajeda shared that finding a table in a conference room was "no different from a real camp." He continued, "You step in a classroom and you try to sit next to your friends." VirBELA has recreated the in-person training room in a virtual space. Another referee noted, VirBELA was "the closest to a classroom we [could] get. Here, there is more interaction. I really like about this. It's more personal. You feel like you are there, walking. I really like that" (Vazquez 2020). Enabling referees to feel as if they were with their peers helped achieve PRO's intangible goals.

VirBELA's ability to provide interactions and engagement was significant. Vazquez noticed that VirBELA was "a little more complicated than Zoom or RingCentral but was more social." Referees were able to move around, sit down at a table, and interact with each other. While a conference call system can have breakout rooms, chats, and polls, as Vazquez noted, "on Zoom, you cannot really move. You're stuck in one place. Here you feel more freedom to move." In some instances, referees were instructed to walk to different parts of the room depending on their decision on an incident, e.g., no foul or a foul. Such flexibility enabled more classroom-like interactions. In his interview, Vazquez frequently characterized VirBELA as "just like a camp" (Vazquez 2020). Both in terms of technical features and emotional connections, referees felt that their community continued to exist despite the pandemic.

The virtual environment afforded more flexibility with breakout sessions. During a regular face-to-face camp before the pandemic, referees would break into small groups to discuss a clip or an incident. Reserving small conference rooms can be expensive. As a result, these breakout sessions would happen in hotel rooms. Walking to a room, finding a place to sit, and configuring a bedroom for a breakout session can take time. Even after a session, walking back to the main conference room takes extra time. With a few clicks on VirBELA, referees found themselves in their respective breakout room, minimizing the time lost while achieving the relocation. Vazquez noted that even though virtual breakout sessions were possible on a conference call system, moving from one room to another virtually made these sessions more realistic (Vazquez 2020).

The ability to communicate among referees was also crucial. VirBELA allowed different ways of communication: such as chat, speech, file sharing, screen sharing, and video sharing. Diverse communication methods are vital in virtual instruction (Vlachopoulos and Makri 2019). Referees could choose to talk only with those sitting at the same table or present their opinion about a game incident to everyone in the room. Audio-based communication allowed for a realistic, articulate, participative experience (Trespalacios and Uribe-Florez 2019). From having a small discussion at a table to having breakout room discussions, and to presenting in front of a larger group, participating referees turned themselves into a positive, communicative community of learners, a key component for successful virtual training (Wragg 2019).

Challenges and Countermeasures

The referees had varying degrees of familiarity and fluency with technology in general. Geiger stated, "anytime you introduce a new technology to a new group of people with all different levels of experiences with using different technologies," some technical troubles are unavoidable (Geiger 2020). Users may feel overwhelmed by technology or may be less enthusiastic about learning a new technology (Dickey 2011; Dayag 2018). At the beginning, it was common to have an avatar stand up by accident during a class when a user accidentally hit a wrong key. Depending on the Wi-Fi quality, one might get disconnected from a session and have to log back on. One's Internet bandwidth, hardware, firewalls, client interface, and more simple issues may impact the quality of learning (Warburton 2009; Dickenson, Burgoyne, and Pedler 2010). While VirBELA includes various setting options to ensure low-performing computers could still handle the software, the potential for technical difficulties is inherent to any technology-mediated communication.

One of the major concerns for PRO was the quality of video feed, because video clips are a fundamental part of referee training not only to reflect on the accuracy of a decision but also to analyze numerous topics including the severity of a foul, point of contact, and speed of a tackle. A choppy or of low-resolution video clip due to a poor internet connection or a low computer specification will impact the quality of training. Although participants generally agreed that videos ran with less latency on VirBELA than on Zoom and its equivalents, there still were some. On this point, Webb argued that, "all platforms have limits" (Webb 2020). The key to realizing a successful camp was to understand the limits associated with the platform and generate a countermeasure. PRO uploaded all the video clips to BOX, a cloud-based file sharing service, so that referees could watch and download them in advance. They could also watch the clips on their device while in a virtual classroom.

Another difficulty with VirBELA was associated with equipment. Unlike full-time referees, PRO's assistant referees did not have a PRO-issued laptop. Although the PRO staff and full-time referees had a laptop with which they could use VirBELA, some assistant referees only had a laptop issued by their employer. Without their own personal laptop, some were unable to download the software to their work laptop. Consequently, a clinic cannot happen exclusively on VirBELA when these assistant referees are invited. For some assistant referees, meeting PRO staff on VirBELA was not an option and they had to rely on RingCentral or phone calls.

Not being able to see each other's faces posed a unique challenge to instructors. Geiger, who had previously taught in high schools for seventeen years, was careful with calling on his referees. He recognized that some feel uncomfortable being singled out or cannot be called upon for their special needs. However, in a face-to-face setting, someone's facial expression may suggest they have something to share. This was the case both with high school students and referees. "A lot of the ways I teach is based on the feedback I am getting, the body language I am getting from individual students in the classroom or the referees in the session. And that is one thing you miss in this," said Geiger (2020). Fortunately, having known PRO officials for many years, in some cases for over a decade, he knew who was generally willing to share their ideas, who would not mind being called upon, and who he needed to wait for to speak up.

In general, referees felt that the sense of space that VirBELA provided gave them a stronger feeling of being together with their peer referees than simply seeing each other's faces. Despite the challenge posed by not being able to see each other, Webb learned that while some participants preferred to see other people's faces, not all referees felt so (Webb 2020). Similarly, Grajeda noted that he and his fellow referees enjoyed using avatars. While the avatars looked like them, there were some differences. He jokingly stated that he liked that his avatar was slimmer than he was. His peers looked for what others' avatars would be dressed in for the second day of a training session. They could try to make the avatar look as close to themselves as possible, or they could make it completely different. Referees enjoyed the flexibility.

BEYOND FORMAL TRAINING

PRO was not only concerned about the content of its referee training but also the psychological and emotional support for its referees. The suspension of the matches and face-to-face training caused a severe sense of uncertainty. For example, Vazquez had just been promoted as a FIFA referee on January 1, 2020. Two months later, the season was suspended. He remembered that initially the suspension was only for a short period of time. But soon, it was extended. It did not take long until referees started feeling as though the season might not happen at all (Vazquez 2020). Grajeda was already on his way to a match in Orlando, Florida, when he was told the game was canceled. Just like everyone else, he did not know if the suspension would be only for a few weeks, a few months, or longer. He found the experience to be "surreal" and "scary" (Vazquez 2020). PRO had to make sure the referees felt supported and heard.

As early as April 15, PRO instructors started offering virtual office hours. They set 2 p.m. to 3 p.m. from Monday to Thursday as their office hours so referees could join to discuss anything. Beyond regular learning, online formats can offer a more personalized feel that can lend itself to a teacher-learner mentor style relationship (Thomson 2010). Without having face-to-face camps where a referee could approach one of the instructors for advice or where referees might find themselves talking to a referee coach in a hallway, referees could have easily felt the support system disappeared as the season was suspended. PRO's countermeasure was to offer office hours on VirBELA where they could bump into each other more naturally.

Webb's contact with referees increased during the lockdown. Before the lockdown, referees could have spoken to Webb by phone and he would have welcomed such calls. But few referees did so. With VirBELA, Webb noted, more referees were willing to swing by to chat during his office hours (Webb 2020). Vazquez agreed. He found it was easier to use VirBELA office hours than making a phone call. He felt a phone call was more casual and "social." VirBELA office hours provide a "more professional atmosphere" (Vazquez 2020). As Juan and Steegmann (2010) noted, professionalism is a key component of online learning. Grajeda also took advantage of the office hours held by PRO staff. He has shared his feelings with both Webb and Geiger that on VirBELA, "it [felt] just like when we got together." He continued to feel togetherness and support. He has swung by Webb's office to talk about the clinic. He felt as if he had been at a hotel in Dallas and met Webb in the lobby. Office hours on VirBELA felt professional and private. Especially for the younger generation of referees, a virtual system of this kind came naturally (Grajeda 2020).

OTHER BENEFITS

Using avatars also created a unique engagement experience. For one of the sessions, referees were told to dress their avatars in a particular color shirt. The shirt color designated each referee's breakout group for the day. Avatars were used as a strategic tool to increase engagement and collaboration, key components to realize quality training (Sullivan and Freishtat 2013; Barnett 2015; Vlachopoulos and Makri 2019). In addition, after a breakout session, the instructor was able to call on referees from different breakout groups, simply based on the color of their shirt (Geiger 2020).

The use of avatars also avoided privacy concerns. A webcam might disclose people's private lives more than they choose to, from what the inside of their house looks like, to having other members of the household accidentally jumping in front of the camera. Zoom's virtual background and other functions address some of these issues, but even the question of whether one should feel obliged to have their camera on or off, or if a moderator can or should make participants turn on a camera, have caused some controversy (Lorenz, Griffith, and Isaac 2020; Marks 2020). VirBELA enabled its participants to stay clear of such privacy concerns. Because there was so much interaction among referees before, during, and after training sessions, referees experienced high levels of interactions and engagements without compromising their privacy (Webb 2020).

Vazquez also explained that on VirBELA, because of its mobile flexibility, he did not have to miss any instruction. When a referee needs to leave a physical meeting room for whatever the reason, including going to the bathroom, they would miss at least a few minutes of instructions. Especially during the period when a referee juggled their professional and personal responsibilities at home, this was important. On VirBELA, they could even walk to the bathroom or kitchen with their laptop, allowing them to not miss any instruction.

Not having to travel every two weeks also came with its own advantages. Webb reflected that purely from the carbon footprint perspective, not having face-to-face camps for which referees flew from all over the country was a significant positive. Additionally, referees did not have to spend time away from home. Webb noted even those who liked traveling appreciated being able to stay at home and having to dedicate a smaller amount of time for a clinic (Webb 2020). Vazquez commented that not having to travel was "huge" (Vazquez 2020). Grajeda concurred by calling the reduced traveling "fantastic." Virtual training can significantly increase time with family (Grajeda 2020). Reflecting upon his final years as an active referee, Geiger remembered having spent more than 200 days away from home. Although many of these travel days were for international tournaments and games, many were for camps. From the perspective of life-work balance and minimizing fatigue associated with traveling, having clinics on VirBELA was viewed positively by both instructors and referees.

The financial savings from canceling even just one face-to-face camp and holding it on VirBELA can be significant for PRO. Flying twenty-six referees to Minnesota or Texas for a multiple-day camp can be "incredibly costly." From airfare and hotel rooms, to meals and conference rooms, costs quickly add up. The savings may allow PRO to supply laptops to assistant referees who were unable to download VirBELA on their work computers. Because the cost of a referee camp on VirBELA is so low, PRO could offer more training opportunities to different groups of referees. PRO's video assistant referees, for example, only have three clinics in a year. Referee assessors' clinics are also limited in number. Similarly, Geiger stated that future PRO referees in training—so called "PRO2" referees—could also listen in at VirBELA clinics (Geiger 2020).

Conclusion

The lives of MLS referees are unique. Even though they work with a select small group of colleagues, they only work with each other on a match a few times a year. Physical distance prevents them from seeing each other except for at a game or at a camp. However, in interviews, PRO staff and referees repeatedly highlighted their strong sense of community. As athletes themselves, losing training opportunities even for a few months can have damaging consequences to their career. It was vital that referees continued to feel supported and be trained without any quality compromises.

Grajeda summarized his experience eloquently by stating, "we became successful by spending time together, not away from each other. We got to know each other's spouse, parents, siblings, dogs, brothers, and sisters [VirBELA] was a very good option to give us a sense that we were still together. We can hear each other's voices. Avatars might be a little off, but the voices are still there." He continued, "This would not have happened on RingCentral. They will block their camera. They will put a fake picture. This one, you see a face [though] it might not be a human face." But one can feel they are among their peers (Grajeda 2020). Similarly, Vazquez commented, "I feel incredibly supported. It always feels like that they're there supporting you. [Feeling not supported] never even crossed my mind" (Vazquez 2020).

Months of training on VirBELA hints what might happen with virtual training for PRO referees in the future. Geiger suggested, "if we are going to have the same outcome, same learning happening [on VirBELA that we can achieve face-to-face], then [continuing to use it] is something that we can certainly do" (Geiger 2020). In any referee training, being deliberate about training methods and content is important (MacMahon et al. 2007; Samuel 2017). Having clear views on what a session should achieve, as PRO already does, will enable the group to maximize its financial investment and time investment. As Geiger characterized, "Is [VirBELA] perfect? No. Perfect is meeting in Dallas or Minneapolis like we have done for the past eight years. But this has become a viable resource going forward for us. We are not losing much at all" (Geiger 2020).

REFERENCES

Armenteros, M., Anto J. Benítez, R. Flores, M. Sillero-Quintana, M. Sánchez Cid, and J.A. Simón. 2018. "The Training of Soccer Assistant Referees Beyond On-field Experience: The Use of the Interactive Video Test." *International Journal of Computer Science in Sport* 17 (2): 163-174. https://doi.org/10.2478/ijcss-2018-0009.

Burnett, Cathy. 2016. "Being Together in Classrooms at the Interface of the Physical and Virtual: Implications for Collaboration in on/Off-Screen Sites." *Learning, Media and Technology* 41 (4): 566-589. https://doi-org/10.1080/17439884.2015.1050036.

Carpenter, Jeffrey P., and Jennifer S. Pease. 2012. "Sharing the Learning: Instead of Pushing More Responsibility for Learning onto Teachers, Let's Consider New Models in Which Students Assume Greater Responsibility for Their Own Learning. (New Styles of Instruction)." *Phi Delta Kappan* 94 (2): Gale Academic OneFile.

Dayag, Joseph Decena. 2018. "EFL Virtual Learning Environments: Perception, Concerns and Challenges." *Teaching English with Technology* 16 (4): 20-33. EBSCOhost.

Dickenson, Mollie, John Burgoyne, and Mike Pedler. 2020. "Virtual Action Learning: Practices and Challenges." *Action Learning: Research and Practice* 7 (1): 59-72. Taylor & Francis Online.

Dickey, Michele D. 2011. "The Pragmatics of Virtual Worlds for K-12 Educators: Investigating the Affordances and Constraints of 'Active Worlds' and 'Second Life' with K-12 in-Service Teachers." *Educational Technology Research and Development* 59 (1): 1-20. ProQuest.

Dickey, Michele D. 2005. "Three-Dimensional Virtual Worlds and Distance Learning: Two Case Studies of Active Worlds as a Medium for Distance Education." *British Journal of Educational Technology* 36 (3): 439-51. BERA.

Etherington, Nicole, Linda Baker, Marlene Ham, and Denise Glasbeek. 2017. "Evaluating the Effectiveness of Online Training for a Comprehensive Violence against Women Program: A Pilot Study." *Journal of Interpersonal Violence*. https://doi-org/10.1177/0886260517725734.

Fernandez, Manuel. 2017. "Augmented-Virtual Reality: How to Improve Education Systems." *Higher Learning Research Communications* 7 (1): 1-15. https://doi-org/10.18870/hlrc.v7i1.373.

Geiger, Mark. 2020. PRO Director of Senior Match Officials. Interview by authors. July 2, 2020.

Genç, Zülfü, and Hasan Tinmaz. 2016. "The Perception on Fundamentals of Online Courses: A Case on Prospective Instructional Designers." *European Journal of Contemporary Education* 15 (1): 163-172. EBSCOhost.

Grajeda, Chico. 2020. MLS Referee. Interview by authors. July 1, 2020.

Gregory, Sue, Sheila Scutter, Lisa Jacka, Marcus McDonald, Helen Farley, and Chris Newman. 2015. "Barriers and Enablers to the Use of Virtual Worlds in Higher Education: An Exploration of Educator Perceptions, Attitudes and Experiences." *Journal of Educational Technology & Society* 18 (1): 3-12. Gale Academic OneFile.

Gulec, Ulas, Murat Yilmaz, Veysi Isler, Rory V. O'Connor, and Paul M. Clarke. 2018. "A 3D Virtual Environment for Training Soccer Referees." *Computer Standards & Interfaces* 64: 1-10. https://doi.org/10.1016/j.csi.2018.11.004.

Jan, Shazia K., and Panos Vlachopoulos. 2018. "Influence of Learning Design of the Formation of Online Communities of Learning." *International Review of Research in Open and Distributed Learning* 19 (4). https://doi.org/10.19173/irrodl.v19i4.3620.

Juan, Angel A., Cristina Steegmann, Antonia Huertas, M. Jesus Martinez, and J. Simosa. 2011. "Teaching Mathematics Online in the European Area of Higher Education: An Instructor's Point of View." *International Journal of Mathematical Education in Science and Technology* 42 (2): 141-53. Taylor & Francis Online.

Jung, Insung, and Ilju Rha. 2000. "Effectiveness and Cost-Effectiveness of Online Education: A Review of the Literature." *Educational Technology* 40 (4): 57-60. JSTOR.

Kizilet, Ali. 2011. "Using Distance Physical Education in Elite Class Soccer Referee Training: A Case Study." *The Turkish Online Journal of Educational Technology* 10 (3): 328-339.

Lorenz, Taylow, Erin Griffith, and Mike Isaac. 2020. "We Live in Zoom Now: Zoom is Where We Work, Go to School, and Party These Days." *New York Times*, March 17, 2020. https://www.nytimes.com/2020/03/17/style/zoom-parties-coronavirus-memes.html.

MacMahon, Clare, Werner F. Helsen, Janet L, Starkes, and Matthew Weston. 2007. "Decision-making Skills and Deliberate Practice in Elite Association Football Referees." *Journal of Sports Sciences* 25 (1): 65-78. https://doi.org/10.1080/02640410600718640.

Marks, Gene. 2020. "On CRM: Should You, or Should You Not Turn on Your Camera for That Zoom Meeting?" *Forbes*, March 1, 2020. https://www.forbes.com/sites/quickerbettertech/2020/05/01/on-crm-should-you-or-should-you-not-turn-on-your-camera-for-that-zoom-meeting/#7e062491bb06.

Nunes, Felipe Becker, Aliane Loureiro Krassmann, Liane Margarida Rockenbach Tarouco, and José Valdeni De Lima. 2018. "A Teaching Method Based on Virtual Worlds and Mastery Learning." *Journal for Virtual Worlds Research* 11 (3): 1-15. EBSCOhost.

Samuel, Roy David. 2017. "Training Prospective Soccer Referees Using a Deliberate Practice Perspective: The Israeli Excellence Program." *Journal of Sports Psychology in Action* 8 (3): 184-196. https://doi.org/10.1080/21520704.2017.1287798.

Samuel, Roy David, Yair Galily, Or Guy, Elad Sharoni, Gershon Tenenbaum. 2019. "A Decision-making Simulator for Soccer Referees." *International Journal of Sports Science & Coaching* 14 (4): 480-489. https://doi.org/10.1177/1747954119858696.

Schweizer, Geoffrey, Henning Plessner, Daniela Kahlert, and Ralf Brand. 2011. "A Video-based Training Method for Improving Soccer Referees' Intuitive Decision-Making Skills." *Journal of Applied Sport Psychology* 23 (4): 429-442. https://doi.org/10.1080/10413200.2011.555346.

Soffer, Tal, and Rafi Nachmias. 2018. "Effectiveness of Learning in Online Academic Courses Compared with Face-to-Face Courses in Higher Education." *Journal of Computer Assisted Learning* 34 (5): 534-543. Wiley Online Library.

Sullivan, Timothy M., and Richard Freishtat. 2013. "Extending Learning Beyond the Classroom: Graduate Student Experiences of Online Discussions in a Hybrid Course." *Journal of Continuing Higher Education* 61 (1): 12-22. Taylor & Francis Online.

Svendsen, Lisbet, and Margrethe Smedegaard Mondahl. 2013. "How Social-Media Enhanced Learning Platforms Support Students in Taking Responsibility for Their Own Learning." *Journal of Applied Research in Higher Education* 5 (2): 261-272. Emerald Insight.

Thomson, Dana L. 2010. "Beyond the Classroom Walls: Teachers' and Students' Perspectives on How Online Learning Can Meet the Needs of Gifted Students." *Journal of Advanced Academics* 21 (4): 662-712. Gale Academic OneFile.

Trespalacios, Jesús, and Lida J. Uribe-Flórez. 2020. "Case Studies in Instructional Design Education: Students' Communication Preferences During Online Discussions." *E-Learning and Digital Media* 17 (1): 21-35. Sage Journals.

Vazquez, Rubiel. 2020. MLS and FIFA referee. Interview by authors, June 26, 2020.

Vlachopoulos, Dimitrios, and Agoritsa Makri. 2019. "Online Communication and Interaction in Distance Higher Education: A Framework Study of Good Practice." *International Review of Education* 65 (4): 605-632. Springer Link.

Wagner, Nicole, Khaled Hassanein, and Milena Head. 2008. "Who Is Responsible for E-Learning Success in Higher Education? A Stakeholders' Analysis." *Journal of Educational Technology & Society* 11 (3): 26-36. ProQuest.

Webb, Howard. 2020. PRO General Manager. Interview by authors. June 12, 2020.

Webb, Tom. 2020. "The Future of Officiating: Analysing the Impact of COVID-19 on Referees in World Football." *Soccer & Society*. https://doi.org/10.1080/14660970.2020.1768634

Wragg, Nicole. 2019. "Online Communication Design Education: The Importance of the Social Environment." *Studies in Higher Education*: 1-11. Taylor & Francis Online.

Wrzesien, Maja, and Mariano Alcañiz Raya. 2010. "Learning in Serious Virtual Worlds: Evaluation of Learning Effectiveness and Appeal to Students in the E-Junior Project." *Computers & Education* 55 (1): 178-187. Science Direct.

Yang, Dazhi. 2017. "Instructional Strategies and Course Design for Teaching Statistics Online: Perspectives from Online Students." *International Journal of STEM Education* 4 (1): 1-15.

Individual Sports

CHAPTER 13

Between Self-Interest and Solidarity: European Football and the Covid-19 Lockdown

Alan McDougall

INTRODUCTION

The 2020 European Football Championship should have been a celebration of the world's most popular sport. For the tournament's sixtieth birthday, the Union of European Football Associations (UEFA) organized a continent-crossing tribute to what the tournament's founder, Frenchman Henri Delaunay, once called "a footballing Europe" (Goldblatt 2006, 399). Matches in Euro 2020 were scheduled for twelve cities in twelve countries, from Bilbao in Spain to Baku in Azerbaijan.

Long before China began to report cases of Covid-19 in December 2019, critics felt that Euro 2020 might be a European vanity project too far. Football Supporters Europe, the continent's largest fan network, rejected what then UEFA president Michel Platini described as a "zany" but "good" plan when he announced it in 2012 (Riach 2012). Industry insiders raised questions about infrastructural costs, diminished sponsorship and tourism opportunities, and a fracturing of the "euphoric" sense of community often seen at major sports events (Stura et al. 2017, 30-34).

As Covid-19 infections spread from Asia to Europe in early 2020, a tournament designed around cross-border travel looked increasingly problematic. UEFA initially held firm. On March 3, Platini's successor Alexsander Čeferin deflected fears that Euro 2020 would be postponed: "Let's be optimistic and not talk about dark scenarios" (Klosok 2020). European football's collective denial lasted another week. On March 11, the day that the World Health Organization declared Covid-19 a global pandemic, Liverpool F.C. hosted Atlético Madrid in a round of sixteen clash in UEFA's flagship club competition, the Champions League. The crowd of 52,000 included 3,000 Atlético supporters, allowed to enter the United Kingdom despite the fact that Madrid was a Covid-19 hotspot and Spain in partial lockdown. Evidence later suggested a spike in Covid-19 cases in Liverpool a few weeks after the game (Thorp 2020).

Events moved rapidly beyond UEFA's control. Within days of the WHO proclamation, leagues across Europe were suspended. On March 17, UEFA bowed to the inevitable and postponed Euro 2020 until 2021. Acknowledging "the biggest crisis" in the game's 160-year history, Alexsander Čeferin now sang from a different hymn sheet. "There is no more time for selfishness," he warned. "This is a reset for world football" (R. Smith 2020).

This essay examines the unprecedented global shutdown of football in March and April 2020, focusing on the sport's historical and commercial heartland, Europe. It places Čeferin's call for a "reset" in the context of the competing but overlapping interests of European football's stakeholders—the Fédération Internationale de Football Association (FIFA), UEFA, national associations, clubs, players, supporters, and broadcasters—in this period. After brief scrutiny of previous disruptions to the football calendar, there is an overview of the crisis as it unfolded in March and April. Using cross-continental examples, and a suitably international array of scholarly and media sources, the essay then explores how a mixture of self-interest and solidarity presented a rhetoric of unity in the European football family that did not always survive close inspection.

European football's "time out" created an uncertain landscape, in which the sport's embrace of late capitalism—an economic model that concentrates wealth in a few hands and radically widens the gap between rich and poor—was questioned but not rejected. While stakeholders protected their interests, there were encouraging signs of solidarity, from a rapprochement between FIFA and UEFA to community projects across the continent. In the spring of 2020, possibilities existed for a reimagined football world, built (in the words of Liverpool manager Jürgen Klopp) on "sound judgment and morality" (Klopp 2020). But these possibilities were harder to enact than to discuss, especially amid the anxious instability of these months. Though it remains too early for definitive conclusions, European football's Covid-19 hiatus, I argue, was most likely just that—a temporary interruption to the norm, when ideas about structural reform or wealth redistribution mattered less than one-off acts of charity and the first divisive rumblings about restarting football. In this, the game reflected wider European responses to the pandemic. Market orthodoxies ensured that the show went on.

THE BIGGEST CRISIS IN FOOTBALL'S HISTORY?

European football had faced major disruptions before 2020. The First World War stopped international matches and domestic competitions across the continent. Two thousand of Britain's 5,000 professional players enlisted, as the country's leading sport became an effective propaganda and recruitment tool (Walvin 1994, 93). The influenza ("Spanish flu") pandemic that killed fifty million people worldwide between 1918 and 1920 exacerbated the wartime disturbance. At the virus's peak in Switzerland in the autumn of 1919, fifty-five of seventy matches in the national football league were canceled (Jost and Attwood 2020).

By the Second World War, governments were reluctant to shut down football, which had attained global popularity during the inter-war years. A British Mass Observation report noted in 1939 that "people find the war at present completely unsatisfactory as a compensation for sport" (Goldblatt 2006, 297). But no competition in combatant countries survived unscathed. In Poland, ground zero of the Nazis' war of racial extermination, league football disappeared between 1939 and 1946. In another Nazi-occupied country, Norway, there was no championship between 1940 and 1947. With Dynamo Moscow atop the table, the outbreak of war with Germany forced the cancellation of the 1941 Soviet league after ten games. National competition did not return until 1945 (Tovar 2020, 2-4).

Football, then, had been interrupted before—and not only due to war. Bitterly cold winters in 1946/47 and 1962/63 played havoc with fixtures in England. Player strikes delayed seasons in Norway (in 2002) and Italy (in 2011). None of these stoppages prepared the football world for Covid-19. During the influenza pandemic, matches in England and Spain continued in front of large crowds, regardless of the public health implications. Ninety thousand people watched Rapid Vienna's 4-3 defeat of Schalke 04 in the German championship final on June 22, 1941, the day that the Wehrmacht invaded the Soviet Union (McDougall 2020, 151). The ball kept rolling, even in the unlikeliest settings. Soldiers played football in No Man's Land on the Western Front in 1914. Prisoners played at Auschwitz thirty years later.

There was no leeway in 2020. In the absence of a vaccine, the most effective measure to counter Covid-19 was social distancing. This made travel and team training impossible and large crowds in stadiums dangerous. The blanket nature of the Covid-19 lockdown pushed football into uncharted waters. Alexsander Čeferin was not alone in describing the challenge in cataclysmic terms. On March 14, Borussia Dortmund president Hans-Joachim Watzke called the pandemic "the biggest crisis" in German football history (kicker 2020a).

THE GREAT SHUTDOWN, MARCH-APRIL 2020

When Alexsander Čeferin counselled optimism about Euro 2020 on March 3, European football's mantra was still business as usual. Covid-19 headlines announced cosmetic changes, such as the English Premier League (EPL) prohibiting pre-match handshakes between teams or Bayern Munich's ban on players signing autographs. The Swiss Super League was suspended on March 2, but, as of March 10, only three European leagues had followed suit, in Austria, Italy, and Portugal. On March 9, the U.K. government—advocating a "herd immunity" approach to Covid-19 and led by a Prime Minister, Boris Johnson, who boasted of shaking hands "with everybody" (Mason 2020)—insisted that there was "no reason" to cancel sports events (BBC Sport 2020).

The WHO declaration of a global pandemic on March 11 transformed the situation. The shutdown of European football was as sudden as it was unparalleled. Worldwide, 105 countries canceled professional football between March 12 and 18 (Tovar 2020, 5). This included almost every country in Europe, from England, which suspended the continent's wealthiest competition, the Premier League, on March 13, to the Faroe Islands, where the start of the new season in the Betri League (scheduled for March 8 then March 15) was indefinitely delayed. This hectic period saw the postponement of every forthcoming men's international tournament, including the European Championship, the Copa América, and the Africa Cup of Nations. UEFA canceled all games in its club competitions, the Champions League and the Europa League. The finals, scheduled for May, were not assigned new dates. Europe's governing body earned cautious praise for its flexible and inclusive management of the March crisis (Conn 2020; R. Smith 2020). In truth, it had few other options. Football's vulnerability to the pandemic demanded a united response.

The last major European league to close down was Turkey's Super Lig on March 19. After that, the only competition left standing was the Belarusian Premier League. The new season opened on March 19, as Energetik-BGU Minsk defeated BATE Borisov 3-1 in front of 730 people. The country's president Alexander Lukashenko claimed that "there are no viruses here" and advocated sport, saunas, and vodka as remedies for Covid-19. No restrictions were placed on attending live sport. Belarus's top division soon attracted football-starved international audiences. The country's football federation announced television deals with ten countries, including India, Israel, Russia, and Ukraine (Kostin and Vasilyeva 2020).

While Belarusian football enjoyed an unlikely moment in the spotlight, the rest of the football world struggled into an alien landscape. In the short term, debate concentrated on how, when, and if European domestic seasons could be finished. Approaches varied. Some competitions, including the EPL, Spain's La Liga, the Bundesliga, and Serie A, kept options alive for a return to action. Others, often controversially, cut their losses. In early April, Belgium's Pro League became the first top-flight competition to cancel the 2019/20 season. Leaders Club Brugges were declared champions. France's Ligue 1 did likewise at the end of the month, as Paris Saint-Germain claimed the championship. Relegated Amiens subsequently started legal proceedings against the Ligue de Football Professionnel (LFP) for what club president Bernard Joannin called the "unjust" decision to freeze standings with ten games to play (J. Smith 2020). Second-placed Rangers publicly questioned the digital vote to end the Scottish Premier League season, a decision that paved the way for rivals Celtic to claim a ninth straight title. The Dutch FA meanwhile angered affected clubs by voiding the Eredivisie season, with no champion and no promotion or relegation.

Discussions about completing seasons shaded into larger economic concerns. UEFA claimed that an outright cancellation of Euro 2020 would have cost the organization €400 million. Postponement until 2021 still cost €300 million (Marcotti 2020). Spanish giants Barcelona announced that Covid-19 had cost €50 million in ticket sales, €39 million in TV income, and up to €25 million in commercial income (Kuper 2020b). However, Barcelona's annual revenue in 2017/18 topped €1 billion, a record figure for any sports club. In the same year, UEFA earned more than €2.5 billion from its club competitions (UEFA 2018). It was hard in either case to cry poverty.

Crisis came lower down the pyramid. Small clubs, reliant on gate receipts rather than television to cover expenses (chiefly wages), faced dire prospects. On March 30, seven-time Slovakian champions MŠK Žilina became the first top-level European club to declare bankruptcy during the Covid-19 crisis, after players allegedly rejected wage cuts of up to 80%. A few weeks later, second-division Belgian club Lokeren went bust, after failing to find an investor to cover debts of €5 million. Off the field, the suspension of matchday operations devastated the small businesses (concession stall owners, food vendors, local pubs and cafes) and club staff (cleaners, receptionists, stewards) that made up modern football's gig economy. The women's game, one of European football's success stories, faced new uncertainties. FIFPro, the world players' union, warned on April 16 that the Covid-19 crisis left many female players "at great risk of losing their livelihoods" (FIFPro 2020). A week later, UEFA postponed the 2021 Women's European Championship—now in direct competition with the rescheduled men's tournament—until 2022.

In the men's game, economic concerns were sometimes disguised as claims about football's cultural importance. Martin Kind, the majority shareholder at German second division (2. Bundesliga) club Hannover 96, asserted in early April that football's return would give people "trust and hope." He compared the scenario to the emotional boost that the 1954 World Cup victory gave post-war West Germany (Willeke 2020). As Covid-19 death tolls mounted across Europe, such statements seemed absurd. Television stations offered re-runs of classic matches. Housebound footballers competed against each other in FIFA 20 video games. Nothing adequately replaced live football, but the game's sudden cultural marginalization was widely accepted and understood. Economically, it was a different matter. As Peter Ahrens wrote in *Der Spiegel* on April 2: "football might be at a standstill, but the football business is not allowed to be" (Ahrens 2020).

"AT THE END OF THE DAY, IT IS ABOUT MONEY": SELF-INTEREST AND SURVIVAL

After the Bundesliga's shutdown on March 13, Bayern Munich president Karl-Heinz Rummenigge expressed his club's desire to continue the season as soon as it was safe to do so. "At the end of the day," he stated, "it is about money" (kicker 2020b). Media reports that week claimed that German football might lose €770 million in television, ticket, and sponsorship money were the last nine Bundesliga matchdays not played (FAZ 2020). EPL chief executive Richard Masters informed the U.K. government on April 6 that "we face a £1 billion loss, at least, if we fail to complete Season 2019/20" (Masters 2020). Co-dependency between elite competition and television meant that clubs and leagues were not the only stakeholders in trouble. Enders Analysis predicted in late March that Sky and BT Sport, the U.K.'s leading EPL broadcasters, would lose a combined £928 million if matches were not resumed before August (Sweney 2020).

These examples suggest an image of European football that critics would have long recognized: a dominant, market-driven elite concentrated on safeguarding its interests and profits as part of "a Faustian bargain with money and power, the price of which was the game's soul" (McDougall 2020, 192). In March and April 2020, however, self-interest was not just a pejorative term for protecting the reduced but still sizeable revenues of mega-clubs such as Manchester United and Real Madrid. For a far greater number of clubs and individuals, it was a question of survival.

Self-interest and solidarity were not mutually exclusive categories during the lockdown. In mid-March, Borussia Dortmund president Hans-Joachim Watzke drew criticism for questioning whether wealthy Bundesliga clubs, including his own, should support their poorer peers: "At the end of the day, the clubs who have made the effort to put a bit of money aside these past years can't reward those who have not... We're running businesses in a market, and we're in competition" (Marcotti 2020). The club soon changed its tune. On March 26, Borussia Dortmund joined fellow Champions League participants Bayern Munich, Bayer Leverkusen, and RB Leipzig in providing a €20 million aid package to Bundesliga and 2. Bundesliga clubs. Players and management accepted pay cuts of up to 20% to support the club's 850 non-playing staff. By early April, part of Dortmund's Westfalenstadion was a Covid-19 treatment center.

As Dortmund's U-turn suggested, the perception of self-interest was not a good look in the spring of 2020, especially for Europe's wealthiest clubs. Deloitte ranked Dortmund the world's twelfth richest club in 2019. At number seven on the list was Liverpool F.C., a club with a turnover in the 2018/19 season of £533 million. On April 4, the six-time European champion announced that it would take advantage of a government scheme—whereby the state paid 80% of the wages of workers unable to work due to Covid-19—to furlough half of its non-playing staff, a total of 200 people. The backlash was immediate. The idea that such a wealthy club, marketed around community values and the slogan "this means more," would use public money to save a few dollars (approximately £1.5 million) aroused fierce criticism. Supporters' union Spirit of Shankly wrote the club an open letter, recounting the "overwhelmingly negative fan reaction" to the announcement and the damage it did to "our club's reputation and values" (Steinberg 2020). On April 6, Liverpool backtracked. Chief executive Peter Moore admitted that "we came to the wrong conclusion," issued a public apology, and promised to find other ways to protect the club's "entire workforce" from the pandemic's financial fallout (Moore 2020).

Acts, or perceived acts, of selfishness were closely scrutinized in the early months of the lockdown. Old and new media censured footballers—such as Real Madrid's Luka Jović, Douglas Costa (Juventus), and Kyle Walker (Manchester City)—who broke quarantine guidelines. Television companies garnered equally little sympathy. Canal+, one of two channels that screened France's Ligue 1 and Ligue 2, announced in late March that it would withhold a €110 million payment to the LFP after the French season was suspended. "We are not a bank," stated chairman Maxime Saada (L'Equipe 2020). The other provider, Qatari-owned beIN Sports, also suspended payments. After vainly disputing Canal+'s claims, the LFP took a state loan to cover the €224.5 million hole in its budget, thereby easing pressure on the country's forty professional clubs.

For those at the wrong end of European football's late capitalist economy, a place where Lokeren's €5 million debt was less than two months of Brazilian star Neymar's annual salary at Paris Saint-Germain, cutbacks were painful necessities and shortfalls inevitable. Dependent on gate receipts, League of Ireland clubs such as Sligo Rovers and St Patrick's Athletic laid off all playing and non-playing staff. In Croatia, only the ten-team First Football League was professional. Most footballers were considered self-employed. They lacked the legal protections that gave many workers a state-funded minimum wage during the lockdown. The Croatian Football Federation had no common fund to support struggling clubs. First division teams received their share of outstanding broadcast revenues, but this amounted to a modest €1.5 million each (Colucci, Cottrell, and Sethna 2020, 36-38).

In late April, third-tier A.F.C. Fylde became the first women's club in the U.K. to disband due to the pandemic. Though the decision was reversed a month later, Fylde's struggles showed how Covid-19 threatened the growth narrative that had defined the women's game in the past decade. FIFPro urged investment not cuts but conceded that "due to its less established professional leagues, low salaries, narrower scope of opportunities, uneven sponsorship deals and less corporate investment," the Covid-19 crisis exposed "the fragility of the women's football eco-system" (FIFPro 2020).

In the 2020 lockdown, Europe's richest clubs—like the world's largest banks during the 2008/09 financial crisis—were "too big to fail." Restart priorities followed the money, reaffirming the primacy of football as a televisual commodity and elite project. Even if Covid-19 were to reduce the total income of European clubs from its record high of €28.4 billion in 2017/18 to the 2008/09 figure (€15.7 billion), it would hardly be calamitous for the clubs that took most of these profits (Kuper 2020a). There were no certainties for those who got smaller pieces of the pie. In the lower leagues and the women's game, self-interest made solidarity axiomatic. Survival required generous actions and a lowering of the drawbridge that separated the elite men's game from the rest of the sport. The Covid-19 crisis forced powerful stakeholders, however reluctantly or temporarily, to examine the inequities at the core of European football.

Solidarity is Not Lip Service: A Collective Response?

As Covid-19's impact became clearer by the day, a new sense of sobriety entered the football industry. This started at the top. The world game's two most powerful organizations, FIFA and UEFA, had long been at loggerheads over many issues, most notably FIFA president Gianni Infantino's plans to introduce an expanded Club World Cup—a move which clashed with UEFA's plans to consolidate the global hegemony of the Champions League. As late as March 3, Alexsander Čeferin defended UEFA's 38% increase in revenue in 2018/19, calling European football "the greatest success story of modern-day sport," and made veiled criticisms of his FIFA counterpart for putting "profit over purpose" (UEFA 2020a). Turf wars, political posturing, and an ever-expanding schedule seemed to be irremovable features of football geopolitics.

Then, almost overnight, everything changed. Faced with Covid-19, hubris gave way to modesty and competition to cooperation (Conn 2020). Two weeks after his truculent speech of March 3, Čeferin announced the postponement of Euro 2020, negotiated with national associations to extend domestic seasons, and publicly thanked Infantino for showing flexibility about a new football calendar: the shifting of the European Championship to 2021 meant the postponement of Infantino's pet project (and Čeferin's *bête noire*), the Club World Cup. In public statements, both leaders struck conciliatory notes. Infantino's words to Italian newspaper *Gazzetta dello Sport* on March 23 would have been unthinkable a few weeks earlier: "Perhaps we can reform football by taking a step backwards. [There would be] fewer but more interesting competitions, maybe fewer teams but for a better balance, fewer but more competitive matches to preserve players' health" (Kunti 2020). Both organizations established emergency funds for member associations. FIFA announced a €139 million Covid-19 relief fund on April 24. Three days later, UEFA released €236.5 million to its 55 member associations.

The FIFA-UEFA rapprochement highlighted world football's new watchword: solidarity. Across Europe, Liverpool manager Jürgen Klopp's injunction to "think about the vulnerable in our society and act where possible with compassion for them" (Klopp 2020) struck a chord. Enders Analysis had predicted in late March that negotiating players' salary reductions would be "like herding cats" (Sweney 2020). Conservative Health Minister Matt Hancock took aim at the same target. He insisted in early April that Premier League footballers "play their part" in the fight against Covid-19 by accepting pay cuts (Ellen 2020), a shame-inducing request made to no other elite profession in the U.K.

In fact, with occasional exceptions, footballers' responses to the lockdown belied stereotypes about greed and self-absorption. Barcelona announced on March 30 that its players would take a 70% pay cut during the Covid-19 crisis. Italian club Roma declared the following week that its squad would waive four months' wages, effectively a 33% cut to annual salaries. In both cases, the cuts were player-led initiatives. In England, the captains of the twenty EPL teams, spearheaded by Liverpool's Jordan Henderson, announced on April 8 a charitable fund (#PlayersTogether) that sought to raise £4 million for the National Health Service (NHS). VfL Bochum's Simon Zoller partnered with two grassroots organizations to raise funds for Germany's amateur football clubs (DFB 2020). Borussia Dortmund's Marco Reus donated €500,000 to local businesses. These examples were the tip of the iceberg.

Clubs were equally keen to show goodwill. Around the continent, they started community outreach projects, donated money to foodbanks, set up call centers for quarantined fans, and opened facilities to health workers. Real Madrid's Santiago Bernabéu Stadium became a storage and distribution center for medical supplies.

Chelsea made its Millenium Hotel (situated on the site of the club's stadium, Stamford Bridge) available to NHS workers for free. My uncle, a Watford season ticket holder, had a thirty-minute chat with the club's ex-defender, Steve Palmer, one of many phone calls organized by the club's Community Trust in March and April. Every EPL club established systems to connect with elderly and isolated supporters.

Community work was not confined to Europe's wealthiest leagues. In Azerbaijan, players and staff at F.C. Sabah raised more than €25,000 for a national Covid-19 fund. In the Czech Republic, North Bohemian rivals Jablonec and Slovan Liberec donated the proceeds from ticket sales for their postponed derby to a local hospital. The national stadiums in Northern Ireland (Windsor Park in Belfast) and Wales (Cardiff's Principality Stadium) became, respectively, a Covid-19 testing center and an emergency field hospital (UEFA 2020b).

After the Bundesliga's Champions League entrants announced their €20 million donation to fellow clubs on March 26, the CEO of the German Professional League (DFL), Christian Seifert, proudly declared: "This campaign underlines that solidarity in the Bundesliga and 2. Bundesliga is not lip service" (kicker 2020d). Such claims were sincere. Even if they made for good PR, solidarity actions undertaken by top European clubs and players during the Covid-19 crisis were well-intentioned, often generous, and usually beneficial to the recipients, at least in the short term. But what did they ultimately signal?

FIFPro noted in mid-April how the communal rhetoric engendered by the pandemic could benefit women's football. The sport's position "on the margins," the players' union argued, meant that it had long cultivated "non-monetary forms of value," "including important forms of social capital, ties to local communities, player solidarity, and opportunities for education" (FIFPro 2020). It was harder to make such a case for the elite-level men's game, at least with a straight face. Lockdown solidarity there, I would argue, was gestural rather than structural. As more widely in late capitalist societies, feelgood acts of charity functioned as substitutes for, rather than bridges to, substantive redistributions of wealth and power in European football.

Conclusion

In an international survey on football and Covid-19 published on May 5, 2020, the Sports Law and Policy Centre and LawInSport argued that the pandemic offered a chance to make football "more sustainable" (Colucci, Cottrell, and Sethna 2020, 3). The survey proposed three measures to achieve this goal: the creation of emergency reserve funds (financed by clubs proportionate to wealth and ranking); a "revisiting" of the amounts payable in "solidarity mechanisms and training compensation" to provide greater support to clubs "at the grassroots/lower levels"; and a reform of accounting procedures at all clubs that made executives "really and effectively responsible for the budget at their disposal" (Colucci, Cottrell, and Sethna 2020, 10-11).

That think tanks and policy advisors made such prompt recommendations speaks to the apparent appetite for change in European football during the lockdown. It was not only Gianni Infantino and Alexsander Čeferin who bandied around such terms as "reform" and "reset." The entire football industry grappled with existential questions in similar language. Ex-Bayern Munich president Uli Hoeness predicted on March 25 "a new football world": "I can't imagine €100m transfers in the near future" (kicker 2020c). Football podcasts carried titles such as "Covid 360 Where does football go now?" and, more simply, "What next?" It became something of a truism to argue that football might never be the same again.

Was Čeferin's call for a "reset" of world football a rhetorical device, or a harbinger of change? It is worth remembering the cautionary note in the same March 17 interview, where the UEFA president emphasized the "extreme solidarity" in football's response to the Covid-19 crisis: "So I'm optimistic. But let's see. You know, when the crisis hits, we act sometimes a bit differently than we do after the crisis finishes" (R. Smith 2020). Fevered discussion about the future of European football was, in part at least, a diversion unto itself, i.e., a means of filling the void created by the absence of on-field action. It did not necessarily have to lead anywhere. As the Mexican writer Carlos Monsiváis once wrote: "Football is first. The craziness around football is second. Then there is the rest of the world" (Goldblatt 2019, 1).

Nobody writing in 2020 can confidently forecast how the Covid-19 lockdown will change football. But it is possible to suggest what a "reset" of the European game might, and might not, mean. First, there was undoubtedly a reset for the players. Whether this was welcome or not related to earning capacity. For superstars such as Lionel Messi (Barcelona) or Mohamed Salah (Liverpool), the opportunity to recharge batteries after years of almost never-ending club and national team commitments was a happier prospect than it was for English non-league footballers such as midfielder James Comley, who was furloughed by his seventh-tier club Maidenhead United in mid-March and faced worries about the long-term viability of his chief source of income (Hunter, Ames, and Doyle 2020).

There was, second, an enforced restructuring of the football calendar, as major tournaments such as the men's and women's European Championship were pushed back a year to 2021 and 2022, respectively. Improved relations between FIFA and UEFA headlined a cooperative, flexible approach to new logistical challenges. Whether the makeover heralded a more streamlined and equitable international calendar, or merely created a nightmarish backlog of fixtures, is open to debate. With the 2022 World Cup still scheduled for November and December in Qatar, the latter seems the likelier scenario.

Finally, and less tangibly, the lockdown gave football time to take stock and confront its sudden lack of relevance. Whatever the results of this period of self-examination, it was no bad thing, given the UEFA and big-club arrogance typical of what David Goldblatt in 2019 termed "the age of football." For two or three months in 2020, football as a live and lucrative entity was not first or second, but nowhere. In these extraordinary circumstances, and through a range of community actions, the

European football family recovered some of its togetherness, and perhaps a little of its soul.

In the final reckoning, though, new-found solidarity always had to contend with entrenched self-interest, much of it driven by money. Financial calculations meant that the EPL, or what chief executive Richard Masters now called "the behind closed doors product" (Walker 2020, 34), was always likely to restart. There was no equivalent clamour for the completion of the 2019/20 Women's Super League season. Football's eventual return—the Bundesliga was the first major competition to come back on May 16—was not business as usual: the absence of spectators, the face-masked substitutes, and the cavernous echoes in the stadium made that abundantly clear. But it was still business. The inequality hardwired into twenty-first century European football meant that skepticism about its capacity for reform (still less revolution) was warranted. The game reflected a wider truth of the late capitalist age. Governing bodies and leading clubs, like national governments and international organizations, pumped in money during times of crisis to shore up tottering systems, not to overturn them. For the powerbrokers of European football, the lockdown rhetoric of unity and solidarity may have been genuine, but they sought damage limitation and the status quo ante, rather than radical transformation.

REFERENCES

Ahrens, Peter. 2020. "Nimm dich nicht so wichtig." *Der Spiegel*, April 2, 2020. https://www.spiegel.de/sport/fussball/fussball-in-der-corona-krise-nimm-dich-nicht-so-wichtig-a-8b4116b0-de50-4718-a620-f79aade4f35a.

BBC Sport. 2020. "Coronavirus: British Sporting Events to Continue as Normal, Says Culture Secretary Oliver Dowden." March 9, 2020. https://www.bbc.com/sport/51777154.

Colucci, Michele, Sean Cottrell, and Rustam Sethna. 2020. "Coronavirus and its Impact on Football: A Sports Law and Policy Centre and Lawinsport Joint Survey." Version 2.0, May 5, 2020. https://www.lawinsport.com/topics/covid19-impact/item/coronavirus-a-and-its-impact-on-football-a-sports-law-and-policy-centre-and-lawinsport-joint-survey.

Conn, David. 2020. "Football's Leaders Put Squabbles Aside to Strike Heartening Tone in a Crisis." *The Guardian*, March 19, 2020. https://www.theguardian.com/football/blog/2020/mar/19/uefa-fifa-football-leaders-coronavirus-david-conn.

Deutscher Fußball-Bund (DFB). 2020. "Zoller: 'Amateurfußball ist die Basis für alles.'" dfb.de, April 13, 2020. https://www.dfb.de/news/detail/zoller-amateurfussball-ist-die-basis-fuer-alles-214848/.

Ellen, Barbara. 2020. "Matt Hancock Scored an Own Goal with his Cheap Shot at Footballers." *The Guardian*, April 4, 2020. https://www.theguardian.com/commentisfree/2020/apr/04/matt-hancock-scored-an-own-goal-with-his-cheap-shot-at-footballers.

L'Equipe. 2020. "Maxime Saada (Canal +) sur la suspension du versement des droits TV: 'On n'est pas une banque.'" April 6, 2020. https://www.lequipe.fr/Medias/Actualites/Maxime-saada-canal-sur-la-suspension-du-versement-des-droits-tv-on-n-est-pas-une-banque/1125281.

FIFPro. 2020. "Covid-19: Implications for Women's Professional Football." April 16, 2020. https://www.fifpro.org/media/zp3izxhc/fifpro-wf-covid19-new.pdf.

Frankfurter Allgemeine Zeitung (*FAZ*). 2020. "Bundesliga droht Ausfall von 770 Millionen Euro." March 14, 2020. https://www.faz.net/aktuell/sport/fussball/bundesliga/fussball-bundesliga-droht-ausfall-von-770-millionen-euro-16679059.html.

Goldblatt, David. 2006. *The Ball is Round: A Global History of Football*. London: Penguin.

———. 2019. *The Age of Football: The Global Game in the Twenty-First Century*. London: Macmillan.

Hunter, Andy, Nick Ames, and Paul Doyle. 2020. "Football and Coronavirus: 'This Could Be the End of the Grassroots Game.'" *The Guardian*. May 7, 2020. https://www.theguardian.com/football/2020/may/07/football-coronavirus-this-could-be-the-end-of-grassroots-game-change-non-league.

Jost, Christophe and Tony Attwood. 2020. "The Last Pandemic was 100 Years Ago. But the Effect on Football This Time is Different." *Untold Arsenal*. April 12, 2020. https://untold-arsenal.com/archives/80358.

kicker. 2020a. "Watzke sieht 'größte Krise': Die Stimmen aus der Bundesliga." March 13, 2020. https://www.kicker.de/772170/artikel.

———. 2020b. "Rummenigge für Austragung: 'Es geht am Ende des Tages um Finanzen.'" March 13, 2020. https://www.kicker.de/772149/artikel.

———. 2020c. "Hoeneß: 'Es wird eine neue Fußballwelt geben.'" March 25, 2020. https://www.kicker.de/772797/artikel.

———. 2020d. "BVB, Bayern, Leipzig und Leverkusen stellen 20 Millionen Euro zur Verfügung." March 26, 2020. https://www.kicker.de/772858/artikel.

Klopp, Jürgen. 2020. "Jürgen Klopp's Message to Supporters." liverpoolfc.com. March 13, 2020. https://www.liverpoolfc.com/news/first-team/390397-jurgen-klopp-message-to-supporters.

Klosok, Aleks. 2020. "UEFA Says Let's 'Not Talk about Dark Scenarios' about Euro 2020 and Coronavirus." CNN.com. March 3, 2020. https://www.cnn.com/2020/03/03/football/coronavirus-euro-2020-uefa-aleksander-ceferin-spt-intl/index.html.

Kostin, Vladimir and Maria Vasilyeva. 2020. "Fans Turn to Belarus to Fill Void as Virus Puts Sport on Hold." Reuters. March 30, 2020. https://uk.reuters.com/article/uk-health-coronavirus-soccer-belarus/fans-turn-to-belarus-to-fill-void-as-virus-puts-sport-on-hold-idUKKBN21G0DN.

Kunti, Samindra. 2020. "Infantino Suggests Coronavirus Could Lead to FIFA Reforms Even After Health Crisis Subsides." Forbes. March 24, 2020. https://www.forbes.com/sites/samindrakunti/2020/03/24/fifa-ponders-swooping-reform-with-fewer-competitions-after-coronavirus/#8c3a6d82acf5.

Kuper, Simon. 2020a. "How the Coronavirus Will Change Soccer: Cheaper Transfer Fees, Swap Deals and Takeovers." ESPN. April 24, 2020. https://www.espn.com/soccer/english-premier-league/story/4087556/how-coronavirus-will-change-soccer-cheaper-transfer-feesswap-deals-and-takeovers.

———. 2020b. "Barcelona in Crisis: Club's VP Talks Coronavirus, Wage Cuts, Infighting and When Messi & Co. Might Return." ESPN. May 4, 2020. https://www.espn.com/soccer/barcelona/story/4091666/barcelona-in-crisis-amid-coronavirus-clubs-vp-talks-wage-cutsinfighting-and-when-messi-and-co-might-return.

Marcotti, Gabriel. 2020. "UEFA's Biggest Challenge of the Coronavirus Crisis: Easing the Economic Impact on Clubs, Nations." ESPN. March 18, 2020. https://www.espn.com/soccer/blog-marcottis-musings/story/4076049/uefas-biggest-challenge-of-coronavirus-crisis-easing-the-economic-impact-on-clubsnations.

Mason, Rowena. 2020. "Boris Johnson Boasted of Shaking Hands on Day Sage Warned Not To." *The Guardian*. March 5, 2020. https://www.theguardian.com/politics/2020/may/05/boris-johnson-boasted-of-shaking-hands-on-day-sage-warned-not-to.

Masters, Richard. 2020. "Letter to Mr Julian Knight, MP, Chair, Digital, Culture, Media and Sport Committee." April 6, 2020. https://committees.parliament.uk/publications/597/documents/2452/default/.

McDougall, Alan. 2020. *Contested Fields: A Global History of Modern Football*. Toronto: University of Toronto Press.

Moore, Peter. 2020. "A Letter from Peter Moore to Liverpool Supporters." liverpoolfc.com, April 6, 2020. https://www.liverpoolfc.com/news/announcements/392368-a-letter-from-peter-moore-to-liverpool-supporters.

Riach, James. 2012. "Fans Reject Michel Platini's 'Zany' Plan for Continent-Wide Euro 2020." *The Guardian*. December 7, 2012. https://www.theguardian.com/football/2012/dec/07/fans-reject-michel-platini-euro-2020.

Smith, Jeremy. 2020. "'This is Unjust': Amiens President Rails Against Relegation from Ligue 1." *The Guardian*. May 21, 2020. https://www.theguardian.com/football/2020/may/21/this-is-unjust-amiens-president-relegation-ligue-1.

Smith, Rory. 2020. "In Pausing Their Sport, Soccer's Leaders Put Everyone on the Clock." *New York Times*. March 18, 2020. https://www.nytimes.com/2020/03/18/sports/soccer/uefa-euro-2020.html.

Steinberg, Jacob. 2020. "Liverpool Challenged by Spirit of Shankly Fan Group Over Staff Furlough." *The Guardian*. April 5, 2020. https://www.theguardian.com/football/2020/apr/05/liverpool-challenged-by-spirit-of-shankly-fan-group-over-staff-furloughs.

Stura, Claudia, Christina Aicher, Robert Kaspar, Carina Klein, Susanne Schulz, and Stefan Unterlechner. 2017. "The UEFA Euro Championship 2020: A Path to Success or a Mistake in the Making?" In *Routledge Handbook of International Sport Business*, edited by Mark Dodds, Kevin Heisey, and Aila Ahonen, 26-36. London: Routledge.

Sweney, Mark. 2020. "Sky and BT Will 'Lose £1Bn if Sporting Events Stay Shut Until August.'" *The Guardian*. March 30, 2020. https://www.theguardian.com/business/2020/mar/26/coronavirus-sky-and-bt-will-lose-1bn-if-sporting-events-stay-shut-until-august.

Thorp, Liam. 2020. "Liverpool Coronavirus Deaths Soared After Atletico Madrid Match." *Liverpool Echo*. June 3, 2020. https://www.liverpoolecho.co.uk/news/liverpool-news/liverpool-coronavirus-deaths-soared-after-18354705.

Tovar, Jorge. 2020. "Soccer, World War II and Coronavirus: A Comparative Analysis of How the Sport Shut Down." *Soccer & Society*. Published ahead of print, April 14, 2020. https://doi.org/10.1080/14660970.2020.1755270.

UEFA. 2018. UEFA Financial Report 2017/18. https://editorial.uefa.com/resources/024e-0f842e7cd20b-39675a5dd261-1000/2017_18_uefa_financial_report.pdf.

———. 2020a. "UEFA President Aleksander Čeferin: 'Purpose Over Profit. That Is the Key.'" UEFA.com, March 3, 2020. https://www.uefa.com/insideuefa/news/newsid=2640460.html.
———. 2020b. "European Football Stands United Against COVID-19 Crisis: A–Z Guide." UEFA.com, April 20, 2020. https://www.uefa.com/insideuefa/about-uefa/news/newsid=2641389.html.
Walker, Ben. 2020. "On the Pitch." *London Review of Books* 42 (12): 34.
Walvin, James. 1994. *The People's Game: The History of Football Revisited*. Edinburgh: Mainstream.
Willeke, Andreas. 2020. "'Klein bisschen wie nach dem Krieg': 96-Profichef Kind sieht in Geisterspielen Mutmacher." Sportbuzzer. April 2, 2020. https://www.sportbuzzer.de/artikel/hannover-96-corona-pandemie-geisterspiel-profichef-martin-kind-mutmacher/.

CHAPTER 14

Covid-19: How Football Closed in South America

Jorge Tovar

INTRODUCTION

On March 11, 2020, the World Health Organization (WHO) declared the Covid-19 outbreak a pandemic. The implication for football across the globe was beyond what anyone in this generation had seen. The speed and breadth of the virus spread had an effect not seen in other major catastrophes, including World War II (Tovar 2020). South America, relatively distant from the globalization network, viewed for much of January and February the virus as part of the international news section. None of the ten members of the South American Football Confederation (Conmebol) had stopped its activities before the WHO declaration.

Up to March 11, there was no apparent reason why the subcontinent's football should be particularly worried. At that point, there was only one reported fatality in South America. By March 17, however, all ten South American football associations had issued orders to shut down all football-related activities. Five of them closed March 13, two on March 15, two on March 16, and finally Argentina on March 17. On that same day, Conmebol postponed the nation's most important regional tournament, Copa América, to 2021. This followed the March 12 announcement that the upcoming matches of Copa Libertadores, the South American equivalent to the UEFA's Champions League, were also postponed. In less than a week, South America witnessed the unbelievable. There was no football in the region. Never in history had South Americans witnessed so many silent stadiums simultaneously.

This chapter reviews the response to the pandemic in South America with particular emphasis on Argentina, Chile, Colombia, and Peru. It first contextualizes South American football and the pandemic. It uses the case studies to explore how the Covid-19 impacted the club finances and reviews the response given by football authorities. It also discusses how female football has confronted the virus. The final section discusses main findings and notes that football clubs cut costs at the expense of the players, its most important asset. The clash of interests is not unprecedented, but the universality of the Covid-19 pandemic gave it another dimension. The pandemic showed that despite technological advancements (e.g., VAR, high tech football boots and balls, cutting edge pitches), football proved to be a labor-intensive industry with a loyal base far more potent than in any other industry. Moreover, Covid-19 confirmed that female football still lacks full support from the sport's administrators. When facing an unparalleled shock, much of the words backing women's football were carried away by the wind.

The research faced two methodological challenges. First, it is a novel topic with little published material yet. Second, due to the ongoing pandemic, research cannot rely on traditional libraries, nor could the researcher visit or travel to acquire information on the field. Thus, for the most part, the investigation relied on online material exploiting the speed at which information travels in cyberspace. Indeed, web research can facilitate research on ongoing events (Dogruer, Eyyam, and Menevis 2011). However, there is plenty of misleading and incomplete news and stories on the internet (Aldwairi and Alwahedi 2018). To deal with this possibility, Lazer et al. (2018) suggest evaluating the news, either by reviewing credible news sites or fact-checking information across websites. The analysis in this chapter is therefore based on well-known websites and double-checked with different sources when deemed necessary.

SOUTH AMERICA IN CONTEXT

South Americans are very proud of their football. For over one hundred years, football has allowed South America to conquer its miseries and become equal with wealthier nations, as, for instance, Galeano (2006) and Wilson (2016) show when discussing how *criollo* football was born and what it represents. Indeed, not only can the region compete with Europe, they can beat them. Covid-19 changed history because never, not even during World War II, did the region's weekly football games stop. In part, this explains the initial reactions of Conmebol and the region's football association.

While football shut down in distant countries, such as China in January, Kuwait, Japan, and Switzerland in February, and Thailand and Iran in early March, these events seemed far away to South Americans. Things changed drastically when Italy instituted a lockdown on March 9, effectively shutting down football across the country. *Serie A*, closely followed by South American fans, is among the top leagues in Europe, and the world.

Moreover, given the proximity of the March 26 start of the South American World Cup qualifiers, the situation in Italy had an enormous impact on how the region approached the virus. There were two games scheduled for each national team, the second one on March 30. It would be a mistake to underestimate the importance of the qualifiers in South America. Not only are they a chance to represent the region in the, arguably, major sporting event in the world, they also represent a unique opportunity for South Americans to see in their homeland the football stars that play in Europe. Many of them, of course, play in Italy, and it was obvious that, sooner rather than later, other countries in Europe would probably close their leagues. In the eyes of the

South American football authorities, press, and fans, this meant one thing: would the qualifiers had to be played without the "Europeans"?

At the time, the idea of canceling the qualifiers seemed unthinkable. However, on March 9. FIFA postponed the first stages of the Asian qualifiers. At that point, South American football fans and authorities understood that canceling the first two matchdays was but a matter of days away. Still, on March 10, Lionel Scaloni, the Argentinian manager, announced the names of the players that would defend the national team in the upcoming games. Others, like Brazil and Venezuela, had made their announcements before Italy had shut down *Serie A*.

On March 11, President Vizcarra of Peru announced that incoming travelers from Italy, Spain, France, and China would have to quarantine for fourteen days. The direct implication was that at least four potential players could not play for the national squad considering that Trauco (Saint Etienne) and Advincula (Rayo Vallecano) would definitely be considered and others, such as Prado (Nantes) and Benavente (Nantes) had a good chance. Argentina and Chile faced a similar problem. World stars such as Lionel Messi (Barcelona), Arturo Vidal (Barcelona), or Gary Medel (Bologna) would have to quarantine for fourteen days upon return to South America because the government determined such measures for everyone coming from Spain or Italy. At this point, Conmebol requested that FIFA postpone the first two matchdays, which was granted on March 12.

At the same time, Conmebol suspended the Copa Libertadores. A week later, the suspension was extended until May 5. In mid-September, jointly with FIFA, Conmebol decided that Matchday 3 of the round-robin format qualifiers would take place on October 8. The Copa Libertadores started, with no fans in the stadiums, on September 15.

The situation with the continental tournaments reflects how football executives in South America understood the incoming pandemic. Despite the news from abroad, it was an unexpected event. No one in the continent was able to anticipate that the circumstances would alter football in ways never seen before. In fairness, as in other areas of society, no evidence suggests that anyone should have expected such a disaster. Consequently, decisions were made based on limited information.

ARGENTINA, CHILE, COLOMBIA, AND PERU

South American nations tend to cheer for each other when competing beyond their borders but are intensely competitive otherwise. This section focuses on four representative countries in the South American context to understand the key factors that emerged as the pandemic advanced across the globe. The fundamental changes, maybe not surprisingly, tended to move uniformly across the four countries, but there were some specific differences in how football responded.

The Virus is Coming

During the early stages of the crisis, no country thought that they would have to stop their domestic football competitions. This was even true for government authorities. Still, on March 6, the Peruvian Health Ministry did not outline any ban on large gatherings, including attendance at football games (Fútbol Peruano 2020a). With just one Covid-19 case at the time, there seemed no reason to declare a state of emergency. Its Colombian counterpart took a similar approach on the day the first case was confirmed. In Peru, the great derby between historic Lima rivals Universitario and Alianza Lima took place as planned on March 8. Nevertheless, the virus was a concern for the game; some fans wore facemasks and used the antibacterial gel dispensers placed around the stadium (Gestión 2020).

On March 7, Boca Juniors became the new Argentinian league champions after beating their fierce rival, River Plate, on the final day of the season. The virus seemed unimportant on that date, despite the fact that Argentina had confirmed a second case. Similarly, in Chile, football carried on relatively uninterrupted by the virus, despite the government announcing on February 25 that up to 260 individuals were self-isolating because of Covid-19 related symptoms and confirming the first case on March 4.

The situation radically changed the following weekend. Peru announced that schools would not start as planned. Argentina and Chile partially closed them on March 14, Colombia on March 15. These measures implied that large gatherings were now a significant issue. Football authorities, however, expected to solve the problem by playing behind closed doors. On March 12, the Chilean Ministry of Health announced jointly with the Chilean Football Association that no fans would be allowed in stadiums between March 19 and April 19 (Diario Concepción 2020). However, on March 18, Chilean football was suspended entirely. Colombia and Peru had no time to plan football without fans; they suspended immediately all matches.

Argentina, as ever, had its own story. Initially, as in Chile, the idea was to play with no fans in the stands. However, River Plate announced on Friday evening, March 13, that the club would be closed indefinitely as from March 14 (Irigoyen 2020). That day, they had to play Atlético Tucumán, which should have been the start of the new season. According to the regulations of *Superliga*, the Professional Football League, River Plate should have been awarded a loss, have points deducted, and received a fine. What bothered many people was the unilaterality of the decision. Both sets of players expressed their unwillingness to play, but Atlético Tucumán announced that the club would nevertheless travel to Buenos Aires. Playing at home, River Plate closed the stadium, and when the referees arrived and found the doors closed, they called the notary's office to officially confirm that access was denied. Although Atlético's players were still at the hotel and did not have to go to the stadium, the club did intend to play.

Having played a couple of games without fans, and following River Plate's decision, footballers in Argentina pressed for the suspension of the *Superliga*.

However, Argentinian President Alberto Fernández, among others, pushed for football to remain open. The president's argument was justified by the importance of keeping people happy and connected to the sport, a statement that mirrored others in the past, such as actions taken in England (Tovar 2020) and Germany (Hesse 2003) during the Second World War. Former player, Diego Maradona, a loud voice in the Argentinian context, and Falcioni, a 63-year-old coach who had previously suffered from cancer and pneumonia, also supported the suspension (Rodríguez 2020). Finally, on March 17, the Ministry of Tourism and Sport decided to postpone all games until March 31, while also proposing that training should also be canceled (EFE 2020). A day later, it was announced that football was indefinitely suspended.

On Finances and Labor Disputes

With football indefinitely suspended, the very survival of the clubs was a cause for concern. Early in 2020, the debate in Colombia revolved around the new pay-per-view scheme because, for the first time in history, there would be no free-to-air TV games. At some point in the debate, a congressman proposed a law to broadcast at least one game for free due to the social value of the sport and the importance of guaranteeing football on TV to low-income households (El Espectador 2020). The response of the President of Dimayor, the Colombian Professional Football Association, was to remind the government that football was a private business. He added that the only option to follow the sport would be to pay to attend live at the stadium, or the fee for the pay-per-view channel. Moreover, he insisted, if the government was interested in having one game on TV, they should pay for it.

But when Covid-19 arrived, the tables turned. On March 30, Dimayor officials sent a letter to Colombian President Iván Duque asking for government support. Among other requests, Dimayor leaders asked for a loan using systems already in place for other institutions. The Ministry of Sports responded swiftly. The priority was to protect the Olympic cycle (excluding football, which had not qualified for Tokyo 2020) while reminding Dimayor that as a private business, it should seek funding from the private sector (Forbes 2020).

The impact of the lockdown had a short-term effect on matchday revenues, a mid-term effect on broadcasting revenues, and expected long-term effects on merchandising revenues. Table 1.1 reports the revenue composition for clubs in Argentina, Chile, and Colombia. There is no such information for Peru where media reports state that broadcasting revenues for eleven teams represent around 70% of the total (Gestión 2018). The primary revenue source in Argentina and Chile is television, while in Colombia it is merchandising. The main picture is that shutting down broadcasting and matchday revenues will impact between 40 to 55% of total revenues. Moreover, transfers are not a constant source of income for every club, because the ability to sell players varies depending on the market, and it can be very volatile.

Table 1.1: Professional Football Revenues: Sources

	Argentina: 2018/19	Chile:2018	Colombia:2018
Broadcast	35.7%	37%	20.4%
Merchandising	17%	29%	26.4%
Matchday	32.3%	16%	17.9%
Transfers	15%	16%	21.7%
Others	0%	3%	13.7%

Sources: Argentina: Informe de clubes Fútbol 2019. Chile: Anuario Financiero del Fútbol Chileno. Temporada 2018. Colombia: Comportamiento Financiero de los 36 clubes de fútbol colombianos Supersociedades 2019. Note: Others in Chile include prizes obtained in international competitions. In Colombia, others contain "participation in events." It is not clear if it includes domestic tournaments. It also includes transfers from Dimayor, donations, and other non-operational revenues.

Broadcasting companies, for the most part, kept honoring their deals with the football associations during the initial phases of the pandemic. Exceptions are Chile's Mediapro and CHV, which owns the rights to broadcast the Chilean national team and which partially stopped paying in March (Parker and Barrera 2020). In contrast, the premium channel (as in Colombia), which owns the rights to the first division, decided to stop charging its subscribers for football that was not played and paid the agreed amounts to the football association (Chócale 2020). In general, broadcasting firms kept paying during the first months of the pandemic. However, during the first week of July, the Colombian teams complained that the TV network had decided to partially withhold payments, as did the sponsor that gave its name to the league (El Tiempo 2020). In Argentina, the *Superliga* negotiated with the broadcasting company to continue payments for at least three months, until June (Colombo 2020). The money from the television contracts was an important source to help football survive the crisis, although in Peru, the story differs in an important way.

Most Peruvian teams were able to negotiate contracts with the broadcasting company. However, four first division teams did not manage to finalize the deal. As a consequence, while some clubs like Universitario received broadcasting rights income, others had no expectations regarding that important source of funds.

As the crisis deepened, clubs sought help from FIFA, Conmebol, and their respective governments. On April 24, FIFA announced that it would transfer $500,000 to each of its 211 football federations, plus some outstanding funds from 2019 and 2020 (FIFA 2020). In late March, Conmebol announced that participant clubs in Copa Libertadores and Copa Sudamericana (the second-rated continental tournament) would receive their participation fee in advance (Conmebol 2020a). In April, Conmebol announced another aid package valued at around $1.4 million to each of its ten members (Conmebol 2020b). By late June, Conmebol added another $6 million, evenly distributed among the ten members (As 2020a). There was a further $2 million to be used for Covid-19 testing to facilitate restarting of the game, and the remainder could be used according to each country's specific needs. Some independent attempts, such as Chile's ANFP, the professional association, to negotiate a $27 million-dollar bank loan to distribute among first and second division teams, failed due to managerial and political tensions (ESPN 2020a).

Among the initial strategies of clubs around the world was a move to cut wages. Early in the crisis, talk of reducing salaries rumbled across the industry. FIFA defended such measures in March 2020, in exchange for keeping contracts alive and avoiding layoffs (Semana 2020).

In Argentina, the reduction of salaries was initially understood as a process that had to be jointly agreed between players and clubs (García 2020). In Peru, several players also assumed that they might need to lower wages (Cruzado 2020). Chilean players, in contrast, despite some exceptions, did not agree with such proposals.

In Colombia, the first division team Jaguares suspended the contract of all its players and staff arguing "force majeure" (As 2020b). If players cannot provide their services, the employer cannot pay. Bucaramanga replicated such measures. However, they were the exception.

Colombian club Deportivo Cali agreed with its players in late April to proportionally reduce their salaries for the duration of the crisis (Garcés 2020). Millonarios, another top team in the country, agreed to pay the contract for those earning up to COP 8 million (around $2,100) and reduce the salaries of everyone else up to COP 10 million (around $2,600). Interestingly, according to the team's President in a interview in Navarrete (2020), around 86% were included in the first group. Other significant clubs followed suit in Colombia and elsewhere, Universidad de Chile, and Sporting Cristal and Cienciano in Peru, for instance. Under most agreements, players would receive their income as soon as football restarted. As time passed, though, the general thinking was that such agreements were sustainable only after fans were allowed back into the stadiums.

Cutting costs by reducing wages became a typical dispute between employers and employees. Deportivo Coopsol, for instance, a second-division team in Peru, fired all its players and managerial staff in mid-April. In May, Binacional, the 2019 Peruvian champions, suspended all wage payments having failed to reach an agreement with players (El Comercio 2020). By late April, only five teams in Argentina had paid their staff salaries on time. In Chile, Colo Colo, one of the most popular and successful clubs in the country, went from negotiating salary reduction with the players, to temporarily deleting the pictures of all players from the club's website (La Tercera 2020).

In Chile and Peru, several teams filed for government resources to deal with salaries. In the former, the *employment protection law*, in the latter, the *perfect suspension of work*. The Chilean law allows workers to retain social security when a pact for the temporary reduction of working hours is agreed between employers and workers. The Peruvian instrument authorizes employers to suspend workers without having to pay any compensation, although low-income workers receive some government subsidy. However, this led to a media and social debate on whether football clubs should use economic measures designed to support employment in troubled firms.

In Chile, even as some teams filed for protection, the TV network was still paying as agreed, but this source only covers parts of the clubs' income (Table 1.1). The government stated that the clubs had the right to file for protection, as the players were workers, but that they should do it under the law. By late June, up to eighteen clubs in Chile, between first and second division teams, had filed for the employment protection law. Without any doubt, the historic and only Chilean club to win the Copa Libertadores, Colo Colo was the most significant (Dote 2020).

The Peruvian law, the *perfect suspension of work*, developed as a response to the Covid-19 pandemic, had Carlos A. Maucchi as the first Peruvian team to apply to it in late April as a result of inconclusive negotiations between the club and the players. Two of the top-three teams in Peru, Alianza Lima and Universitario, also applied for the perfect suspension, albeit differently. The latter did it conventionally for the entire team in early May (As 2020c). The former did it in June but only for one player, Carlos Ascues, as he was the sole member of the team that did not settle with the salary reduction agreement (ESPN 2020b).

In Argentina, Racing was the first, in early April, to agree with players to reduce salaries. Within a month, Talleres and Velez followed. Moreover, the Argentinian Football Association (AFA) and non-football player unions settled in late May to 20% cuts in May and 25% in June. In mid-June, the Football Players Union agreed with the AFA to pay for players' salaries (both male, up to fourth division, and female) until December when their contract expired on July 1, and when they were unable to sign a new contract.

Boca Juniors, one of the two most influential clubs in Argentina, agreed to a 30% salary cut. However, the club was able to pay full salaries and 60% of earned bonuses in large part because 75% of the 200,000 club members have met their monthly membership fees (Telam 2020). The other major club, River Plate, agreed in early May to pay some variable upper limit to high earners while the team was not playing, and reinstate complete payment when the competitions resumed. As is the case of Boca Juniors, River Plate benefits from its large number of members, 80% of which kept paying the monthly membership fees during the pandemic (Clarin 2020).

The Forgotten: Female Football

Female football in South America has progressed in the last few years, but it still lags well behind its male counterpart. Money is low, sponsors are scarce, and the tournaments are irregular. The 2019 Copa Libertadores, for instance, was played over just two weeks in October. The 2020 version was postponed. Due to the pandemic, Conmebol suspended in early June the licensing process for the tournament (El País

Colombia 2020). The licensing process was being implemented for the first time to support, professionalize, and develop female professional football. The Covid-19 crisis, however, threatened to undermine progress; as of September there was no official decision on the fate of the 2020 Copa Libertadores.

The unique Covid-19 situation has had an impact on everyone, not only those within the football community. Many male players, particularly those that are not part of the elite, have been affected financially. However, it is also true that among those that suffered the most were the women trying to push for a higher quality of professional football in South America.

Early in the pandemic, Santa Fe, one of the top clubs in Colombia, announced that the male professional team's salaries would be partially paid. The contracts for the female players, on the other part, would be suspended (As 2020d). The decision made worldwide headlines as a team in Colombia was paying its male players while firing the female players. The other team in Bogota, Millonarios, had an easier situation: they had not signed any contract with female footballers when the pandemic was declared, everything was verbal (Navarrete 2020). Thus, they did not need to fire players who were not yet, legally, part of the club.

The women's football league in Colombia, like others in the world, had substantial uncertainties over its viability in 2020. Indeed, according to Colombia's football players union, only two of eighteen clubs maintained the contractual conditions agreed during the preseason (As 2020e). Nevertheless, by late May, the Minister of Sports had claimed that the football league should start by September. A bit behind schedule, Dimayor officials announced on September 10 the format of the league which started on October 16th (Dimayor 2020).

However, the lack of sponsors in Colombia and the rest of South America is a significant constraint on the development of female football. On April 29, 2020, in a press bulletin, AFA announced the suspension of all tournaments in Argentina. The last article, number 11, stated that the suspension included the entire 2019/20 female football season (AFA 2020). In 2019, AFA had announced a twelve-month financial support for female football, up to ARS2.8 million (around $40,000) to the seventeen first division teams. When the suspension of female football was announced, the AFA said that it would not renew the contract whereby it subsidized the female league, as it was due to expire on June 30 and had become an unsustainable financial burden. The underlying assumption being that the female league would likely not take place and that, if it did, fewer teams would participate. Upon the announcement, Sergio Marchi, the Secretary General of Unionized Argentine Soccer Players, stated that they would strongly defend the female players (Ole 2020). AFA's decision not to continue supporting female football stirred resentment in the country, leading the AFA to announce that they would keep subsidizing female professional football for another year (Ole 2020). Players were allowed to start training in September in preparation for a short transition league competition (El Femenino 2020)

In Chile, the decision on female football was swiftly made on March 31. The ANFP canceled the league until August, while the male football league was put on standby pending the developing nature of the Covid-19 crisis (ANFP 2020). In June, football authorities announced that the tournament that had barely begun in March was expected to be played as a short transition league starting in October, though details were not formalized. The main constraints were the biosecurity protocols that the ANFP needed to implement (Emol 2020).

In contrast to Argentina, Chile, and Colombia, where female football has some level of professionalism, in Peru, it is mostly amateur with just a few players receiving enough compensation to be considered professional (Fútbol Peruano 2020b). As such, even Universitario, a major club in the country, and the current female champions, excluded female players from the *suspension perfecta* that applied to its male counterparts.

The amateur status is double-edged. On the one hand, because most players either study or have another job, the salary cuts that rippled across professional football potentially will have less impact on their financial situation. On the other hand, as the Peruvian Football Federation discusses when and how to reopen male football, they will not restart female football because of its amateur status. Consequently, its activities can only start in phase four of the governmental recovery program, when the country moves to a new normal state (Fútbol Peruano 2020c).

DISCUSSION

Covid-19 swept South America as other regions in the world: silently, harshly, and unexpectedly. Football, an integral part of society, initially faced the challenge of following what other institutions did, including governments. Officials first denied the danger, then closed the activity and, lastly, sought funding to guarantee survival. In that sense, football officials' response to the pandemic was similar to leaders in other industries.

Having football stop, however, reflects the magnitude of the crisis in a region were the sport represents the essence of happiness, pride, and entertainment. This chapter discussed the impact of the situation on two related areas: club finances and the ensuing labor disputes.

Modern football clubs are like other businesses (Leach and Szymanski 2015). They have workers who are protected by law, no matter how weak these are in the region, and the flow of money is dependent on the ability to sell the product on a weekly basis. Put simply, with no product, there is no revenue. Hence, upon a severe adverse shock, employers need to cut costs, which for clubs are mostly wages. It turns out that no matter how embedded technology is, football is still a labor-intensive industry.

However, football differs from other businesses in its ability to engage with supporters and consumers. Indeed, modern sports organizations are keen to connect with fans using traditional and new means, such as social media or cell phones, to increase loyalty (Byers 2018). But football clubs go beyond brand loyalty. Some authors refer to it as attitudinal loyalty: a unique and robust engagement between supporters and the institution that, in some cases, may even impact their way of life (Maderer and Holtbrügge 2019). Others speak of brand equity, the added value that a football club can have on consumers behavior in terms of brand awareness, perception, loyalty, and association (Manoli and Kenyon 2018).

While other industries, restaurants, for instance, were forced to close as they were unable to pay rents and salaries due to a constraint in the flow of money, football revenue streams did not entirely stop. Of course, football clubs have a comparative advantage. Despite the historical tendency for professional clubs around the world to return financial deficits annually and grow their debts, they have managed to have abnormally high survival rates (Storm and Nielsen 2012). Regardless, when facing such a unique crisis, football clubs were forced to cut costs via the reduction of wages. Such actions led to a unique dispute, due to its global nature, between soccer players and managers.

Still, significant sources of cash remained in place from sponsors and broadcasting companies which, at least during the first three months of the crisis, stood by most of their obligations. Money has also poured from FIFA and Conmebol, where the accumulated wealth in the past has served a useful purpose in the most unexpected scenario. Moreover, some clubs have a source of income based on fan loyalty. Boca Juniors and River Plate are the prime examples where members keep paying despite there being no product. It is difficult to imagine another industry with such strong loyalty among its customers or members, where the latter go beyond product purchasers, and are active participants in the life of the institution.

Covid-19 has revealed the duality of football. An industry whose strength lies in the people that support it, more than on the money that it generates, even in the midst of a pandemic. However, football has evolved, and romanticism may be enough to keep money flowing in the short run. In the long run football needs to open and allow fans to fill the stadiums.

This chapter also analyzed the reaction towards female football. Covid-19 reminded the world that women's football in South America lags behind its European counterparts, and its progress is strongly dependent on external decisions. Indeed, it is not an exaggeration to state that it is currently entirely dependent on male football, which, in principle, is not necessarily worrisome. The main problem is if women's football is seen as a burden that the associations bear due to social pressure rather than by a genuine conviction of supporting its development. Many female players did not manage to sign their contracts because they were last in line, given the irregularity and short span of their competitions. Moreover, when having signed a contract, they were among the first to be fired, ironic because their salaries are much lower than their male counterparts. Lastly, in some, if not in all countries studied, there were some threats to cutting "subsidies" towards the female league.

Overall, the crisis has brought out some of the best and the worst about South American football. It is clear that the sport remains embedded in the heart and soul of the population. Football remains part of daily life, despite its financial growth over the past decades. However, industry leaders have not responded in the most consistent manner towards players, whether male or female. Even today, footballers are surprisingly the weakest link in the football chain.

Six months after the declaration of the pandemic, male football opened in empty stadiums, while its female counterpart remained closed. Empty stadiums prevail, and financial uncertainties persist. It remains to see how the region responds in the long run to the crisis.

REFERENCES

AFA. 2020. Campeonatos oficiales de la Asociación. Boletín No. 5768. Accessed August 22, 2020. https://www.afa.com.ar/upload/builder/NuevaCarpeta%201/NewFolder/Bolet%C3%ADn%205768%20(27-4-2020%20).pdf.

Aldwairi, Monther, and Ali Alwahedi. 2018. "Detecting Fake News in Social Media Networks." *Procedia Computer Science* 141: 215-222.

ANFP. 2020. "ANFP y Clubes Acuerdan Suspender Fútbol Joven Y Fútbol Femenino Y Programar Su Regreso Para Agosto." *As,* March 31, 2020. http://www.anfp.cl/noticia/35233/anfp-y-clubes-acuerdan-suspender-futbol-joven-y-futbol-femenino-y-programar-su-regreso-para-agosto.

As. 2020a. "Conmebol Reparte 6 Millones De Dólares Entre Las Federaciones." *As,* March 6, 2020. https://as.com/futbol/2020/06/23/internacional/1592932980_118665.html.

———. 2020b. "Jaguares Suspende Contratos a Jugadores Por El COVID-19." *As,* March 28, 2020. https://colombia.as.com/colombia/2020/03/28/futbol/1585352563_975306.html.

———. 2020c. "Administración De La "U" Aplica Suspensión Perfecta A Sus Jugadores." *As* May 9, 2020. https://peru.as.com/peru/2020/05/09/futbol/1589023027_272489.html.

———. 2020d. "Acuerda Salaries Con Jugadores Y Suspende Contratos Del Femenino." *As* April 7, 2020. https://colombia.as.com/colombia/2020/04/07/futbol/1586225095_808201.html.

———. 2020e. "Carta Abierta De Jugadoras Colombianas Ante La Crisis." *As* April 13, 2020. https://colombia.as.com/colombia/2020/04/13/futbol/1586787439_409107.html.

Byers, Terri. 2018. "Trends in Professional Sport Organisations and Sport Management and Their Market Impact." In *the Palgrave Handbook on the Economics of Manipulation in Sport*, edited by Markus Breuer and David Forrest, 55-70. Palgrave Cham: Macmillan.

Chócale. 2020. "CDF Suspenderá Cobros De Sus Canales Premium, HD Y Estadio Durante Abril." *Chócale*, April 3, 2020. https://chocale.cl/2020/04/suspension-cobros-cdf-coronavirus/.

Clarin. 2020. "Fútbol En Crisis. River Plate Llegó a Un Acuerdo Con El Plantel Y Habrá Un Tope Salarial Mientras Dure La Pandemia." *Clarín*, May 7, 2020. https://www.clarin.com/deportes/futbol-crisis-river-llego-acuerdo-plantel-tope-salarial-dure-pandemia_0_AjrRQIoUs.html.

Colombo, Agustín. 2020. "¿Qué Harán Los Clubes Si La Televisión Deja De Pagar O Paga La Mitad?" 442, June 27, 2020. https://442.perfil.com/noticias/futbol/que-haran-los-clubes-si-la-television-deja-de-pagar-o-paga-la-mitad.phtml.

Conmebol. 2020a. "CONMEBOL Anticipará Pagos a Clubes Para Mitigar El Impacto Del Covid-19." *Conmebol,* March 26, 2020. http://www.conmebol.com/es/conmebol-anticipara-pagos-clubes-para-mitigar-el-impacto-del-covid-19.

———. 2020b. "CONMEBOL Entrega 14 Millones De Dólares Del Programa Evolución a Las Asociaciones Miembro Para Afrontar El Impacto Del Covid-19." *Conmebol.* March 30, 2020. http://www.conmebol.com/es/conmebol-entrega-14-millones-de-dolares-del-programa-evolucion-las-asociaciones-miembro-para.

Cruzado, Rinaldo. 2020. "¡Enorme Gesto! Futbolistas De Alianza Lima Aceptarían Reducción De Sueldos Debido a La Para Por El COVID-19." *RPP*, March 28, 2020. https://rpp.pe/futbol/descentralizado/coronavirus-alianza-lima-enorme-gesto-futbolistas-del-cuadro-intimo-aceptarian-reduccion-de-sueldos-debido-a-la-para-por-el-covid-19-noticia-1254933.

Diario Concepción. 2020. "Por Coronavirus: Suspenden Eliminatorias Sudamericanas Y La Libertadores Mientras El Fútbol Chileno Será Sin Público." *Diario Concepción*, March 12, 2020. https://www.diarioconcepcion.cl/deportes/2020/03/12/futbol-chileno-se-jugara-sin-publico-por-al-menos-un-mes-como-prevencion-ante-coronavirus.html.

Dimayor, 2020. "Calendario de la Liga Femenina Dimayor 2020." *Dimayor*, September 10, 2020. https://dimayor.com.co/2020/09/calendario-de-la-liga-femenina-dimayor-2020/.

Dote, Sebastián. 2020. "18 Clubes De Fútbol Se Acogieron a La Ley De Protección Al Empleo." *El Dínamo*, June 10, 2020. https://www.eldinamo.cl/deportes/2020/06/10/coronavirus-chile-18-clubes-de-futbol-se-acogieron-a-la-ley-de-proteccion-al-empleo/.

Dogruer, Nazan, Ramadan Eyyam and Ipek Menevis. 2011. "The Use of the Internet for Educational Purposes." *Procedia-Social and Behavioral Sciences* 28:606-611. https://doi.org/10.1016/j.sbspro.2011.11.115.

EFE. 2020. "Argentina Suspende El Fútbol Hasta El 31 De Marzo Por El Coronavirus." *EFE*, March 17, 2020. https://www.efe.com/efe/america/deportes/argentina-suspende-el-futbol-hasta-31-de-marzo-por-coronavirus/20000010-4198104.

El Comercio. 2020. "Binacional, Rival De LDU En La Copa, Suspende Salarios Por Coronavirus." *El Comercio*, May 22, 2020. https://www.elcomercio.com/deportes/binacional-peru-liga-pago-jugadores.html.

El Espectador. 2020. "¿Es El Fútbol Un Tema De Interés Nacional? El Debate Que Se Abrirá En El Congreso." *El Espectador*, June 22, 2020. https://www.elespectador.com/noticias/politica/es-el-futbol-un-tema-de-interes-nacional-el-debate-que-se-abrira-en-el-congreso-articulo-900958/.

El Femenino. 2020. "Se Postergó El Regreso." *El Femenino*, September 6, 2020. http://www.elfemenino.com.ar/se-postergo-el-regreso/.

El País Colombia. 2020. "Suspendida Licencias De Clubes Femeninos Para La Copa Libertadores 2020." *El País*, August 22, 2020. https://www.elpais.com.co/deportes/futbol-internacional/suspendida-licencias-de-clubes-femeninos-para-la-copa-libertadores-2020.html.

El Tiempo. 2020. "Nuevo Golpe Para Las Finanzas De Los Clubes." *El Tiempo*, July 2, 2020. https://www.eltiempo.com/deportes/futbol-colombiano/win-sports-y-betplay-reducen-sus-pagos-a-los-equipos-de-la-dimayor-513638.

Emol. 2020. "¿Qué Pasa Con El Fútbol Femenino En Chile? En Un Año Los Equipos Han Jugado Un Solo Partido." *Emol*, September 17, 2020. https://www.emol.com/noticias/Deportes/2020/09/17/998212/futbol-femenino-chile.html.

ESPN. 2020a. "Crisis En ANFP Tiene Frenado Los Créditos a Los Clubes." *ESPN*, May 25, 2020. https://www.espn.cl/futbol/chile/nota/_/id/6977164/crisis-en-anfp-tiene-frenado-los-creditos-a-los-clubes.

———. 2020b. "Alianza Lima Le Aplicó La Suspensión Perfecta De Labores a Carlos Ascues." *ESPN*, June 9, 2020. https://www.espn.com.co/futbol/peru/nota/_/id/7027394/alianza-lima-le-aplico-la-suspension-perfecta-de-labores-a-carlos-ascues.

FIFA. 2020. "FIFA Starts Immediate Financial Support to Member Associations in Response To COVID-19 Impact." *FIFA*, April 24, 2020. https://www.fifa.com/who-we-are/news/fifa-starts-immediate-financial-support-to-member-associations-in-response-to-co.

Forbes. 2020. ""No Tenemos Dinero Para El Fútbol Colombiano": Ministro del Deporte." *Forbes*, April 2, 2020. https://forbes.co/2020/04/02/actualidad/no-tenemos-dinero-para-el-futbol-colombiano-ministro-del-deporte/.

Fútbol Peruano. 2020a. "¿Se Puede Suspender La Liga 1 Por La Llegada Del Coronavirus A Perú?" *Fútbol Peruano*, March 6, 2020. https://www.futbolperuano.com/liga-1/noticias/se-puede-suspender-la-liga-1-por-la-llegada-del-coronavirus-263164.

———. 2020b. "Fútbol Femenino. ¿Retorno Del Fútbol En Perú Involucra Al Fútbol Femenino?" *Fútbol Peruano*, May 22, 2020. https://www.futbolperuano.com/peru/futbol-femenino/futbol-femenino-retorno-del-futbol-en-peru-involucra-al-futbol-femenino-270985.

———. 2020c. "¿La Liga De Fútbol Femenino Verá La Luz En 2020 En Perú?" *Fútbol Peruano*, August 13, 2020. https://www.futbolperuano.com/peru/futbol-femenino/la-liga-1-de-futbol-femenino-peruano-vera-la-luz-el-2020-277690.

Galeano, Eduardo. 2006. *El fútbol a sol y sombra*. Madrid: Siglo XXI de España Editores. Primera edición de bolsillo.

Garcés, Marco A. 2020. "Cali Rebaja Salarios Por Emergencia De Covid-19, Pero Por Un Acuerdo." *Fútbolred*, April 2, 2020. https://www.futbolred.com/futbol-colombiano/liga-aguila/atencion-cali-rebaja-salarios-en-acuerdo-con-jugadores-por-la-crisis-115128.

García, Hugo. 2020. "¿Qué Dice La Ley Sobre Hacer Recortes a Los Sueldos De Empleados Del Fútbol?" *Mundo D*, March 23, 2020. https://mundod.lavoz.com.ar/futbol/que-dice-la-ley-sobre-hacer-recortes-a-los-sueldos-de-empleados-del-futbol.

Gestión. 2020. "Universitario Vs Alianza Lima: Las Medidas De Prevención En El Estadio Monumental Para Evitar El Contagio Del Coronavirus En El Perú." *Gestión*, March 8, 2020.

https://gestion.pe/tendencias/coronavirus-en-peru-universitario-de-deportes-vs-alianza-lima-las-medidas-de-prevencion-en-el-estadio-monumental-para-evitar-el-contagio-en-el-clasico-del-futbol-peruano-fotos-nczd-noticia/.

———. 2018. "Clubes De Primera División Generan Ingresos Hasta Por US$60 Millones Al Año, Según La FPF." *Gestión*. November 18, 2020. https://gestion.pe/economia/clubes-primera-division-generan-ingresos-us-60-millones-ano-fpf-nndc-250631-noticia/?ref=gesr.

Hesse, Ulrich. 2003. *Tor! The Story of German Football*. London: WSC Books Limited.

Irigoyen, Juan I. 2020. "Coronavirus: River Se Planta." *El País*, March 14, 2020. https://elpais.com/deportes/2020-03-14/coronavirus-river-se-planta.html.

La Tercera. 2020. "Colo Colo Borra La Foto De Sus Jugadores En Medio De La Guerra Por Los Sueldos." *La Tercera*, April 27, 2020. https://twitter.com/latercera/status/1254851558740811783.

Lazer, David M., Matthew A. Baum, Yochai Benkler, Adam J. Berinsky, Kelly M. Greenhill, Filippo Menczer, and Michael Schudson. 2018. "The Science of Fake News." *Science* 359 (6380): 1094-1096.

Leach, Stephani, and Stefan Szymanski. 2015. "Making Money out of Football." *Scottish Journal of Political Economy* 62 (1): 25-50.

Maderer, Daniel, and Dirk Holtbrügge. 2019. "International activities of football clubs, fan attitudes, and brand loyalty." *Journal of Brand Management* 26 (4): 410-425.

Manoli, Argyro E., and James A. Kenyon. 2018. "Football and Marketing." In *Routledge Handbook of Football Business and Management*, edited by Simon Chadwick, Daniel Parnell, Paul Widdop and Christos Anagnostopoulos, 88-100. London and New York: Routledge.

Navarrete, Juan S. 2020. "El Acuerdo Al Que Llegaron Los Jugadores De Millos En El Tema Salarial." *El Tiempo*, March 28, 2020. https://www.eltiempo.com/deportes/futbol-colombiano/habla-presidente-de-millonarios-sobre-salarios-en-medio-del-coronavirus-478172.

Ole. 2020. "Idas Y Vueltas. ¿Qué Pasa Con El Fútbol Femenino?" *Diario Ole*, April 30, 2020. https://www.ole.com.ar/futbol-femenino/futbol-femenino-contratos-afa-barios_0_PaswLlbjc.html.

Parker, Matias and Christian Barrera. 2020. "Dos Meses Impagos: Chilevisión Pide 60 Años Para Regularizar Su Deuda Con La ANFP." *La Tercera*, May 20, 2020. https://www.latercera.com/el-deportivo/noticia/dos-meses-impagos-chilevision-pide-60-dias-para-regularizar-su-deuda-con-la-anfp/AWOXKSPACFDZTEJUFYJ3HUOGZM/.

Rodríguez, M.A. 2020. Falcioni: "Tuve Neumonía Y Cáncer Y El Viernes Tuve Que Trabajar Igual" *Marca*, March 16, 2020. https://www.marca.com/futbol/argentina/2020/03/16/5e6fb4aae2704e209c8b456d.html.

Semana. 2020. "FIFA Pide Acuerdos Sobre Salarios." *Semana*, April 6, 2020. https://www.semana.com/deportes/articulo/fifa-pide-acuerdos-sobre-salarios-y-recomienda-renovar-contratos/661808/.

Storm, Rasmus K., and Klaus Nielsen. 2012. "Soft Budget Constraints in Professional Football." *European Sport Management Quarterly* 12 (2): 183-201.

Telam. 2020. "Boca Abonó Los Sueldos Completos Y Está Al Día Con El Plantel." *Telam*, May 19, 2020. https://www.telam.com.ar/notas/202005/465516-boca-coronavirus-sueldos.html.

Tovar, Jorge. 2020. "Soccer, World War II and Coronavirus: A Comparative Analysis of How the Sport Shut Down." *Soccer & Society*, 1–9. https://doi.org/10.1080/14660970.2020.1755270

Wilson, Jonathan. 2016. *Angels with Dirty Faces: The Footballing History of Argentina*. New York: Hachette U.K.

CHAPTER 15

The Zwift Pace: How Elite Cycling Faced the Covid-19 Lockdown

Bertrand Fincoeur, Serena Bongiovanni, and Vincent Gesbert

Like almost any sport during the Covid-19 lockdown, elite cycling had to suddenly interrupt most of its activities. On March 14, the 2020 Paris-Nice edition finished day early after the final stage was canceled, while seven elite teams had previously decided to not even start. All subsequent races were canceled and/or postponed due to the global pandemic. After an intensive consultation process involving the principal representatives of elite road cycling, the International Cycling Union (UCI) draw up a revised 2020 UCI WorldTour and decided to fit all major races into a tight schedule from August 1 until October 31, 2020. Importantly, elite riders had to face various training situations during the lockdown. While the lockdown in several countries (e.g., France, Italy, Monaco, Spain) prevented elite riders from training in their usual conditions, other countries granted alternative regulations allowing elite riders to train (e.g., Belgium), or did not impose a strict lockdown at all (e.g., Switzerland).

The at-home virtual training app Zwift has been extensively used to help riders maintain good fitness and deal with uncertainty about the rest of the season. It was also intended to help reduce the negative effects of the lockdown on the well-known precarious business model of elite cycling (Van Reeth 2016). Yet, several elite cycling stakeholders were prompt in providing new avenues in order to cope with the expected difficulties. In particular, Zwift was used to organize a series of virtual cycling races involving some of the best riders of the peloton as early as April.

In this chapter, we will show that virtual races: 1. have been primarily used to guarantee elite cycling sponsors some exposure during the lockdown, with the aim of keeping (at least part of) the economics of elite cycling alive, 2. have switched from an entertainment tool to a valuable resource for training and self-fulfillment, 3. may contribute to bringing cycling fans and recreational cyclists closer to elite riders, and 4. have the potential to develop as an ever-growing sports activity, either self-sustaining or complementary to traditional elite road cycling.

Due to the difficulties associated with the Covid-19 crisis and the very recent development of virtual cycling during the lockdown, this contribution focuses on and analyzes topical online media sources primarily published during the lockdown in English, French, Dutch, and Italian languages. We then followed the rules of purposeful sampling, a method that is widely used in qualitative research for the identification and selection of information-rich cases related to the phenomenon of interest (Palinkas et al. 2015). Given that this research field is very recent and ongoing, we are aware of the limitations of our exploratory perspectives that will need further exploration in the next few months.

What is Zwift?

Although different online cycling platforms have been developed, we focus on Zwift in this chapter simply because it has been the most used application for virtual races during the lockdown. Zwift is a massive, multiplayer, online cycling training program that enables users ("Zwifters") to interact, train, and compete in a virtual world. The application was released in September 2014 and became a paid product with a fee of $10 per month in October 2015. Zwifters may cycle freely around the game world and join organized group rides, races, or workouts with other users. "Smart" home trainers, which include a built-in power meter, permit accuracy in the measurement of watts, as well as enabling an immersive technology experience, where resistance is applied or lessened to simulate the gradient encountered on the virtual course.

GUARANTEEING EXPOSURE TO ELITE CYCLING SPONSORS THROUGH VIRTUAL RACES

The business model of elite cycling worldwide is fragile. Indeed, sponsorship revenues amount to as high as 94% of elite cycling teams' budgets (Aubel and Ohl 2014). As a result, teams' budgets primarily rely on one client, or a small group of clients, since teams generally have a main sponsor, which names the team, and smaller sponsors that associate to form it. Marketing officers of companies investing in an elite team estimate that the visibility offered by cycling races yields a six to eight times higher return than does advertising in the media (Claveau 2015). Sponsoring an elite team may also be part of a soft power strategy. For example, three out of nineteen UCI World Team teams in 2020, which are sponsored by "emerging countries" in international sports (i.e., Astana ProTeam, Bahrain-McLaren, Israel Start-Up Nation). Looking for exposure is also crucial for companies that choose to bypass the title sponsorship of a team and buy space directly at the cycling events. Large companies such as Carrefour or Skoda then have a massive marketing presence at the most valuable races on the cycling calendar (Martin 2017). Finally, race organizers also obtain most of their revenues from broadcasting (Lagae 2016).

No matter their provision of capital, the various sponsors and organizers definitely need the visibility offered by the races. This is why, when faced with the race cancellations, several race organizers decided to associate with Zwift in order to reduce the negative impact of the lockdown on the global economics of sport in general, and elite cycling in particular. The first race, the virtual Tour of Flanders, was broadcast in Belgium and had a record viewer market share of 57%. It attracted more than 600,000 viewers, quite similar to the average per stage viewing for the Tour de France in Belgium, which gets about 700,000 people each year (Van Reeth 2019). Surprisingly, the limited mileage (only the last thirty-two kilometers of the real race) and the few runners at the start (13) did not discourage cycling fans. "I think we all had fun despite the frustration of not being pushed by the crowd," said Belgian winner Greg Van Avermaet. "In these difficult times, it was a very good idea for the runners and their sponsors" (Archyde 2020). Similar initiatives then followed in subsequent weeks, such as the virtual Giro d'Italia and Tour de France.

It is worth noting that not only the Zwift platform organized cycling races during the lockdown. Unlike the created digital world of Zwift, another app, Rouvy, used augmented reality, placing riders' avatars into a real-world environment created with footage of actual races. Hence, the Digital Swiss 5, replacing the 2020 Tour of Switzerland, was organized during five days in late April 2020. Although major promoters that are part of larger media conglomerates, like the Tour's *Amaury Sport Organisation* (ASO) and the Giro's *RCS Sport*, suffered from the Covid-19 crisis, other events might not overcome a one-year absence. Going virtual might therefore be a serious future option to consider (Lindsey 2020). The Digital Swiss 5 was the result of a partnership made in December 2019 between Rouvy and Tour of Switzerland promoter Cycling Unlimited. But when the pandemic occurred, the organizers decided to shift to an entirely virtual version of the race for elite riders.

Importantly, cycling fans frustrated with the absence of the Tour de France in July could follow a multi-stage virtual Tour, featuring six stages including the final stage on Paris' Champs Elysees. The format of each stage was designed specifically for the virtual platform, with Zwift CEO Eric Min revealing that he believed an hour of racing was the ideal length for virtual racing to ensure spectators remain engaged throughout,

> Most bike races often see people tuning into the last 50km of racing, and we've limited these races to an hour, both due to the viewing demands of consumers but also the training demands of the riders, as they are actively preparing for the Tour and might arrive at our race having already done 3 hours on the bike. (Lindsey 2020)

The virtual Tour de France was set to be broadcast live internationally across a wide range of channels and mainstream networks, such as SBS in Australia, NBCSN in the U.S., BBC Sport in the U.K., and Eurosport across Europe. "We know that eSports has undergone big development during COVID-19 as riders have spent time on the home trainer during lockdown," Media Director at ASO said, "we will have to see how things go with the event in terms of the broadcasting, the viewing figures, and of course the riders and teams, but of course e-sports is something we're looking at" (Gaskell 2020).

Aside from other considerations we will develop further in this chapter, it is thus clear that e-racing gained credibility during the lockdown as there has been a tangible growth in usage. For several riders, it might be that such events primarily served as a warm-up for the bigger races to come. Although it is too early to draw conclusions about their real economic impact, it is equally clear that those Zwift and Rouvy races between April and July 2020 were aimed at downsizing the economic catastrophe due to the various race cancellations. They were intended to provide some exposure to sponsors, without which the whole business model of elite cycling would just collapse. "You keep your (team) name a little bit in the front of the public mind and the sponsor might get a bit of the bounce out of that, (although) quite often the platforms and race organizers don't want the team sponsors to be prominent; they want their own sponsors to show up," said Velon CEO Graham Bartlett (Lindsey 2020). Velon is an organization made of elite cycling teams, created in 2014. Its tagline is "to create a new economic future for the sport and bring fans closer to the riders, races and teams—by working together and in partnership with others" (www.velon.cc). However, virtual races do not get money from host towns, there are no fans at the roadside to market to, and it remains unclear if there will be enough viewers to justify broadcast contracts. Further, prize money was so far missing from virtual races. Other incentives therefore explain why e-races have been so successful during the lockdown and in the weeks after. In particular, more psychological and training-oriented dimensions of the Zwift races need to be considered.

ZWIFT: FROM AN ENTERTAINMENT TOOL TO A VALUABLE RESOURCE FOR TRAINING AND SELF-FULFILLMENT

Home trainers have been used for years by riders aiming to keep their condition over the winter months, although such training options were not always appreciated by several elite riders. French rider Yoann Offredo summarized his mixed feelings vis-à-vis this kind of training tools,

> I did use a lot a home trainer when I was a young rider. I was a student and I came back home late. I had two options: training outside in the dark, or train at home. But at that time there was no Zwift and eCycling, I only had headphones and my wall in front of me. Home training was just pissing me off! (Poisson 2020)

Since its development, Zwift has promoted a new approach to home training thanks to its virtual environment and various interactive properties. Its slogan "Serious Training Made Fun" is indicative of its intrinsic nature: Zwift blends the fun of video games with the intensity of serious training. However, many riders had never used Zwift before the Covid-19 crisis: less than half of the peloton had a Zwift account in December 2019 (Baheux 2019). Yet, this application has basically switched from being seen as an entertainment tool, although already pretty demanding, to a resource increasingly perceived by riders as valuable for maintaining fitness and, even further, reaching milestones in their season. In fact, Zwift provided riders with a reason to stay engaged in usual training and elite riders' activities. Covid-19 has raised and highlighted a new concern for elite riders: the need to train without having clear and specific objectives, such as competitions, reaching peak form, etc. In this context, virtual races on Zwift have created a field of opportunities (Reed 1993) encouraging riders to keep active. This has had two main outcomes: the first of which relates to training, the second one has to do with riders' identities and motivations.

Impact on Training

Overall, training activities of elite riders may be considered hard and monotonous. Hard because they are time-consuming and they require considerable investment in order to reach or keep a high level of performance. Hard conditions are basically the result of the interaction between the structure (e.g., intensity-based training) and the nature (e.g., weather conditions) of the training sessions. Monotony comes from the repeated routes, races, training camps, and overall efforts that do not stimulate much innovation. Home trainers, then, primarily accentuate such effects. However, being an elite rider also demands fulfillment in order to remain committed to the expectations and requirements of an elite rider's career. It is worth considering that the development of Zwift's virtual training and racing program has likely contributed to reducing monotony associated with usual home trainers. Otherwise, how to best explain that elite riders were keen to pedal for hours on Zwift? This is suggestive of the difference between *deliberate practice* vs *deliberate play,* as various riders emphasized the funny side of virtual competitions on Zwift or similar others. While the theory of deliberate practice is based on the idea that proficiency in any domain is tied explicitly to the amount and type of training performed and is motivated by the goal of improving performance (Ericsson, Krampe, and Tesch-Römer 1993), deliberate play can be defined as activities in sport designed to maximize inherent enjoyment and provide immediate gratification (Côté 1999). Clearly, the Zwift app echoes deliberate play. According to Irish rider Nicolas Roche,

> It was nothing like riding outdoors together; it was the social side that was important. We attacked each other on the climbs, got annoyed with each other, laughed together. Before, the time limit for me to spend on the home trainer was an hour-and-a-half, maximum. I didn't even have Zwift but was set up on it on the first day of containment. My trainer was so old that, because of the noise it made, my neighbors thought I had a jacuzzi on my balcony. But then [presumably having gotten a new home trainer] I really started getting into it and was averaging more than 20 hours a week. (Cyclingnews 2020a)

Interaction and pleasure provided by training and/or competing on Zwift were therefore mentioned as key success factors of such virtual activities during the lockdowns.

Various riders then showed how Zwift helped them increase the number of daily training hours during the lockdown. Similarly, virtual competitions have allowed several riders to set an objective or follow a training plan in order to reach peak performance at some stage of the season. Due to their social and interactive properties, and their realistic design, virtual races tend to portray actual constraints experienced by elite riders. They provide two major opportunities to re-think the effectiveness of several training programs in the post-lockdown period. First, the short mileage of Zwift competitions (i.e., about a one-hour effort) could help riders better understand the key kilometers in races. "This is really ideal to practice the final of a stage," admitted French rider Valentin Madouas (Proux 2020), even though the impact of such training activities, particularly intensity-based training, on real performance will need to be assessed in the near future. The second main implication of the increasing use of virtual home trainers is that training facilities could be reconsidered under bad weather conditions or in order to reduce the risks associated with traffic and falls. According to Nicolas Roche,

> Up to now, I preferred to ride under the rain than to use a home trainer. Today, I know I can use Zwift for a 4- or 5-hour session. Next year, instead of climbing a pass at the beginning of the season, with my muscles being frozen, I will presumably take part in several virtual races. This COVID-period made clear how beneficial this new technology may be. (Bouhier 2020)

Zwift has also had an impact on aspects of elite cycling other than training, especially on riders' identities and motivations.

Impact on Identity and Motivation

During the lockdown and the no competition period, virtual training and racing helped riders maintain their identities as elite athletes, that is the degree to which an individual identifies with the athletic role (Brewer, Van Raalte, and Linder 1993). The competitive drive of riders may then explain their engagement in eCycling. Yet, riders' days and weeks are organized around specific objectives, consisting of training and recovery phases. They also include about 70-80 days of competition per year. The lockdown and the cancellation of all races during more than four months, thus, importantly modified riders' daily lives by preventing them from competing and sometimes even from training in countries where lockdown measures were undertaken. Riders then faced an unusual and uncomfortable situation: to keep training without clearly established objectives. Riders' identities were consequently weakened because riders struggled to make sense while there was a lack of correspondence in action and consequence. Despite the lack of available data, it might be that the social and interactive properties of applications such as Zwift contributed to mitigate several negative outcomes of the lockdown in terms of mental health and overcome the loss of motivation. A major beneficial effect of smart home trainers has therefore been to allow riders to improve their fitness in readiness for the various virtual races that took place between April and July 2020. "I had prepared myself for the Digital 5. I'm a competitor, I like to have goals to reach. I need goals, just like any athlete. It helped me to keep going and concentrated when I was locked at home," reported Nicolas Roche (Today Cycling 2020). In fact, competitions require cyclists to set up and follow a training program and these elements are part of the riders' identities. If training plans are not intended to reach competitive objectives, they become meaningless for athletes (Lamont-Mills and Christensen 2006). Consequently, and importantly, Zwift races then served as alternative competitive goals, which in turn fostered athletes' identities.

Additonally, most virtual races require serious short-distance efforts, several elite riders (e.g., Mark Cavendish, Luke Rowe, Emanuel Buchmann, Lachlan Morton) used Zwift during the lockdown to take part in some quality workouts such as the Everest Challenge, which consists in an extreme ride of 8,848m on the same climb. "I was cooked, completely empty," Italian rider Giulio Ciccone told *La Gazzetta dello Sport*,

> I can't even remember exactly how long I rode. I lost 2.1kg and consumed about 9,000 calories. I'd promised myself two pizzas if I finished but was so tired I could only eat one. The ride gradually wore me down, hour after hour. I've never felt as bad, even after cracking in a race in the cold and rain. (La Gazzetta dello Sport 2020)

In the same vein, on March 20, Belgian rider Laurens De Vreese racked up more than eleven hours and 368km on Zwift,

> I started at 6.30am. After 125km, my jersey was soaked. No one could imagine what I drank: four bottles of energy drink, four one-liter bottles of water, one Ice Tea, and one coffee. Even my girlfriend resupplied me with sandwiches. (…) Next step, 500km would be a fantastic mileage on a home trainer. (La Dernière Heure 2020)

These examples illustrate how the various challenges on Zwift contributed to helping individuals feel like elite riders—and pain is part of that athletic identity (Weinberg, Vernau, and Horn 2013) and the subsequent self-fulfillment.

Many who compete in cycling, whether as an amateur or a professional, are particularly concerned with statistics. For example, riders fret over their power output or their weight. From a rider's perspective, such considerations are all crucial, and they are at the heart of virtual racing platforms such as Zwift. Virtual races could even provide considerable gratification to several riders who are usually not that familiar with victories on the roads. So, it was South-African rider Louis Meintjes who won the final men's race and the points-based general classification of the Zwift *Tour for All*. Meintjes had not won on the road in five years. He said, revealing his emotions to be back racing and winning,

> It's been frustrating but the team has been keeping us competitive and I've enjoyed this racing. I was prepping like for a normal race, going all nervous before the start and going through my normal race route. It's something to keep you busy and make you feel like a professional bike racer. (Cyclingnews 2020b)

Virtual races on Zwift not only helped elite riders fulfill their athletic identity and needs for performance and success. They also contributed to bring cycling fans and recreational cyclists closer to their idols.

ONLINE TRAINING PROGRAMS: BRINGING CYCLING FANS AND RECREATIONAL CYCLISTS CLOSER TO ELITE RIDERS

Since Zwifters consist of both elite and (especially) recreational riders, virtual training and racing contribute to putting them in touch with each other. Obviously, apart from the WorldTour and the various competitions organized by the International Cycling Union (UCI), which are limited to elite riders, there were already numerous ordinary races mixing elite with non-elite riders. Criteriums and, in particular, kermesses, i.e., two popular styles of cycling races (especially in Belgium and the Netherlands) in which competitors ride a number of laps of a short circuit. Entering a kermesse, however, usually requires holding a license with UCI. Unlike kermesses, eCycling on Zwift is open to all interested riders as long as they have a home trainer, and they pay the monthly fee to the Zwift company. As a result, Zwift races form an opportunity for any avid rider to virtually compete with athletes he/she usually only sees from the sidewalk or on television. Although Zwift's basic principle is not to differentiate its users while taking part in virtual rides, the company has established a distinction between elite riders, who benefit from free access to the application, and their recreational counterparts, who need to pay a subscription.

Elite teams also try to get support and/or create links with recreational riders through Zwift. For example, during the lockdown, the website for the Dutch Team Jumbo-Visma mentioned,

> Our riders will take part in several group rides, our eCompetition and training sessions at Zwift. Do you want to know when you can join and train together with, for example, Tony Martin or Primoz Roglic on Zwift? Keep an eye on the program of our riders and our team! (https://www.teamjumbovisma.nl/)

Likewise, Australian team Mitchelton-Scott invited its fans on the Internet to "the unique opportunity to become teammates with the professionals, in an exclusive and private fan ride on Zwift" (https://www.greenedgecycling.com/). In June 2020, Zwift itself organized four virtual "social rides"—any rider interested could take part in them—each of which was supported by "cycling stars," such as multiple Tour de France winner Chris Froome or one-hour record holder Victor Campenaerts (Cyclingnews 2020c). Zwift then highlighted the fact that each Zwifter could send the cycling stars messages while riding. Latvian rider Tom Skujins confirmed that virtual ride-alongs have seen increased interest, "I'm learning a new skill: pedaling and typing. I'd done a few Zwift rides (with fans) like that pre-pandemic, but now there are more people on the platform and looking for a conversation instead of just smashing the pedals" (Lindsey 2020). According to EF Pro Cycling team manager Jonathan Vaughters, "with racers sidelined, the team's media outreach has focused heavily on rider bio content and lifestyle fare, and web traffic and social engagement are higher than they've ever been" (Lindsey 2020).

No matter the actual reasons people join the "Zwift community," the full range of which remain unknown, Zwift had more than 285,000 fans on the social media site Facebook in July 2020. Although the total number of Zwift subscribers is difficult to find out, there seemed to be no fewer than 200,000 users in December 2016, about one million two years later, and presumably 1,500,000 users in December 2019 (Baheux 2019). To date, we found no clear estimates about the number of users in the post-lockdown period. We did, however, observe that the use of the interactive mode on Zwift increased from 2% (before) to 8% after the lockdown in most parts of Europe (that is, between mid-March and mid-May 2020). Moreover, the total daily average number of kilometers of all users worldwide increased from ~1,000,000 to ~3,500,000 over the same period. This is therefore suggestive of an impact of the lockdown and the subsequent large publicity given to Zwift and other virtual platforms on the desirability of these applications. It might be that such success simply illustrates the converging interests of elite riders—we already discussed the implications on their training activities and athletic identity—teams—for which virtual cycling could represent a new source of revenue through sponsors interested in the large exposure provided by the increasing development of e-sports in general—and companies like Zwift, which gained much from having elite riders confined at home for several weeks. However, the future of virtual races remains uncertain and it is unclear whether and how eCycling will continue to develop, either as a self-sustaining phenomenon or as a complement to traditional elite road cycling.

Can Zwift Be the Future of Cycling?

Attributing the growing development of Zwift races only to the Covid-19 crisis would be a serious misunderstanding of the success factors surrounding virtual platforms. Indeed, one cannot neglect the overall evolution of the eSports landscape. Debates on the opportunity to include them in the Olympics are increasingly taking on importance

(Miah and Fenton 2020) since there is strong evidence that eSports are often more popular than various Olympic disciplines, with a range of professional leagues playing to packed stadiums (Gaskell 2020). eCycling is no exception, and in 2019 Zwift launched the first professional cycling eSports League (KISS Super League), with the participation of different elite teams. Although we emphasized the impact of the lockdown on the development of virtual racing, this should not dwarf the structural grounds that underpin such evolution. In fact, the lockdown has primarily served as a window of opportunity for companies like Rouvy or Zwift, the latter being ranked fifth by the website Fastcompany.com in 2019 Most Innovative Companies of the Sports Sector.

The increasing development of eCycling raises the question of its independence vis-à-vis traditional road cycling. Until recently, Zwift was used by a limited number of elite riders. In December 2019, Zwift announced that seventy-four of 176 participants of the 2019 Tour de France had a Zwift account (Baheux 2019). However, "today it is clear that eRacing is a distinctive discipline of cycling, with its own tools and strategies," reported the manager of elite team Alpecin-Fenix (Ienco 2020). The nature of racing in Zwift has led to a new form of teamwork, strategy, and even a new skillset. For instance, the platform today offers various gamification elements, such as draft and weight bonuses. Unsurprisingly, the most successful riders since the lockdown are those who have spent the most time familiarizing themselves with the platform and its nuances. "On the road, you have to focus on the tactics, being in a good position in crucial moments, saving energy whenever you can, and being at your best at key moments of the race," said American rider Lawson Craddock. He continued,

> On Zwift, it's more and less, "who's the strongest guy over the course of the whole race." It's pretty incredible how you can see all these incredible racers on the road, just not having that ability to translate that into Zwift racing, and of course you see that both ways too. I think both are great forms of racing, it's hard to compare, but it leaves room for different skills which is cool. (Gaskell 2020)

Numerous elite riders took part in the 2020 Tour de Zwift. However, the top ten was made up of riders from eCycling teams. In the near future, it is very likely that eCycling will develop under its own specialists (Le Soir 2020).

Nevertheless, Zwift may facilitate the career of elite riders. In early 2016, Zwift launched the Zwift Academy program, which utilizes the platform to test would-be riders for their suitability for elite cycling. 1,200 women cyclists entered in the inaugural competition. Former marathon runner Leah Thorvilson was crowned and consequently secured a contract with an elite team. In 2017, the Academy expanded, adding a men's competition. New Zealander Ollie Jones defeated 9,200 other cyclists and could, in turn, join Team Dimension Data for Qhubeka one year later (SBS 2017). This appears to be evidence that cycling and eCycling could reinforce each other, and that eCycling might expand the sport in unexpected directions, likely attracting new audiences and talent. Of course, not every road rider will become a passionate Zwifter but the Covid-19 crisis has perhaps offered cycling an opportunity to re-think part of its business model, if elite teams and/or riders succeed in attracting new sponsors and a possibly new public for such sports events. Importantly, this will also depend on the capacity of virtual races to coexist when the Covid-19 period passes and traditional road cycling races take over. Paradoxically, elite road cycling could also suffer from some competition with eCycling if it struggles to integrate virtual races in its development. In the meantime, the UCI established a new body of rules concerning eCycling and built a partnership with Zwift to organize the first eCycling World Championships in September 2020. While the "world after Covid-19" remains unknown in many respects, the future of cycling seems to be moving forward at a swift pace.

REFERENCES

Archyde. 2020. "Tour de Flandres: Audience Success for the Virtual Edition." *Archyde,* April 6, 2020. https://www.archyde.com/tour-de-flandres-audience-success-for-the-virtual-edition-fil-info/.

Aubel, Olivier, and Fabien Ohl. 2014. "An Alternative Approach to the Prevention of Doping in Cycling." *International Journal of Drug Policy* 25 (6): 1094-1102.

Baheux, Romain. 2019. "Zwift: l'application qui entraine stars du peloton et cyclistes du dimanche." *Le Parisien*, December 3, 2019. https://www.leparisien.fr/sports/cyclisme/zwift-l-application-qui-entraine-stars-du-peloton-et-cyclistes-du-dimanche-03-12-2019-8208588.php.

Bouhier, Maxime. 2020. "Nicolas Roche: 'Le home trainer ne doit pas être un ennemi.'" *Today Cycling*, May 2, 2020. https://todaycycling.com/nicolas-roche-le-home-trainer-ne-doit-pas-etre-un-ennemi/.

Brewer, Britton W., Judy L. Van Raalte, and Darwyn E. Linder. 1993. "Athletic identity: Hercules' muscles or Achilles heel?" *International Journal of Sport Psychology* 24 (2) : 237-254.

Claveau, Philippe. 2015. *Management de projets événementiels*. Grenoble: Presses Universitaires de Grenoble.

Côté, Jean. 1999. "The Influence of the Family in the Development of Talent in Sport." *The Sport Psychologist* 13 (4): 395-417.

Cycling Central. 2017. "Kiwi Jones selected as Zwift Academy winner." Last modified November 22, 2020. https://www.sbs.com.au/cyclingcentral/article/2017/11/22/kiwi-jones-selected-zwift-academy-winner.

Cyclingnews. 2020a. "Nicolas Roche on Life Alone in Monaco During Lockdown." *Cyclingnews,* May 13, 2020. https://www.cyclingnews.com/news/nicolas-roche-on-life-alone-in-monaco-during-lockdown/.

———. 2020b. "Zwift Tour for All: Meintjes Wins on Alpe du Zwift." *Cyclingnews,* May 8, 2020. https://www.cyclingnews.com/races/zwift-tour-for-all-2020/stage-5-men/results/.

———. 2020c. "Ride on Zwift with Froome, Dygert and Campenaerts for World Bicycle Day." *Cyclingnews,* June 3, 2020. https://www.cyclingnews.com/news/ride-on-zwift-with-froome-dygert-and-campenaerts-for-world-bicycle-day/.

Dernière Heure. 2020. "Laurens De Vreese réalise un entraînement de 368 kilomètres de chez lui." *Dernière Heure,* March 21, 2020. https://www.dhnet.be/sports/cyclisme/laurens-de-vreese-realise-un-entrainement-de-368-kilometres-de-chez-lui-5e762a0df20d5a29c678fceb.

Ericsson, Anders, Ralf Krampe, and Clemens Tesch-Römer. 1993. "The Role of Deliberate Practice in the Acquisition of Expert Performance." *Psychological Review* 100 (3) : 363-406.

Gaskell, Adi. 2020. "Is the Virtual Tour De France The Next Stage in The Evolution of ESports?" *Forbes,* July 7, 2020. https://www.forbes.com/sites/adigaskell/2020/07/03/is-the-virtual-tour-de-france-the-next-stage-in-the-evolution-of-esports/#7dcddb207f73.

Gazzetta dello Sport. 2020. "Ciccone e l'Everest sui rulli: 'Persi 2 kg, bevuti 3 litri d'acqua in 11 ore.'" *Gazzetta dello Sport*, April 20, 2020. https://video.gazzetta.it/ciccone-everest-rulli-persi-2-kg-bevuti-3-litri-d-acqua-11-ore/0e178d64-833d-11ea-9204-899568ffe6f8.

Ienco, Grégory. 2020. "Quand le virtuel vient au secours du cyclisme." *Cyclisme Revue*, April 4, 2020. https://cyclismerevue.be/2020/04/04/cyclisme-virtuel-zwift-confinement/.

Lagae, Wim. 2016. "Peculiarities of Sponsorship in Professional Road Cycling." In *the Economics of Professional Road Cycling,* edited by Daam Van Reeth and Daniel Larson, 83-98. London: Routledge.

Lamont-Mills, Andrea, and Steven A. Christensen. 2006. "Athletic Identity and its Relationship to Sport Participation Levels." *Journal of Science and Medicine in Sport* 9 (6): 472-478.

Le Soir. 2020. "Le triathlete canadien Lionel Sanders gagne l'édition virtuelle du Tour de Zwift cycliste." Last modified April 5, 2020. https://www.lesoir.be/292469/article/2020-04-05/le-triathlete-canadien-lionel-sanders-gagne-ledition-virtuelle-du-tour-de-zwift.

Lindsey, Joe. 2020. "Bike Racing Goes Virtual, But Will It Stick?" *Bicycling,* April 23, 2020. https://www.bicycling.com/news/a32251011/bike-racing-goes-virtual/.

Martin, Spencer. 2017. "Analysis: Is a Pro Cycling Sponsorship Worth the Cost." *Cyclingtips*, August 11, 2017. https://cyclingtips.com/2017/08/analysis-pro-cycling-sponsorship-worth-cost/.

Miah, Andy, and Alex Fenton. 2020. "Esports in the Olympic and Paralympic Games: The Business Case for Integration." In *Routledge Handbook of the Olympic and Paralympic Games*, edited by Dikaia Chatziefstathiou, Borja Garcia, and Benoit Seguin. London : Routledge.

Proux, Jeremy. 2020. "L'application "Zwift", le salut des coureurs professionnels?" *Ouest-France*, March 19, 2020. https://www.ouest-france.fr/sport/cyclisme-coronavirus-l-application-zwift-le-salut-des-coureurs-professionnels-6785143.

Palinkas, Lawrence, Sarah Horwitz, Carla Green, Jennifer Wisdom, Naihua Duan, and Kimberly Hoagwood. 2015. "Purposeful Sampling for Qualitative Data Collection and Analysis in Mixed Method Implementation Research." *Administration and Policy in Mental Health and Mental Health Services Research* 42 (5): 533-544.

Poisson, Guillaume. 2020. "Yoann Offredo: L'e-cycling? Je comprends l'engouement mais ce n'est pas le même sport." *France TV Sport,* July 3, 2020. https://sport.francetvinfo.fr/cyclisme/yoann-offredo-le-cycling-je-comprends-lengouement-mais-ce-nest-pas-le-meme-sport.

Reed, Edward S. 1993. "The Intention to Use a Specific Affordance. A Conceptual Framework for Psychology." In *Development in Context. Acting and Thinking in Specific Environments*, edited by Robert H. Wozniak and Kurt W. Fischer, 45-76. Hillsdale: Erlbaum.

Van Reeth, Daam. 2016. "The Finances of Professional Cycling Teams." In *the Economics of Professional Road Cycling*, edited by Daam Van Reeth and Daniel J. Larson, 55-82. London: Routledge.

Van Reeth, Daam. 2019. "Forecasting Tour de France TV Audiences: A Multi-Country Analysis." *International Journal of Forecasting* 35 (2): 810-821.

Weinberg, Robert, Daniel Vernau, and Thelma Horn. 2013. "Playing Through Pain and Injury: Psychosocial Considerations." *Journal of Clinical Sport Psychology* 7 (1): 41-59.

CHAPTER 16

Analyzing Boxing's Most Extended Break Between Rounds: The Impact of the Covid-19 Pandemic on National Boxing Federations and Innovative Responses

Ria Ramnarine and Kalyn McDonough

INTRODUCTION

The World Health Organization characterized and officially declared the Covid-19 outbreak as a pandemic on March 11, 2020. One hundred and fourteen countries had already reported cases of Covid-19 and the virus was continuing to spread throughout the world rapidly. Similar to other fields such as trade, business, and travel, the sphere of sport was also affected on a global scale in an unprecedented fashion. The sport of boxing was no exception.

The effects of the pandemic on boxing were increasingly complex due to the close-contact nature of the combat sport and as such it was one of the first activities to be halted and will be slow to resume. As Olympic hopefuls prepared for the 2020 Olympic Games, several elite competitions and qualifying tournaments were canceled or postponed. For example, the European Olympic Qualifier started on March 14, 2020, in London and was due to end on March 24, 2020. However, the International Olympic Committee (IOC) Boxing Task Force decided to suspend the event on March 16, 2020, amid growing concerns about the safety of the participants, increasing travel restrictions, and quarantine measures. The Americas Continental Qualifiers, World Qualifiers and other major events, such as the International Boxing Federation (AIBA) 2020 Congress, were also postponed.

This pandemic has presented an entirely unforeseen and unexpected dilemma for the sport of boxing and those who govern it. The way forward is seemingly unpredictable, and there will undoubtedly be numerous strategies that will reshape the world of boxing. The authors of this chapter have over twenty-five years' experience in elite sport, including as a former world boxing champion and 3-Star AIBA coach. They believed it was critical to explore the impact of the lockdown and measures undertaken by Boxing's National Federations (NFs) to mitigate the effects of the pandemic, identify valuable lessons to inform decision-making in the sport moving forward, and contribute to the broader understanding of emergency and crisis management in sport.

BACKGROUND

International Boxing Association and National Boxing Federations

To better understand the impact and actions of NFs throughout the Covid-19 lockdown, it is worthwhile to identify the governing system of the sport, function of the NFs, and how boxing historically was influenced by a crisis of comparable nature.

Similar to other sports, amateur boxing is governed by an International Federation (IF), the International Boxing Association (AIBA), and by NFs within each country. While boxers on the professional circuit are overseen by various organizations, such as the World Boxing Association and the World Boxing Council, AIBA is the only governing body that oversees amateur boxers. Although the term "amateur" has been replaced with "AIBA Open Boxing," it is still a commonly used term and will be referenced throughout this text. During the past decade, AIBA also included in its ambit semi-pro and professional boxing, with the aim to provide a complete career pathway for pugilists from novice to world champion.

AIBA is comprised of 203 NFs and each NF is responsible for managing the sport in their respective country; including over 9,000 registered elite boxers and 5,000 officials. The Constitution of each NF must reflect that of AIBA, while also being in accordance with particular nuances of their region and nation. An NF works on behalf of all the amateur boxers, coaches, officials, and stakeholders within the respective country, and manages the sport from grassroots to elite level. Some of the main objectives of the NFs are to:

1. Promote the sport in light of its health, educational, cultural and sports values, to all possible participants.

2. To initiate programs designed to attract, encourage and support young athletes.

3. To provide the best training options possible, especially for members of the national teams.

4. Ensure the holistic development and well-being of the athlete—physically and psychologically.

5. To secure and maintain the interest of the athletes, and to provide an environment of camaraderie, discipline and trust.

6. To organize competitions and events and promote fairness and proper sport practices.

7. To ensure the safety and welfare of the boxers.

8. To train and improve the quality of coaches and officials by regularly hosting development courses.

(AIBA 2018; Boxing Federation of India 2016)

Boxing and Historical Crises

Similar to its unequivocally tough athletes, the sport of boxing has withstood the test of time as it has developed from a backyard pastime to a professionally organized sport despite a number of historical crises (Barnum 2000). Yet, systematic documentation of the influence of global crises on the sport, and the response by sport administrators, remains limited. This is despite the fact that the popularity of the sport was well documented in pop culture, films, books, and photography during such crises as the 1918 "Spanish Flu" pandemic, the Great Depression, and World War II (WWII).

AIBA was founded in 1946, just over two decades after one of the world's most devastating pandemics, the Spanish Flu. Although the international and national organizations were not yet formed, there are lessons that can be drawn broadly on the impact of the 1918 Pandemic and the resilience the sport displayed.

The Spanish Flu pandemic spread worldwide between 1918 and 1919, infecting an estimated 500 million people (one-third of the world's population), with a death toll of at least 50 million (CDC 2019). The highly contagious nature of the flu, coupled with the absence of a vaccine, meant that leaders in some countries ordered citizens to wear masks, banned large gatherings, and closed schools and businesses (NIH 2007). Boxing was not isolated from the impact of the pandemic. An iconic photograph taken aboard the USS Siboney, on one of its many transatlantic trips carrying troops from the United States to and from Europe in 1918-1919, shows a boxing match underway as surrounding troops wear face masks amid the pandemic.

Figure 1: Boxing aboard the USS Siboney, 1918-1919

Source: Williams, 1975. U.S. Naval Historical Center Photograph.

An article in the New York Times on October 13, 1918, describes the impact of the pandemic on boxing in the U.S. in further detail,

> Boxing in the East is now at a standstill, because of the epidemic of Spanish influenza. Promoters in Philadelphia, Boston, and New Jersey, in compliance with requests issued by their different Health Departments, have agreed to close up shop. How long the sport will be idle remains to be seen, but it is positive that no matches of any importance will be undertaken while the epidemic continues. (NY Times, 1918)

Boxing resumed in the U.S. a month later in November 1918, and the sport saw several boxers succumb to the virus (Zidan 2020). Now, just over a century later, our world and the sport of boxing have been thrust into another global pandemic. Thus, it is important to learn from the past, and document more recent processes, to support the health and well-being of the sport of boxing and most critically, its participants.

As shown by the example of the 1918 pandemic, and experienced during the Covid-19 pandemic, sports do not operate in a vacuum and are impacted and influenced by both natural and humanmade disasters. Amplified by increased globalization, it is becoming more important for sport leaders to understand the influence of such global crises on their particular organization and have a plan for preparedness to minimize risk. However, in a review of relevant literature on crisis and emergency management in sport, Shipway and Miles (2020) found few studies and limited development of conceptual frameworks in this topic area. Furthermore, they showed that international frameworks for disaster risk reduction, such as the Sendai Framework for Disaster Risk Reduction 2015-2030 (Sendai Framework) (United Nations 2014), include "non-State stakeholders" such as business, professional associations, and the private sector, but do not include the sport industry.

The Sendai Framework was endorsed by the United Nations (UN) General Assembly following the 2015 Third UN World Conference on Disaster Risk Reduction (UNDRR 2020). The framework outlines actionable steps to protect development gains from the risk of disaster, with the ultimate goal to,

> Prevent new and reduce existing disaster risk through the implementation of integrated and inclusive economic, structural, legal, social, health, cultural, educational, environmental, technological, political, and institutional measures that prevent and reduce hazard exposure and vulnerability to disaster, increase preparedness for response and recovery, and thus strengthen resilience. (UNDRR 2015)

In order to achieve this goal, the framework outlines four priority areas: 1. Understanding disaster risk, 2. Strengthening disaster risk governance to manage disaster risk, 3. Investing in disaster risk reduction for resilience, and 4. Enhance disaster preparedness for effective response and to 'Build Back Better' in recovery, rehabilitation and reconstruction (*ibid.*). Included within each of the priority areas are actionable steps to help achieve these overarching objectives. Specifically, under Priority 1 and 2 are recommendations to systematically record and evaluate disaster loss to understand the economic, social, health, education, environmental, and cultural heritage impacts (*ibid.,* 15); and mainstream disaster risk reduction across all sectors including the promotion of mutual learning and exchange of good practices (*ibid.,* 17-18).

Recognizing that the sport industry is not included as a "non-State stakeholder" within the Sendai Framework, and that currently there are limited studies that integrate crisis and emergency management in sport (Shipway and Miles 2020), this study was designed to explore themes in Priority 1 and 2 of the framework as it pertains to the sport industry. In particular, the immediate impact of the Covid-19 lockdown on elite boxing and the response of Boxing's NFs to the lockdown. Findings will be used to help inform decision-making in policy and practice and provide preliminary data to support the integration of crisis and emergency management in sport.

Methodology

The study was conducted with eighteen key informants from eighteen different NFs from across the five continental confederations. The qualitative interviews focused on exploring two main themes: 1. the impact of the Covid-19 lockdown on NFs, and 2. the response of NFs during the lockdown. The study was approved by the Institutional Review Board (IRB) of the University of Delaware, and both researchers (university-affiliated and non-university affiliated) obtained the required human subjects training to interview participants in the study. To protect the privacy of interview participants, confidentiality was maintained in the reporting of findings.

The eighteen key informants held positions within their federation including: Executive Director, President, Vice President, Secretary General, Communications Manager, High Performance Director, Board Members and Head Coaches. An interview guide was used to explore the research themes but also allowed for flexibility for respondents to highlight pertinent themes not previously identified by the researchers.

Since the research themes are of an exploratory, descriptive nature, open-ended qualitative interviews were conducted as they produce in-depth responses concerning people and/or organization's experiences and knowledge that supports construction of understanding around the issue (Patton 2015). Key informants were utilized as they are individuals with knowledge, expertise, and influence in the topic area (*ibid.*).

Although the interview guide did outline pre-determined categories, such as "immediate impact" and "response" informed by the Sendai Framework, these sections were kept very broad, and thus inductive analysis was conducted. Inductive analysis includes evaluating the qualitative data for patterns and themes without applying preconceived frameworks, concepts, and/or theories (*ibid.*). A strategy of triangulating analysts was used in which both researchers analyzed the data independently and compared their findings to strengthen the credibility of the study's findings (*ibid.*).

Findings and Discussion

The findings and discussion have been organized by immediate impact and response as recorded in the interviews. Due to a number of diverse variables (e.g., size of federation, financial status, and organizational culture) that were out of the scope of the study, there appeared to be a broad range of responses from NFs. As such, it is noted that a number of NFs were not been able to respond or take any action during the lockdown. The strategies of those that were able to take action are provided to promote mutual learning and inform decision-making among other NFs, as well as providing a base for future research in this area.

Immediate Impact

"Canceled"

Around the world, NFs reported a similar immediate impact of the Covid-19 lockdown: cancellations. From the cancellation of Regional Events to National Championships to the Olympic Qualifiers, NFs reported an immediate freeze on boxing. Along with these cancellations came a number of other disruptions to NFs. One team (including a team manager, coach, and boxer) were in transit to attend a qualifying event abroad but had to return home just before Covid-19 was declared a pandemic. A Secretary General reported working closely with travel agents, the team, and the National Olympic Committee to bring the team immediately back home before borders closed. This disruption also influenced coaches who were working full-time in a foreign country; NFs reported that many of their foreign coaches immediately left for their home countries to avoid being stranded during the lockdown.

Financial Challenges

As a result of the lockdown and numerous event cancellations, a number of NFs reported a "severe economic setback." One Executive Director said that, "The Covid-19 pandemic has for now crippled the entire functioning of the boxing ecosystem in [their country]." NFs reported a significant portion of their financial support comes from membership fees, but since all boxing events were on hold, they had lost that revenue. Similarly, the cancellation of events led to a loss in revenue from registration, ticket sales, and sponsorships. An NF Executive Director stated,

> These mass cancellations have led to the sponsors withdrawing their support or asking for a deferment until business betters. As a sports federation where the only revenue source has been the government funding as well as the sponsorships, such pull outs have not only affected the training programs but it has also put a complete stop to the funding and support that the state bodies enjoyed.

The severity of financial hardship appeared to differ among NFs that reported a larger portion of government-funded support. One NF stated, "so far it has not had an impact. We have not lost funding because our main income comes from our government grants as, yet they are still honoring that although I do expect cut backs will be imminent."

This finding is important as it displays the expansive economic impact of the Covid-19 lockdown on elite boxing, including the loss of membership fees, event registration, ticket sales, and sponsorships. In addition, it appeared that NFs that reported a larger portion of government-funding support did not experience the same level of economic impact. Further research is needed to determine if additional government-funded support, or diversity in funding streams, could be a disaster risk resiliency strategy for NFs (see Priority 3 of Sendai Framework).

Athletes

The cancellation of events and the financial hardship inflicted upon some NFs has been challenging, but respondents were quick to identify the considerable struggles facing their boxers. These struggles were related to a loss of opportunity to compete and train in-person, as well as feelings of isolation. One respondent described,

> [The] immediate impact of travel restrictions due to Covid-19 resulted in loss of opportunities for athletes to compete in international and regional competitions as well as overseas training camp opportunities. This is what our boxers rely on to gain the necessary development, exposure and experience to achieve required preparations for qualification.

In a more drastic example, a President of one NF reported that four of their boxers were stranded in a foreign camp, and at the time of the interview, they still had not been able to get confirmation from the government of when they could return home. The respondent stated that they were maintaining communication with the boxers, but they were "broken and disheartened."

Along with lost opportunities to compete, there have been challenges related to training. Boxers were unable to train in-person and NFs reported several challenges related to virtual training sessions as some athletes did not have the space, proper devices, or online capabilities. There were also challenges related to training schedules and timelines. An NF President said, "Boxers, like other sports, train to peak for competition and since no one knows when next there will be any competition, the boxers training is limited. Difficult to train without purpose." The Secretary General of another NF spoke on the same issue, "[the] demotivation of athletes not having confidence in when they will be able to compete or go for training camps given the challenges of hosting a local competition." This finding begins to outline the impact of the lockdown on individual boxers, including the social, health, and economic implications (see Priority 1 of Sendai Framework), but additional research is needed to systematically evaluate these impacts on a larger scale.

Response

NFs' responses amid the lockdown varied considerably. Some NFs reported taking on a significant role of governance and acting in full coordination with clubs and boxers, while other NFs were unable to respond in any capacity and waited for the lockdown to lift before resuming activities. The responses described here are of NFs that reported substantial activity during the lockdown as a means to promote mutual learning and exchange of good practices.

Governance and Guidance

NFs that reported a very active role during the lockdown discussed operating in a role of governance and providing guidance to their boxing community. One respondent stated that early on in the lockdown their "Club Support Officers" phoned each club in their region to conduct a needs assessment and offer support. Similarly, another federation unified their provincial associations, clubs, athletes, coaches, and staff, and acted as a coordinator to streamline communication and address the challenges of the pandemic.

A number of NFs also spoke about advising pertinent parties on the most recent updates and recommendations surrounding Covid-19 and the implications for boxing. One respondent described this role, and highlighted that collaboration was strengthened between provincial associations and across combat sports to address a common problem,

> [Our] main goal was to ensure all provincial associations had the right resources, and right information to know what to do and what the recommendations were. So there were monthly calls with the provincial associations, so everyone was able to share their own experience in their province, able to get regular updates on how the situation was progressing in each province, they were able to share tips and ideas, what different measures could be implemented. Created great collaboration between provincial associations, which was there before but having to work on a common situation, strengthened the collaboration between each province. There was great communication with other combat sports and other NFs, since we had to discuss similar states because combat sports were facing similar restrictions. [It was a] great outcome. National federations also had greater collaboration.

Safety

Paralleling these efforts to provide accurate information and recommendations was guidance around safety measures. NFs reported maintaining communication on safety procedures through emails and closed social media groups with members and clubs, and through regular phone calls with coaches. One Board Member stated that their National Olympic Committee hosted regular meetings on safety guidelines and the NF was responsible to duly pass on the information to the member clubs. A Communications Manager shared that their NF provided proper signage on safety guidelines that could easily be printed from their website. These signs included guidelines on how to properly wash hands, the use of equipment, and what to do when entering a gym.

Respondents, including Presidents, Secretaries, and Coaches, stated that they strongly emphasized to members that there should not be any sparring or hand-pad sessions during training sessions. These particular types of sessions involve close contact between coach and athlete or two athletes, and therefore were not permitted. Additionally, one coach responded that the boxers who exercised outdoors or did their track work were told to wear appropriate masks or face shields and maintain strict physical distancing.

Financial Guidance and Support

Six NFs outlined how they provided financial guidance and support to their members. NFs communicated with provincial associations and clubs to make sure they were informed on any possible funding opportunities. One NF had their officers help clubs complete grant applications for emergency funding and were successful in helping 271 clubs secure an average of approximately $4,000 per club. This same NF also launched a campaign to encourage clubs to set up their own online funding campaigns, which ultimately resulted in raising approximately $148,000.

The actions of NFs to step into a more substantial role of governance as it pertained to sharing updated information on the virus, streamlining communication between levels of the organization, and conducting and responding to a needs assessments of stakeholders including financial support is in strong alignment with the Sendai Framework's Priority 2 (Strengthening disaster risk governance to manage disaster risk) and should be considered as an example of good practice among NFs.

Actions/Strategies Directed at Boxers

Virtual

Among the first responses by NFs during the lockdown was connecting virtually with their boxers, coaches, support staff, referees, and judges. The virtual strategies took on a variety of different forms including online workouts, trainings, educational webinars, live chats, Facebook resource pages, as well as comprehensive databases. The majority of NFs that went "virtual" started with a focus on their national teams and then grew the virtual boxing community to include their other members.

The High-Performance Director and the Communications Manager of one NF outlined their virtual support for the national team,

> The National Federation made sure that a reliable web platform was sourced and obtained to stay in contact with the athletes, even if not physical. We started to group the people that surround the national team (e.g., specialist, psychologist, physiologist, strength and conditioning), and started to provide strength and conditioning plans from the conditioning coach. Twice a week athletes did the program remotely at home, but with the strength and conditioning coach monitoring via computer, paying attention to what they did. Every week or two, the nutritionists sent recipes and nutrition advice, creating a system where they monitor the athletes remotely through apps and verified by the physiologist. A sport psychologist was accessible to all

athletes on the team and the physiotherapists stayed in touch with them to see about injuries. Video analyses was being done with the athletes every week and meetings were held every week with all the high performance athletes, and information was shared accordingly. The main goal was to keep athletes involved in the program to prevent a big shock when they return to training.

Numerous NFs reported maximizing the use of technology; including the production of training videos, skills identification videos, tactic videos, and videos related to maintaining fitness, health, and nutrition.

In a similar fashion, a Director reported on a special online class for qualified and elite boxers training for the World Qualifiers. The boxers had been connected to a single platform where Head Coaches posted special workout schedules to boxers, and the coaching staff was able to monitor their training. Athletes were encouraged to post videos of their trainings which were then evaluated by the coaches and Performance Director.

Engagement

Several NFs expressed a concern over isolation among their boxers and a resultant lack of motivation to train. In order to combat that, a few NFs discussed the development and distribution of mental health tools and resources, and implemented creative strategies for engaging their boxers and the wider boxing community. A Manager at one NF detailed the provision of a mental health indicator to boxers as well as resources outlining trauma and dealing with trauma. This same NF developed an online mental health tool that offered a series of free, online sessions focused on increasing awareness of mental health issues specifically in the boxing community and information on where to access support.

To help decrease isolation and increase engagement, a Communications Manager described how their NF created a social media campaign around "staying active" and encouraged members to send in examples of how they accomplished that. They shared these videos on their social media platform. A President of another NF tried to keep boxers engaged by hosting "mini" competitions, such as "best shadowboxing video." The winner would be awarded a small prize. Lastly, another NF encouraged their boxers to share videos on social media as a means of keeping them motivated as well as generating interest among fans.

General Boxing Community

Along with activities for elite boxers, NFs reported on strategies they implemented for juniors, sub-juniors, and the public. An NF's Executive Director described a virtual training class for juniors and sub-juniors that focused on teaching proper fitness techniques to avoid injury in the future. Such classes were operated live and were also available to the wider public as a means of outreach and promotion of the sport across the country. Similarly, an NF started a social media campaign where their elite boxers would showcase various facets of their lives during the lockdown and post "how to" home training videos for fans and the general public.

One Communications Manager described how student-athlete boxers helped keep the wider boxing community engaged. They created videos that could assist with training in lockdown, including an interactive virtual pad work session. Boxers could practice "hitting" the pads according to the instructions in the video or how the pad was positioned. These videos were shared on the NF's website and YouTube, for the use of a broader audience.

Furthermore, the pause in training allowed one NF the opportunity to complete construction of its national boxing center, which will be used for a variety of boxing-related activities and stakeholders. The President stated,

> The completion of the center had lagged for a few years, but the NF got permission for contractors to work on the structure as the boxers were not training for the period. The new facility boasts areas for training, hosting of events, conferences and most importantly, proper facilities for female boxers. The NF is very excited about the center and the opportunities that exist now with regards to female participation in the sport, unhindered training for national teams, and resumption of after-school programs. This was a positive that came out of the pandemic.

Collectively, the diverse strategies in response to the pandemic display an effort of resilience among NFs to reduce the negative effects of the lockdown on individual boxers including supporting their mental health, sport-specific performance, as well as income. These strategies again reveal the governing role that several NFs played in alleviating disaster risk (Priority 2) and highlight NFs as important entities in mitigating disaster risk in the boxing industry.

Joining the Fight

A particularly interesting and inspiring finding from the interviews was the work of one NF and its boxing community to directly support the fight against Covid-19. The respondent stated,

> The [country's] boxing federation launched a hotline in support of [country's] sport, which for two months provided assistance to ex sports personnel, athletes, coaches, referees, as well as veterans of the war, pensioners and large families during restrictions related to the prevention of the spread of the coronavirus infection. Boxers helped hospitals by giving them personal protective equipment and working on re-equipping building. Volunteers became blood donors, representatives of regional federations visited orphanages and boarding schools, delivering

food packages. Our volunteers delivered more than one and a half million masks and 122,000 liters of antiseptic hand wash, as well as 11,080 food packages.

This response by the NF and its boxing community was beyond the original conceptualization of the study, as the researchers were concerned with the response as it related to the sport and the support of its participants. Yet, this example underscores the critical governing role that NFs played, which in this case expanded beyond their boxers as they assumed the role of an organizing agent among their members to directly respond to the disaster in their country. This passionate response by the NF and its members, to support its wider community during a pandemic, helps to outline what is possible as we conceptualize the role of NFs in disaster risk resilience.

Conclusion

Findings from the study identified a substantial impact of the Covid-19 lockdown on NFs including immediate and widespread cancellations of competitions, events, and training with severe disruptions and implications for the health, safety, and financial stability of athletes, coaches, and clubs. Along with the substantial impact, additional findings revealed wide-ranging responses among NFs to the Covid-19 lockdown. Several NFs were able to take on a strong governing role which ultimately provided very different systems and supports for boxers in those countries and may have played a role in mitigating additional risk from the lockdown. From the study's limited sample, it appeared that the ability to take on this role was influenced by a variety of contextual variables including size of federation, financial status, and organizational culture, but additional research is needed to explore the presence and influence of these variables in a larger sample.

The range of responses is an important finding as it highlights a potentially inequitable system and structure in which elite boxers operated. Virtual strategies were continually highlighted as pivotal to working through barriers of the lockdown, but not all NFs and their boxers were able to acquire the equipment and online capabilities to conduct virtual training. Furthermore, due to the lockdown, boxers lost the opportunity to travel which is more critical for those that do not have the infrastructure to support elite performance in their country; further revealing an inequity exacerbated by the Covid-19 lockdown.

For NFs that were in a good position to respond, the findings revealed that many took on a strong role of governance to help manage the disaster response among their stakeholders. This included distributing up-to-date information on the virus, streamlining communication between levels of the organization, and conducting and responding to needs assessments of stakeholders. These findings display the potential role of NFs in mitigating disaster risk among their stakeholders as their work falls in alignment with the Sendai Framework.

In this governing role, NFs reported that the lockdown forced them to become more creative and implement a number of strategies to promote resilience among their organizations and stakeholders. It appeared that the "cancellation" of boxing allowed space for federations to brainstorm new ways of doing business, required greater efficiency under economic turmoil, and enhanced the skills required to support both elite athletes and the wider boxing community. Many of these newly-designed strategies could serve as good practices to inform decision-making among other NFs.

Collectively, these findings revealed the role that NFs can, and arguably should, play in mitigating risk of disaster among their stakeholders. Following guidance from the Sendai Framework to support federations in this role, it is important to mainstream and integrate information in disaster risk reduction into policies and administrative procedures of NFs. This can help to support NFs' responses in times of disaster, and potentially decrease the inequity experienced by boxers. This role can also be supported by documenting and sharing good practices that promote resilience among organizations and stakeholders. Future research should focus on building a more nuanced understanding and knowledge across crisis and emergency management in sport.

References

Barnum, Phineas Taylor. 2000. *The Life of P.T. Barnum*. Illinois: University of Illinois Press.
Boxing Federation of India. 2016. "Memorandum of Association." Accessed August 24, 2020. http://boxingfederation.in/wp-content//2017/12/BFI_Constitution.pdf.
Centers for Disease Control and Prevention, National Center for Immunization and Respiratory Diseases. 2019. "1918 Pandemic (H1N1 virus)." Accessed July 20, 2020. https://cdc.gov/flu/pandemic-resources.
International Boxing Association. 2018. "AIBA Statutes." Accessed July 24, 2020. https://d21c25674tgiqk.cloudfront.net/2019/01/20181109-Final-AIBA-Statutes_Approved-on-November-3-2018-reviewed-by-CR.pdf.
Miles, Lee, and Richard Shipway. 2020. "Exploring the Covid-19 Pandemic as a Catalyst for Stimulating Future Research Agendas for Managing Crises and Disasters at International Sport Events." *Event Management* 24 (4): 537–552. https://doi.org/10.3727/152599519X15506259856688.
National Institutes of Health. 2007. "Rapid Response was Crucial to Containing the 1918 Flu Pandemic." Accessed July 20, 2020. https://nih.gov/news-events/news- release/rapid- response-was-crucial.
New York Times Archives. 1918. "Influenza Halts Boxing Activity; New Jersey Health Authorities Latest to Put Ban on Fight Organizations." Accessed July 21, 2020. https://www.nytimes.com.
Patton, Michael Quinn. 2015. *Qualitative Research & Evaluation Methods*. California: Sage.
Roşca, Vlad. 2012. "The Political Economy of World Heavyweight Boxing During the Great Depression." *Theoretical and Applied Economics* 566 (1): 127-142.
Shipway, Richard, and Lee Miles. "Bouncing Back and Jumping Forward: Scoping the Resilience Landscape of International Sport Events and Implications for Events and Festivals." *Event Management* 24 (1): 185-196.
United Nations. 2015. "Sendai Framework for Disaster Risk Reduction." Accessed on September 15, 2020. https://www.undrr.org/publication/sendai-framework-disaster-risk-reduction-2015-2030.
United Nations Office for Disaster Risk Reduction. 2020. "Implementing the Sendai Framework" Accessed on September 15, 2020. https://www.undrr.org.
Williams, Clarence. 1975. "Boxing on Siboney." Accessed on July 20, 2020. Donated by Mrs. Clarence Williams. U.S. Naval Historical Center Photography.
Zidan, Karim. 2020. "What UFC Can Learn from Mistakes Made During Spanish Flu Outbreak." *The Guardian*, April 16, 2020. https://www.theguardian.com/sport/2020/apr/16/what-ufc-can-learn-from-boxings-mistakes-during-the-spanish-flu-outbreak.

CHAPTER 17

The Lift Seen Around the World: Hafþór Björnsson and Legitimacy in Strongman

Conor Heffernan

INTRODUCTION

It was a lift watched, streamed, and shared, around the world. Hafþór Björnsson, the Icelandic strongman and former *Game of Thrones* actor, stood before a barbell weighing over 1,100 lbs. In the months leading up to the May 2 event, which saw Hafþór lift a barbell from the floor to his waist (a "deadlift"), the athlete spoke confidently of his ability to set a record that would mark him as one of the world's greatest strongmen (McNulty 2020). Hafþór's goal had been to compete in a live competition against his peers, cheered on by fans. When it became apparent that the Covid-19 pandemic made such plans impossible, Hafþór, and his managers, set about devising a compromise, one which would allow him to complete the record safely. A decision was thus taken for Hafþór to complete the world record from his private gym in Iceland (Blechman 2020). It seemed a relatively unproblematic solution. After all, lifting heavy weights should be relatively objective. If the weights are measured before competition, there can be little doubt whether or not an individual has truthfully competed. The sport of strongman has rarely, however, abided by simple logic. On announcing his decision to attempt the record, Hafþór was met with a wave of criticism from fellow strongmen and fans who claimed the lift was illegitimate and a cheap publicity trick (Salmon 2020).

At the heart of such questions were issue of fairness and legitimacy. Understanding legitimacy, in this context, as something conferred by the adoption of regulatory processes akin to other sports, this chapter examines the absence of legitimacy for athletes and fans of strongman. Without an overarching federation or agreed upon set of rules, many advanced the idea that Hafþór's world record should was illegitimate. Those arguing against Hafþór's attempt claimed that done outside competition, in comfortable surroundings, with familiar equipment which may—or may not—have been altered, meant that such an exercise could not be counted as a record but rather as an exhibition (Ellis 2020). Critiques of athletes attempting to set records during the pandemic were not uncommon (Dure 2020) but the unique nature of strongman marked such disapproval as special. Unlike other sporting organizations, strongman is not a regulated sport. Numerous competitions exist, drug use is tolerated, and little standardization exists. Claims that Hafþór was acting in an untoward manner simultaneously highlighted and ignored the sport's uneasy foundations as a sport. Strongman has never been a formalized sport in, a point which this chapter explores. In doing so, this chapter argues that Hafþór's lift, and the controversy it attracted, highlighted the strained nature of legitimacy in a sport which operates on the nexus between sport and entertainment. Put another way, Hafþór's lift inadvertently highlighted the dysfunctional and unorganized nature of a pursuit still struggling to establish itself as a recognized sport. To do so, the chapter opens with a discussion of strongman's origins which, aside from a handful of works (Webster 1993), has yet to be explored. Following this, mention is given to a push for legitimacy in strongman before finishing with Hafþór's world record, set on May 2, 2020. The Covid-19 pandemic, and Hafþór's effort to circumvent its repercussions, began a debate about strongman as a sport that has yet to be resolved.

CIRCUSES, CELEBRITY, AND CONTESTS

Strength sports, as an endeavor, are simultaneously a modern, and pre-modern, sport. Accounts of men engaging in contests date back to the Chinese practice of lifting heavy stones and cauldrons in 6000 BC (Hai-sheng 2012). Likewise, Ancient Greece, Rome and Egypt, among other regions, had strength cultures (Crowther 2007). That withstanding, strength contests and feats, like Hafþór's deadlift, trace their immediate history to the late nineteenth and early twentieth century, when "physical culture" emerged as a new recreational movement. Defined by Michael Anton Budd as a late nineteenth and early twentieth century phenomenon concerned with the "ideological and commercial cultivation" of the body, physical culture marked the beginning of mass gym cultures (Budd 1997). Originating in Europe and spreading to the United States, physical culturists included strongmen and women who routinely competed against one another for prestige and popularity.

Tellingly, these early strength competitions were marked by their disorganized and deceptive nature. When Eugen Sandow travelled to London in 1889 to face fellow strongman Samson, he insisted on using his own equipment lest Samson attempt to cheat (Chapman 1994, 86-99). Sandow later brought fellow strongman, Arthur Saxon, to court over claims that Saxon deliberately cheated in a contest between the pair (Chapman 1994, 100-109). Unlike other sports, which codified during the nineteenth century, strength competitions remained a largely unregulated enterprise. Strongmen and women performers were found predominately in circuses, music halls and Vaudeville theaters. They often performed by themselves, lifted odd objects (anything from canons to bags of lime) and typically labelled themselves the strongest performer in the industry (Kent 2012). Early strongmen and women became synonymous with the objects they could lift. Speaking in a documentary, Professor Terry Todd noted that performers chose to lift odd objects, such as horse carts or cannons, because the public had an immediate frame of reference for how heavy an object was (Rogue Fitness 2017). Between performers, little incentive existed to challenge one another for fear of losing a claim to strength. When competitions did occur, deception was often attempted. This partly explains why Randy Roach's history of this period is ingeniously titled *Muscle, Smoke and Mirrors* (Roach 2008).

It became difficult to test whether or not a record was legitimate. In a different field Josh Boyd's (2009) study stressed the role of utility and responsibility in sporting legitimacy. If an organization or athlete is seen to act irresponsibly in the governing of a sport, and if rules are not applied uniformly, suspicions arise. Such was the incredulity which often met feats in the early 1900s that efforts were made by the 1920s to create some form of regulated strength competitions. Owing, in part, to the growing importance of weightlifting as an Olympic sport—which began in 1896—federations in Britain, Europe and the United States were created around various weightlifting movements (Bonini 2001). Unlike the strength shows found in the Music Hall or circus, such contests included specific equipment, namely barbells and/or dumbbells. These groups accurately measured equipment before competition, divided competitors into divisions, had verifiable records and used judges in their competitions. They were modernized in the Allen Guttmann (1978) sense of the word. Although critiqued now for its determinism about what was, and was not, a sport (Guttman 2001), Guttman's emphasis on records, contests and standards as a prerequisite for modern sport holds true. Such groups ensured that one strain of physical culture was formalized in the form of Olympic weightlifting and, in time, powerlifting (Todd 2003).

Absent from such worlds was the circus performer who continued to operate in a largely peripheral role throughout this period. Included in this was the Highland Games competitions found in the Scottish sporting calendar that combined athletics and strength contests (Jarvie 2004). Although the Highland Games came to influence the development of strongman, their largely unregulated nature and fluid governing structures mark it as a localized, rather than a national sport (Jarvie 2004). Despite the growth of weightlifting and powerlifting during the twentieth century, dedicated strongman shows remained the preserve of the circus. It was only in the 1970s that a strongman competition, based on odd lifts and strange objects, was held. Critical in this regard was the development of powerlifting in the 1960s. Also important was the popularity of *Superstars*, an American television show produced in 1973 that pitted famous athletes and celebrities against one another in competition (Pesca 2012). Powerlifting, which focused on the lifting of heavy weights using three specified movements, heightened discussions about who was, and who not, the strongest athlete in the United States. Testing athletes in the squat, bench press and deadlift, powerlifting was very much a modern sport defined by standardization and rules.

Where powerlifting intensified debates about strength, *Superstars* opened a space for new athletic spectacles on television. Previous discussions of *Superstars*, a television show that sought to determine the world's best athletes, have noted its immense popularity, as well as its legacy (Pesca 2012). Produced by ABC in the early 1970s, the program proved so successful that a series of spin-off shows were produced around the world (Pesca 2012). The idea that a multi-faceted athletic contest could take place, and command a great deal of television interest, partly explains the development of annual strength competitions. *Superstars* helped normalize the concept of somewhat eccentric athletic contests. One such example was the *World's Strongest Man* (henceforth: WSM) contest created in 1977. It was this competition that marked the creation of strongman and strongwomen competitions.

Produced by CBS, as part of Trans-World International, the WSM sought to do for strength sports what *Superstars* had done for sport more generally. Inviting athletes from several different sports, the contest sought to discover the world's strongest athlete (Todd 2002). Critically those involved in the creation of WSM marked a hodgepodge of sporting organizers and television executives. Two of the key organizers were David Webster and Douglas Edmunds, both of whom had been involved in athletics, Highland games and physical culture for decades (Webster 1994). This added some respectability to the event but the need for entertainment meant that their suggestions were often modified to make them palatable for television audiences (Todd 2002). Thus, strongmen were tasked with carrying refrigerators over long distances, lifting mock stages holding several women and bending iron bars. This, more than anything else, marked the beginning of strongman and in this beginning, a tension between sport and entertainment existed. This tension later fed into the legitimacy concerns surrounding Hafþór's deadlift.

The inaugural WSM was a commercial success and became an annual contest. From 1977 to the present day, the event has continued to be aired on television and still attempts to entertain audiences with strange sights. That commercial concerns have dominated this activity explain why, in the past, dominant competitors have been barred so as to avoid predictability, strongmen have faced off in sumo wrestling competitions and, in one-year's contest, deadlifted heavy blocks of cheese (Webster 1994). The interference of television concerns into the sport's actual competitive element is somewhat unique to strongman. Advertising has undoubtedly impinged the length of matches in the NFL, but marketing concerns have not changed the sport's rules (Goldsberry and Rowe 2020). Herein lies the sport's problem. Strongman's initial growth did not stem from a sporting federation, but rather a mishmash of athletes and advertisers. This has largely prevented the emergence of a dedicated governing body because the creation of such a group would likely limit the variability demanded by television audiences.

This tension between sport and spectacle has remained in the sport from 1977. Since the WSM's first contest, a series of other strongman events have been created but, owing to the sport's unregulated nature, no formal governing body exists in the same way that FIFA, for example, oversees world soccer. Returning to the issue of legitimacy, this has influenced debates about what is, or is not, an acceptable feat of strength. Regional, national and international contests exist, whose rules and standards are entirely subject to the whims of the organizers. In some instances, organizers have competed in their own events, which leads to claims of cheating (Art 2018). Without delving into the subsequent spread of strongman contests, many of which had a short life cycle, it is worth mentioning that it was only in the early 2000s that some form of regulation came to the sport through the growth of international strongman leagues, which served as qualifier events for the WSM and the creation of the Arnold Strongman Classic (henceforth: ASC). It was the ASC, and its subsequent association with Rogue Fitness, which serve as the backdrop for Hafþór's attempt as they helped normalize some form of consistent rule-setting and record breaking.

The Arnold Strongman Classic and the Drive for Respectability

The Arnold Strongman Classic, first held in 2002, is, alongside the WSM, one of the premier events of the strongman calendar. Part of the Arnold Sports Festival named after its creator Arnold Schwarzenegger, the ASC takes place each year in March. Significantly the ASC is one of the few strongman competitions that has not only competed with the WSM for legitimacy but has proven itself to be a sustainable contest. Work in extreme sports (Kim 2010) has stressed the importance of creating standard organizing bodies in the quest for legitimacy and recognition. The ASC has provided a small, but sustained, example of why this is important in strongman. One of the points which distinguishes the ASC is its unique focus on strength above all else. This was not an accident, but a deliberate move made at the contest's inception. The ASC was created in 2002 following a meeting between Arnold Schwarzenegger, his business partner Jim Lorimer and Professors Jan and Terry Todd. As retold by Terry Todd, the purpose of the ASC was to create a regulated test of strength that was contrasted with the WSM. As the WSM was equal parts sport and spectacle, similar in one sense to the "sport's entertainment" model found in professional wrestling (Atkinson 2002), challenges involved lifting heavy weights for long periods of time and often over a distance. Such feats made for excellent television footage but often failed to provide a true test of strength. Rather than discovering the strongest competitor, the WSM inadvertently created a competition to uncover the strongest, and most athletic, individual (Todd 2002).

It was a subtle difference but one the ASC exploited. Seeking to discover the strongest competitor, the ASC hosted contests which involved once off feats of strength undertaken in short and strict time limits. In this way, the ASC represented a truer form of competition for strongman competitors, one which cared more about competitiveness than television viewers. Critically, the ASC displayed a keen interest in records, and strict rules, two factors underpinning legitimacy in sport (Boyd 2009). Part of this stemmed from the involvement of Professor Terry and Jan Todd, as well as David Webster, formerly of the WSM. As historians of physical culture, and accomplished strength athletes in their own right, the Todds succeeded in incorporating events based on historic lifts. This explains why, at the inaugural 2002 contest athletes were challenged with the "Apollon Wheels," a barbell used by French strongman Louis Uni in the late 1800s (Todd 2002).

The WSC's reliance on television spectacles had largely divorced the sport from the earlier strongman shows from the 1900s. Rarely did the WSC attempt to utilize historic lifts, which meant that, in essence, its form of contest was born in 1977 and operated on the border of sport and entertainment. The ASC, in contrast, used verifiable weights, which held a historical record. In this way, the ASC attempted to legitimize the sport by using historical records, verifiable competition and record keeping as part of the contest (Todd 2002). This, more than anything else, has defined the ASC and explains why many within the sport regard ASC winners as stronger than WSM winners when discrepancies arise (Todd 2003). Later contests included the Inch Dumbbell used by strongman Thomas Inch in the early 1900s, the Cyr Dumbbell used by French-Canadian strongman Louis Cyr and a host of other objects. The ASC became a means of contest, spectacle and historic comparison. This explains why, from 2016, the ASC became to formalize, even further, its association with record keeping and legitimate competition.

In 2012 Rogue Fitness, an American barbell manufacturer, became the official supplier and sponsor to the Arnold Strongman Classic. Founded by Bill Henniger in 2007, the company is one of the fastest growing equipment manufacturers in North America (Anon. 2016). Working alongside the ASC's organizers, Rogue developed a keen interest in the history of strength, a point evidenced by the several historic documentaries created by the company on famous strongmen and strongwomen from the early twentieth century (Rogue Fitness 2017). Aside from documentaries, Rogue also created an online database of historical documents in conjunction with Professors Jan and Terry Todd, while also producing its own line of strength equipment said to mimic old strongman devices. To somewhat labor the point, the company's keen interest in the history of strength surpasses many of its competitors, even companies like York Barbell which has produced equipment since the early 1930s (Fair 1999). Rogue's creation of an annual Rogue Record Breaker contest at the ASC—an annual contest designed to break historical records—from 2016 furthered this interest (Todd 2016).

Driven primarily by the ASC, strongman competitions, including the WSC, began to record more and more records. Previously a sporadic concern, legitimate records now became a driving focus. Athletes, in turn, began to explicitly target new records as a means of increasing their popularity, and it is no coincidence that such athletes often did so on social media. Eddie Hall, the man whose record Hafþór ultimately broke, spent several months detailing his training and ambitions on social media platforms as a means of generating interest and sponsorship. For a sport firmly rooted in entertainment and spectacle, greater efforts were made to set tangible records distinct from the carnivalesque WSM approach. Thus in 2014 Icelandic strongman Benedikt Magnússon set a new world record in the deadlift at a Europe's Strongest Man Competition. The commentary and reporting surrounding Magnússon's lift, especially online, revitalized efforts to break the deadlift record. Prior to 2014, the last record had been set in 2011, again by Magnússon. As a recognizable strongman, Magnússon's record encouraged other strongmen to challenge the record. The first athlete was Eddie Hall, an English born strongman who, in 2015 broke Magnússon's record by 2.2 pounds at the Arnold Expo in

Melbourne, Australia. That the new record was set at an event sponsored by Arnold Schwarzenegger points once more to the change effected by Arnold's involvement with strongman. The deadlift record next rotated between Eddie Hall, Benedikt Magnússon and another strongman Jerry Pritchett. The rivalry culminated in 2016 when Eddie Hall set a new deadlift record of 1,102 lbs. or 500 kilograms. Surpassing his rivals, and in Hall's own testimony nearly killing him, the record established Hall as one of the strongest men in recorded history (Tao 2018).

HAFÞÓR AND THE LIFT SEEN AROUND THE WORLD

Largely absent from this story, so far, has been Hafþór Björnsson, the Icelandic strongmen who currently holds the world record in the deadlift. To understand why Hafþór's record proved so controversial, it is necessary to understand the shaky foundations and recent modernization of the sport of strongman. Hafþór's own career is deeply related to these issues. More famous for his role as "The Mountain," a mute but violent knight, in the HBO series *Game of Thrones*, Hafþór's strongman career has always likewise couched in sport and entertainment (Hibberd 2020). As relates to the current state of the sport, much of Hafþór's training, philosophies and rivalries have been played out in the public arena, especially in the case of Hafþór's relationship with Eddie Hall.

Since 2017, Hafþór and Hall have publicly feuded online and in person. The cause of this conflict stems from that year's WSM competition in which Hall narrowly defeated Hafþór to win the contest. In the aftermath of the decision, Hafþór argued poor judging decisions handed Hall the contest, a claim the Englishman denied. That Hall officially retired from strongman competitions after 2017 did little to temper their arguments. Using social media platforms like Instagram and YouTube, the two have continually accused one another of lies, unsportsmanlike behavior and, on more than one occasion, of "unmanly" attitudes. Hall's labelling of Hafþór as "unsportsmanlike and unprofessional," "the world's weakest liar," and a "scum bag" provide some indication of the vitriol exchanged (Cooper 2020). There is, much like professional wrestling or boxing, a degree of showmanship in all of this. Done online, such feuds boosted both athletes' public profile and, in the case of Hall, allowed him remain relevant. That, at the time of writing, both men have signed a lucrative contract to compete in a boxing match provides some indication of the calculated, or profitable, nature of this rivalry (Chapman 2020).

Others in the sport have also capitalized on this rivalry. Since 2018 Hafþór has been continuously challenged, and encouraged, to break Hall's deadlift record. At the 2018 ASC, Hafþór set a new record in the elephant bar deadlift, a specialized piece of equipment designed by Rogue Fitness (Horaczek 2019). Although less than Hall's record, the record signaled a growing movement to challenge Hall's feat, with Hafþór cast as a frontrunner. It is telling that Rogue were one of the most vocal and supportive players in this regard. Aside from providing equipment, the firm offered huge prize monies for Hafþór to defeat Hall's record as individual contests began bidding for Hafþór's involvement. In February 2020, it was announced that Hafþór would attempt the feat at a World's Ultimate Strongman contest that April in Dubai (Lockridge 2020). This did not, however, prevent others from attempting to woo the strongman. At the 2020 ASC, held in March, Hafþór was offered $101,000 to defeat the deadlift record (GI Team 2020). The size of the prize money was reflective of the strain placed on the competition by the outbreak of Covid-19—a late decision was made to ban crowds from attending.

Hafþór declined the offer, claiming he wanted to focus on winning that year's competition, which he ultimately did. Cognizant of the expectations placed on him, his camp announced that, as planned, Hafþór would break the record at the upcoming WUS contest the following month. The announcement was naïve in hindsight. The ASC struggled to run due to Covid-19, and although few fully appreciated the extent of the virus's transmission, it was unlikely to have vanished in four weeks. The WUS show was canceled on April 11, 2020. In the days preceding the WUS cancellation, Hafþór toyed with the idea of attempting the feat from his home gym in Iceland (Cooper 2020). This decision was later formalized after the April 11 announcement.

Former strongman and current referee Magnus Ver Magnusson would adjudicate while spectators could watch the attempt online or through American broadcaster ESPN. Objections to this compromise arose even before the official announcement. On April 5, Eddie Hall claimed during a YouTube video that he did not trust Hafþór or those managing him to conduct the lift fairly. Citing objections made about Hall's 2017 WSM victory—in which Hafþór cited poor refereeing judgements—Hall claimed that the same scrutiny should be placed on Hafþór (Cooper 2020). The tone of Hall's comments was undoubtedly accusatory, a point he admitted during a subsequent apology (Cooper 2020). The underlying sentiment of his complaint, that Hafþór needed to complete the lift in competition, and not in private, nevertheless initiated a great deal of soul searching within the sport. In the absence of a recognized organizing body the legitimacy of individual records could be challenged or deemed illegitimate with relative ease. As the sport was now providing ever increasing prize monies for world records, a risk now existed that certain records could be disregard based on a public consensus that it was illegitimate.

Hall had the most to lose from Hafþór's challenge. Many with less at stake still, however, echoed his views. Fellow strongman, Brian Shaw, was one such example. Having worked with Hall on a short-lived *Strongest Man in History* show for the History Channel, Shaw's support for Hall was unsurprising but powerful (Cooper 2020). A multiple time WSM winner, Shaw's reputation in the sport was beyond reproach. His objections were echoed, and supported by others within the sport like Mark Bell, who runs a successful podcast which hosted both Eddie Hall and Hafþór during this time (Bell 2020). Significantly in the age of social media, a great deal of the debate was played out online, on popular platforms like Reddit and Twitter (Reddit 2020). At the heart of these criticisms was the idea that for a record to be valid, it needed to be done in competition. In the absence of an independent judge or federation, competitions were presented as the most impartial platform the sport had to offer. Taking such criticisms to extremes, some argued that without spectators, other competitors and standardized equipment, Hafþór's lift was open to critique but also suspicion to the point of being illegitimate. That Hafþór was attempting to break a world record, rather than win a contest, from his own gym did little to quell such claims.

Those supporting Hafþór put forward a number of important points. In the first instance several strongmen had broken records without being in a competition. Rogue's Record Breakers series often featured one strongman attempting to break a record in a variety of different lifts. While this was done in front of a crowd, it was done outside of competition (Reddit 2020). Next many noted that although Hafþór was going to execute the lift from his own gym, a registered, although unaffiliated, strongman judge would attend, all of his equipment would be weighed and individuals could watch online or on television (Reddit 2020). It was presented as a clever solution to the problem of Covid-19 and the need for social distancing. Finally, and this point stemmed from the sport's origins, that there was no set standard for the sport (Cooper 2020; Reddit 2020). There was no rulebook and hence no guidelines as to what was, and was not, legitimate.

There was no one formal strongman organization. Where soccer has FIFA or American Football has the NFL, strongman is, in reality, a hodgepodge of different organizers who roughly follow the same patterns. Among these groups there is no hierarchy between organizers save, of course, for popularity. This does not make for an objective, or arguably legitimate, framework. When individuals claimed a lack of legitimacy, it made no sense in the context of a sport with no federation. Legitimacy in sport is premised, largely, on adherence to a set grouping of rules (McFee 2004). Strongman did not have this owing to its history as a music hall, and later television spectacle. Jan Todd, the physical culture professor and ASC organizer even commented as much. Detailing her dismay at the unsportsmanlike conduct exhibited on the part of Hall, Todd noted that,

> there is no all-encompassing association for Strongman that legitimates world records as the International Weightlifting Federation (IWF) does for Olympic weightlifting. And, unlike weightlifting where the rules plainly state that world records can only be set in specific IWF competitions, in front of certified referees, and following exacting rules, Strongman has no standardized rules that apply to all competitions. (Todd 2020)

Instead, Todd claimed that legitimacy in strongman has always come from the acceptance of other athletes and spectators. Put another way, Todd argued that if others believed the lift was genuine, that was enough. Todd was not alone in this point. Andy Bolton, a former powerlifter and strongman competitor, endorsed this view on Facebook. Bolton himself was a one-time world record holder in the deadlift when he became the first man to deadlift 1,000 lbs. That Bolton and Todd publicly claimed legitimacy on Hafþór's behalf was shared enthusiastically in the days leading up to the event.

Hafþór and his team remained quiet on this point, aside from occasional comments that anyone could challenge Hafþór if they so wished (Cooper 2020). It was clear, however, that anxieties about the attempt's legitimacy were not to be ignored. On ESPN and an internet live stream hosted by Hafþór, commentators emphasized the event's transparency (ESPN8 2020). Weights were measured, commentators celebrated the accuracy of the measurements, and fans were allowed to engage with one another using a live stream. In a 'behind the videos' scene uploaded the day after the event, spectators were shown Hafþór's team meticulously weighing each weight. The same video showed the referee for the record, Magnus Ver Magnusson, running through all the requirements for the lift (Björnsson 2020). As much as a strongman event could be legitimate, this was it.

Ultimately successful, Hafþór's attempt nevertheless highlighted a vacuum which existed in strongman. It is telling that in other sports, with impartial federations, world records produced in during Covid-19 isolation were ratified and seen as legitimate. Strongman, on the other hand, had no such organization. This meant that when Hafþór announced his intention to attempt the record from his home gym, there were no guidelines. Likewise, when Hall and others disputed his attempt, there was no formal adjudicator outside of the sport's fandom. That the sport has not yet evolved from its music hall and television spectacle origins, that it has not yet modernized (Guttman 1978), encouraged controversy over a relatively straightforward issue. In effect, Covid-19, and attempts to continue strongman during the pandemic, highlighted the still strained nature of strongman as a sporting spectacle and the need to formally organize. As the sport continues to privilege new records, the absence of a formal federation means that no record is beyond reproach and can, as shown by Hafþór, be challenged as illegitimate by those one's rivals.

CONCLUSION

That strongman struggles to balance its music hall origins with a more serious sporting identity was showcased in more ways than one during Hafþór's record. Immediately after breaking the record, Hafþór told viewers that his next great feat would be a boxing match with Eddie Hall. This, perhaps unsurprisingly, led to a great deal of suspicion that Hall's objections were made as a means of exciting interest in a fight between the two men, rather than any innate desire in codifying his sport. Regardless of the, somewhat cynical, efforts used to excite interest in a boxing bout, the Hall/Hafþór disagreements spoke to both the problems caused in the sporting world by Covid-19 but also the fragility of strongman as a respectable sport. The fragility of strongman, as understood in its lack of organizing body and ever-changing rules, was not created by the pandemic but rather exacerbated by it.

In other sports, like soccer, challenges to games played without spectators often centered on the argument that it is too unlike the "real" experience (Sports Illustrated

2020). Important though such criticisms were, they were largely superficial. There was little objection to events undertaken during Covid-19 induced social distancing. This was because in many other sports a general structure, or general apparatus, for sport and competition not only exists, but has done so for several decades. Strongman has no such apparatus and this issue does not stem from its relatively recent origins. Other sports, most notably mixed martial arts or mixed martial arts were formalized after strongman and, for the most part, operate from a largely clear set of practices overseen by federations. Strongman lacks a set rulebook, no overarching federations exist, athletes are effectively freelancers, and contests vary in their motivations and executions. Until now, such points rarely, if ever, caused problems. It was only in times of crisis fundamental questions began to be asked about legitimacy and fair play. The answers have yet to be found but it is likely that strongman's soul-searching over what is, and is not, a legitimate feat, has only just begun.

REFERENCES

Anon. 2016. "Rogue Fitness Partners with Arnold Strongman Classic." *UCW Newswire*. February 26, 2016. http://press.ucwe.com/2016/02/26/rogue-fitness-partners-with-arnold-strongman-classic/.

Atkinson, Michael. 2002. "Fifty Million Viewers Can't Be Wrong: Professional Wrestling, Sports-Entertainment, and Mimesis." *Sociology of Sport Journal* 19 (1): 47-66.

Bell, Mark. 2020. "Mark Bell's Power Project." YouTube, April 24, 2020. https://www.youtube.com/watch?v=VjKGLwxoeTg.

Björnsson, Hafþór. 2020. "WORLD RECORD DEADLIFT 501KG! Behind the scenes!" YouTube, May 2, 2020. https://www.youtube.com/watch?v=4e8azCO3seg.

Blechman, Phil. 2020. "ESPN to Broadcast Hafthor Bjornsson's 501kg Deadlift World Record Attempt." *Barbend*, April 15, 2020. https://barbend.com/hafthor-bjornsson-501kg-deadlift-espn/.

Bonini, Gherardo. 2001. "London: The Cradle of Modern Weightlifting." *Sports Historian* 21 (1): 56-70.

Boyd, Josh. 2009. "The Legitimacy of a Baseball Number." In *Rhetorical and Critical Approaches to Public Relations II*, edited by Robert L. Heath, Elizabeth L. Toth, and Damion Waymer, 154-169. New York: Routledge.

Budd, Michael A. 1997. *The Sculpture Machine: Physical Culture and Body Politics in the Age of Empire*. New York: NYU Press.

Chapman, Anthony. 2020. "Hafthor Bjornsson vs Eddie Hall Boxing Match CONFIRMED with The Mountain to Fight the Beast in September 2021." *The Sun*, May 4. 2020. https://www.the-sun.com/sport/779895/hafthor-bjornsson-eddie-hall-boxing-confirmed-date/.

Chapman, David L. 1994. *Sandow the Magnificent: Eugen Sandow and the Beginnings of Bodybuilding*. Chicago: University of Illinois Press.

Cooper, Edward. 2020. "Fighting for 501: The Bizarre, Fascinating and Fierce Feud Between Strongman's Eddie Hall and Hafþór Björnsson." *Men's Health*, April 17, 2020. https://www.menshealth.com/uk/fitness/a32157739/eddie-hall-hafthor-bjornsson-deadlift/.

Crowther, Nigel B. 2007. *Sport in Ancient Times*. Westport: Greenwood Publishing Group.

Dure, Beau. 2020. "U.S. Rowers Fight Back Against COVID-19 in Real World and Virtual World." *NBC Sports*, April 22, 2020. https://olympics.nbcsports.com/2020/04/22/us-rowing-covid-19-virtual/.

ESPN 8: The Ocho. 2020. "The Mountain Hafthor Bjornsson Deadlifts 1,104 Pounds to Set New World Record." YouTube, May 2, 2020. https://www.youtube.com/watch?v=Z1F0bEQ5L5E.

Fair, John D. 1999. *Muscletown USA: Bob Hoffman and the Manly Culture of York Barbell*. Pennsylvania: Penn State Press.

GI Team, 2020. "Hafthor Bjornsson Breaks World Record With 501KG Deadlift." *Generation Iron*, May 2, 2020. https://generationiron.com/hafthor-bjornsson-world-record-deadlift/.

Goldsberry, Kirk and Katherine Rowe. 2020. "How Much Football is Even in a Football Broadcast?" *Five Thirty-Eight*, January 31, 2020. https://fivethirtyeight.com/features/how-much-football-is-even-in-a-football-broadcast/.

Guttman, Allen. 1978. *From Ritual to Record. The Nature of Modern Sports*. New York: Columbia University.

———. 2001. "From Ritual to Record: A Retrospective Critique." *Sport History Review*, 32 (1): 2-11.

Hai-sheng, Q.I.N. 2012. "The Research on the Weightlifting Sports of Ancient China." *Journal of Anyang Institute of Technology* 2: 26.

Hibberd, James. 2020. "Game of Thrones Actor on His Next Goal: Winning the Heaviest Boxing Match Ever." *Entertainment Weekly*, June 4, 2020. https://ew.com/tv/game-of-thrones-hafthor-bjornsson-mountain-interview/.

Horaczek, Stan. 2019. "Building a Barbell For 1,000 Pound Deadlifts Takes Careful Engineering and Lots of Testing." *Pop Sci*, January 9, 2019. https://www.popsci.com/rogue-elephant-bar-deadlift-barbell/.

Jarvie, Grant. 2004. "Lonach, Highland Games and Scottish Sports History." *Journal of Sport History* 31 (2): 161-175.

Kent, Graeme. 2012. *The Strongest Men on Earth: When the Muscle Men Ruled Show Business*. London: Biteback Publishing.

Lockridge, Roger. 2020. "Hafthor Bjornsson Will Attempt 501kg Deadlift in Bahrain." *Barbend*, February 24, 2020. https://barbend.com/hafthor-bjornsson-501kg-deadlift-bahrain/.
McFee, Graham. 2004. *Sport, Rules and Values: Philosophical Investigations into the Nature of Sport*. London: Routledge.
McNulty, Rose. 2020. "Hafþór Björnsson Sets Deadlift World Record at 1,104 Pounds." *Muscle & Fitness*, May 2, 2020. https://www.muscleandfitness.com/athletes-celebrities/news/hafthor-bjornsson-sets-new-deadlift-world-record/.
Michael, Kim. 2010. "Mixed Martial Arts: The Evolution of a Combat Sport and its Laws and Regulations." *Sports Law Journal*, 17: 49-71.
Pesca, Mike. 2012. "Olympians Were 'Superstars' In ABC Sports Show." *NPR*, February 22, 2012. https://www.npr.org/2012/02/22/147247325/olympic-athletes-were-superstars-in-abc-sports-show.
Philip, Ellis. 2020. "Strongman Eddie Hall Is Beefing with Hafthor Bjornsson Over His Upcoming 501 Kg Deadlift." *Men's Health*, April 11, 2020. https://www.menshealth.com/fitness/a32114726/strongman-eddie-hall-hafthor-bjornsson-501-kg-deadlift-dispute/.
Reddit, 2020. "Thor's 501kg Deadlift: Legitmate World Record?" *Reddit*, April 29, 2020. https://www.reddit.com/r/Strongman/comments/fzp4hw/thors_501kg_deadlift_legitimate_world_record/.
Roach, Randy. 2008. *Muscle, Smoke, and Mirrors*. Bloomington: AuthorHouse.
Rogue Fitness. 2017. "The Rogue Legends Series Chapter 2: Louis "Apollon" Uni." YouTube, October 11, 2017. https://www.youtube.com/watch?v=kdZZm1f4RvY
Salmon, Jonathan. 2020. "Eddie Hall Apologizes While Top Strongmen React to Hafthor Bjornsson Deadlift Challenge." *Generation Iron*, April 14, 2020. https://generationiron.com/eddie-hall-strongmen-react-hafthor-bjornsson/.
Sports Illustrated. 2020. "Fake Crowd Noise on Soccer Broadcasts Provides Comfort, But It's Disingenuous." *Sports Illustrated*, May 27, 2020. https://www.si.com/soccer/2020/05/27/fake-crowd-noise-soccer-tv-broadcasts-bundesliga
Tao, David. 2018. "Breaking: Eddie Hall Makes History, Becomes First Man to Deadlift 500kg." *Barbend*, October 17, 2018. https://barbend.com/eddie-hall-makes-history-becomes-first-man-deadlift-500kg/.
Terry, Art. 2018. "Why You Need to Pay Attention to The Sport of Strongman." *Joker Mag*, August 10, 2018. https://jokermag.com/why-you-need-to-pay-attention-to-the-sport-of-strongman/.
Todd, Jan. 2003. "Chaos Can Have Gentle Beginnings: The Early History of the Quest for Drug Testing in American Powerlifting: 1964-1984." *Iron Game History: The Journal of Physical Culture*, 8: 17-18.
———. 2020. "Records, Vitriol and Hafthor Bjornsson's Quest for the 501 Kilo Deadlift." *Stark Center*, April 30, 2020. https://starkcenter.org/2020/04/records-vitriol-and-hafthor-bjornssons-quest-for-the-501-kilo-deadlift/?fbclid=IwAR3i2eMae7SIeKpNAyWPvVs4WzOL4vXnOhjwnHpRpFGpptwAvNLwuZD6nGs.
Todd, Terry. 2002. "The Arnold Strength Summit." *Iron Game History* 7 (2-3): 4-11.
———. 2003. "Arnold's Strongest Man." *Iron Game History* 8 (1): 3-8.
———. 2016. "The 2016 Arnold Strongman Classic." *Rogue Fitness*, March 3, 2016. https://www.roguefitness.com/rogue-equipped-events/2016-arnold-strongman-classic.
Webster, David P. 1993. *Sons of Samson*. Glasgow: D.P. Webster.

CHAPTER 18

Rise of the Machine: On the Prevalence of Indoor Rowing Records Under Covid-19

Alec S. Hurley

INTRODUCTION

In mid-April of 2020, a rising star on the Australian National Women's rowing team sat down on her indoor rowing machine to get in a long Saturday quarantine workout. Seventy-nine minutes later, she emerged having unknowingly bested the world record for the half-marathon on the stationary ergometer with a time that shattered the previous mark set in 2014. In the weeks that followed, records on indoor rowing machines continued to fall around the world. Restless Olympic hopefuls, alongside disheartened oarsmen and women at all levels, reluctantly turned to indoor training in response to the 2020 competitive racing season's postponement. What has been revealed during this trying time has been an appreciation of the ulterior motives for participation in an athletic contest. This work will analyze the impact Covid-19, and its disruption to traditional training programs, had on the rewriting of record books as rowers of all levels faced the loss of traditional constructs such as communal physical space while uniting around a shared global homogeneity.

There is little in modern history that one might equate to the current pandemic wrought by Covid-19. Scholars have compared the Olympic disruptions of Tokyo 2020 with the 1920 Antwerp Games held during the outbreak of the infamous Spanish Flu (Constandt and Willem 2020, 2). The current pandemic, however, has cost the postponement or cancellation of athletic events in a way the "forgotten" epidemic of a century ago did not (Honigsbaum 2013, 167). As athletes were forced inside during the Spring of 2020, competition and the pursuit of records remained, albeit restricted to isolated practice sessions and digital communication. As with any historical project involving an ongoing and evolving situation, this piece relied heavily upon rowing "trade publications" such as the renowned website row2k.com as well as national team news publications for primary data. To provide proper historical grounding on both the pursuit of records and indoor rowing the works of Allen Guttmann (2004), Volker Nolte (2005), and Hans Bonde (2009)—among others—were essential.

Previous studies on the pursuit of records—from Guttmann (2004) to Brohm (1978), Bale (2003), and Loland (2001)—have focused on competition. Few sports, if any, have the capacity to set formally recognized records in practice sessions except for rowing, which makes this a novel area of inquiry. The indoor rowing machine known as an ergometer is, and always has been, a training tool—akin to a treadmill for runners or NordicTrack for skiers. However, records in the latter two have been celebrated far less feverishly due to those who compete internationally rarely using the machines as official testing apparatuses in their training processes. The same is not true for rowing, where elite and recreational competitors alike use the same equipment for regular physiological testing purposes. What also differentiates rowing is the accepted variation within machine-based training records. Different versions of the ergometer, from the quintessential stationary machine to the recently developed dynamic ergometer, all possess records validated by *FISA*, the international governing body of rowing, with elite athletes and lower rungs of competitors lumped together separated only by age and sex. Therefore, the pursuit of these "training records" are the closest to a level playing field that sport has.

The history of the indoor rowing machine—colloquially known as an "erg" or "ergo" for those outside the United States—traces its roots to roughly the fourth century B.C. In Athens, naval recruits would be trained on the proper technique on land via wooden frames adjacent to the shore before sending them out to sea (Heffernan 2016). Variations of the device evolved over the course of the first two millennia A.D. with one particularly ill-fated version commissioned for the Titanic's opulent gym (Garber 2012). The device turned from tortuous training machine into an exciting competitive apparatus in 1980. Denied an Olympic appearance, an eclectic mixture of frustrated senior members of the United States National rowing team—men and women—along with a couple of the Harvard varsity and friends set up the then brand-new Dreissigacker indoor rowing machines in the cramped Newell Boathouse on the Charles River in Boston and raced (Rosenbladt 2018). What started as a small-scale way to vent bitterness amidst once-in-a-generation circumstances has evolved into the world's largest indoor rowing event. The current pandemic has offered the latest generation of athletes a chance to write their own unique chapter to this story.

In an op-ed for the BBC, Matthew Syed presented the current Covid-19 pandemic as an opportunity; a rare upside to "reimagine the world and our place within it" (Syed 2020). As such, sport and leisure face a moment of reflection regarding traditional practices (Lashua, Johnson, and Parry 2020, 2). The possible upside to this catastrophic pandemic is the opportunity to see sport in an entirely new light, to foster new avenues in the pursuit of long-established benchmarks. In his influential thesis on the quantification and obsession with records, Allen Guttman postulated that sport would continue to exist in the absence of an audience. Facilitating a more in-depth exploration into the emergence of machine- or indoor-based records under global isolation orders can thereby provide insight into both the human fascination with records and the transformation of sport during a global pandemic.

RECORDS AND MEANING

Guttmann's bold proclamation in 1978 that "sports have existed, do exist, and will continue to exist in situations without an audience," seemed untestable even at the time of his revised edition in the early 2000s (Guttmann 2004, 12). Under the current pandemic, not only have sports continued to play—when safe—but all manner of creative endeavors were made to fill the stands (Fernandez 2020). Even endurance sport persevered. The natural isolated training environment provided a smoother transition into quarantine than ball sports and the ever-looming presence of records provided the necessary motivation. To break a record—or even the attempt—defines sport. Record breaking mirrors society's constant quest for "more" and quantifies its passion for "progress." Through the celebration of milestones, exemplified by records, sport embeds itself within the minds of the population (Lopez-Gonzalez 2014, 353).

This is not to say that the meaning behind records has been static. Rather it has consistently found itself to be a hotly contested point of discussion within sport scholarship. In a recent attempt to scientifically analyze the history of records, a Danish historian concluded that there is no such thing as a "bad record" (Bonde 2009, 1321). In an explanation which highlighted the singular nature of "time sport," Bonde argued that any given record merely represents the quantifiable high point within a given discipline. As such records can never be canceled, merely surpassed. Therefore records, even the most rigidly guarded, carry a somewhat arbitrary nature. The prioritization of time over a distance rather than distance over a time simply happened (Guttmann 2004, 2). However, debates over the arbitrary nature of records miss the point. Records allow athletes and fans alike to sift through the increasingly endless stream of statistical data to uniformly decide which performances are worth remembering (Lopez-Gonzalez 2014, 357). Their central importance is their function as a tool to help distinguish "the 'forgettable' from the 'unforgettable'" (Roche 2003, 109).

Shift to Quantification

The shift towards quantification can be traced back as early as the eighteenth century but did not reach a point of intellectual dominance until the middle of the nineteenth century. Guttmann links the emergence of sport records with the "Theory of Progress," which simply stated is the "linear concept which assumes that every improvement can be improved upon" (Guttmann 2004, 53). A sociologist later critiqued that stance, positing that the most salient feature of quantification was its ability to "reduce complex events into intelligible, manageable information for mass audiences" (Giulianotti 2005, 21). Sport, therefore, represents a form of knowledge—its own epistemology. As such sport competitions can be equated with a scientific experiment in which performances are ranked and recorded. Quantification then is simply the process through which two or more participants in an athletic contest can be compared and measured (Jonasson 2014, 1310). Performance measurements and an exact standardized framework are the necessary requirements for what Sigmund Loland described as "record sport." The absence of one or the other relegated a physical activity to the "quasi-record sport" category (Loland 2001, 128).

This framework nicely suits the dual-natured position of rowing. Competitions and training which take place on the water clearly fall under Loland's second category as there is not an exact standardized framework because varying bodies of water create a multitude of possible locations. However, indoor rowing fits both criteria necessary for "record sport" classification. Standard performance measurements are easily verified as the indoor rowing machine are manufactured by only a few companies worldwide that adhere to international standards. The exact framework is also determined by the machine as concerns about external conditions are nullified by its indoor placement. While the specific type of indoor location may vary (gym, garage, or even a driveway) the differences in conditions are not recognized as a significant factor. Therefore, despite on-water rowing being the primary avenue of competition, indoor rowing is better equipped to embrace the pursuit of records.

Formalization of Progress

In the twentieth century the spatial aspects of progress came under increased scrutiny alongside its temporal counterpart. The dictionary definition of progress alludes to that spatial characteristic, as it is derived "from a Latin word meaning 'step forward'" (Bonde 2009, 1322). Part of the "step forward" in the progress of sport is the tendency towards homogeneity and globalization. Often coming at the cost of local customs and folk sport, the modern evolution towards the "sameness" of space prioritizes interchangeability over unique regional difference (Bale 2003, 148). The technological advancements have, however, generated a unique global community. During the Covid-19 pandemic, elite level rowers have been able to assess their training levels quickly and accurately compare with those of their teammates due to the widespread availability of identical equipment and similar environments ("George Relishes Record" 2020). Consequently, full rosters of Olympic eligible athletes have been able to adhere to the same training program knowing the conditions and apparatuses are equal across the board.

The ability to obtain and clarify measurable achievements is a cornerstone of a theory towards the progress of sport proposed by Guttmann's contemporary Jean-Marie Brohm. His conceptualization of progress within elite sport relied less on the record itself than on the increasing sophistication of processes for measuring improvement. Homogenization of sport was to Brohm, unlike Bale, something to be desired. It could guarantee the standardization of records across the globe or between varying sets of rules (Lopez-Gonzalez 2014, 349). The standardization of records allowed athletes to construct a deeper connection with their sport. Performances, especially in "record sport," enabled elite athletes to identify with "the product of their work" as would a craftsman or tradesman (Guttmann 2004, 76).

As the athletes grew more closely connected to their labor, some on the edge of elite sport feared the growing connection between the athletes and the pursuit of records was a dangerous and possibly reckless endeavor. At the 1912 Olympic Games a Danish medical doctor in attendance feared that the obsession with records—specifically how fast one could cover a distance—would lead to a corruption of the sporting gentleman. The "cult of speed," as termed by the doctor, transformed the means of sport into its end. A growing fear persisted that if athletes were not careful the pursuit of records could cost one his life or health (Bonde 2009, 1324). The "cult of speed" ultimately prevailed and as the twentieth century progressed the obsession and drive for records continued. Exploring the limits of one's physical capacity enthralled not just the athletes, but academics as well. Arguing for the connection between speed, power, and progress, the French philosopher Jacques Derrida wrote, "every invention is the invention of a process of acceleration or at least a new experience of speed" (Penz 1990, 162). Achievements on the field are witnessed in a universal language. It is through extraordinary demonstrations that the athlete can "present himself" to the world in a way that others cannot. Records allow the athlete to transcend the "circle of specialists" to become a part of the larger social discourse and global community.

The extent of the transcendental nature of records presented a dilemma offered by Loland in his classification of record-sport categories. His concern was that the obsession with records was "built on the impossible quest for unlimited growth in limited systems" (Loland 2001, 130). Perhaps an acknowledgement of the limitations of the system explains the surprisingly laissez-faire attitudes prevalent among the athletes who broke over one-hundred-thirty indoor rowing records since March of 2020. If the nature of sport does not necessarily subsist on the desire for records, then it follows that any pursuit of them should be muted.

The Essential Nature of Records

If, as Loland suggested, the nature of sport does not imply the will for records, what is left of the relationship between the two. One solution proposes that the relationship between sport and records exists as a paradox. Drawing from his literary background, Guttmann proposed that the quest for records is the embodiment of the ultimate Faustian drive, an "extraordinary manifestation of the Romantic pursuit of the unattainable" (Guttmann 2004, 89). Sport, through dynamic physical expression, speaks to the human contract (Barthes 2007, 63-65). Sport is inherently irrational and paradoxical, embodying the "slow development of an empirical, experimental, mathematical *Weltanschauung*" (Guttmann 2004, 85). The contradictory nature at the heart of modern sport might best be summarized by Jonasson's rough distillation that "modern sport is a set of formalized, physical contests among human beings" (Jonasson 2014, 1307-308).

Leaving the metaphysical complexity of Barthes and Guttmann, other scholars have taken a decidedly more scientific approach to determine the essence of the relationship between the pursuit of records and modern sport. With Barthes answering his own questions with further questions, Bonde looked to modern science to ascertain the fundamental nature of records. Relying on Einstein, Bonde presented an argument for the importance of socially accepted "fixed time" (Bonde 2009, 1321). In simplified form, he works backward to determine that through Einstein's theory of relativity our fixed conception of time is fiction as it is only based on temporal rhythms. If time—or our perception of it—is just a social construction, what use are records? His answer is that our perception shapes our reality and since that reality governs our collective materiality, records, and the technology to measure and compare them, are an integral part of our human consciousness. Records represent a fulfillment of the human desire to understand and manipulate time.

Using language that translates beautifully to the world of elite sport, the French cultural theorist Paul Virilio argued in 1997 that the "'tyranny of distances' has given way to the 'tyranny of real time'" and that geographic space would yield to electronics (Virilio 1997, 115). In the realm of elite sport, records can be set and verified within a matter of minutes. Teammates can track training progress as they complete separate workouts. Competition is no longer essential to the pursuit of records. So long as the machine can provide standard measurements and an accurate list is maintained, the interactive sport dynamic is no longer essential. Therefore, in contrast to Jonasson's assessment that the essence of modern sport relies on contests among human beings, the Covid-19 pandemic has raised an intriguing case for the essence of sport to redefine itself as human versus machine.

RECORDS SPIKE UNDER QUARANTINE

For elite rowers, the Spring of 2020 represented the peak of their four-year training cycle for the Olympic Games. Then, in March, the pandemic struck with global lockdown orders that preceded the first World Cup event by just two weeks. Facing the disappointment of the loss of championship racing and viable training alternatives, the athletes turned indoors. The sheer volume of elite competitors venting frustrations on the ergometer resulted in 131 new records in just seventy-five days ("Headspinning" 2020). The "indoorization" of rowing altered how national teams trained for the now delayed Olympics as well as offering a new look at an open-competition model via digital platforms.

One of the initial challenges faced was the isolation for athletes who usually train in team boats ranging from one partner to eight other teammates in close proximity. For athletes used to dedicating full-time hours to a sport where they are rarely recognized as professionals, the sudden outbreak of isolated indoor training proved to be a significant disruption at first. However, if professionalism is measured by the dedication to one's craft rather than money, by late April rowers across all categories proved themselves capable professionals (Guttmann 2004, 39). With more time than ever allocated to the erg—often avoided as much as possible by rowers beneath the elite ranks—the allure of indoor records swept through the community. Along with new records set in the elite category, youth and para records fell at an unprecedented pace. Occasionally the record books were single-handedly rewritten. Australian Paralympic rower Erik Horrie, for instance, owns five world records in the para category at the time of writing ("Headspinning" 2020). During the two and a half months following when lockdowns began being imposed in Europe, roughly early March to mid-May, Australia lead the world with thirty-six new world indoor records, besting the second place United States by ten.

It should also be noted the commitment to the hastily prepared indoor rowing training programs faced resistance in the early stages. Most of the objections came from athletes who wished to continue on-water training in single sculls (one-person rowing shells). Those boats, by virtue of their design, would keep individual athletes at the desired one and a half to two meters of separation while on the water. However, as recreational authorities determined, such protocols could not be maintained within the clubhouses and therefore the rowing ban, along with other water-based activities, was upheld (Simpson 2020, 4). In addition to training obstacles due to isolation, the physical limitations of the ergometer became more pronounced. Although erg tests are commonly used by coaches to evaluate rowers and are part of athlete selection for many senior and junior national rowing teams, "the data suggest that physiological and performance tests performed on a rowing ergometer are not good indicators of on water performance" (McNeely 2012, 5). More recent data suggest a more compelling case for the indoor rower. The creation of the "dynamic erg"—one which more closely mimics the flow found on the water—can calculate scores to within 0.5% of on-water speed. A claim which was tested and verified by the Dutch National Men's 8+ and the University of Washington Men's Varsity who competed in the world first virtual team-based dual race in January ("Separated by an Ocean" 2020).

Once the severity of the pandemic became abundantly clear, world and Olympic champion rowers began laying their claim to some of the rowing community's most prestigious indoor records. Athletes with previous on-water records to their name such as Hamish Bond of New Zealand and Martino Goretti of Italy have now claimed indoor records as well ("Headspinning" 2020).

Accidental Records

The reverence with which elite sporting records are discussed and pursued has been replaced under the current Covid-19 pandemic with genuine disbelief or subdued acceptance. When Georgie Rowe, a member of the Australian Women's eight-oared crew that took the silver medal at the 2019 World Championships, sat down to "get some kilometres up" for her standard Saturday workout she had no intention of chasing, let alone breaking, a world record ("Accidentally Beats World Record" 2020). In fact, Rowe openly admits that she had no idea what the world record for the half marathon on the ergometer was before starting the workout. Despite her ignorance of the standing record, by the time she finished she had smashed the previous mark, set by American Olympic champion Esther Lofgren in 2014, by more than forty seconds. All told she was simply participating in the workout plan generated by the Australian National Rowing Federation, which was making attempts to keep their athletes motivated in the early weeks of isolated training. Aside from the standard distance session, the national federation also assigned head-to-head virtual duals to keep the competitive fire burning while the team was under strict travel restrictions. ("Accidentally Beats World Record" 2020).

Praise for Rowe came too quickly, however, as her record was quickly scrutinized by the record keepers at Concept2—the rowing equipment manufacturer that keeps the list of world records set on their machines. The dispute concerned the official recognized distance of the half marathon in meters, the standard unit of measurement on the erg. The exact half-marathon distance is 21,097.5m and wanting to be cautious, Rowe set her machine to 21,098m unaware that the recognized standard distance for the half-marathon indoor record is actually 21,097m. This minute difference has held up her record from being officially rubber-stamped, and her mark is still recorded as "unofficial" at the time of writing ("Row, row, row" 2020). For all the technological advancements to facilitate the pursuit of records, the persistence of human error remains a constant (Lindell 2018, 340).

Another athlete whose record-breaking performance was unusually subdued was Tom George of the United Kingdom who became the first man in the country to break the five-minute-forty-second barrier over two-thousand meters. The two-thousand-meter ergometer piece is the crown jewel of rowing records as it is the standard on-water championship distance. Despite being just the tenth man ever to break the barrier, the twenty-five-year old was nonplussed, simply walking back into his parents' house to shower, telling them the piece went "okay" ("British Rower" 2020). He did admit that the absence of screams of support and congratulations at the conclusion of the piece was "a bit weird" and that it was unusual to register such a performance in a garage rather than the official national rowing center. While he was in contact with his training partners both before and after the physiological test, the record setting moment occurred under isolated circumstances. Only the allure of the viability of achieving the record as he crossed the halfway point drove him to the record setting mark ("Tom George Breaks Record" 2020). The record alone is accomplishment enough, but George first had to overcome the pain of missing out on his first Olympic contest to which he had been selected just two days prior to the U.K. lockdown.

For both Rowe and George, their records were accomplished shortly after being named to their first Olympic teams. Staring down a long fifth year of preparation, the governing bodies of the Australian and U.K. teams relied on the presence of records—whether known or not—to generate world class performances from athletes desperate to regain a sense of normalcy. As one world champion stated, "I don't think [about lockdown] too much. I prepare as if it was going to be the Olympics" ("Olympic Champions Back" 2020). In the meantime, indoor records continue to fall.

Deliberate Records

Not all the world records set during the Covid-19 pandemic were done under a veil of ignorance. As early as March, the Chinese national rowing team made a deliberate effort to stage virtual championships and dual competitions to break up the monotony of training for their men's and women's squads. At a national indoor rowing event, nearly the entire Chinese Olympic squad entered including several on-water world and Olympic medalists. The star entrant was the thirty-three-year old Liang Zhang who entered with the explicit purpose of breaking the world record for the "Men's Marathon Erg on Slides" in the 30-39 age category. A little over two hours later he had not only decimated the age category record by over thirty minutes, but he was confirmed to have pulled the fastest overall "Marathon on Slides" time in history ("China" 2020). His victory was quickly turned into promotion for the Chinese squad eager to break into the upper echelon of the international rowing community. Additionally, his record in the endurance category, not often contested at the elite level, was promoted by the president of the Chinese Rowing Association as a stereotype-busting performance that would change attitudes about "Chinese athletes regarding stamina and stress" ("China" 2020).

Outside of nationally funded support for elite level record-setting pursuits, a young American rower has spent the entirety of 2020 consuming every age category record available to him. At age sixteen, Isaiah Harrison currently "owns all thirteen indoor rowing world records for his age group—from 500m to the marathon—most of them being broken during the lockdown" ("Headspinning" 2020). Having set eight age-category world records by thirteen, he has bested his own marks in every category since the start of 2020, including the benchmark two-thousand meter American record with a time most high performance collegiate athletes would be envious of ("Force on the Erg" 2020). As someone who was introduced to the sport via an ergometer in his house, the pandemic has not disrupted his training the way it has for so many others. The "pursuit of the unattainable" is the driving factor behind his zeal for the record books. Though at his current pace there may not be much left in the unattainable category.

RENEWAL OF THE SPECTACLE

Following Guttmann's prescient claim that sport would continue in the absence of spectators, he offers a scathing moral attack, criticizing athletes who value audience attention more than the actual activity. Chastising the athlete-as-entertainer, he wrote that "the athlete who performs for the fans, violates the code of sports and frequently suffers under the mockery of purists." (Guttmann 2004, 12) However, under Covid-19, there has been a revisioning of what a broadcast sports spectacle can be. China was the first to adapt to digital forms of training and competition. Within a few weeks of a WeChat app called "Online Erging" going live, over one hundred recreational enthusiasts were participating with other similar set-ups sponsored by local boat clubs

("China" 2020). Building off the success of the small-scale communities, the Chinese Rowing Association launched a live broadcast of the Chinese Indoor Rowing Extreme Challenge in early June. The event, a part of the larger competition which saw Zhang set the world's marathon erg record, was broadcast on CCTV5, the national sports television channel, in ultra-high-definition format. It was also the first sport event held in China since the outbreak began in late December 2019 and counted the director of the General Administration of Sport China among its attendees ("China" 2020). Unlike the entertainment or competition focus of pre-Covid-19 sporting events, the donations raised from the over 1.25 million viewers provided enough money to generate assistance to the Wuhan Jinyintan Hospital.

In the United States, a consortium of boat manufacturers and repair companies called *Rower's Choice* partnered with U.S. Rowing to sponsor a virtual U.S. National Championship erg competition. The tournament, with age categories for junior, collegiate, and elite athletes, was modeled after the March Madness style basketball brackets ("U.S. Virtual Championship" 2020). Every round featured a different distance challenge based on legendary racecourses from the United States and the United Kingdom. With the goal to inject some fun back into what had been a season of despair, the champions were eventually crowned on April 23 after a month of knockout competition ("2020 Virtual March Mania" 2020). With limited access to the material world and traditional sport opportunities inaccessible due to Covid-19, "athletes flocked to opportunities through the digital world" (Bond et al. 2020, 3).

CONCLUSION

The disruptions posed to the sport world by the Covid-19 pandemic are unprecedented in scale. Rather than despair, athletes—along with their coaches, equipment manufacturers, and savvy marketers—found a way to persevere. If prior examples of barriers overcome are any indication, this generation of rowers will push a centuries old sport firmly into the digital age, with a whole new slate of records to come. One of the key takeaways from this brief examination of indoor rowing records under the Covid-19 pandemic has been the emergence of ulterior motives for participation in an athletic contest. First, the ergometer records demonstrate that it is not necessary to be physically together to compete, which runs counter to the necessity of human interaction proposed by Jonasson. Second, the concerns of homogeneity of sport at the expense of regional differences espoused by Bale turned out to be the common linking factor in fostering a sense of global community when one was cut off from their immediate physical community. Third, Loland's concern about the limitations in the pursuit of records remains a valid concern, but with elite athletes only recently making a concerted effort to pursue indoor records—typically reserved for training—there seems to be a fair distance left before his theoretical limits are reached. Indeed, there seems to be some support for Guttmann's claim that there must be more to competition than just profiting as the victor (Guttmann 2004, 76).

The most common theme articulated by those who have established new records so far during the pandemic has been a longing to reunite with teammates and competitors. Perhaps the community of competition, therefore, is the silver lining to sport under Covid-19 restrictions. Support for the pursuit of records is bolstered not through external praise (i.e., live spectators), but rather through the camaraderie of one's peers. As one historian wrote recently, "records are the result of an honest belief in progress, a deeply embedded hope for a better hereafter," a hope the world shares as we attempt to contain and eventually emerge from the current pandemic (Lopez-Gonzalez 2014, 354).

REFERENCES

"Australian Woman Accidentally Beats Rowing Machine World Record." *New Zealand Herald*, April 15, 2020. https://www.nzherald.co.nz/sport/news/article.cfm?c_id=4&objectid=12324992.

Bale, John. 2003. *Sports Geography*. London: Routledge.

Barthes, Roland. 2007. *What is Sport*. New Haven: Yale University Press.

Bond, John Alexander, Paul Widdop, David Cockayne, and Daniel Parnell. 2020. "Prosumption, Networks and Value During a Global Pandemic: Lockdown Leisure and COVID-19." *Leisure Sciences*. DOI: 10.1080/01490400.2020.1773985.

Bonde, Hans. 2009. "The Time and Speed Ideology: 19th Century Industrialisation and Sport," *The International Journal of the History of Sport* 26 (10): 1315-1334.

Brohm, Jean-Marie. 1978. *Sport, a Prison of Measured Time: Essays*. Translated by Ian Fraser. London: Ink Links Ltd.

Constandt, Bram and Annick Willem. 2020. "Hosting the Olympics in Times of a Pandemic: Historical Insights from Antwerp 1920." *Leisure Sciences*. DOI: 10.1080/01490400.2020.1773982.

"Coronavirus: Row, Row, Row Your Boat to an Indoor World Record," *The Straits Times*, Apr. 15, 2020. https://www.straitstimes.com/sport/coronavirus-row-row-row-your-boatto-an-indoor-world-record.

Fernandez, Gabriel. 2020. "Look: KBO's Hanwha Eagles Pack Stands with Stuffed Animals in Lieu of Live Fans." *CBS Sports*, May 27, 2020. https://www.cbssports.com/mlb/news/look-kbos-hanwha-eagles-pack-stands-with-stuffed-animal-in-lieu-of-live-fans/.

Garber, Megan. 2012. "Picture of the Day: The First-Class Gym of the Titanic." *The Atlantic*, April 13, 2012. https://www.theatlantic.com/technology/archive/2012/04/picture-of-the-day-the-first-class-gym-of-the-titanic/255836/.

Giulianotti, Richard. 2005. *Sport: A Critical Sociology*. Cambridge: Polity Press.

Guttmann, Allen. 2004. *From Ritual to Record: The Nature of Modern Sports*. New York: Columbia University Press.

Heffernan, Conor. 2016. "The History of the Indoor Rower." *Physical Culture Study*, May 6, 2016. https://physicalculturestudy.com/2016/05/06/the-history-of-the-indoor-rower/.

Honigsbaum, Mark. 2013. "Regulating the 1918-19 Pandemic: Flu, Stoicism and the Northcliffe Press." *Medical History* 57 (2): 165–185.

Jonasson, Kalle. 2014. "Modern Sport Between Purity and Hybridity." *Sport in Society* 17 (10): 1306-1316. DOI: 10.1080/17430437.2014.850807.

Lashua, Brett, Corey W. Johnson, and Diana C. Parry. 2020. "Leisure in the Time of Coronavirus: A Rapid Response Special Issue." *Leisure Sciences*. DOI: 10.1080/01490400.2020.1774827.

Lenk, Hans. 1973. "Leistungssport in der Erfolgsgesellschaft." In *Leistungssport in der Erfolgsgesellschaft*, edited by Frank Grube and Gerhard Richter, 147-168. Hamburg: Hoffmann & Campe.

Lindell, Lisa R. 2018. "Cuckoo Collins: The Crooked Path of a Nineteenth-Century Professional Sprinter." *Journal of Sport History* 45 (3): 334-351.

Loland, Sigmund. 2001. "Record Sports: An Ecological Critique and a Reconstruction," *Journal of the Philosophy of Sport* 28 (2): 127-139. DOI: 10.1080/00948705.2001.9714608.

Lopez-Gonzalez, Hibai. 2014. "Quantifying the Immeasurable: A Reflection on Sport, Time and Media." *Journal of the Philosophy of Sport* 41 (3): 347-362. DOI: 10.1080/00948705.2013.832265.

McNeely, Ed. "Rowing Ergometer Physiological Tests Do Not Predict On-Water Performance." *The Sport Journal*, January 2, 2012. https://thesportjournal.org/article/rowing-ergometer-physiological-tests-do-not-predict-on-water-performance/.

Nolte, Volker. 2005. *Rowing Faster*. Champaign, IL: Human Kinetics.

Penz, Otto. 1990. "Sport and Speed." *International Review for the Sociology of Sport* 25 (2): 157-167. DOI:10.1177/101269029002500205.

Roche, Maurice. 2003. "Mega-Events, Time and Modernity on Time Structures in Global Society." *Time & Society* 12 (1): 99-126. DOI: 10.1177/0961463X03012001370.

Rosenbladt, Oli. 2018. "CRASH-B: Past, Present, and Future." *Row2k.com*, February 26, 2018. https://www.row2k.com/crashb/features/2018/183/CRASH-B--Past--Present--and-Future/.

———. 2020. "Isiah Harrison: A Force on the Erg." *Row2k.com*, March 2, 2020. https://www.row2k.com/crashb/features/2020/198/Isaiah-Harrison--A-Force-on-the-Erg/.

Row-360. 2020. "Tom George Breaks GB Rowing Team 2k record in lockdown." Accessed June 21, 2020. https://row-360.com/tom-george-breaks-gb-rowing-team-2k-record-in-lockdown/.

Rowers' Choice. 2020. "2020 Virtual March Mania." Accessed June 20, 2020. https://www.rowerschoice.com/marchmania.

"Rowing: Olympic Champions Back on the Water as Croatia Eases Lockdown." *Reuters*, May 5, 2020. https://www.reuters.com/article/us-health-coronavirus-sinkovic/rowing-olympic-champions-back-on-the-water-as-croatia-eases-lockdown-idUSKBN22H16E.

Simpson, Brian. 2020. "Mass Hysteria, Manufacturing Crisis and the Legal Reconstruction of Acceptable Exercise during a Pandemic." *Leisure Sciences*. DOI: 10.1080/01490400.2020.1774002.

Syed, Matthew. 2020. "Coronavirus: The Good That Can Come Out of an Upside-Down World." *BBC News*, March 3, 2020. https://www.bbc.co.uk/news/world-us-canada-52094332.

Team GB. 2020. "George Relishes Rowing Record Broken in Parents' Garden Shed." Accessed June 21, 2020. https://www.teamgb.com/article/rowings-george-relishes-lockdown-record/2hbLvf68FgEJ7FFkHGLI0Q.

"Tom George: British Rower Breaks 2km Indoor Rowing Record During Lockdown." *BBC Sport*, June 22, 2020. https://www.bbc.com/sport/rowing/53118747.

US Rowing. 2020. "Rowers Choice Partners with US Rowing to Create the First-Ever U.S. Virtual National Championship." Accessed June 15, 2020. https://usrowing.org/news/2020/3/30/events-rowers-choice-partners-with-usrowing-to-create-the-first-ever-us-virtual-national-championship.aspx.

World Rowing. 2020. "Indoor Rowing Records Set in China." Accessed June 20, 2020. http://www.worldrowing.com/news/indoor-rowing-records-set-china.

———. 2020. "Separated by an Ocean, Racing Each Other." Accessed August 30, 2020. http://www.worldrowing.com/news/separated-ocean-racing-each-other-watch-the-netherlands-university-washington.

———. 2020. "The Head-Spinning Statistics of Indoor Rowing During the Lockdown." Accessed June 20, 2020. http://www.worldrowing.com/news/the-head-spinning-statistics-indoor-rowing-during-lockdown.

CHAPTER 19

A Handbrake Turn in Mexico: Crisis Management of a Global Motorsport Event

Hans Erik Næss

INTRODUCTION

This chapter examines the crisis management of a global motorsport event. Amidst Covid 19-related cancellations everywhere else in the world of motorsports, Rally Guanajuato Mexico, the Mexican round of the 2020 FIA World Rally Championship (WRC), went ahead from March 12 to 15. Despite worried statements from global health authorities, the organizers argued as long as they did not have any local cases of illness the rally was not in a risk zone. The International Automobile Federation, usually known by its French name Fédération Internationale de l'Automobile (FIA) even in English-speaking countries (the governing body) and WRC Promoter GmbH (the commercial rights owner) supported this stance. However, the rally, as one of the few major sporting events to be held despite the outbreak, suddenly had to be shortened from three to two days because international travel constraints accelerated the need to get the Europe-based teams home. Then strong criticism followed because the organizers did not call off the event immediately.

Since motorsport is a non-contact sport it is reasonable to believe that the organizers considered it less risky to continue with their sport than was the case in contact sports, although the major concern, as it would turn out, was the spectators and the locals of Guanajuato. The Mexican race of the 2020 WRC, therefore, provides an example for conceptual research into the aspect of crisis management in sport that concentrates on communicative strategies for organizational repositioning. Key themes connecting studies on crisis management in sport are the occurrence of negative incidents related to athletes' behavior (Hambrick, Frederick, and Sanderson 2017), integrity flaws in sporting organizations (Onwumechili and Bedeau 2016), and the dark sides of stakeholder involvement (Lagree, Wilbur, and Cameron 2019). While previous studies generally examined these themes based on data gathered after a crisis occurred, which in some cases is logical because the consequences of these crises only become visible subsequently, this chapter examines crisis management and communicative strategies of a major event as the Covid-19 situation unfolded. Analyzing crises only once the event has occurred excludes the chance to grasp the processes: as *the situation of an issue transforming into a crisis* remains unexplored" and presents "a clear gap in sport communications research" (Kitchin and Purchell 2017, 662, emphasis added).

This study used Google Alert ("WRC Mexico") to gather secondary data related to the 2020 Rally Guanajuato Mexico (the Mexican WRC event) as the event was turning into a crisis. I was mostly interested in the views of the championship's main stakeholders: the local organizer, the WRC's official promoter, the three WRC manufacturer teams (Toyota, M-Sport (Ford), and Hyundai), and the FIA. In the period March 1 to May 1, 2020, I received sixty-five Alerts by email, in both Spanish and English. By creating a timeline of events and searching for turning points, a manual coding process revealed that the Mexican event involved three phases of response negotiations: denial, realization, and making amends. As a result, the implications of this study are twofold. First, it demonstrates the complexity of a world-class sporting event—not complex in terms of size, but in the type of relations involved in its organizational management. Second, as the complexity of the case enables a sociological approach to system shocks, it provided a stepping-stone for additional empirical studies of risk management in sport.

Conceptual Framework

An organizational crisis is "a threat or challenge to an organization's legitimacy where stakeholders question if an organization is meeting normative expectations" (Coombs and Holladay 1996, 281). These challenges include "unpredictable events" which can "seriously impact an organization's performance and generate negative outcomes" (Coombs 2015, 2). For communication-oriented research, an often-underestimated premise is that the complexity of the event conditions the ability of the organization to handle the situation. Although not focused on either crisis or risk management per se, Parent's conceptual framework (2010) is relevant here in considering how the decision to continue, and then cancel, the Mexican WRC event came about. In her study of the Pan American Games, Parent identified four drivers of decision-making: structural dimensions, stakeholder interactions, information management and personal characteristics. According to Parent (2010, 292), examining this process unravels the relationship between what strategies lie behind decisions and the parameters that influence the decisions themselves.

The first driver, structural dimensions, is about who makes decisions and at what level. At a WRC event the chain of command is usually decentralized when it comes to the high number of decisions that are necessary to make prior to, during, and after an event (Næss 2014). However, centralization of the Mexican WRC intensified as only four parties joined to make the decision to first continue, and then to cancel the event. Parent's (2010) second driver, stakeholder interactions, is equally relevant as the event's local organizing committee, the FIA, the WRC Promoter GmbH, and the rally teams cooperated in what came to be the result of the week-long discussions of the event's fate. At the same time, the FIA, for example, could not or would not intervene and demand the event be called off. Ultimately, the decision was left to the organizer, who relied on regional authorities when it came to the third driver identified by Parent (2010)—information management. The final driver, personal characteristics, relates more specifically to skills, experience, and networks (*ibid.*). In this case, the organizers—particularly the event's Chief Medical Officer, Pablo Escalera—diverged from their usual internal handling of medical questions to draw upon government advice to assess the situation.

In light of this conceptual framework, it is reasonable to view the WRC rally as a "complex project." The term draws on Piperca and Floricel's (2012) conceptualization of unexpected events and how they impact the project itself and the circumstances that influence decisions made about it. Rooted in sociology, this typology is the result of reconciling two perspectives on organizational response to system shocks: those based on individual actions and those on system capacity. Drawing on the sociological theories of Niklas Luhmann, Piperca and Floricel (2012) understand social systems as networks of "communicative couplings" between actors. In a project like a WRC event, these couplings interfere with the behavioristic ideas of rational choice theory as they "assume a certain level of mastery over objects, whereas unsuspected properties or a different level of complexity from what was expected are frequent occurrences in projects" (Piperca and Floricel 2012, 255). What is less debated in this approach is complexity itself and how to handle it on individual and organizational levels when crises occur.

Urry (2005) made a crucial distinction between complexity and complication and emphasized the understanding of the movable parts of the system as crucial: "Such complex social interactions are likened to walking through a maze whose walls rearrange themselves as one walks through" (Urry 2005, 3). The question is how an event can meet this challenge and move with the rearrangements of the environment rather than against them. To be prepared for crisis, this configuration of activities has to be matched with the event's risk management capabilities, which according to Geraldi, Lee-Kelly, and Kutsch (2010, 548) is the ability "to assess and manage uncertainty in advance—to define responses to risks that may have an adverse impact on the project outcome before they materialize." To outline the interaction between the project and the environment in this case, the case context as well as the three negotiation phases of the WRC event are explored below.

Case Context

The organization of a WRC event involves four stakeholders—the local organizing committee, the FIA, the commercial promoter, and the teams. Taken together, this group of core stakeholders is a mobile construction that negotiates terms and responsibilities in various cultural and political settings, as the WRC is a championship with events in fourteen countries each calendar year. Second only to Formula 1 in terms of fan popularity, media interest, and sponsor investment, the WRC has developed a rich history since its first world championship event in 1973 (Næss 2014).

In this study, I focus on the Rally Guanajuato Mexico, the third event of the 2020 season. First held in 2004, the Mexican event has become an important partner to local businesses and a hub of South American motorsport culture (*ibid*). Counting 550.000 spectators in 2016 (WRC 2017) and experiencing significant growth in 2019 (WRC 2019), the Mexican event is one of the WRC's most popular in terms of spectator attendance. Of all incoming visitors, rally fans attend in greater numbers than those coming to other events and spend more money than other tourists on local franchises (UNWTO 2016). For these reasons, cancellation seemed like the last resort for the organizers, and with neither the commercial owners nor the FIA giving any indication that they would call the event off, the teams also followed suit. While the earliest signs of the ramifications of Covid-19 on sport came in February 2020, the WRC community was divided in its coverage. Some sources claimed that all parties were keeping a close eye on the outbreak (Dirtfish 2020a; 2020c; WRC 2020a). Other actors prepared for the event without making any mention of the virus (Holmes 2019; Toyota 2020).

It is, however, important to underline that the WRC community was not alone in its reluctance to make a swift judgment. For example, the International Olympic Committee (IOC) did not announce the postponement of the 2020 Tokyo Summer Olympic Games to 2021 until March 24. At the same time there were three other issues related to the Mexican WRC rally that impacted the aftermath. First, the FIA, in the person of its Medical Commission president Professor Gérard Saillant, had assured the world in January 2020 that it was "closely monitoring the evolving situation with relevant authorities and its Member Clubs" (Yahoo!Sport 2020a). Second, the cancellation of the Australian Formula One Grand Prix the very same weekend as the Mexican WRC event and the debate surrounding it, which I will come back to below, gave clear indications of how things were developing. And third, the Argentinian WRC event planned for April 23-26, was postponed prior to the Mexican WRC event, due to new measures put in place by the Argentinian government to contain the virus. Yet the Mexican organizers decided to push on, backed by the FIA and supported by its national government. The next three sections analyze the consequences of this choice.

Phase I: Denial

Prior to the event, there were discussions among the core event stakeholders about the degree to which the Covid-19 outbreak would affect the participants (Dirtfish 2020c). Yet when the Europe-based manufacturer teams, which had the power to discuss the matter with the FIA and the local organizers, prepared to leave for Mexico a week before the event, there was little concern in the Rally Guanajuato Mexico's service park. On March 9, one senior team representative said: "We have travelled normally to Mexico, following the advice from the team doctor. There are not many cases, very few cases in Mexico and the same with Argentina" (Dirtfish 2020c). Another senior team person thought it was only a matter of precaution,

> There's no advice against travelling to Mexico and no need for any self-isolation when we go home from here (...) The last time I looked, the world was still turning. (Dirtfish 2020c)

One of the team principals, usually not afraid to speak his mind, was even bemused about the developments: "The panic is the worst thing I am seeing spreading around at this moment, this is worse than the virus" (Dirtfish 2020c).

Unlike Australia, Mexico—or more precisely the Guanajuato region—had no major problem with Covid-19, although the first confirmed case was recorded on March 10 (Padilla-Raygoza et al. 2020). Similar to the earlier cases of health-imposed troubles such as the SARS outbreak that threatened World Badminton championships in Birmingham, U.K., in 2003 (Elliott 2004) and the impact of the zika virus on the 2016 Rio Olympics (Hamilton et al 2019), Covid-19 was not considered a risk because of a geographically determined understanding of it. Medical risk assessments of alternative virus scenarios, however, were seemingly considered less important. Hence, the Mexican event solved what Elliot (2004) called the pre-crisis stage in what crisis management research would consider a predictable manner: inappropriate staffing, or a focus on profit to the detriment of safe working practices (Elliott 2004, 416).

Ignoring external safety reviews, in particular, became an issue when some WRC insiders expressed a wish to close the service park to public access, only to be met with Mexican officials pointing to their record of no outbreaks (Dirtfish 2020d, 2020e). What then crept up on the organizers were not medical worries, but logistical trouble. The rally was intended to last from March 12 to 15, but in the U.S., where many of the international WRC community had their connecting flights back to Europe, the closure of airports was due to take place on 16 March. WRC teams were therefore concerned about being able to dismantle the service park and get out of the U.S. before the lockdown was enforced. Rally Director Patrick Suberville then claimed that the decision was not due to the worsening of the Covid-19 situation in Mexico, but the teams' collective concern about being stuck in the country (Mediotiempo 2020). For the organizers, this was the point of no return: shorten the event.

Phase II: Realization

In phase II, when it became clear that the rally could not be completed in its original form, it was shortened because of logistical issues just enough to make it count as a point-awarding event in the WRC and wrapped up in a hurry. When the event entered this phase, it overlapped what Elliot (2004, 416) called "the immediate period of the crisis, between the crisis taking place and the resumption of operations or activities." Outwardly, the key stakeholders emphasized *consensus*. Diego Sinhue Rodríguez Vallejo, Governor of Guanajuato said on March 14,

> In coordination with the organising committee of Rally Guanajuato México, and due to the closure of some destination airports for teams and visitors from foreign countries, the decision to move forward the awards and closing ceremony of the event to this evening has been confirmed. (WRC 2020)

Apart from leaving out the fact that the first confirmed Covid-19 case in the state of Guanajuato was registered on March 10 (Padilla-Raygoza et al. 2020), it seems like in light of the increasing complexity of the event, as discussed above, the core stakeholders decided to move with the changes in the environment rather than against it. Similar to Vallejo, Yves Matton, FIA Rally Director thus said,

> The decision to finish the event tonight has been taken unanimously by the Rally Mexico organisers, with the support of the governor, the WRC Promoter and the FIA. We are all very sad that the rally has to end prematurely but due to the rapidly evolving situation and the various travel restrictions being implemented in the different parts of the world, the priority was to ensure a safe return home for the teams and personnel. (WRC 2020b)

This was also the view of Patrick Suberville, Rally Guanajuato Mexico Director, stating that the cancellation would "allow teams and the media to return to their countries with the anticipation of the imminent closure of their borders because of COVID-19" (WRC 2020b). Using two central elements of crisis communication—the credibility of the communicator (WRC's core stakeholders instead of using a PR person) (Yang, Kang, and Johnson 2010) and the "enactment of the narrative of control (or at least its appearance) in the face of high uncertainty" (Heath 1997, 317), the comments above illustrate the event's managerial turn towards parts of the situation that could be mastered (responding to travel restrictions) instead of neglecting the ones that were steeped in uncertainty (outbreak developments).

Phase III: Making Amends

The third, and final, stage refers to "the period in which an organisation seeks to consolidate and then reposition itself. Of course, stage three feeds back into stage one as organisations may or may not learn from their experiences" (Elliott 2004, 417). Apart from the confirmed case of one German journalist, who tested positive for Covid-19 before the event (which took five days to make public; see RevistaScratch 2020) and the same for one staff member of the WRC Promoter on March 21 shortly after the event (Speedcafe 2020), criticism came from within and outside the WRC's core stakeholder group. Based on the information and recommendations they had, FIA Rally Director Yves Matton believed "it was the right decision to come to Mexico and do the rally" (Dirtfish 2020e).

Six-time world champion Sebastien Ogier, who won the rally, took a different view. Upon completion of Shakedown (a test run before the rally starts), he expressed doubts: "I almost didn't sleep last night. I was just, I don't know, concerned with this whole world situation at the moment and I really hope that what we do this weekend is right" (Yahoo!Sport 2020b). After the rally, his mood had not changed: "If we put the fans here in danger this victory has no value" (BBC 2020). While FIA President Jean Todt was reluctant to hand out blame when asked whether the FIA and F1 in particular could have handled the situation differently, he was nevertheless convinced that the world of motorsports had learned enough from the crisis so that "we don't face another unpredictable situation and we have experts working on that" (Eurosport 2020). Part of the debate was that the Mexican event was carried out almost as normal apart from eventually restricting access of fans into the service park. In hindsight, the dominant reason seems to have been false assurances from the Mexican government about the low risk of infection and its failure to take proper action, which first came after activist groups obtained court rulings forcing the government to do more (Human Rights Watch 2020).

This political factor, together with the FIA's renewal of the collaboration with International Federation of Red Cross and Red Crescent Societies (IFRC), seemingly helped reposition the governing body in phase III in light of the criticism towards Formula One and the WRC. Already having a six-year long partnership to build upon, a donation of €1 million from the FIA Foundation was made to IFRC's global response to the virus (InsidetheGames 2020). In return, the FIA expects to draw upon the IFRC's expertise to "deliver guidance and preventative health support about COVID-19 to drivers and staff" for the rest of 2020 and remaining motorsport events (InsidetheGames 2020).

Discussion

Above, we saw examples of the four decision-making drivers identified by Parent (2010) applied to the three phases of negotiation that characterized the Mexican WRC event. What seems to unify these four drivers in the Mexican case is the organizer's inability to address potential crisis management issues beyond those related to the event itself. Guanajuato's secretary of health Daniel Alberto Díaz Martínez, for example, put faith in "an epidemiological surveillance system" that was used to "monitor all the drivers and teams arriving from countries where the situation is most serious" (SportBusiness 2020). But the criticism against the organizers concerned the health of the people of Guanajuato, not the health of WRC participants (Mediotiempo 2020). Despite "only" nine cases confirmed on March 11, criticism towards Mexican authorities had at that point begun to grow due to its vague pandemic policy and unreliable statistics on the actual number of cases (Human Rights Watch 2020; Verza 2020; Webber 2020).

In comparison, the F1 race in Australia, which would have taken place on March 14 with all the teams in place in the days before, was going to go ahead as late as few days before the race, similar to Rally Guanajuato. Examinations of the back and forth between March 12 and cancellation the next day revealed conflicting interests between those who would prefer to keep the show on the road and those who addressed health concerns (Benson, 2020). In the end the F1 Grand Prix *was* canceled, as it seems the F1 apparatus finally saw the *uncertainty* of risks associated with Covid-19 as more important than the capacity to deal with calculated risks afterwards. On the one hand, it is impossible to totally de-risk a project (Geraldi, Lee-Kelly, and Kutsch 2010, 548), a well-known fact in motorsports (Elliott 2004; Næss 2020). On the other hand, in the context of Covid-19, the uncertainty of risk factors could not be accepted simply because they were different from the known elements that could have posed a threat to the event. Rather than "known unknowns," they were "unknown unknowns" (Geraldi, Lee-Kelly, and Kutsch 2010). The former are "circumstances, outcomes or events that actors have identified as possibly existing, but do not know whether they will take place or not," while the latter are "those circumstances, events, outcomes that were not identified in the first place" (Geraldi, Lee-Kelly, and Kutsch 2010, 553).

As in practice, evidenced by the different choices made by the Mexican and Australian motorsport event organizers, respectively, scholars disagree on the best way to handle and analyze situations like these. Disagreements concern the role of rationality, information overload, time pressure, complexity, and uncertainty (Phillips-Wren and Adya 2020), in addition to the level of precaution, as demonstrated by the Argentinian government's decision to cancel all upcoming sport events on March 11 due to the growth of Covid-19 cases (Reuters 2020). Both "unknowns" as identified by Geraldi, Lee-Kelly, and Kutsch (2010) are now included in the WHO's guidelines issued in April 2020, as well as in recent studies on the perils related to sport events and mass gatherings (McClosky, Zumla, and Ippolito 2020), requiring future event hosts to assess risk through a different kind of complexity. In the case of Rally Guanajuato, however, its decisions were heavily affected by governmental support and the fact that most other events in Guanajuato at the time, or even Mexico, went on as normal. Only on March 14 did Mexico's Secretariat of Public Education announced that all sporting and civic events would be canceled (El Universal 2020).

By contrast, the decision to cancel the Australian F1 race exemplified Geraldi, Lee-Kelly, and Kutsch's (2010) emphasis on organizational facilitation of human competence as instrumental for project decision-makers to "*create their own luck.*" Successful responses to unexpected events, they argue, are based on three pillars: "a responsive and functioning structure at the organisational level, good interpersonal relationships at the group level and competent people at the individual level" (Geraldi, Lee-Kelly, and Kutsch 2010, 553). Apart from the event-based myopia of the Mexican organizers, encouraged by the government (Webber, 2020), the weak link in the Mexican event—unlike the case of Formula One—was the responsiveness of the organizational structure when the risk assessment changed. At the same time, the complexity of stakeholder relations means that blame cannot be ascribed solely to the Mexican organizers and authorities. The situation might have been different if the FIA or the WRC Promoter or even a major sponsor had intervened. But as the both of them refrained from advising against a continuation of the event, despite the FIA's assurance that it was monitoring the situation, a negative spiral of self-reinforcing decisions led to Rally Mexico being the odd event out when Covid-19 hit the world of sports.

Conclusion

Based on the exploration of Rally Guanajuato Mexico 2020, risk management of sporting events would benefit from a further conceptualization of complexity. The reason is that the WRC event represents a hub in "emergent, dynamic and self-organizing systems that interact in ways that heavily influence the probabilities of later events" (Urry 2005, 3). Because complexity makes it impossible to predict all possible events, this chapter has strengthened the argument from Geraldi, Lee-Kelly, and Kutsch (2010) that "the heart of successful responses to unexpected responses lies with people assets, especially in terms of stakeholder engagement, negotiation and leadership skills" (556). The practical implication is that despite the limitations of this study when it comes to data and theoretical consideration, which ideally would have included interviews with the key participants and further conceptualization of "risk," "complexity," and "management," the more complex the event, the leaner the organizational decision process should be in order to handle a crisis. This conclusion obviously does not provide any guarantees about people making the right decision (how is the "right" decision defined and who is allowed to make this decision?). But the theories, data, and similar cases to the Mexican WRC event it builds upon specify the making of those decisions as uncertainties that are no longer merely attributed to predefined procedures.

REFERENCES

BBC. 2020. "Coronavirus: Sebastien Ogier Unhappy After World Rally Championship Win in Mexico." BBC.com, March 15, 2020. Accessed June 11, 2020. https://www.bbc.com/sport/motorsport/51895556

Benson, Andrew. 2020. "Coronavirus: Australian Grand Prix Called Off." BBC.com, March 13. Accessed June 11, 2020. https://www.bbc.com/sport/formula1/51849163

Coombs, W. Timothy and Sherry J. Holladay. 1996. "Communication and Attributions in a Crisis: An Experimental Study in Crisis Communication." *Journal of Public Relations Research*, 8 (4): 279–295.

Coombs, W. Timothy. 2015. *Ongoing Crisis Communication: Planning, Managing, and Responding.* London: SAGE.

Dirtfish. 2020a. "WRC Heads to Mexico with Eye on Coronavirus Crisis." March 2, 2020. Accessed June 11, 2020. https://dirtfish.com/rally/wrc-heads-to-mexico-with-eye-on-coronavirus-crisis/.

———. 2020b. ""No Risk" to Rally México from Coronavirus". March 3, 2020. Accessed June 11, 2020. https://dirtfish.com/rally/wrc/no-risk-to-rally-mexico-from-coronavirus/.

———. 2020c. "WRC Teams Calm Over COVID-19 as Rally México Begins." March 9, 2020. Accessed June 11, 2020. https://dirtfish.com/rally/wrc/wrc-teams-calm-over-Covid-19-as-rally-mexico-begins/.

———. 2020d. "Mexico Defends Continuation Amid COVID-19 Fears." March 14, 2020. Accessed June 11, 2020. https://www.dirtfish.com/rally/wrc/mexico-defends-continuation-amid-Covid-19-fears/.

———. 2020e. "Opinion: The Final Word on Rally México 2020." March 18, 2020. Accessed June 11, 2020. https://www.dirtfish.com/rally/wrc/opinion-the-final-word-on-rally-mexico-2020/.

El Universal (2020). "SEP cancela eventos deportivos y cívicos en escuelas por coronavirus." *El Universal*, March 14, 2020. Accessed August 2, 2020. https://www.eluniversal.com.mx/nacion/coronavirus-sep-cancela-eventos-deportivos-y-civicos-en-escuelas.

Elliott, Dominic. 2004. "Risk management in Sport." In *the Business of Sport Management*, edited by John Beech and Simon Chadwick, 414-430. Harlow: Prentice Hall.

Eurosport. 2020. "F1 Could Manage to Race Even with Covid-19 Cases, Says FIA." Eurosport.com, May 19, 2020. Accessed June 11, 2020. https://www.eurosport.com/formula-1/motor-racing-f1-could-manage-to-race-even-with-Covid-19-cases-says-fia_sto7753380/story.shtml.

Geraldi, Joana G., Liz Lee-Kelley, Liz and Elmar Kutsch. 2010. "The Titanic Sunk, So What? Project Manager Response to Unexpected Events." *International Journal of Project Management* 28 (6): 547-558.

Hambrick, Marion E., Evan L. Frederick and Jimmy Sanderson. 2015. "From Yellow to Blue: Exploring Lance Armstrong's Image Repair Strategies Across Traditional and Social Media." *Communication & Sport* 3 (2): 196–218.

Hamilton, Bruce, Dan Exeter, Sarah Beable, Lynne Coleman and Chris Milne. 2019. "Zika Virus and the Rio Olympic Games." *Clinical Journal of Sport Medicine* 29 (6): 523-526.

Heath, Robert L. 1997. *Strategic Issues Management: Organizations and Public Policy Challenges.* Thousand Oaks, CA: Sage

Holmes, Martin. 2019. "Preview: 2019 Rally Guanajuato Mexico". *RallySportMag*, March 5, 2019. Accessed June 11, 2020. https://rallysportmag.com/preview-2019-rally-guanajuato-mexico/.

Human Rights Watch (2020). "Mexico: Mexicans Need Accurate COVID-19 Information. López Obrador Misinforms Public on the Health Risks of the Pandemic." *hrw.org*, March 26. Accessed August 2, 2020. https://www.hrw.org/news/2020/03/26/mexico-mexicans-need-accurate-Covid-19-information.

InsidetheGames. 2020. "FIA and Red Cross Team Up to Raise Awareness of Covid-19." Insidethegames.biz, May 15, 2020. Accessed June 11, 2020. https://www.insidethegames.biz/articles/1094270/Covid-19-fia-red-cross.

Kitchin, Paul James and Purcell, Peter A. 2017. "Examining Sport Communications Practitioners' Approaches to Issues Management and Crisis Response in Northern Ireland." *Public Relations Review* 43 (4): 661-670.

Lagree, Danielle, Douglas Wilbur and Glen T. Cameron. 2019. "A Strategic Approach to Sports Crisis Management: Assessing the NFL Concussion Crisis from Marketing and Public Relations Perspectives." *International Journal of Sports Marketing and Sponsorship* 20 (3): 407-429.

Luhmann, Niklas. 1991. *Soziale Systeme: Grundriss einer allgemeinen Theorie*. Suhrkamp: Frankfurt am Main.

McCloskey, Brian, Alimuddin Zumla, and Giuseppe Ippolito et al. 2020. "Mass Gathering Events and Reducing Further Global Spread of COVID-19: A Political and Public Health Dilemma." *Lancet* 395: 1096–9.

Mediotiempo. 2020. "Covid-19. Se adelanta el Rally de México por cierre de fronteras por Coronavirus." Mediotempo.com, March 14, 2020. Accessed June 11, 2020. https://www.mediotiempo.com/automovilismo/Covid-19-adelanta-rally-mexico-cierre-fronteras-coronavirus

Næss, Hans Erik. 2014. *A Sociology of the World Rally Championship. History, Identity, Memories and Place*. Basingstoke: Palgrave Macmillan.

———. 2020. *A History of Organizational Change. The Case of the Fédération Internationale de l'Automobile 1945-2020*. Cham: Palgrave Macmillan.

Onwumechili, Chuka and Bedeau, Koren. 2016. "Analysis of FIFA's Attempt at Image Repair." *Communication & Sport* 5 (4): 407-427.

Padilla-Raygoza, Nicolas, Efrain Navarro-Olivos, Maria de Jesus Gallardo-Luna, et al. 2020. "Clinical Data, Comorbities, and Mortality of COVID-19 in the State of Guanajuato, Mexico until May 20, 2020." *Central Asian Journal of Global Health*, 9 (1).

Parent, Milena M. 2010. "Decision Making in Major Sport Events Over Time: Parameters, Drivers, and Strategies." *Journal of Sport Management* 24 (3): 291-318.

Phillips-Wren, Gloria and Monica Adya. 2020. "Decision Making Under Stress: The Role of Information Overload, Time Pressure, Complexity, and Uncertainty." *Journal of Decision Systems*, https://doi.org/10.1080/12460125.2020.1768680

Piperca, Sergei and Sorin E. Floricel. 2012. "A Typology of Unexpected Events in Complex Projects." *International Journal of Managing Projects in Business* 5 (2): 248-265

Reuters. 2020. "Sport-Argentina Cancels International Sporting Events in March." *Reuters*, March 11, 2020. Accessed August 2, 2020. https://www.reuters.com/article/health-coronavirus-argentina/sport-argentina-cancels-international-sporting-events-in-march-idUSL1N2B41OV

RevistaScratch. 2020. "Un periodista y un miembro de WRC Promoter, infectados por Covid-19 en México." Revistascratch, March 20, 2020. Accessed June 11, 2020.https://www.revistascratch.com/wrc/noticia/un-periodista-y-un-miembro-de-wrc-promoter-infectados-por-Covid-19-en-mexico-55465.

Speedcafe. 2020. "WRC Confirms Positive Coronavirus Test in Mexico." Speedcafe.com, March 21, 2020. Accessed June 11, 2020. https://www.speedcafe.com/2020/03/21/wrc-confirms-positive-coronavirus-test-in-mexico/.

SportBusiness 2020. "Formula E Suspends Season as WRC and FIM Motocross Hit." Sportbusiness.com, March 13, 2020. Accessed June 11, 2020. https://www.sportbusiness.com/news/formula-e-suspends-season-as-wrc-and-fim-motocross-hit/.

Toyota 2020. "*TOYOTA GAZOO Racing* Aims to Continue its Strong Start in the Mexican Heat". Toyotagazooracing.com, March 6, 2020. Accessed June 11, 2020. https://toyotagazooracing.com/release/2020/wrc/rd03-preview.html.

UNWTO (United Nations World Travel Organization). 2016. *Global Report on the Power of Youth Travel*. Accessed June 2, 2020. https://www.wysetc.org/wp-content/uploads/2016/03/Global-Report_Power-of-Youth-Travel_2016.pdf.

Urry, John. 2005. "The Complexity Turn." *Theory, Culture and Society* 22 (5): 1-14.

Valentinov, Vladislav. 2014. "The Complexity–Sustainability Trade-Off in Niklas Luhmann's Social Systems Theory." *Systems Research and Behavioral Science* 31 (1): 14-22.

Verza, Maria. 2020. "Experts Decry Mexico Coronavirus Policy Delay". *America Magazine*, April 1. Accessed August 2, 2020 from https://www.americamagazine.org/politics-society/2020/04/01/experts-decry-mexico-coronavirus-policy-delay.

Webber, Jude. 2020. "The Pandemic Tests Tempers and Tolerance in Mexico." *Financial Times*, May 6, 2020. Accessed June 10, 2020 from https://www.ft.com/content/2603c504-8eab-11ea-a8ec-961a33ba80aa.

WRC 2017. "WRC Crowds Surge." WRC.com, October 19, 2017. Accessed August 2, 2020, https://www.wrc.com/en/news/news-archive/wrc/wrc-crowds-surge/.

———. 2019. "WRC Attendances Top Four Million." WRC.com, March 22, 2019. Accessed August 2, 2020. https://www.wrc.com/en/news/news-archive/wrc/wrc-attendances-top-four-million/.

———. 2020a. "Mexico Organisers Act Against Coronavirus." WRC.com, March 4, 2020. Accessed June 11, 2020. https://www.wrc.com/en/news/season-2020/wrc/mexico-organisers-act-against-coronavirus/.

———. 2020b. "Rally Guanajuato Mexico Confirms Revised Rally Schedule." WRC.com, March 14, 2020. Accessed June 11, 2020. https://www.wrc.com/en/news/season-2020/wrc/rally-guanajuato-mexico-confirms-revised-schedule/

Yahoo!Sport 2020a. "FIA 'Closely Monitoring' Coronavirus Outbreak as Chinese GP Comes Into Question". Yahoo! Sport, January 30, 2020. Accessed June 11, 2020. https://uk.sports.yahoo.com/news/fia-closely-monitoring-coronavirus-outbreak-111503378.html.

———. 2020b. "WRC Rally Mexico Going Ahead Despite Coronavirus Fears." Yahoo! Sport, March 12, 2020. Accessed June 11, 2020, https://autos.yahoo.com/wrc-rally-mexico-going-ahead-222809066.

Yang, Sung-Un, Minjeong Kang and Philip Johnson. 2010. "Effects of Narratives, Openness to Dialogic Communication, and Credibility on Engagement in Crisis Communication Through Organizational Blogs." *Communication Research* 37 (4): 473–497.

CHAPTER 20

Crisis for Sport, Opportunity for eSports?

Hee Jung Hong

INTRODUCTION

Competitive and organized video gaming is known as eSports (Funk, Pizzo, and Baker 2018). eSports has been recognized as a rapidly growing industry worldwide, although it is still debatable whether eSports actually qualifies as sport or not (Hallmann and Giel 2018). It is evident, however, that eSports are closely associated with traditional sport. For instance, the Olympic Council of Asia announced that eSports will be a medal event at the 2022 Asian Games in Hangzhou, China (Morrison 2017). The International Olympic Committee (IOC) and the Global Association of International Sports Federations (GAISF) hosted an eSports forum in 2018 in order to understand the new industry and establish a platform for possible engagement between eSports and the Olympic movement. The IOC and the GAISF have now established an eSports Liaison Group with the aim of developing their relationship with the eSports industry (IOC 2018).

This chapter explores how the eSports industry has responded to the exceptional circumstances of the Covid-19 pandemic wherein traditional sport was largely brought to a halt. Sport was unable to exercise its functions of developing social interaction, promoting physical and mental health, and entertainment during periods of global lockdown. The eSports industry has a unique set of stakeholders. Scholz (2019) identifies key stakeholders in the eSports industry (Figure 1). The current chapter is to provide the various perspectives of key eSports stakeholders, as recognized by Scholz (2019). Compared to stakeholders in traditional sport, game developers may be the most unique and one of the major game developers is involved in this chapter. The IOC, as one of the major stakeholders for one of the largest sport mega events, is also considered to be an eSports stakeholder in this chapter, as either a sport organization or a tournament organizer, depending on context. Perspectives from some key eSports stakeholders were gathered via email questionnaires. The participants included the head of eSports at the International Olympic Committee (IOC), the Global eSports director of Razer (eSports sponsor), and an eSports game publisher, Tencent Esports. In Asian regions, eSports have been accepted part of sport mega events such as the Asian Games (e.g., Jakarta Palembang 2018 Asian Games) and Southeast Asian (SEA) games (e.g., Philippines 2019 Southeast Asian Games), which contributed to the eSports industry developing a closer relationship with traditional sport. Therefore, two practitioners from traditional sport—the National Youth Sports Institute (NYSI) in Singapore and the K-League in South Korea—were also invited to participate in order to provide perspectives from both sides. All participants answered four questions: 1. What are the major changes in the eSports industry? 2. What are the positive/negative implications? 3. Has the relationship with traditional sport been changed? If so, how? and 4. What are future implications for eSports industry in a post pandemic world? Their insights are discussed in following sections. This chapter aims to explore these key stakeholders' views of the implications of the world pandemic for the eSports industry, to understand how the new industry responded to Covid-19, and how this response can be understood relative to traditional sport.

Figure 1: Stakeholders in the eSports industry

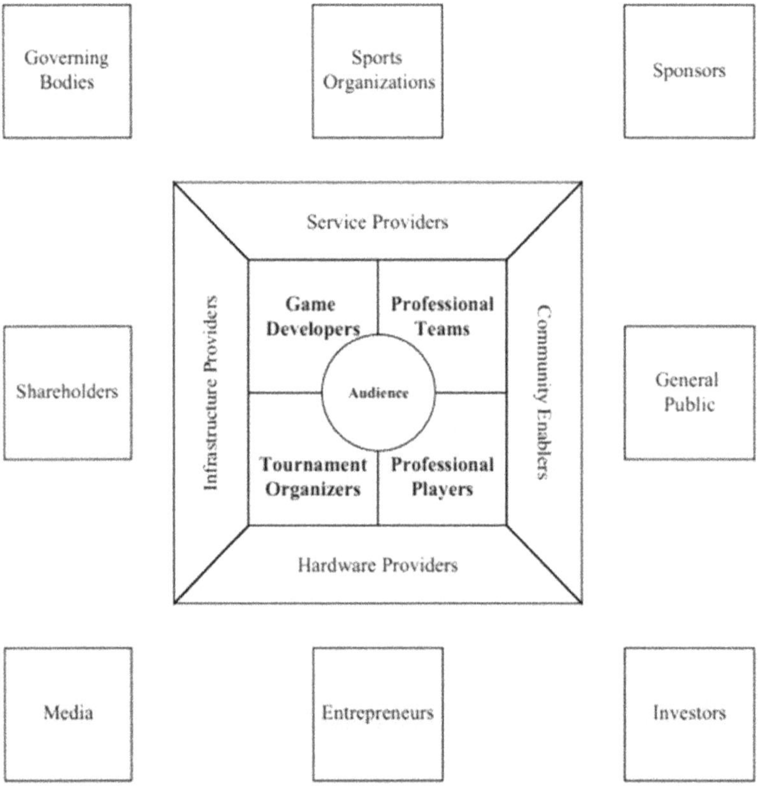

Source: Scholz, 2019.

THE WORLD PANDEMIC AND ESPORTS

Video gaming has been criticized for adverse consequences associated with "excessive gaming." Excessive gaming refers to video or online game addiction (Grüsser, Thalemann, and Griffiths 2007) resulting in social or emotional problems, sedentary behavior, and gaming disorder (Lemmens, Valkenburg, and Peter 2009). Responding to the growing problem of excessive gaming, the World Health Organization (WHO) has classified gaming disorder as an addiction that results in significant impairment of all aspects of a person's life, including the personal, social, and occupational (WHO 2018). The WHO, however, changed its advice on gaming by recommending video games as an effective way to cope with the spread of Covid-19 (Canales 2020). It is worth noting that the experience of sport and exercise has changed due to lockdowns and social distancing measures, such as more people doing exercise alone at home, in outdoor spaces where other people are not around, or through a video screen (Evans et al. 2020). It has also been found that it is becoming more widespread to use technology for tracking and practicing eSports and online courses (Gerrish 2020). In response to this, the eSports industry has taken the opportunity to boost growth. In order to promote messages from the WHO to help slow the spread of Covid-19, eighteen gaming industry leaders have launched a new initiative called #PlayApartTogether to encourage players to follow WHO guidelines (Zynga 2020). Some traditional sports have used eSports as a channel to engage their fans and promote their brand sponsors. The Los Angeles Football Club (LAFC) has produced the LAFC Gaming Charity Challenge Series: a ten game FIFA 20 series streamed live on Twitch in partnership with Allied Esports in order to support Los Angeles-based Covid-19 charities (Duran 2020).

Major Changes in the eSports Industry

The stakeholders identified significant changes in the eSports industry caused by the Covid-19 pandemic. Ms. Merey Tan, a manager of National Youth Sports Institute (NYSI) in Singapore stated, "many youth and national athletes in Singapore had to switch home-based training due to the world pandemic. Some sports such as cycling can be practiced virtually and the use of technology to measure training load and heart-rate velocity has been increased" (M. Tan June 23, 2020). Her statement reflects findings by Gerrish (2020) showing that it was becoming more widespread to use technology for tracking fitness, practicing eSports, and doing exercise via online platforms. Although virtual training itself does not refer directly to eSports, virtual cycling, for example, can be practiced as a form of eSports through "competitive and organized games" (Ruggiero 2019). Mr. Byoungho Kang is currently working as the eSports manager for the K-league but used to work as a manager for the Korea eSports Association. He observed two major changes since the outbreak of Covid-19: 1. an increase in playing time and viewership, and 2. an association with traditional sport. He considered that social distancing and self-quarantine measures contributed to an increase in time spent playing games. He also pointed out that playing video games supports social engagement by creating a climate for people to interact/socialize with one another. He believed that this trend would lead to the growth of sales in the gaming and eSports market. In relation to this, he also highlighted,

> The eSports viewership has spiked up as well because of one of the greatest benefits of eSports, which is that it can be played without the physical presence of participants. So, the current situation increased the content value of eSports rapidly because eSports is the only content that can be consumed at this moment. (B.H. Kang, June 17, 2020)

Mr. David Tse, the Global eSports Director of Razer, also mentioned, "We have seen significant increase in eSports online viewership and with the presence of well-established online casters and streamers in the ecosystem" (D. Tse, June 16, 2020). He added that Razer has led the change with the newly launched South East Asia (SEA) Invitational 2020, with qualifiers and finals to be held entirely online. Therefore, participants are able to compete in their own safe places such as their homes. This indicates that their role as a sponsor has been strengthened by a launching a virtual competition, which would not be affected by the current circumstance by the pandemic.

Mr. Giacomo Modolo, the head of eSports at the International Olympic Committee (IOC) also agreed that social distancing measures have had a significant impact on the eSports industry worldwide. However, Modolo considered that eSports and traditional sport have the same crisis in relation to spectatorship,

> At the end of the day, the core business of eSports is about gathering thousands of fans in an arena to root for their favorite team and enjoy the thrills of live events. In that sense, the impact on live audience is no different than traditional sport. [...] the ability to gather those communities together in a venue is one of the main reasons that the global awareness of eSports skyrocketed during the last couple of years. The success of eSports we observe today, where a video-game competition can fill the Madison Square Garden, makes it hard to ignore. (G. Modolo, June 26, 2020)

These insights are interesting as his organization is also at the core of crises in traditional sport, such as the postponed Tokyo 2020 Olympic Games, of which global spectators and experiences on site are core parts of the sport mega event. Although eSports events seem to take advantage of being hosted virtually, his point should be considered related to players' and spectators' experiences. He also recognized that eSports have an advantage in times like the Covid-19 lockdown. With regard to social distancing measures, he highlighted that people can play video games and practice their skills regardless of social distancing measures due to the nature of video games, which one can practice independently in his/her household. The digital nature of videogames also enables eSports to make a smooth transition into cloud-based production and accommodate competitions that are entirely implemented online. Modolo further described, "you see living rooms turned into production studios, analysts and commentators doing an outstanding job from their bedroom and players competing from their home or training facilities. 90% of the final product remains the same nevertheless" (G. Modolo, June 26, 2020).

As Kang mentioned previously, Modolo also considered that social distancing and quarantine measures contributed to an increase in playing time and attention to forms of digital entertainment. From an economic perspective, he pointed out that the current trend has a significant implication for eSports stakeholders targeting specific audiences who are engaged in gaming: since eSports were the only competitions that people could watch even in early stages of the pandemic, the consumption of gaming content increased. Additionally, he observed, "eSports and gaming are gaining a new momentum, and this will probably lead to another wave of strategic moves from brands, broadcasters and other organizations (in sport as well) to explore and try to add value to the space" (G. Modolo, June 26, 2020).

Tencent Esports also noted that the major change is a transition from offline events to online ones. With regard to this, they refer to Zhang Yijia, the King Pro League (KPL) chairman, "the 2020 KPL Spring Tournament was transferred to be virtual. Zhang Yijia gave a speech that the offline commercial cancellation has negative business consequences, including sponsorship right problems, fixed costs problems, and ticket income losses" (Tencent Esports, July 2, 2020). To deal with such issues, they had to actively communicate with their business partners to set up a plan for how to compensate for their lost rights and interests. They added, "it is the experience of offline-to-online that brings exploration and enlightenment to the traditional eSports business model" (Tencent Esports, July 2, 2020).

Positive and Negative Implications

Stakeholders identified both positive and negative implications of the lockdown period for eSports. Tan, from NYSI, discussed some negative implications for traditional sport linked to eSports. She noted that athletes' performances had been reduced despite home-based training with the use of technology. She also pointed out it might be possible to create a virtual environment for competitions by using technology, but there are things that cannot be replaced virtually such as fan engagement and collective excitement over the unexpected outcomes of the competitions. She commented that eSports would not be the same as a real game, meaning a traditional live match. Tan was also concerned with the limited support services for athletes. Though elite athletes can be supported virtually by sports scientists such as nutritionists and strength and conditioning coaches, some support services such as physiotherapy and sports massage cannot be delivered without face-to-face contact.

On the other hand, Kang from the K-League highlighted that there will be a number of sponsorship opportunities within the eSports industry. This is due to how eSports have grown even during the pandemic while professional sport leagues worldwide were paused and unable to meet the needs of their sponsors. He commented, "on the other hand, the sponsorship value of eSports soared up with high viewership. A variety of natural diseases continue to come out and make a huge negative impact on traditional sport, so more and more brands may possibly set up some new sponsorship strategy with an emphasis in eSports" (B.H. Kang, June 17, 2020). However, he was concerned that the existing criticisms of eSports as a sedentary behavior encouraging young people to spend too much time playing games at home—which may have a negative impact on their social skills, physical and mental health, and even personality—may be highlighted during lockdown. He discussed how socially beneficial attending eSports live events such as meeting with other people and socializing over common interests, which Modolo also emphasized earlier. He noted, "If those live events continue to be canceled, the negative view will be more highlighted" (B.H. Kang, June 17, 2020).

Modolo was also concerned that, "the lack of physical competitions and live audience remains a risk for the whole ecosystem as many stakeholders depend on it to survive" (G. Modolo, June 26, 2020). He remarked that it was strongly recommended to watch a live tournament in an arena where thousands of fans scream and enjoy themselves to understand what eSports are and there could be a negative impact on developing and boosting the industry if eSports fans cannot have the opportunity to participate in such live events to share their passion for eSports. He pointed out a possible issue of competition integrity within the online setting. To overcome such issues, he suggested, "tournament and league organizers must keep several parameters under control to guarantee fair competitions. From stable internet connection to competition manipulation and cheating, there is lot to take into consideration in a remote environment" (G. Modolo, June 26, 2020).

With regard to positive implications, Modolo emphasized that "eSports is inherently social" (G. Modolo, June 26, 2020), which challenges the stereotype of eSports players as solitary and non-social. He maintained that eSports encourage people to play together and interact with one another. In line with what Kang said, he was also aware that one of the major criticisms around eSports is an isolated and sedentary lifestyle. Under the lockdown situation caused by Covid-19, he underlined the importance of organizational support for players,

> If a professional player spends around 8 hours a day practicing his craft, he is very likely to train even more if he can't visit his family and friends or do any other social activities because of social distancing measures. If there is no organizational support and the player does not take care of his physical and mental health, this can have serious negative consequences. (G. Modolo, June 26, 2020)

He also commented on the eSports ecosystem with regard to how quickly it responded to the worldwide pandemic and successfully adapted the given situation. He stressed, "it only took a few weeks for the industry to turn around and propose practically the same products to viewers and fans online. In fact, eSports even extended its offer on linear broadcasts" (G. Modolo, June 26, 2020). He thought this was possible because all the stakeholders in the industry such as game publishers, professional teams, players, and other relevant organizations collectively worked together to keep fans engaged in their games despite social distancing and quarantine measures.

Tse from Razer did not see any major negative impacts on the eSports industry, but he considered it a matter of how to adjust and adapt the given circumstance. As Kang noted, he also highlighted the difference between sports leagues being suspended and eSports tournaments continuing online. For instance, he thought the Razer SEA-Invitational demonstrated the strong adaptability of eSports as both a sport and an ecosystem. He put an emphasis on the role of Razer in the industry as an eSports sponsor by leading upcoming eSports events: "we are definitely witnessing growth and readiness of all the esports federations since 30th SEA [South East Asian] Games last year and believe there will be more progressive development in the region for esports" (D. Tse, June 16, 2020).

Tencent Esports noted that the Chinese government has increased its support of eSports events. The General Administration of Sport of China highlighted ongoing support of scientific guidance for eSports, and Peng Weiyong, deputy director of the Economic Department of the General Administration of Sport of China, also stated that the General Administration of Sport of China will provide continuous support for the development of eSports and promotion of eSports consumer services via e-commerce platforms (Tencent Esports, July 2, 2020). Such support from the government is an indicator of how successfully eSports events have been implemented online. On the other hand, they also noted that in the short term, industrial stagnation was experienced due to canceled or postponed eSports events. In relation to sponsorship, they noted that "due to lost sponsorship rights and tickets fees, eSports events companies face huge commercial losses" (Tencent Esports, July 2, 2020). They also pointed out further challenges that eSports clubs have faced, such as the increasing cost of operations and uncertainty about athlete performances. However, they stressed that such industrial stagnation is short-term and that the eSports industry will find a way to reduce any existing negative impacts.

Changes in the Relationship Between eSports and Traditional Sport

One other aspect related to Covid-19 is how the relationship between eSports and traditional sport changed. Kang stated that the relationship between the two has become stronger because traditional sport recognized the significance of eSports during the lockdown period and traditional sport communities and organizations learned how they could utilize eSports linked to their practice. He described some examples,

> Some professional sport organizations also capitalized on the benefits of eSports to engage with their fans. F1 hosted its eSports events using rFactor2 and F12019 and NBA also utilized NBA2K for their fan engagement. Not only that but many football leagues also hosted eSports events using the FIFA videogame to satisfy the fans' demand for football content. K-League also hosted FIFA Online 4 eSports events in which professional footballers joined, and the events entertained numerous football fans in South Korea. (B.H. Kang, June 17, 2020)

Kang stressed that the FIFA video game was the most common way to host eSports to keep their football fans engaged. The events demonstrated its success as one of the most effective low-cost marketing events. He thought that such success also proved the positive aspects of eSports to the public, particularly to traditional sport fans: "Because of this win-win effect, I think that the relationship between two has been more solid and there will be more collaboration opportunities between them" (B.H. Kang, June 17, 2020). Modolo also commented that traditional sport and society finally saw the growing number of players worldwide and the realized how playing video games/eSports has become more popular and even mainstream. This is due to the industry's quick response to the pandemic and the adaptations to its practice in order to keep its fans and players motivated and engaged. In line with what Kang said, he also remarked, "videogames and other simulations might offer interesting opportunities for sport to increase its exposure and propose new experiences to fans and existing audiences" (G. Modolo, June 26, 2020).

Tencent Esports noted that the communication between eSports and traditional sport has improved since the pandemic began. They gave the same example as Kang, "the suspended F1 held an eSports competition, and there were about 350,000 viewers at the peak of the Bahrain Virtual Grand Prix. This trend brings eSports experiences to traditional sport and inspiration into the development of eSports, as well" (Tencent Esports, July 2, 2020). Tencent Esports also commented on the relationship between eSports and business cooperation during the pandemic to note that there have not been any changes in the relationship. Although a number of different industries are now facing challenges and difficulties caused by Covid-19, they stressed that Tencent Esports' business partners have confirmed their confidence in keeping their investment in the eSports industry, "the eSports industry, as a sunrise industry, still has huge business value, which will not be changed by the epidemic. Therefore, the relationship and business cooperation between sponsors and Tencent Esports remain the same" (Tencent Esports, July 2, 2020).

eSports Industry in a Post-Pandemic World

Respondents also discussed potential changes and implications for the eSport industry following the pandemic. Tan mentioned the world's first global governing body for eSports, the Global Esports Federation (GEF), headquartered in Singapore. Tan commented, "I foresee that the eSports industry will embark on a swift upward trajectory in a post pandemic world. With the proper infrastructure and framework in place, eSports can take on new directions beyond the world of gaming." (M. Tan, June 23, 2020). Based on the positive synergies and effects of the collaboration between traditional sport and eSports, Kang thought such collaboration and partnership would increase in the post pandemic world, "I expect to see the eSports industry increase its partnerships with sports. I also think that more business opportunities will come as eSports demonstrated its greatness to a number of brands and investors" (B.H. Kang, June 17, 2020).

Tse discussed how Razer, as one of the biggest sponsors in the industry, can contribute to the development of eSports at two different levels, professional and amateur. On one hand, they will continue to invest in their professional team—Team Razer—which represents Razer at the top level of eSports competitions worldwide. On the other hand, they are planning to nurture the next generation of eSports talent by providing holistic support to players in order to develop a sustainable career path in the industry. He added, "I believe the way forward is continuing to team up with eSports federations worldwide by aligning ourselves with their national objective of getting eSports recognized as an official sport in their respective countries" (D. Tse, June 16, 2020).

Modolo observed that "it will be interesting to see how the ecosystem balances out online and offline events in the future based on different social distancing measures around the world" (G. Modolo, June 26, 2020). He predicted that events/tournaments at local and regional levels could grow more than global mega eSports events due to the fact that quarantine, social distancing, and lockdown measures may remain localized across the world. He thought it would be an interesting way for the eSports industry to boost its growth by activating local events while planning global events. He also discussed the changes in training for eSports teams,

> eSports teams might also re-consider their operations by encouraging their players to adopt "home training" and "home streaming". However, remote training has proven to have limits in professional eSports, which led to the adoption of gaming houses as standard training facilities. It will be interesting to see if the dynamic of eSports shifts back to "online-first." (G. Modolo, June 26, 2020)

He also remarked on how the fact that there has been a noticeable growth of the numbers of people who play games will affect organizations and brands in establishing their partnerships with eSports professional teams and players. With regard to this, Tencent Esports also stressed business partnerships between the eSports industry and brands post-pandemic. In their view, eSports culture can provide new business ideas to many companies to recover from the current economic stagnation, "In conclusion, it can be a new growth point of the eSports industry through enhancing commercialization and building IP [Intellectual Property]" (Tencent Esports, July 2, 2020).

As noted above, Tencent Esports considers governmental support as a positive outcome given the current circumstance and that communication and cooperation between the government and eSports industry will be strengthened. They also mentioned some schemes driven by the government such as the Beijing eSports Plan 2020: "Beijing government decided to hold the World Champions Cup of the Honor of Kings and build eSports technology experiencing area with Tencent Esports, which is the first local guiding policy for recovery and development of the eSports industry" (Tencent Esports, July 2, 2020). They also indicated that there is a strong possibility of developing an eSports city because eSports has great potential to promote consumption and tourism, particularly in attracting young people and enriching resident's leisure time. As a result, they felt that eSports could contribute to urban economic recovery following the pandemic.

CONCLUSION

While the pandemic presented a unique challenge to sport, it also presented an opportunity for eSports. This was because eSports were able to capitalize on the situation and legitimize themselves as real alternatives to traditional sport. Despite facing some challenges similar to traditional sport, eSports responded to lockdown and social distancing quickly and flexibly—especially by hosting events remotely, which traditional sports was unable to do. However, it should be noted that eSports still need to overcome the criticism related to physical inactivity, sedentary lifestyle, and lack of socialization, all of which may be worsened by the Covid-19 lockdowns. Since it was found that eSports spectators' experiences at live eSports events might be one of the ways that the industry addressed the issue, the eSports industry and stakeholders should consider this aspect as importantly as traditional sport does. Although the game publisher and sponsor included in this chapter responded to the pandemic well and took it as an opportunity rather than crisis, they were in a strong position to take actions to improve on such issues as players and spectators are the ones who contribute to the growth of their and their partners' business in the industry.

Now traditional sport is seeing the value of being flexible and engaging fans in online or eSport settings, potentially leading to new collaborations and ways of presenting and consuming sport. Although the cases of collaboration between eSports and traditional sport have been rising, and eSports is considered to be a good channel for traditional sport to engage young people in sport, it has not been shown how this relationship can positively motivate young people to become more involved in physical activity and sport. This is a crucial point not only for traditional sport but also for eSports. This is an area that researchers should investigate in order to understand the implications for both industries. It is also important for both sides to seek a way to mutually benefit in the long-term, beyond the world pandemic. There is the potential that both industries can provide social benefits to young generation, such as developing social skills both on- and offline and leading healthy lifestyles.

It is worth noting that there might also be a shift in terms of sponsorships due to the increase of eSports viewership, which was evidenced by the stakeholders in this chapter, as the eSports industry has been recognized as a critical partner to the traditional sport sector. It has been observed that many major brands that have sponsored traditional sport have now started to sponsor eSports mega events and professional players. Therefore, it is crucial for traditional sport to manage their competitive values in partnership with the eSports industry while facilitating eSports as a channel to reach out to fans and business partners. As mentioned above, eSports competitions within the Asian Games are a good example of traditional a sports event keeping its values while embracing this new trend. This is another area for researchers to look into what impacts such collaboration have on both industries and their participants economically, educationally, psychologically, and socially. This will give researchers a prospective opportunity to investigate and better understand changing dynamics between these sport sectors.

REFERENCES

Canales, Katie. 2020. "The WHO is Recommending Video Games as an Effective Way to Stop the Spread Of COVID-19, One Year After Adding 'Gaming Disorder' to its List of Addictive Behaviors." *Business Insider*, April 2, 2020. https://www.businessinsider.com/who-video-games-coronavirus-pandemic-mental-health-disorder-2020-4?r=US&IR=T

Duran, H. B. 2020. "Los Angeles Football Club on the Pivot to Esports During Lockdown." *The Esports Observer*, April 17, 2020. https://esportsobserver.com/lafc-interviews-esports/

Evans, Adam B., Joanna Blackwell, Paddy Dolan, Josef Fahlén, Remco Hoekman, Verena Lenneis, Gareth McNarry, Maureen Smith, and Laura Wilcock. 2020. "Sport in the Face tf the COVID-19 Pandemic: Towards an Agenda for Research in the Sociology of Sport." *European Journal for Sport and Society* 17 (2): 85-95. https://doi.org/10.1080/16138171.2020.1765100

Funk, Daniel, Anthony Pizzo, and Bradley Baker. 2018. "eSport management: Embracing eSport Education and Research Opportunities." *Sport Management Review* 21 (1): 7-13.

Gerrish, Dave. 2020. "Together: What Does Coronavirus Mean for the Digital Future of the Physical Activity Sector?" *UK Active*, April 28, 2020. https://www.ukactive.com/blog/together-what-does-coronavirus-mean-for-the-digital-future-of-the-physical-activity-sector/

Grüsser, S.M., Ralf Thalemann, and Mark D. Griffiths. 2007. "Excessive Computer Game Playing: Evidence for Addiction and Aggression?" *Cyberpsychology and Behavior* 10: 290-292.

Hallmann, Kirstin, and Thomas Giel. 2018. "eSports Competitive Sports or Recreational Activity?" *Sport Management Review* 21 (1): 14-20.

International Olympic Committee. 2018. "Olympic Movement, Esports and Gaming Communities Meet at the Esports Forum." *International Olympic Committee*, July 21, 2018. https://www.olympic.org/news/olympic-movement-esports-and-gaming-communities-meet-at-the-esports-forum

Lemmens, Jeroen S., Patti M. Valkenburg, and Jochen Peter. 2009. "Development and Validation of a Game Addiction Scale for Adolescents." *Media Psychology* 12: 77-95.

Morrison, Sean. 2017. "Esports to Join Asian Games as Medal Sport in 2022." *ESPN*, April 18, 2017. http://www.espn.com/esports/story/_/id/19185921/esportsjoin-asian-games-medal-sport-2022

Ruggiero, Adam. 2019. "Zwift, UCI Announce 1st 'Virtual Cycling' World Championships." *Gear Junkie*, September 27, 2019. https://gearjunkie.com/zwift-uci-cycling-esports-world-championships-2020

Scholz, Tobias M. 2019. *eSports is Business: Management in the World of Competitive Gaming*. Cham: Palgrave Pivot.

World Health Organization. 2018. "Gaming Disorder". *World Health Organization*, September 14, 2018. https://www.who.int/features/qa/gaming-disorder/en/

———. 2020. "#HealthyAtHome Physical activity." *World Health Organization*, June 24, 2020. https://www.who.int/news-room/campaigns/connecting-the-world-to-combat-coronavirus/healthyathome/healthyathome---physical-activity.

Zynga. 2020. "Games Industry Unites to Promote World Health Organization Messages Against COVID-19; Launch #PlayApartTogether Campaign." *Businesswire*, March 28, 2020. https://www.businesswire.com/news/home/20200328005018/en/Games-Industry-Unites-Promote-World-Health-Organization.

www.ingramcontent.com/pod-product-compliance
Lightning Source LLC
Chambersburg PA
CBHW040320300426
44111CB00023B/2957